LIFEPRINTS

LIFEPRINTS

Deciphering Your Life Purpose from Your Fingerprints

RICHARD UNGER

Crossing Press
an imprint of Ten Speed Press
PO Box 7123
Berkeley, California 94707
www.tenspeed.com

Distributed in Australia by Simon and Schuster Australia, in Canada by Ten Speed Press Canada, in New Zealand by Southern Publishers Group, in South Africa by Real Books, and in the United Kingdom and Europe by Publishers Group UK.

Cover design by Nancy Austin and Chloe Rawlins
Text design by Laura Milton

Library of Congress Cataloging-in-Publication Data

Unger, Richard.

LifePrints : deciphering your life purpose from your fingerprints /

Richard Unger.

p. cm.

Summary: "A guide to discovering one's life purpose by decoding the map

revealed in our unique combination of fingerprints, based on twenty-five

years of research and fingerprint statistics for more than fifty thousand

hands"—Provided by publisher.

Includes index.

ISBN-13: 978-1-58091-185-6

1. Fortune-telling by fingerprints. 2. Fingerprints. I. Title.

BF1891.F5U54 2007

133.6—dc22

2007016834

Printed in the United States of America
First printing, 2007

1 2 3 4 5 6 7 8 9 10 — 11 10 09 08 07

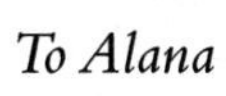

To Alana

CONTENTS

FOREWORD

NOT QUITE TEN YEARS AGO, while I was working on the manuscript for a book considering the evolutionary connections between the human hand and brain, a friend urged me to meet Richard Unger, "a person who looks at people's hands and says things about them." Palmistry was nowhere on the list of research topics for my book, but since I was very much interested in people whose working lives are strongly dependent on the hand, curiosity overcame my professional misgivings; I contacted Mr. Unger and we arranged to meet. A soft-spoken, thoughtful man brimming with Brooklyn wit and enthusiasm, Richard answered a number of questions about his background and work; then, during a moment of quiet when I was trying to account for the somewhat unexpected feeling that I was talking to a highly intelligent man with interesting things to say, he asked me, "Would you mind if I look at your hands?"

Of course you *know* his reading of my hands unmasked me in a trice, but as I subsequently learned, any hand reader worth his salt can do that in his sleep. What mattered more, and what explains why I eagerly accepted his invitation to write this foreword, was that he also agreed to an informal, private test of his interpretive system by reading the hands of a few of my close friends. I was surprised when he said they would not have to meet with him personally; he would only need to see their handprints and fingerprints. He showed me how to prepare an ink print of the hand and its individual fingerprints and told me to bring these to him for a reading as soon as I had collected them.

I returned with the prints about a week later, full of anticipation but totally unprepared for what happened. It was as if I had delivered a medical school quiz on chest X-rays to the chief of the radiology department. Richard didn't tell me who was happily married or who owned a yellow T-bird; instead, he told me what each person was instinctively good at and for each person how a chronic nemesis in his or her life might behave. When he was done, I told him briefly about each individual, still slightly disoriented by how accurately in each instance he had described something essential and distinctive. After my rendering of the life story of one of the five, he looked puzzled, shook his head, and said, "I really missed that one." But I had withheld a piece of extremely personal information about this particular person, and the truth was that Richard had hit five home runs.

At this point I decided that I could not simply dismiss this demonstration; the readings certainly *could* have been a fluke, or a clever charade, but the tables had turned and the burden of explaining his "trick" was now mine. I would have to take my time and learn more about what this man was doing. I studied his system.

Ten years have passed since our first meeting, and Richard and I are now not only close friends but professional colleagues. What I have learned from him during the decade of professional interactions we have enjoyed since our first meeting has both refreshed and intrigued my sense of the hand as both an emblem and an instrument of the human spirit. What he has taught me has also had important consequences for my thinking about a whole class of perplexing disorders regularly encountered in both neurological and psychiatric practice and ultimately convinced me that there was at least a limited role for hand reading in my own practice. As you might guess, I was not merely dubious about offering hand readings to patients in a neurological clinic; there was good reason to expect criticism, or worse, from colleagues. But after the first timid trials, I realized the method was an easy fit with my own style of history taking and in fact could be a powerful catalyst for the airing of personal issues; understandably, patients tend to be cautious with a doctor they do not already know and trust. Yes, a few people balked at having their hands read, but as I gained experience the readings were increasingly welcomed by patients who, once they recovered from their surprise, expressed gratitude that a doctor would actually take the time to tell them what their hands said about them.

At the center of Richard's work is the astonishing assertion that every human hand bears a unique pattern of fingerprints that can be decoded in a psychologically specific and meaningful way. I have been a reluctant, incomplete, and at times extremely difficult, convert to this claim, but I now largely accept it as fundamentally valid. We have had a number of discussions about designing a scientific proof of his method, but since the world is still waiting for any such demonstrations for a host of interpretive systems widely used in clinical psychology and psychiatry, I am content for now with the empirical evidence. Based on a decade of observation, I consider Richard Unger to have produced an objective and straightforward analytical tool with a breathtaking capacity to unmask the sources (and the potent, insistent dynamics) of many of the common frustrations and failures all of us experience in our daily lives.

The single overarching theme common to modern psychology, classical mythology, fairy tales, great novels, and movies—and it is a theme that *everyone* understands—is some version of the narrative concerning what we like and do not like about ourselves. What Richard has found in fingerprints is not simply a fresh way of referencing this inevitable inner dichotomy—what we commonly think of as our strengths and weaknesses—but a compelling argument for treating them as complementary, inseparable, and in fact equally essential agents for healthy psychological development.

As a physician, the most impressive benefit I find in Richard's readings is the implicit invitation to discern in our most intimate and intractable frustrations (and, for some, in unexplained physical disabilities) not bad luck but a unique and intimate code of personal meaning. Learning to read that code can yield entirely unexpected self-understanding and a clear vision of what any particular person, irrespective of life history, can do to move toward a life of real and progressive fulfillment.

Richard's use of fingerprints to unmask the healthy dynamism of inner conflict seems absolutely unique to me, and I think it is not an overstatement to suggest that he may have developed one of the most accessible and fruitful constructs in the history of human psychology. Although I am utterly at a loss to explain how fingerprint patterns could possibly provide such a compass, I am satisfied that the interpretive system he describes in this book is not only psychologically wise but profoundly constructive.

This book represents an extraordinary effort, and achievement, by its author. He may have been working at this for decades, but he is the first to say that it is a work in progress. So be it: if only a beginning, it is already a very mature beginning.

I promise you that if you take Richard at his word, your sense of wonder and appreciation for your own life—not as a sugary confection but with all its foibles, its clumsiness, its retreats, and even its most spectacular crashes, just as they were and are—will grow enormously. Some of you who will read this book will even find, to your great surprise, that your appetite for your own life has become insatiable.

—FRANK R. WILSON, MD, AUTHOR OF *THE HAND: HOW ITS USE SHAPES THE BRAIN, LANGUAGE, AND HUMAN CULTURE* AND FORMER CLINICAL PROFESSOR OF NEUROLOGY, STANFORD UNIVERSITY SCHOOL OF MEDICINE

ACKNOWLEDGMENTS

THIS BOOK HAS BEEN a labor of love, the actual writing of which has spanned fourteen years. During that time, thousands of people have shared their life stories with me, from their highest aspirations to their most hidden secrets. Thank you all for allowing me into your private domain. Your fingerprints are on every page.

Any book of this kind must be a collaboration, and there are many who contributed to the publication of *LifePrints*. To my students who insisted I explain the LifePrints system more clearly and who tested out its principles on tens of thousands of their own clients, family, and friends; to my fellow vision holders: the faculty of the International Institute of Hand Analysis (Alana Unger, Ronelle Coburn, Terry-Linn Snider, Pascal Stoessel, Roberta Coker, Mary DeLave, and Janet Savage); to my colleagues Barbara Schmid, MD, Andre and Teres Studer, Frank Wilson, MD, and John Ward, who supported me in too many ways to list here; to Zen Player, whose ideas ignited my imagination, including the title *LifePrints*; to my friends who generously offered to read and critique early versions of the manuscript, including Harvey Landress, Elijah Nesenboim, and Sandy Lillie; to my editors, including Laura Kennedy, who climbed so deeply into the material that she used it to change her own life, working with you has changed my life as well; to Julie Bennett at Ten Speed Press and to my agent, Rosalie Siegel, thank you for all your efforts and thank you for believing in me; and to my wife, Alana, especially you Alana, not only for loving me and being by my side through this whole process but also for your direct contribution to *LifePrints*: your incisive input courses through the entire book. Thank you all for helping me to see myself more clearly and to live my own life purpose.

INTRODUCTION

THE NEXT EXTRAORDINARY MAP

> *"It is not worth the while to go round the world to count the cats of Zanzibar," says Thoreau. "Be rather the Lewis and Clark . . . of your own streams and oceans, explore your own higher latitudes. . . ." With this metaphor, Thoreau extends the purview of mapping . . . to the self and solitude and the soul. Perhaps the next extraordinary map is not of galaxies or the interior of atoms but something quite different, something Thoreau called "home cosmography."*
>
> —STEPHEN S. HALL, *MAPPING THE NEXT MILLENNIUM*

I am a professional hand analyst.

I estimate that I have read over 52,000 pair of hands thus far in my hand reading career. About half my clients are therapists, counselors, or their clients; the other half are businesspeople, artists, housewives, candlestick makers—anyone who wants to learn more about their life purpose and life lessons.

I know there is an image problem associated with hand reading. "Cross my palm with silver. I see a tall, dark stranger. . . ." When people think of hand reading, if they think of it at all, the image is that of a roadside fortune-teller. Certainly, some fit this description, but most modern hand readers have long since left their crystal balls behind. As far as I have been able to determine, your hands do not know how many children you will have or how long you are going to live. Your hands do, however, have a very specific picture of your life purpose printed out in your fingerprints.

THE BIRTH OF LIFEPRINTS

In the summer of 1969, having just finished the active duty portion of my National Guard commitment I needed something to revive my spirits. Neil Armstrong was about to take "one small step for mankind," but I had a different adventure in mind. I set out to explore America.

On that trip, in a little bookstore in Boulder, Colorado, a used palmistry book somehow caught my attention. According to its diagrams, I was the type of person who needed a mission in life. You could say that about anybody, I thought, but I bought the book anyway thinking it would be fun. Two days later, I was totally hooked on hands.

I was amazed at how accurate hand reading was, even if only 10 percent of what was visible in someone's hands made sense to me. I was delighted to have such meaningful conversations with people with whom I probably wouldn't have talked for more than five minutes otherwise. More importantly, reading hands gave a part of me that I barely knew an opportunity to emerge. The more hands I read, the more this "me" came forward and I liked the way that felt.

Returning to college that fall, I devoted myself to studying hands. I would carry around *The Laws of Scientific Hand Reading* by William Benham, cut classes, and read hands in the snack bar for hours at a time. My sparse knowledge of the subject didn't stop me from being convinced there was something to it, and in the proper spirit of collegiate inquiry, I set out to learn as much as possible. Looking at hands every day, I would tell people a thing or two and ask them to fill in the blanks about their interests, relationships, etc., comparing what they told me to the differing versions presented in my small collection of palmistry books.

ALONE WITH HISTORY

The two concrete lions guarding the Forty-Second Street library stared straight ahead, unconcerned with the passing traffic or the heavy New York City rain. Gaining the entranceway, I proceeded to the main hall, my wet shoes slipping and squeaking on the polished marble floors. The enormous vaulted ceilings always brought out the reverential side of me, so I tried to unload my jacket and notebooks as quietly as possible. Serious thinkers, aged philosophers, and sleeping street people shared the reading tables as I settled in for another day in the archives.

The eyes of Katherine St. Hill, founder of the London Cheirological Society, were staring back at me from the nineteenth century when a woman older still interrupted my reverie. The folded note said I had received permission to view the rare Indagine Book of Palmistry and Physiognomy from 1676.

1676!

To enter this special reading room in the bowels of the library, I had to fill out a three-page questionnaire, wait a day, then swear in writing to not bring pen or pencil with me. I faced possible search and seizure and, I suppose, a lifetime ban on reading if caught *In delicto*.

I made the appropriate vows and signed on the dotted line. The ancient woman, choosing from among fifty two-inch keys, opened the wire caged doors that allowed me into the sepulchral chamber.

I was alone with history.

I felt I was making progress on understanding the message carried in our hands, but I needed to know more. Traveling to the giant public library in New York City, I spent ten glorious days poring through every last word I could find on the subject.

By 1979 I had read more than twelve thousand pairs of hands and had tested the information in pretty much every palmistry book ever written in the English language. Despite holding an honored place in the great universities of Europe through the late sixteenth century, and though taught by scholars from Aristotle to Paracelsus, by the time I got to the literary legacy of this once-grand study, what remained seemed little more than a hodgepodge of outdated opinions, wrong guesses, and intermittently accurate observations. I longed for a palmistic Rosetta stone, some consistent and coherent set of guiding principles that in one elegant swoop would make sense of it all, but it felt as if I was working on a giant jigsaw puzzle without a box cover picture for guidance.

The problem was not a shortage of data, quite the contrary. I had discarded or confirmed numerous interpretations of line formations and hand shapes, using feedback from those whose hands I had read to add to my growing database. The problem, it seemed, was that everybody I met was a mass of contradictions. Whenever I thought I had accurately correlated another hand marking with its specific character trait, the next client's life story would ruin my carefully crafted theory. Either there was another variable in the mix or hands did not offer a full and accurate model of human behavior. Could it be I wasn't playing with all the puzzle pieces?

With no more palmistry books left to read, my unquenchable thirst for hand data eventually brought me to the Texas Medical Center library, part of Houston's huge medical complex. There, nestled in my cubicle, with lab coats and green scrubs passing by in my peripheral vision, I eagerly devoured the extensive literature on hand morphology, palmar lines, and fingerprints.

It wasn't long before a growing city of haphazard piles grew up around me: medical books and genetic journals, anthropological studies and JAMA articles in dizzying towers that threatened to tumble down with each new addition. I moved quickly through article after article. There were thousands, including tantalizing titles not yet translated from German, Chinese, and other languages. The medical literature documented links between fingerprints and lupus disease, Alzheimer's, tuberculosis, heart disease, and cancer. I found numerous studies on fingerprints and mental disorders, hyperactive children, retardation, and schizophrenia. There were twin studies in abundance. Researchers were unanimous: various medical and psychological conditions have certain fingerprint traits in common. Lobbying for an expanded role for dermatoglyphics, researchers had proposed more studies with larger subject groups.

DERMATOGLYPHICS OPENS THE DOOR

Dermatoglyphics: (dermato = skin, glyphics = carvings), a name coined by Harold Cummins, MD, in 1926, is the scientific term for the study of fingerprints and related line and hand shape designations. Its main uses are in population studies, genetic research, and medical diagnostics. Dr. Cummins is commonly referred to as the father of dermatoglyphics, and his seminal work with Dr. Charles Midlo, *Fingerprints, Palms, and Soles*, is considered the standard in the field. Examining embryonic hands, Dr. Cummins documented the emergence of eleven ball-like structures at the eighth week after conception. These "volar pads" will later become the thumb, fingers, and the six sections of the palmar surface. At the fourteenth week, the skin corrugations (fingerprints) begin to appear, forming a topographic-like map of the developing fetal hand.

What? Fingerprints are arranged like a topographic map? I almost fell out of my chair. It was almost too obvious—human fingerprints look like a map. A map is a tool that tells you where you are and how to get where you need to go. How could this have been overlooked for so long?

For ten years, I had been deciphering the personality components of my hand reading clients by comparing the size and shape of their thumbs, palms, and fingers (plus looking at their lines). Each of these factors is subject to change over time. I had gotten pretty good at finding hidden talents and behavioral tendencies, but I still couldn't tell why people with the same traits sometimes behaved so differently. Now, in the medical stacks, I was reading that the fingerprints form *a topographical map prior to birth, a map that will remain unaltered throughout life*. Could this map contain the hidden variable for which I had been searching?

Dermatoglyphics and palmistry both derive from comparative hand topography. Both seek the inner condition based upon outer signs, but there the similarities end. One employs the scientific method, the other is based on folklore and thousands of years of anecdotal experience. One is high tech, the other, ancient wisdom. Arising as they do from such divergent cultures, could a marriage of the two disciplines be possible? When I overlaid the two systems and tested my findings in the human laboratory, it turned out they were made for each other.

DOWN TO THE CORE

After years of searching for isolated jigsaw puzzle tidbits, being in the Texas Medical Center library felt like having access to a giant puzzle-piece warehouse. Ca-chunk, ca-chunk: one new interlocking piece after another! Hours passed in an instant. I couldn't believe the library was closing and I would have to wait until 7:00 the next morning to resume. I was at the door at 6:45.

I learned that each fingerprint is composed of between fifty and one hundred lines, each line having its own signature. There are stops and starts to the lines, forks, and bubbles, a series of easily classifiable formations called pattern minutiae. The FBI does not need all ten of your fingerprints to identify you. Comparing the pattern minutiae of one line of one fingerprint may well do the job. The fact that each fingerprint is unique and unalterable but easy to categorize is what makes fingerprint identification the useful tool that it is.

Interestingly, the same patterning system that appears on fingerprints shows up elsewhere in nature: on sand dunes, for instance. Sand dunes are not smooth; they are ridged, and these ridges have stops and starts, forks and bubbles, just like fingerprint lines. So too at the beach. When the water recedes, we see a ripple pattern in the sand with markings just like those on sand dunes and our fingerprints. Apparently, the ocean waves have left their imprint on the shoreline. Is it only a coincidence that these patterns share the same characteristics with those on our fingertips?

As I stared at the diagrams in *Fingerprints, Palms, and Soles*, a shudder went across my shoulders and up and down my spine. The experience was similar to waking in the middle of the night from the power of a Technicolor dream. I felt sensationally calm, profoundly alert, as though I was remembering something long forgotten. The entire system of fingerprint identification appeared in my brain, whole, intact. And I knew, as I know now in my bones, that fingerprints are a soul-level imprint.

The LifePrints system joins the fingerprint census and arch, loop, whorl sequence of medical literature to the mythic interpretations of hand analysis. The result of this union is a tool as precise as a scalpel and as meaningful as a philosopher's stone: a life-purpose map that can be used as a daily compass to life-scale meaning and fulfillment.

Five months before you were born, a pattern appeared on your body, one with design characteristics similar to the wave impressions left on a beach. Call it a soul map, a holographic image, or a DNA printout, a bar-coded peek at the biological legacy of your ancestors. Consider it your transcript as you begin a new semester at the Earth University.

There are many ways to think about fingerprints, but it doesn't matter how or why fingerprints operate as a map to our core psychology. The fact is they do. The LifePrints system works. It works for me. It works for the thousands of people who have used it already. It will work for you as well.

THE INTERNATIONAL INSTITUTE OF HAND ANALYSIS

Since that life-changing day in the Jessie Jones Medical Library, I have talked with more than forty thousand people about their life purpose. After honing the LifePrints system in these thousands of readings, I then taught it to more than one hundred psychiatrists, counselors, and therapists with various backgrounds and training, who replicated my results. Confident that I had an accurate and specific life-purpose assessment tool, I founded the International Institute of Hand Analysis (IIHA) in Northern California. This was the culmination of a life dream that had its first glimmer when I began reading hands during that trip around America in 1969.

The IIHA began offering yearlong certification trainings in 1985; we had five eager students. Today, the IIHA has five full-time faculty members, dozens of practitioners, and classes in several cities in the United States and Europe. The LifePrints system has been used in a variety of settings: a child development clinic in Switzerland, an inner city high school in Oakland, and in businesses large and small.

Years after my experience in the medical library, a student told me that the Navajo Indians have a saying about fingerprints:

"It was the wind that gave them life. It is the wind that comes out our mouths now that gives us life. When this ceases to blow—we die. In the skin at the tips of our fingers we see the trail of the wind. It shows us where the wind blew when our ancestors were created."

How elegant.

HOW TO USE THIS BOOK

Using information from the study guide that I refined in hundreds of IIHA workshops, *LifePrints* will lead you step by step through the construction of your own life-purpose map. As your life purpose comes into full view, prior events and current circumstances will take on new significance and future prospects will appear in an entirely different light. As you will soon find out, knowing your life purpose will permanently change your outlook on who you really are and where your life is going.

- Chapter One: Life Purpose, Life Lessons, and Soul Psychology Defined—explains the terms and principles you will be using throughout the book to understand your life purpose and life lesson.

- Chapter Two: Identify Your Fingerprints and Find Your School—gets you started on the construction of your life-purpose map.

- Chapter Three: Decipher Your Life Purpose and Life Lesson—helps you translate your fingerprint types into purposes and lessons.

- Chapter Four: Deepen Your Understanding—outlines the significance of each fingerprint's location on the hands. This chapter—along with extensive references to Appendix I: Archetypal Combinations and Case Studies—is where you'll find the book's (and your fingerprints') core information.

- Chapter Five: Create Your Life-Fulfillment Formula and Live a Life on Purpose—brings everything together and presents some journaling exercises to help you integrate this knowledge into your life.

Reading hands is my passion. I have read the hands of babies just born and hands nearly one hundred years old. From successful businesspeople to shamanic healers and from mass murderers to movie queens, each pair of hands presents a sharply focused window into the inner workings of another unique human being. The most unusual work I have done is the study of hands left behind by those no longer on the planet: the petroglyphs of the American Southwest, the Cave of Hands in Argentina, the hands in concrete in front of Mann's Chinese Theatre in Los Angeles, old photos in history books and *Life* magazine, and personal collections—all offer a fascinating record, a Biography channel of their own. Using some of the sources mentioned above, I've read and interpreted the life purpose and life lesson of some very famous people. These are included in Appendix I: Archetypal Combinations and Case Studies and are indexed in the table of contents.

If you want to decipher your life purpose and life lesson as quickly as possible, read chapter one and enough of chapter two to identify your school. Read the section of chapter two that pertains to your school, then skip ahead to chapter three. Decode your life purpose and life lesson, then proceed to chapter four, reading those sections that pertain directly to you as well as the cross-referenced entries in the appendix. You will need to understand the material in chapter five to pull all the parts of your life-purpose map together, and the journaling exercises will help you use what you have learned to bring your life purpose directly into your everyday life.

Or read *LifePrints* straight through.

Either way, I suggest keeping a life-purpose journal as a reference point as you work your way through the book. It will allow you to have your fingerprint chart handy and will offer a home for your thoughts and impressions as you do the journaling exercises at the end of chapter five.

No matter how you use *LifePrints*, whether for self-discovery, to better understand family or friends, or just as a primer on soul psychology, one thing is for sure: knowing your life purpose will change your life in ways you can at this point only barely imagine.

CHAPTER ONE

LIFE PURPOSE, LIFE LESSONS, AND SOUL PSYCHOLOGY DEFINED

Every one of us knows that the content of his life is somehow preserved and sacred.

—VIKTOR FRANKL, *THE DOCTOR OF THE SOUL*

Knowing your life purpose means being clear about your big picture: what your life has amounted to so far and where things are headed. More than a set of core values or a worthy goal, your life purpose is your right life, your reason for being. Finding and living your life purpose is the single most important thing you can ever do.

Robert Goddard, father of modern rocketry, knew his life purpose. At the age of nine, sitting in a tree staring at the moon, he imagined himself building machines that would fly into space. For the next fifty years, on each birthday, he sat in that same tree to re-invigorate the vision that had instilled his life with passion and direction.

Young Geronimo didn't know his life purpose until one day, after fasting and praying naked for two weeks, dehydrated and near exhaustion, he saw a dream deity that promised him battleground invincibility if he would lead the Apaches. Geronimo accepted his call to duty, often invoking his spirit guide for strength and stamina throughout the rest of his life.

Do you know your life purpose?

What if you don't have a tree to stare at the moon from or don't like the fasting-in-the-desert option? What if you are twenty or forty or sixty and have not as yet had any such life-altering revelation; how in this world are you supposed to find *your* life purpose? And say a map with your life purpose on it mysteriously appeared before your very eyes, a life-purpose map with absolute proof of your identity. Would you have the good sense to follow where it led?

Luckily, you do not have to be as smart as a world-class scientist nor as brave as Geronimo to find and pursue your true path. Instead, you can read the life-purpose map printed on your body five months before you were born—your fingerprints. Long associated with identity, your fingerprints contain another level of personal information infinitely more fascinating. Like examining the acorn to know the type of oak tree that may emerge someday, by looking at your fingerprints you can see a coded picture of the person it was always in you to become.

Your life-purpose map is literally at your fingertips.

LIFE PURPOSE IS . . .

Before we look at your life-purpose map, let's start by looking at what life purpose really is. The first thing to know about life purpose is that it is not about getting your life into some ultimately optimal arrangement. Nor is it about matching your capabilities and inclinations to the marketplace. Life purpose is bigger than that. It goes beyond improving your circumstances or even improving yourself. Living your life purpose means developing a state of consciousness that naturally and regularly unfolds into right life.

To illustrate, let's assume that your life purpose is one of the service-oriented ones discussed later in this book. There are four main categories of life purposes that you will learn about in chapter two; service-based life purposes are one of the four. Assuming that you are in a service-oriented life purpose, does that mean that doing something for your family is on purpose for you? Maybe yes, maybe no, maybe maybe. Imagine this scenario: you are the mother of three and you accept an invitation to go out on Tuesday night with some friends. When you announce your plans, your entire family complains. Under pressure, you decide to stay home.

A month later another invitation arrives, and this time you are determined to accept it. As you prepare for your night out, your family unleashes the big guns. "If you don't help me with this most-important-of-all-time homework assignment, I'll know for sure what a bad mother you really are." "Honey, you aren't leaving me alone with the kids when the Smith proposal is due this Friday?" Since your life purpose is service based, does that mean it is in your best interests to stay home again? Absolutely not. Stay home if that is what you decide to do, but staying home under duress is not service. It is servitude.

So you make it out the front door, a chorus of "I never did like your apple pie anyway!" following you to the street. Surprise, the sun rises as usual the next morning. A new attitude starts to pervade your life, and from now on, if you decide to do something for your family, it is much more likely that it will be a real honest-to-goodness service rather than a guilt-motivated obligation. As this simple story demonstrates, it is not what you *do* that makes something on purpose. It is not the outcome engendered. It is the mind set, the attitude involved in the doing that is the difference between (in this case) a life-affirming service and a life-numbing burden.

Looked at this way, all experiences—those that have a happy ending and those that don't—all experiences that bring you closer to a clear recognition of your life purpose are absolutely on purpose for you. Agonizing over how much to do for spouse and children and feeling guilty no matter what you decide are just as much a part of a service-oriented life path as devoting your life to a cause and receiving a Lifetime of Good Deeds Award. Like everyone else, you are not getting into your right life without going through the requisite training program.

Life Purpose Is Ongoing

The second crucial concept about life purpose is a logical outgrowth of the first. If life purpose is a consciousness to inhabit as opposed to an action to take or a set of circumstances to arrive in, then life purpose is a process, a life-sized journey, rather than a final destination. Like Goddard reaching to outer space or Geronimo fighting for freedom, each day you are alive presents new possibilities for discovery and self-expression. Life purpose is always a work in progress.

Already present before your birth, your life purpose is continually being refined and shaped by your experiences. Recognizing your life purpose in its nascent form allows you to take advantage of opportunities you might otherwise miss. Consider Divaldo Franco's story.

At the age of sixteen, this young Brazilian had a dream in which he was shown a photograph of an old man surrounded by smiling children. He was told to look carefully at the photograph and remember it because this was his life purpose: to assist those who had no one else to help them. Although deeply moved, the young man could make no sense of the dream and it soon receded into a corner of his mind.

Five years later, while walking down an alley past a garbage dump, Divaldo heard an infant's cry. There, wrapped in rags, was an abandoned baby boy. Shocked and confused, he picked up the child and, looking into its eyes, remembered the dream from years before. Not knowing what to do, he took the baby home. Months passed. Incredibly, he came across another infant in similar circumstances. What else could he do? He took this child home as well.

Word of his caring and compassion spread, and within a few years his household of orphaned children had grown to five, eventually evolving into a children's center with dozens of abandoned boys and girls. Now, over fifty years later, that first child from the garbage dump has become the doctor of that center, and the boy who dreamt his life purpose is the old man in the photograph, surrounded by smiling children.

Divaldo, Geronimo, and Goddard; a humanitarian, a warrior, and a scientist: one found his heart, another his power, the third the clarity upon which to build a career. Like the Blues Brothers on their Mission from God, things didn't always work out as planned, but knowing their life purpose meant that at least they had an idea of where they were trying to go.

Life Purpose is Non-Circumstantial

Life purpose is a lifelong process devoted to increased self-awareness and the pursuit of meaning. As such, living your life purpose is possible no matter what circumstances you find yourself in today. For instance, if your fingerprints reveal your life purpose to be The Leader, it does not matter if you are too young to be president of the United States or too short to be captain of the basketball team. Your life assignment is to inhabit your leadership consciousness right here, right now, dealing with whatever life sends your way. That is what you came to do in this lifetime. That is where you can find your greatest fulfillment.

Living a leadership life purpose can occur in any number of ways: a prison philosopher holding court in C block, a CEO running a major corporation, a child stopping a fight in a school yard. Leadership can thrive in any environment. You were only a fetus when your fingerprints took form; you've had those same fingerprints all through your life, and you'll have them until you die. The ability to live your life purpose is never a function of current circumstance.

Life Purpose Seeks Meaning

Does my life have significance?

At the center of each person is an essential, irreducible ME that yearns for deeper meaning. Whether this presence is the material-world expression of an eternal spirit or merely the result of bio-receptors triggered by chemicals in the brain, Living on Purpose means being in direct and continual contact with this part of yourself.

Hidden or known, this ME is the guiding force behind all the events of your life, the voice of your destiny calling out to you from your soul. This ME lies within you, constantly seeking to awaken you to its message. It is elusive, it is always there; it is oceanic, it is concrete; it is real, it is a dream. When this ME fully infiltrates your life, a whole new level of satisfaction becomes available and an unselfconscious aliveness takes over. Ray Charles singing, Amelia Earhart flying, your Aunt Mathilda baking her apple pie—like true art, life purpose in action is not easy to define, but you know it when you see it.

James Hillman, psychotherapist and coauthor with Michael Ventura of *We've Had a Hundred Years of Psychotherapy*, knows what life purpose is:

> *If [Jung is right and] at the soul's core we are images, then we must define life as the actualization over time of that original seed image, what Michelangelo called the* imagine del cuor, *or the image in the heart, and that image—not the time that actualized it—is the primary determinant of your life.*
>
> *Do you see what this means?*

It means that our history is secondary or contingent and that the image in the heart is primary and essential. If [this is so]. . . then the things that befall us in the course of time (which we call development) are various actualizations of the image, manifestations of it, and not causes of who we are. I am not caused by my history—my parents, my childhood, my development. These are mirrors in which I may catch glimpses of my image.

This *imagine del cuor* is your life purpose. It is not only visible in fleeting images but is printed right there in full view on your fingertips. And the problems you face, the problems that can make a life so difficult, many of these can now be understood as essentially uncaused, the natural outcome of your life purpose seeking expression. As such, they are not to be changed or overcome as much as to be accepted, integrated, reframed as allies. *LifePrints* is full of stories of people doing just that (or failing to).

Life Purpose Is Objective, Life-Scale, and Personal

There are many ways to learn more about your inner nature. You can go at it from the inside out: meditate, keep a dream journal, take self-development courses. All of these have something to offer, but each is subjective. None offers independent verification, a source outside your inner dialogue with which to measure your own picture of yourself. None guarantees that the insight you've gained will still feel relevant ten years from now.

In search of objectivity, many have turned to the Meyers-Briggs Personality Test. Millions are done every year, and Meyers-Briggs has a reputation for accuracy. But what will it tell you about life purpose and the search for meaning—what Viktor Frankl calls the ultimate human motivator? Nothing.

Historically, religion has claimed this territory. But, if every true believer shares the same call to cosmic duty, then at best all we have is a mass-produced life purpose, identical for millions of people. How then shall we make decisions about this invisible, hard-to-quantify realm of human experience? Is truth merely what any person chooses to believe?

For a life-purpose map to be useful, it needs to be specific to each person, yet it must address the universal question: Why am I here? It needs to resonate with personal experience yet not be too subjective. It must be life-scale yet pertinent to current circumstance. *LifePrints* offers just such a map.

Life Purpose Is Practical and Specific

At the beginning of every life-purpose workshop I teach, participants are asked to write *My Life Purpose Is . . .* at the top of the page and see what written response comes forward. Let's peek in at one workshop and see how everyone is doing trying to define their life purpose.

"Okay, pens down. Tina, please read out loud what you've written about your life purpose."

"Ahem . . . my life purpose is to be a good wife and mother and do everything I can to make my community a better place to live . . . oh, and to visit all the continents before I die . . . but not Antarctica." Tina is glowing, proud of her work. She takes a deep breath and sits down.

"Mathilda."

"My life purpose is to love everyone and to shine my light."

Smiles abound, except for Jim, who sits curmudgeon style, arms folded. When it is his turn, he rises into a Bill Murray stance, somewhat above it all. Everyone is curious to hear what he has to say. "My life purpose is to just once beat my brother at chess." Nervous laughter ricochets around the room. No one is exactly sure what to do about Jim.

Carol is next. She also wants to love, grow, and be a good person. Carson's number one priority is his family. Jules wants to go public by March of next year and canoe the entire Yukon River. Donna is a multidimensional evolving enterprise. Jean is just trying to be happy.

At this point in the seminar, people are shifting in their seats, staring out the window, cleaning their eyeglasses. What can it all mean? Each person's statement seems sincere enough, but when you put them all together they sound repetitious, pleasant but vague, like a junior high school essay contest.

This kind of discomfort often surfaces whenever I lead a life-purpose workshop. The responses you have read are a composite from classes in California. New York participants tend to include more business goals—not as much being and evolving in the Big Apple. Texans often focus on family themes. I get a slightly different set of answers in Europe, but overall the effect remains the same. An unsettling recognition fills the room as it becomes clear that no one has a good answer to the question What Is My Life Purpose?

By the end of the opening exercise it is clear that those in attendance are going to be asked to consider their life purpose in an entirely new way: a way that is practical and specific, one that brings clarity to life choices. We all want to continue growing as people, to have healthy finances and loving relationships. That said, is there any *particular* reason *you* are on this planet?

I believe there is.

Life Purpose Defines What Is Important

Where did we come from and what are we doing here? Whole civilizations were born, grew up, and died around their answers to these two questions. From the ancient Egyptians through the Renaissance, from Romeo and Juliet to you and me, each person and each society defines what is important, and therefore how to order life and resources.

Context is everything.

Imagine the commitment of time and energy necessary to build the pyramids. Did the Egyptians (or their captives) gladly march to Giza, eager contributors to their Pharaoh's immortality, or were they coerced, baking miserably in the Saharan sun? For one each day was slavery, while another exalted in the culmination of a life's dream.

And you, are you baking or exalting? On a macro scale, the governing ethos defines a civilization; on a micro scale, life purpose defines what is important in an individual life.

Look around you. A new worldview is aching to emerge, and with it a new definition of what is important. Like all preceding worldviews, from Cleopatra's to Newton's, our current version, advanced though it may be, has been found confining and incomplete: confining in that too many people live with little or no connection to their life purpose; incomplete in that the current worldview has disregarded or politicized humanity's universal hunger to contribute to something greater than ourselves, to connect to soul, both collectively and as individuals.

Adapt or perish. Any country, company, or person that cannot or will not acknowledge this emerging spiritual reality is doomed. The Information Age will self-destruct, stillborn, choking on a glut of lifeless data if it cannot help individuals better define and manifest that which has lifelong meaning, if it cannot help us all to a higher standard of self-realization.

It is time for humanity to get to its right life before it finds that it is too late to do so. Getting to your own right life is your contribution.

YOUR LIFE LESSON

Knowing your life purpose is your first step toward achieving it. The second step, integrating your life lesson, is where the magic happens.

Like a treasure map torn in two, neither half having the full picture, your soul-psychology map has two components that must be viewed together for its message to become clear. These two halves are your life purpose and your life lesson. Your life purpose is you, effortlessly living the life you were made to be living. Your life lesson is the shadow aspect of your soul psychology, your blindest blind spot, your weak backhand in the Wimbledon of Life. Since your life purpose cannot flourish without your coming to terms with your life lesson, *learning to turn your life lesson from nemesis to ally is the secret passage to life-purpose satisfaction.*

To get a clearer picture of what life lessons are all about, consider this analogy. You are in a hallway with thirteen mirrors—truth mirrors, each one a bit more difficult to look into than the last. "Mirror, mirror on the wall, show me something about myself that I have not been willing to see before." When you get to the thirteenth mirror, the mirror after which there are no more parts of yourself left unexposed—you see revealed the part of you called your life lesson.

Though commonly experienced as an embarrassing inadequacy, this oh-so-human, can't-get-rid-of-it part of your soul psychology is actually an essential contributor and dynamic organizer of your life. Without stumbling into the "problems" your life lesson sets in motion, how would you ever have the growth experiences your life purpose requires?

It is not so easy to think this way when your life lesson is doing its job, as a recent client can attest. Carmen came in for her reading hoping for a clue that might put an end to the frustrating family upsets that (it seemed) were messing up her whole life. Instead, the reading she received challenged her to look at her life from a perspective she had never considered.

Carmen's life purpose was The Artist and her hands were certainly creative enough for such a life path. But her life lesson was Family Connection. As I looked up from her hands, I saw the sad eyes of someone resigned to either becoming a lone wolf or struggling forever with a family that didn't appreciate her special gifts. "I'll never have the family connection I want," the sad eyes cried. "Why can't they accept me as I am? What is wrong with me?"

Where did this terrible ache for family connection and the sense of its impossibility come from? Who knows the source, but there it was in plain view in her fingerprints. The truth is, Carmen felt a creative urge too strong to ignore. But, without a family to appreciate her efforts, something big was missing. Worse, in trying to connect to her family, she felt unseen, and that was devastating. What a dilemma! "Either be me and be alone or give up me so I can join my family. Either way, I lose." At least, that is how it looked to my client. Was there any chance she could see her struggles as a function of her own inner process?

Lights ... Camera ... Action. The delicious dilemma enters the stage. Carnegie Hall is on line one: "We want you for a one-woman show." But Dad is on line two: "Mom is sick. We need you at home." What to do? Without a life-purpose map as her guide, it appears as if Carmen's circumstances have put her in a terrible bind, but from the fingerprint perspective we can see that it is one more inescapable iteration of Carmen's soul psychology expressing itself in still one more disguise.

Seeing the seemingly paradoxical life quest (her family vs. her art) for what it is puts to rest the idea that there is some perfect solution that she must find that will end this tug-of-war once and for all. Carmen's fingerprints say it is her destiny to face recurring choices of this kind. The choices are hers to make, the consequences real. The only question is: what will she learn about herself from the choices that she makes? Recognizing this fact is the beginning of turning her life lesson from nemesis to ally.

THE BENEFITS OF KNOWING YOUR SOUL PSYCHOLOGY

I have seen many people grasp the significance of their life lesson's role in their lives and, in so doing, access the fulfillment that only living their life purpose can bring. I am still surprised, however, when on occasion someone asks me, "What good is knowing your life purpose?" Isn't that self-evident, I wonder. Apparently not.

For me, knowing the life purpose in my fingerprints has confirmed my own sense of who I am and what my life is all about. The more choices that become available to me, the more often I check in on my life-purpose map to keep things in perspective. Knowing my life purpose has afforded me a certain grace under pressure; it has made it easier to take responsibility for life-size errors without being crushed by paralyzing self-criticism. Feeling on purpose has been a blessing, a golden anchor, my guaranteed safe harbor no matter what is happening in my life. Without getting too far ahead of ourselves, let's take a closer look at how knowing your life purpose can improve your life.

Direction and a Sense of Purpose

Finding your life purpose has obvious benefits for your sense of direction, but there are some not-so-obvious directional benefits as well. Three different types of life purposes will serve as examples.

One group of life purposes is dualistic in nature: Tycoon Doing World Service, for instance. In a case like this, completely different skill sets must be used in tandem to find fulfillment. A life spent as a tycoon, without an accompanying element of service to others, is bound to frustrate such a person, as would a life of service to others without a chance to exercise his or her worldly abilities. It is like rowing with only one oar in the water. No wonder you feel you are going in circles. You are. Rowing faster is not going to get you to your destination.

Another group of life purposes is singular: The Teacher, The Artist, or let's say, The Therapist. Often, The Therapist will spend hours on the phone with his or her Aunt Mathilda, providing therapeutic services but without the sense of purpose and satisfaction promised by the fingerprints. Water-cooler amateur psychiatrists may find themselves in the same boat: already doing what their life purpose asks, but on the periphery instead of at the center of their lives. Maybe all you need to do is make it official. If you are on the brink of your life purpose, what will it take for you to make the leap?

For a third group, the life question is not "What?" but "How?" For example, if Live Your Passions is your life purpose, it doesn't matter what you do. Do whatever you want. Just make sure you really want to be doing it. (If you think this is a piece of cake, you obviously are not the owner of these fingerprints. You will find more about this and the other life-purpose possibilities in chapters two through five.)

A Proper Estimation of Possibility

Lots of people tell me they already know their life purpose. Checking their fingerprints, hearing their life stories, sometimes I completely agree. Other times, my client is mostly on purpose, with a bit of tweaking perhaps all that is called for. Most often, however, those who tell me they are on purpose actually mean that they have a goal they are after, like Jules from the life-purpose workshop who wanted to canoe the Yukon. Or I hear something lacking in directional value, like Mathilda shining her light. Fingerprints point the way to the real questions at the very base of your existence.

Another issue that often impedes the discovery of life purpose is the habitual underestimation of possibility. "I am the fellow who couldn't find my keys the other day. I have messed up X, Y, and Z in my life. What right do I have entertaining such a grandiose image of myself? Anyway, it would be egotistical to think I could . . . Besides, I am too young, too old, too tall, too short. . . ." Marianne Williamson put it nicely when she wrote, "Our deepest fear is not that we are inadequate, our deepest fear is that we are powerful beyond measure." Perhaps you need to consider the possibility that you are capable of more than you ever imagined.

Seeing Your Limitations in a New Light

LifePrints is a system of dynamic polarities in which personality inconsistencies and repetitious struggles (life lessons and delicious dilemmas) do not imply character defect or sin, nor is triumph the end point. Instead, difficulties and failure are integral parts of the quest for meaning, and success is measured by the awareness you have gained.

Carmen, The Artist, can't know how long her current family difficulties will continue. But given her life purpose and life lesson, choices involving family and her creativity (whether debilitating or life affirming) are bound to be what she comes up against. Knowing this, perhaps she will not be so hard on herself upon her next encounter, one of those acausal moments that psychotherapist James Hillman suggests is a chance to catch her soul's image peeking out at her from the truth mirror.

In the movie *As Good as It Gets*, Jack Nicholson tells Helen Hunt that being with her has made him want to be a better man. Maybe cleaning up your act because now there is a reason to do so is the true benefit of knowing your life purpose. Shortly, you will gain your own life-purpose map. You will track its path over earlier events in your life. You will consider your future possibilities and come to your own conclusions.

THE PRINCIPLES OF SOUL PSYCHOLOGY

Soul psychology is a term I use to differentiate the information in your unalterable fingerprints, your life purpose and life lesson, from your personality psychology as revealed in the evolving lines on your hands and the ever-changing shape of your palms and fingers. The idea that each person has two psychologies, independent yet inextricably linked, underlies the LifePrints system.

One's soul psychology is permanent, indelibly hardwired into the psyche. Its goals are life-scale. Meaning and fulfillment are its prize. Conversely, the personality is ego driven, as well it should be. With its shifting motivational patterns and learned behaviors, it is constantly in flux. The dance between these two psychologies makes life the interesting drama that it is.

LifePrints' focus is on the soul psychology side of the ledger. With this in mind, we now examine the three principles at the heart of soul psychology that will help you to understand your life-purpose map as you begin its construction in chapter two.

Principle One: Experience Required

Any experience is capable of unlocking your life purpose.

This is a central tenet of soul psychology. To illustrate, let's look at two people reacting in their own ways to a similar set of circumstances. Bob from Boise has a leadership-based life purpose and a history of abuse. His father beat him, physically and emotionally. At school, Bob got bullied by the bigger kids; even his parakeet showed him no respect. Twenty-five years later, while accepting the Citizen of the Year Award, Bob credits his early experiences as pivotal in his development. Having been on the wrong end of the stick in his early life, his threshold for stoic resignation gone, he could not sit idly by watching one more instance of injustice. Someone needed to set things straight. Surprising himself with his assertion, Bob rose to the occasion and took the actions that led to his award.

Fred from East Frasalia had a similar childhood; however, Fred moved in the opposite direction: he became a power abuser. He was too controlling in relationships. He had power battles with legitimate authorities in the world and at work. He treated his parakeet badly. Then an incident occurred that turned his whole life around. "Oh my God, what have I done?" It hurt Fred deeply to realize the pain he had caused. He made amends where amends needed making. He became particularly sensitive to any possibility that his actions might cause discomfort in others. When life presented him with leadership opportunities, Fred, having learned from past mistakes, was still assertive but now he was empathetic as well.

In these two examples, similar origins led to the emergence of a leadership-based life purpose in different ways. Of course, there is always the alternative possibility: Bob and Fred might learn nothing from their earlier experiences. Unconsciously trudging through life, they might make no progress toward the leadership purpose they share in common. If this were the case, Bob and Fred would both live in their life-purpose inverses (powerlessness for Bob, tyranny for Fred).

Life being the messy business it is, rarely does a straight-line diagram describe a person's life. In retrospect, we can see The Leader slowly going through its developmental phases in both Bob and Fred's lives, while in the short term, each zig and zag seems random and all consuming. The thing to remember is that any experience can serve a person's progress.

Problems Are Part of the Process Let's say that you do learn from your experiences sufficiently for your life purpose to clearly emerge. Like Picasso discovering his passion for art, you have opened the door into the main sequence of your life purpose. You are gaining satisfaction points on a regular basis.

Congratulations. Does this mean that everything is now automatically rosy? No. You have problems (or you do not) like everyone else in the world. However, now, Picasso, when you have a problem you have an Artist problem, the exact type of problem you are supposed to have.

Let's put Jacques Cousteau into our illustration, assuming he was right on purpose with his life. Was Jacques Cousteau's existence trouble free? What do you think? As the world's most famous ocean explorer, he got to explore the toughest ocean environments, to address challenges beyond the scope of anyone else. Difficulties abounded. Nor did Jacques want a life free of all difficulties. When he got to the Gates of Heaven (however you interpret that phrase), Jacques would have wanted a good story or two about how tough things were in his day so he could hold his own with the ancient mariners already there. "We had to make our own boats," one would say. "That's nothing," an even more ancient one would suggest, "We had to invent sailing itself."

The point is that for Jacques boat problems were the type of problems that he was supposed to have. Factory problems ("I can't take another day on this assembly line") were not problems that would have moved Jacques's life purpose along. If he were lucky, an old salt might have set him straight. "The problem, Jacques, is that you are in the wrong life here. Go find you a boat."

So *you* find *your* boat. Are you done now, is your life purpose complete? Not at all. You are just beginning. Welcome to your right life. Now, what are you going to do about the mutiny in the Miami office? What about time for your family now that you are so busy? And so on. Similarly, when Picasso unlocks The Artist within, has he finished his life purpose? Of course not. Now it is his job to have a lifetime of Artist experiences and express this life on his canvas of choice.

The more consciously you gain in experience, the more your true self emerges. The more your true self emerges, the more your life purpose blossoms. The more your life purpose blossoms, the more you will like the life you are living.

The Goldilocks Rule: Too Much / Too Little Leads to Just Right You know the fairy tale. Goldilocks is lost in the woods and comes upon a house. Going inside, she finds a table set for breakfast: three bowls of porridge, steam rising. (What, no cappuccino?) Hungry, Goldilocks tastes the first porridge: too hot. The second is too cold, but the third is just right. She goes into the next room where she finds three beds. The first one is too hard, the next is too soft, but the third is just right. If you don't know what happens when the three bears come home to find her asleep in their bedroom, you can look it up on the Internet.

Goldilocks, though only a child, is a true master of this three-dimensional plane. Look at her experimental method: she tries something out. It is too this or that. She tries again, this time going to the opposite extreme. Again she goes too far. But she perseveres and finds that which is just right. Too much, too little, just right—that's the master's formula.

To gain experiences, humans go too far and not far enough on their way (hopefully) to just right. The trick is to learn from your experience, to follow the Goldilocks Rule and not to get stuck forever playing ping-pong between uncomfortable extremes that represent inappropriate responses to circumstances. To make this as clear as possible, let's see if we can spot the Goldilocks Rule at work in the next story.

Gilda is totally infatuated with George. I guess that is why she agreed to give him the money she had been saving for college. The plan is for Gilda to meet up with George in Alaska in a few weeks, where he will be building a cabin for them to live in. They will start an organic farm and live happily ever after. Arriving in Alaska, Gilda finds no cabin, no George, no zucchinis. Maybe next time she won't be so trusting with someone she has just met.

Fast-forward fifteen years: Gilda has not had a serious relationship since George. In effect, she has locked the barn door after the horses have gone, but she's not complaining. "I don't need a man to be happy," she says, and who wants to argue with that? Then Phil shows up. Gilda helps Phil to sobriety. Phil is grateful. They fall in love. Phil moves into Gilda's townhouse. Somehow, Phil loses his job. UH-OH. One and a half years later, Phil is still not gainfully employed.

Did you spot the Goldilocks Rule working its inevitable influence over Gilda's life? Gilda's life lesson, it turns out, is Surrender Skills. As such, early attempts at surrender will be the attempts of a novice. Big errors are to be expected. So, fifteen years old, she surrenders to George. Sex, drugs, rock and roll; I guess Gilda surrendered too much. Phase II: fifteen years later, she finds she has been unable to say the words "I love you" to any man. Here is surrender error #2: surrender too little. She meets Phil: surrender error #3: surrender too much again. This is the Goldilocks Rule in action. Too Much, Too Little. Repeat as necessary.

Two years after breaking up with Phil, Gilda has resumed dating again. At least this time she didn't need a fifteen-year hiatus. She is still looking for her first good relationship, but the barn door is neither carelessly flung open nor is it nailed shut. This is progress, and progress on your life lesson is what opens the door to life purpose. After all, how is Gilda going to learn except through trial and error?

As your experience level increases, your ability to make choices improves and your outcomes will be more in your favor. However, you cannot gain experience without trial and error. You are not supposed to get it right the first time. Progress is the key. You have permission to learn.

Principle Two: The Paradox Principle

The quest for any life purpose automatically puts one into direct contact with its opposite.

People come into my office. I read their hands. Inevitably, each personal history follows the prescribed possibility formula imprinted in the fingerprints five months before birth. As I listen to my clients' descriptions of their lives, it's easy to identify the life purpose *and* the life-purpose inverse in the events and circumstances they choose to share. That's it, each and every time. Incredible.

It is as if we are playing out our lives on a giant personal game board with the game squares preprinted. Your personality is like the top hat, race car, or other token. You roll the dice, move forward nine spaces. Boardwalk and Park Place, Go to Jail; as you circle the board, the squares stay the same and your chosen destiny, your life purpose and its inverse, come into focus. As your skills improve, time spent in your life-purpose inverse may decrease, but it never reduces to zero. Nor should it.

Gilda, our Prisoner of Love, needs to learn what love and closeness are *not* before she is ready for a fulfilling relationship. The path to power implies bone-crushing bouts with humility. Healers must deal with their unhealthful behaviors. The list goes on. As these examples suggest, the Paradox Principle pervades our lives just as assuredly as does the law of gravity. All life paths follow this route, as we will witness time and again throughout the remainder of this book.

Principle Three: The Validity of the Personality

It is incumbent upon each of us to let our personality emerge in its inherent form, to work with this personality on the goals that are selected from a soul level for this lifetime. Errors arise when we either attempt to ignore the personality completely or when we seem to forget that it is only the vehicle for our life purpose, not the purpose itself.

For instance, you may have a business career, yet your life purpose asks you to become The Mentor if you are to find your highest fulfillment. In this case, being a successful businessperson fulfills the personality need, but by itself will not bring life-purpose satisfaction.

Or you may be hiding your true talents, like Will Hunting, the math genius in *Good Will Hunting*. For people such as these, life-purpose satisfaction is elusive. The validity of the personality says you must be the you that you really are for your life purpose to emerge.

Other people have life purposes and personality styles totally in harmony with each other, like Carmen, our Artist with family issues from a few pages back. She has all the talent in the world with which to manifest her life purpose and she is actively engaged in doing so. Still, there is a developmental process her personality must go through before her life purpose can take its ultimate form.

See if you can apply the validity of the personality to the character in the following case study.

The Personality Is the Vehicle; The Soul Sets the Agenda Shelly was a slightly built woman, angular in appearance and serious in manner. Clearly, all unnecessary fat molecules had disappeared from her body years ago, banished in disgrace. A trace of mirth remained behind her eyes, slightly amused at the process of having her hands read. The rest of her face seemed haggard, as if she alone were responsible for taking inventory at the world's largest Wal-Mart.

Shelly's fingerprints revealed one of The Artist–type life purposes, and auspiciously enough her line markings revealed a Star of Apollo, the perfect sign in the palm for high creativity. Unfortunately for Shelly, her Star of Apollo was missing one of its six component parts. It is not easy to earn a Star of Apollo. To find one in your hand, even an imperfect one, is still good news, like finding a Lamborghini in your garage, only to learn later that it needs engine work. This particular five-sixths Star of Apollo was being towed to the garage because the line that represents discipline and due diligence was nowhere to be found. The irony was that Shelly couldn't be more exacting in her personal accountability if she were head timekeeper at Greenwich. What was going on?

The Personality Is Attracted to and Resistant to the Life Purpose Here before me was a person with all the discipline she could possibly need, yet none of it was devoted to creative endeavors (hence the absence of one-sixth of the Star of Apollo). This might all be fine and dandy if Shelly's life purpose were not to express her creative nature. Since The Artist was Shelly's life purpose, as long as this aspect of her self was ignored, the door into her right life would remain shut, satisfaction would elude her, and she would spend her days in the big gaping hole (life without meaning). Shelly's Star of Apollo held the key to her life purpose, but would she use it?

The Personality Can Animate the Life Purpose or Suppress It Imagine Shelly at the Cosmic Laboratory, mixing the ingredients into the cauldron that eventually would be her personality makeup for this lifetime. "Let's see, I'll pour in a lot from the Jar of Creativity (after all, I want to devote myself to creative pursuits), but let's add a solid dose from the Jar of Responsibility (I don't want to just dabble, you know). Oops, maybe that's too much responsibility. Oh well . . ." Next thing you know, Shelly is walking through Wal-Mart with a clipboard, light years away from the art classes that energized her in high school.

In this case, the personality has taken over. Instead of being the lieutenant to her creative side, keeping her studio neat, cleaning her brushes immediately after use, the conservative side of Shelly's nature is acting like the General in Charge, making the big choices, defining her life. Then again, Shelly is only in her early thirties. There will be plenty of time for breakdowns and breakthroughs. We'll just have to wait and see how this one turns out.

ESCAPING THE BIG GAPING HOLE

The big gaping hole is the phrase we use at the International Institute of Hand Analysis to signify life without meaning, life without purpose. Most people have visited the big gaping hole at some point or other, but to feel stuck there with no possibility of escape—what could be worse? Perhaps one of the biggest benefits of knowing the life purpose revealed in your fingerprints is that it provides a way out of the big gaping hole.

In the first few months of my hand reading career, I was wrestling with my own big gaping hole. My dreams were particularly vivid during that time and in one of them I was at the end of my life, faced with a panel of judges. I had to prove that I had done enough, loved enough, learned enough to justify my life. Next morning, as I prepared for the first reading of the day, the judges were still staring down at me. Oh yes, I had made mistakes. I could have done any number of things better. And what hadn't I done? I was gripped by the need to not waste this lifetime living in the big gaping hole.

The doorbell brought me back to reality. Time to read another pair of hands, another set of hopes and fears. I dissolved into the pattern of the hands before me and started to sense the life revealed therein. Usually I am the one to talk first, but that day was different. She was crying before anything was said. Catching her breath, she told me her story. The particulars are not important; more important was the wave of feeling that swept the room. Her dam had broken; words came flooding out, and I felt the overarching ache of her life—not lost love, as utterly painful as that can be; not lost direction or being overwhelmed at life's difficulties, as deeply troublesome as those are; not the death of a loved one. No. It was the big gaping hole that was consuming her: life without meaning and the feeling that it would always be thus. Nothing would ever amount to anything—a wasted life.

That was what engulfed her and filled my office and half a city block for all I knew. I let it wash over me and held on to my chair, like Ulysses tied to the mast. Then it subsided. The storm had passed, though it would surely come again. I didn't want to be glib; what use were words in the face of such emotion? But she had come for a reading, and it was my turn to speak. I revealed her life purpose, her life lesson, and her delicious dilemma. Her circumstances matched up, she informed me. We completed the reading. I wish it had been on video so she could have seen her before-and-after pictures. Believing that her life might actually have a purpose and that it was potentially within her grasp, she looked ten years younger.

Back at my desk, my judges were still there. They didn't say anything, but I felt a lot better than I had an hour and a half before.

Every life has its own story, a life-scale battle royal in the inner theater of mind and soul. Nobody, it seems, just waltzes through life. Or maybe some do. I just haven't met them yet.

And the by-a-fingernail escapes from the big gaping hole, the perseverance in the face of life-lesson dilemmas—we are all wrestling each day with such matters. On a different scale than my client that day perhaps, but the battle is just as real. Great men and women of history get their biographies written, but for the rest of us, where besides our fingerprints are such epic tales told of victory and loss?

FROM THEORY TO PRACTICE

It is time to move from theory to practice. In the next chapter, you will begin to construct your life-purpose map by identifying your ten fingerprints and finding your school, an essential element in both your life purpose and life lesson. Chapter three will teach you how to identify your life purpose and life lesson. Chapter four will give you a deeper understanding of your life purpose and life lesson by going into more detail on the meanings of the fingerprints and the fingers on which they appear. Chapter five will pull all the aspects of your soul psychology together in a life-fulfillment formula and offer exercises to apply what you have learned to your own life. At that point, as you look over your past and current circumstances, there is no telling what you might realize about yourself.

CHAPTER TWO

IDENTIFY YOUR FINGERPRINTS AND FIND YOUR SCHOOL

These new maps are charting the world all over again. They reinvent our idea of frontier. They push back the boundaries of what we know and what we might explore. They are changing our notions, not only of what the future might hold, but where we are likely to find that future, which in some ways is the most important geographic question of all.

— STEPHEN S. HALL, *MAPPING THE NEXT MILLENNIUM*

Constructing and interpreting your life-purpose map requires that you complete the following five steps:

STEP 1 Identify and record your ten fingerprints.

STEP 2 Identify your school at the Earth University.

STEP 3 Identify your life purpose.

STEP 4 Identify your life lesson.

STEP 5 Create your life-fulfillment formula.

This should take you about sixty to ninety minutes for the first set of fingerprints you look at, five to ten minutes for the next several sets, and less than a minute after you get familiar with the system. Chapter two covers the first two steps. Steps three through five are covered in the next three chapters. At the end of chapter five, there is a series of journaling exercises designed to help you use your life-purpose map as a daily compass to meaning and fulfillment.

STEP 1: IDENTIFY AND RECORD YOUR TEN FINGERPRINTS

Your first assignment is to identify the type of each of your ten fingerprints. A good light and a magnifying glass will greatly simplify this process. Slowly rotate the tip of each finger ever so slightly from side to side and aim your eye to the middle of the pattern. If you are having any difficulty, step outside. Sunlight is better than any light you have in the house. What if your fingerprints are very faint? What if stray lines make your fingerprints hard to see? What if you forget to take off your gloves? Relax. Take a breath. You will be able to read your fingerprints. You may have to take two minutes to see all ten. That's OK.

The Four Main Fingerprint Types

Each of the four main fingerprint types has a meaning that will be covered later in this chapter. There is an additional layer of meaning depending upon the finger on which the fingerprint appears. This will be discussed in chapter three.

Whorl with circular center | Whorl with S center | Whorl with spiral center

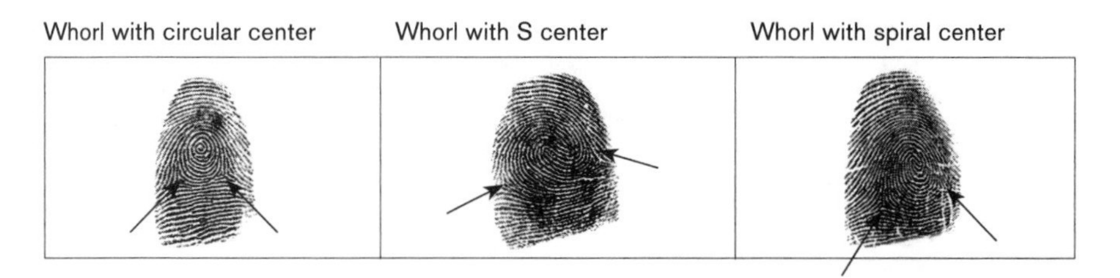

Whorls have two triradii, points where the pattern splits into three directions (see above). The center of the whorl pattern may look like a circle, an S pattern, or a spiral.

Loops

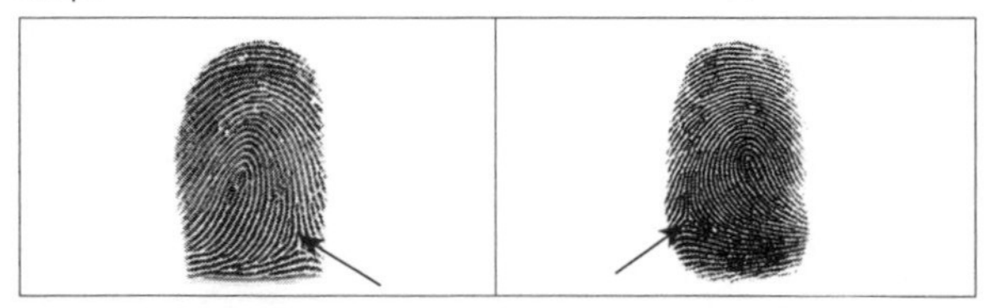

Loops have one off-centered triradius (see above). Loops that open away from the thumb are called *ulnar loops*. Loops that open toward the thumb are called *radial loops*. The significance of the ulnar and radial loops is discussed on page 60.

Tented arches

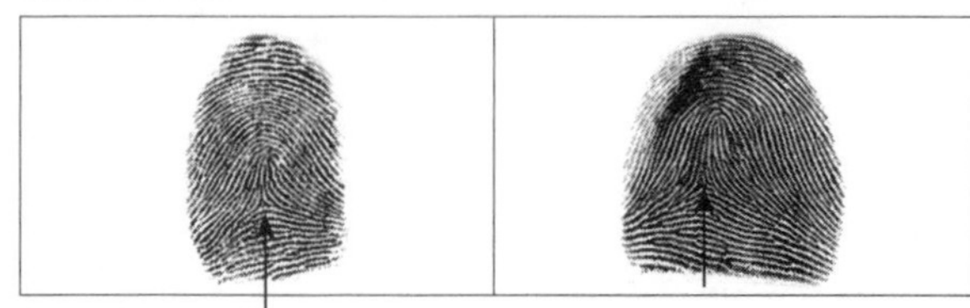

Tented arches have a single, centralized triradius and a vertical tent pole (see above).

Arches

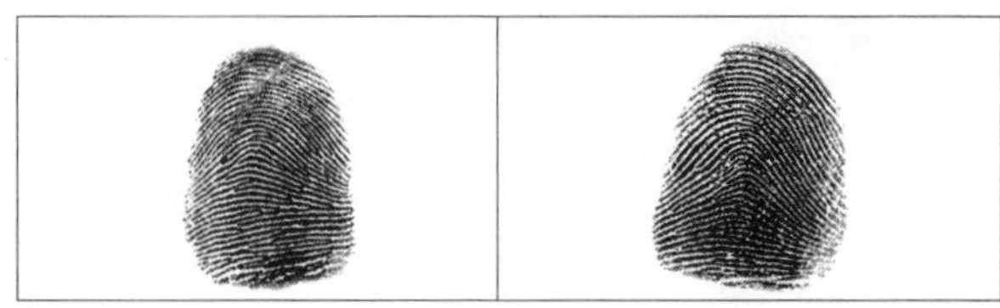

Arches do not have any triradii. There is a bump in the middle of the fingerprint, but no tent pole.

The following chart shows the four main fingerprint types. The last column contains the written symbol you will use to record your ten fingerprints on page 23.

FOUR MAIN FINGERPRINTS

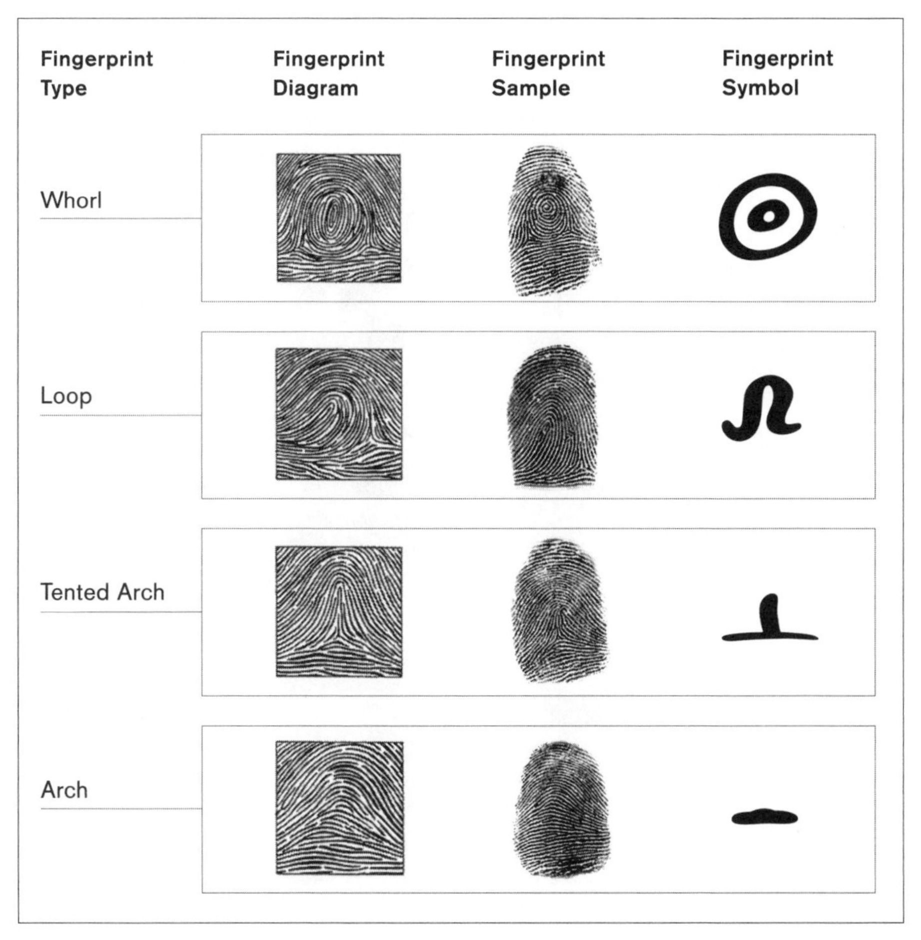

Fingerprint Variations

Sometimes one or more of your fingerprints won't look like one of the four main types. In this case, you probably have a fingerprint variation. The most common fingerprint variations are the composite whorl, the peacock, and the loop/tented arch.

- The composite whorl forms an S pattern.
- The peacock is a hybrid: part whorl and part loop.
- The loop/tented arch is also a hybrid: it looks like a tented arch, but the tent pole is slightly off center and not vertical.

The following chart shows the three fingerprint variations. The last column contains the written symbol you will use to record your ten fingerprints on the chart opposite.

THREE FINGERPRINT VARIATIONS

Fingerprint Type	Fingerprint Diagram	Fingerprint Sample	Fingerprint Symbol
Composite Whorl			
Peacock			
Loop/ Tented Arch			

Record Your Fingerprints

As you identify each of your ten fingerprints, write the symbol for that fingerprint in the appropriate box on the chart below (if you don't want to write in the book, copy the chart into your life-purpose journal and note your fingerprints in the appropriate boxes). For example, in the sample set of fingerprints, the person has a whorl on the right thumb, a tented arch on the right index finger, a loop on the right middle finger, and so on. When you have identified all ten of your fingerprints and written down their appropriate symbols, you are ready for step two.

SAMPLE FINGERPRINTS

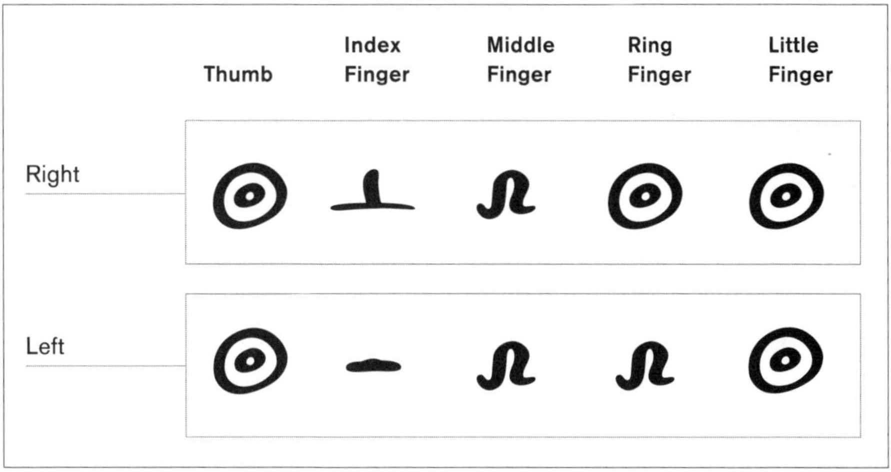

	Thumb	Index Finger	Middle Finger	Ring Finger	Little Finger
Right					
Left					

MY FINGERPRINTS

	Thumb	Index Finger	Middle Finger	Ring Finger	Little Finger
Right					
Left					

STEP 2: IDENTIFY YOUR SCHOOL AT THE EARTH UNIVERSITY

Your school, which you will identify shortly, is a soul-level initiation, a life-scale training program that works its way into every corner of your life. At your best, the experiences you garner in your school are highly rewarding and become an integral part of living your life purpose.

The four schools, each represented by one of the main fingerprint types (see chart below), correspond to four themes of human development, ranging from the most basic (feeling safe in your body), to the development of awareness and intellect, to the recognition of heart and empathy, and finally to the inclination to serve others. Each person is challenged to grow in each of these four areas. *None is more or less important than the others*, but the school you are in represents the area of development worthy of your extra attention. As your life-purpose map comes into full view, you will gain a greater perspective on the pivotal role this developmental theme has played, and continues to play, in your personal growth.

THE FOUR SCHOOLS OVERVIEW

School	Fingerprint	Theme	Developmental Focus
Service	Whorl	Spirit	Self vs. others
Love	Loop	Heart	Emotional growth
Wisdom	Tented Arch	Mind	Issues of commitment
Peace	Arch	Body	A life in balance

To identify your school, you will count the number of each type of fingerprints you have and then compare your results to the Number Necessary column in the chart below. If you have the "borderline" number of prints, you will experience some of the issues of the listed school, but not to the extent that you would if you had a "yes" number of prints. If you have two borderlines, then you are in both schools. Three borderlines means you are in three schools. (See page 47 for more information about belonging to multiple schools.)

School	Fingerprint	Symbol	Number Necessary
Service (page 28)	Whorl		4 = Yes 3 = Borderline
Love (page 33)	Loop		8 = Yes 7 = Borderline
Wisdom (page 37)	Tented Arch		2 = Yes 1 = Borderline
Peace (page 42)	Arch		2 = Yes 1 = Borderline

If you have one of the three fingerprint variations, count them as directed below.

- Composite whorls count as regular whorls toward the School of Service.
- Peacocks count as half whorls and half loops or, in other words, a half point toward the School of Service and a half point toward the School of Love.
- Loop/tented arches count as half loops and half tented arches or, in other words, a half point toward the School of Love and a half point toward the School of Wisdom.

Let's practice with some sample fingerprints before you identify your own school.

EXAMPLE 1

	Thumb	Index Finger	Middle Finger	Ring Finger	Little Finger
Right					
Left					

The person in example 1 above has one whorl and nine loops. This is not enough whorls to qualify for the School of Service (at least four whorls are needed) but is enough to get into the School of Love (at least eight loops are needed). This person has no tented arches or arches, which rules out the School of Wisdom and the School of Peace.

Thus, this person is in the School of Love.

EXAMPLE 2

	Thumb	Index Finger	Middle Finger	Ring Finger	Little Finger
Right					
Left					

The person in example 2 has three whorls, two peacocks, and five loops. Four whorls are required to be in the School of Service, so with three whorls and two peacocks (peacocks count half toward the School of Service and half toward the School of Love), the total count for whorls is four. This is enough to qualify for the School of Service. Eight loops are required for the School of Love, so a count of six (five loops plus two half loops from the peacocks) is not enough to qualify. This person has no tented arches or arches, which rules out the School of Wisdom and the School of Peace. Thus, this person is in the School of Service.

Refer to your fingerprint chart on page 23 or consult the chart you recorded in your life-purpose journal. Count up each type of fingerprint and find your school. Be careful of jumping to premature conclusions about your soul psychology. You will need to complete steps three, four, and five to get the full picture.

I have _4_ whorls (including composite whorls).
I have ___ peacocks (which count one-half toward a whorl).
Therefore, I have _4_ points toward being in the School of Service.

I have ___ loops.
I have ___ peacocks (which count one-half toward a loop).
I have ___ loop/tented arches (which count one-half toward a loop).
Therefore, I have ___ points toward being in the School of Love.

I have ___ tented arches.
I have ___ loop/tented arches (which count one-half toward a tented arch).
Therefore, I have ___ points toward being in the School of Wisdom.

I have ___ arches.
Therefore, I have ___ points toward being in the School of Peace.

Checking my totals, I am in the school(s) of _Service_________.

Now that you have identified your school(s), let's find out what that means.

THE SCHOOL OF SERVICE

WHORL

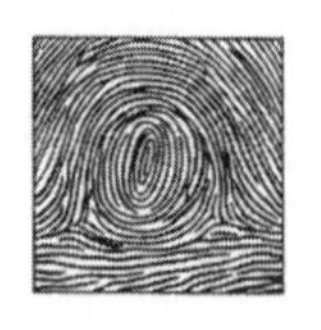

OBJECTIVE: To become a master of service consciousness
REQUIREMENT: Four fingerprints of the whorl category (three whorls is borderline)
SKILL NEEDED: Knowing when to do and when not to do for others

- True service comes from a desire to help others, not control them.
- It empowers both the giver and receiver.
- It feels good regardless of outcome.
- The activity itself is reward enough.

Overview

Helping others can make a person feel good. Really good. It is part of what it means to be human. Knowing you have contributed, that you helped make the world (or someone's world) a better place, can bring meaning and life-scale satisfaction to anyone. However, for those whose fingerprints include four or more whorls, the theme is central and unending. If this is your school, there is not one major incident in your life, not one key relationship, that does not at its core involve issues of service. It is your challenge to awaken to this part of yourself and, in so doing, learn its value as a compass on your life's journey.

This is perhaps the most paradoxical of the four major soul initiations available at the Earth University. Before service can become the fully integrated part of your life that it was meant to be, certain experiences, *experiences seemingly at odds with service*, must be encountered. It is one thing to understand the concept of service. It is quite another matter to live it joyously.

On the road to service consciousness, you must experience all aspects of yourself that are not aligned with service. Your self-absorbed side (and its cost) becomes apparent, as does the inclination to misinterpret obligation for service. In this way, all un-service-like components are brought to conscious awareness. The process of dealing with and learning from service errors ultimately reveals the unique true service that craves expression.

It does not matter who plays which role in your life movie. You may be too selfish in one part of your life, the martyred do-gooder somewhere else. Perhaps you get to live with the king or queen of self-indulgence, or your child is too generous in trying to gain approval points at school. No matter: "If it is in your hands, it is in your life," we like to say at the IIHA. For you to make progress in your service training, all niches of the subject must be studied thoroughly.

As you make progress, as servitude and self-indulgence decrease, life satisfaction increases. As life satisfaction increases, your ability to do service gets better as more of your personal talents emerge. The particular service for which you are most suited comes into focus.

Four Steps to Service Mastery

If you have four or more whorls, the service vs. servitude theme takes form as your life unfolds. This happens automatically whether you are aware of it or not. As you read steps one through four, try to see yourself as the causative agent in your story, not the victim. If you can, you are already making good progress.

Step 1: The Setup Life presents you with a circumstance and you get to do something for somebody. (In the School of Service, it is your assignment to practice "being of service.")

Step 2A: All Goes Well "Thank you." "You're welcome." No complications.

or

Step 2B: Complications Arise You do everything to assist, but the more you do, the lousier things get. Your load is feeling heavier and appreciation is not forthcoming. As you serve ever more fervently, you may even face rejection for not doing enough, not doing it sooner, or some other objection. Service training means practice, and practice means trial and error.

You are now experiencing service error.

All is proceeding as planned.

Step 3: Escalation Demands escalate.

Your mother wants you to do something for her, that wonderful woman who worked three jobs to get you through medical school. She wants to move in with you. With her new boyfriend. And his mariachi band, including dancers. You'll have to sleep on the porch; no, they need the porch. You'll have to sleep in the backyard. In the rain. And while you're out there, could you. . . ? The Escalation Clause has worked to perfection. Now you definitely know you are in servitude . . . again.

Things are not always as black and white as in the example above, but if your first and last thoughts each day are about how to get out of this hole you have found yourself in, you are probably in servitude. Things can remain this way indefinitely, until you arrive in service backlash: "Get off my back! I ain't doin' nothin' for nobody no more 'cept me." It is ironic that those on the path of service must first learn to become selfish, but without a sense of self there can be no true service.

Step 4: Breakthrough Service backlash provides some measure of relief and is an important step on your road to true service, but it still falls short on life-scale satisfaction. Consciously experiencing this shortfall is crucial. It is your opportunity to learn the difference between self-indulgence and an appropriate sense of personal identity. So, leaving service backlash behind, you change strategies, embracing your mother and the whole mariachi band from the bottom of your heart. No regrets. As the song says, "They ain't heavy, they're my family."

Unfortunately, two weeks of sleeping out in the rain with mariachi music coming from the porch is too much for most service trainees. You re-enter service backlash and repeat steps one through three several more times until, magically it seems, your entire outlook shifts of its own accord.

"I do what I darn well please," you declare, "and I darn well please to be of service."

So, service diploma in hand, you tell your mom that she and the band can stay, but you are keeping your room and the music has to quit at 10 P.M. Or you join the band yourself and eventually play at the old folks' home each Christmas. Or you help your mom some other way that better fits your lifestyle. No matter what selection you make, you find a way to be of service without feeling controlled by the needs of everyone around you. It works out well for your mom, and it works out well for you. Good going! You are now properly prepared for the next set of challenges on your service path, challenges that carry even more meaningful service rewards.

Steps to Service Mastery Summary

STEP 1 The Setup: You do something for somebody.

STEP 2 Complications Arise: You do more and more and things get worse and worse.

STEP 3 Escalation: You finally explode in frustration, deciding you are not going to do any more.

STEP 4 Breakthrough: The energy shifts and doing for others becomes incredibly rewarding.

Remember, your fingerprints do not make you do anything. They are merely the outward and visible map of your inward and invisible soul psychology. See if you can follow the School of Service developmental steps in the following story.

Miss America and the Yellow Rock Gary was hiking on the trail when he came upon Archie, who seemed to be struggling. Gary offered to carry Archie's tent for him. Archie was pleased, and they hiked together. At the top of the hill, Gary gave Archie back his tent.

"Thank you."

"You're welcome."

Another wonderful day at the Earth University.

Next day Gary came upon Sally, a Miss America candidate. Gary offered to take five pounds off Sally's backpack, but pretty soon he had ten pounds, twelve pounds, fifteen pounds. And later, when she remarked how pretty that yellow rock was, Gary found himself with fifteen pounds and a yellow rock. Finally getting to the top of the hill, Gary saw Sally hanging out with her boyfriend.

Gary was stewed. He felt used. But had Sally deceived Gary? Not at all. In Gary's attempt to obligate Sally to him, he had become the obligated party. He could have told Sally he found her attractive. He could have invited her to join him at his campsite. She would have said yes, no, or maybe. Instead, he performed what he deemed a service and wound up in servitude. Had *Archie* asked Gary to carry more pounds, or if Archie thought the yellow rock was pretty, Gary would have reacted differently. Oh well. If carrying one yellow rock up one hill is the worst servitude that Gary winds up in, he will be doing better than 99.9 percent of the service trainees at the Earth University. However, odds are this is not an isolated incident in Gary's life story.

You Know You Are in Servitude If . . .

Training programs at the Earth University are a tricky business. You can be looking right at the issue and still not be sure if what you are doing is service, servitude, or service backlash (it might be some of each). Here is an extra guide to help you.

You know you are in servitude if you are the only one in the canoe (corporate yacht?) who is paddling and the other passengers are complaining that you are splashing too much while they drink all your beer in the back of the canoe.

You know you are in servitude if you go with your friend to the PTA meeting, just for support, and you wind up volunteering to bake cookies for the upcoming fund-raiser. Later you find yourself organizing the entire event as various parents beg off with spurious excuses. It is not much longer before you start getting flak for not taking everyone's hypersensitive feelings into perfect account. And then it hits you like a safe dropped from five stories above: YOU ARE DEFINITELY IN SERVITUDE. Take heart, Master of Service trainee. This is your opportunity for awakening.

If you have gotten rid of all those freeloaders who have been feeding at your trough and finally found some time for yourself, but you notice you are rereading *War and Peace* for the third time (this year) and the only time your phone rings is for a taped sales call—as the parameters of your life get smaller and smaller, maybe you should consider leaving service backlash behind.

Master of Service Checklist

- ☐ Masters of Service are free to say yes or no to requests.
- ☐ Masters of Service take their own needs into account, along with the needs of others.
- ☐ Masters of Service can renegotiate agreements as circumstances warrant.
- ☐ Masters of Service have learned that doing for others is its own reward. The wonderful feeling that joyous service brings is not a function of the reactions or behaviors of other people.

Life-Purpose Maps That Exemplify the School of Service

Appendix I: Archetypal Combinations and Case Studies has life stories that exemplify each of the four schools. If your school is service, check the following three case studies in particular for more information on your school.

- Family Issues in the School of Service/Emily (see page 179)
- Crumb Work (see page 205)
- The Lone Tree on the Plain (see page 261)

THE SCHOOL OF LOVE

LOOP

OBJECTIVE: Emotional mastery, love and closeness
REQUIREMENT: Eight fingerprints of the loop category (seven loops is borderline)
SKILLS NEEDED: Emotional authenticity, vulnerability skills

- Love, as defined here, means the ability to establish and maintain satisfying relationships.
- It includes the ability to feel, display, and communicate a full range of feelings, in the emotional moment, at an appropriate intensity, completely.

Overview

Emotional connection, closeness, love: can you imagine a life without them? Yet how can something so natural, so essential to human existence, something that at times is so easy—how can the world of emotions get so complicated? What does loving someone really mean? One thing is clear: the road to 'emotional mastery involves overcoming whatever barriers may exist in feeling and expressing your genuine emotional self.

Because loops are the fingerprint that occur most often, this is, statistically speaking, the most popular of the four major soul initiations. Yet, it seems to be the one with the greatest degree of misunderstanding. Sure, becoming a Master of Love sounded like a fun class at the Earth University and some of the instructors looked so cute in the faculty guide, but like all trainings, the homework is not always easy and the experiencing process can be a bear.

If the School of Service means developing a service consciousness by unmasking and dealing with your selfish and/or self-indulgent side, expect a similar paradoxical roller coaster ride on the road to emotional mastery. All emotional possibilities, including those seemingly at odds with emotional connection, are grist for your evolutionary mill. Only by pushing up against the boundaries of your emotional tolerance can you expand your awareness and gain the experiences your school requires to emerge and blossom.

This does not mean that the School of Love is only about emotional distress and discomfort, no more than the School of Service is only about servitude. After all, if you make appropriate progress in your studies, the rewards in any of the four schools are well worth the trouble. And the reward here is real-life emotional connection, honest-to-goodness love and closeness, a prize well worth the journey.

Four Steps to Emotional Mastery

Here's how this training program unfolds in terms of the events of your life:

Step 1: The Setup A circumstance occurs that triggers an emotional reaction. (Enrolled in a training program designed to stimulate your emotional growth, you can expect a full range of practice exercises that challenge your heart.)

Step 2A: All Goes Well You are in tune with your feelings. Happiness, anger, guilt, grief, delight: your emotional system operates as intended, informing you of essential inside information. Experiences are real, responses genuine. You register whatever is going on without significant distortion, behaving appropriately under the circumstances.

or

Step 2B: Complications Arise The triggering episode is too much to handle. You're not certain just what you are feeling or the flood of feelings makes you a basket case. Maybe you can't justify your reactions to yourself or you fear uncomfortable repercussions you would prefer to avoid. Pushed beyond your capacity to respond effectively to your environment, your emotional system contracts or goes into inappropriate overreaction, lowering your self-esteem and adding another layer to your protective shell.

Maybe your spouse has just fallen in love with someone else, or maybe you have just returned from military service to a town full of yellow ribbons welcoming you home. Good news and bad news are equally capable of overtaxing a person's emotional system. The likely scenario, however, finds you dealing with one more in a series of day-to-day occurrences that have developed slowly over time: a teenager who doesn't listen, a lingering relationship issue. Any way you look at it, you have arrived at the limits of your emotional mastery. You came into this life to expand your emotional consciousness and being emotionally overwhelmed marks your outer boundary point.

Step 3: Escalation Faced with being emotionally overwhelmed, conscious or unconscious, most School of Love trainees adopt one of the following behaviors: avoidance, blame, denial, hiding out, overreaction, procrastination, going numb, masking a deeper feeling with a shallower one. Which is your personal favorite?

For the beginning student, just knowing what you are feeling is a big step forward. Opening your heart to others, making relationships a matter of importance, allowing feelings, theirs and yours, to be an integral part of life, these are important first steps in the School of Love. For some loop students, one particular emotional arena calls out for attention. You do well in relationships except around issues of money, let's say, or you shut down around your father. For more advanced trainees, dealing with challenging emotions of great complexity or intensity may be the life theme. There is no way to cover all the forms of emotional unconsciousness available to students at the Earth University; however, identifying, expressing, and releasing emotional blocks are part of the training program all loop students must encounter.

Step 4: Breakthrough Progress begins as emotions emerge into conscious awareness. Can you notice as feelings bubble up from inside you? If you are pushing them back down, then who is it in there doing the pushing and why? If feelings are exploding or leaking out inappropriately, can you recognize the process as one not caused by others but emanating from inside you?

Sooner or later, hopefully, you begin to sound and look like a person who is feeling what you are feeling. Early attempts at emotional communications may not go smoothly (overexpressing and underexpressing are to be expected as students learn to navigate the emotional waters), but what other option do you have? So pound your pillows, shout it out, write a letter, face that person or circumstance straight on.

Each one of us must find our own way through the emotional labyrinth. Be smooth or be rocky but somehow let it out, and in the process, learn your own personal formula for honest emotional expression. When the next circumstance occurs you will find you are able to respond with a more genuine and centered emotional presence than before.

Steps to Emotional Mastery Summary

STEP 1 The Setup: You have an emotional reaction.

STEP 2 Complications Arise: It seems more than you can handle.

STEP 3 Escalation: You stuff your feelings or you overreact.

STEP 4 Breakthrough: Your true feelings emerge and deep-down genuine love becomes possible.

Ahhh . . . now you know, a knowing earned through experience, that loving others is the exquisite by-product of loving yourself.

The Master of Love and Closeness Checklist

- ☐ Masters of Love and Closeness have the ability to consciously register any and all emotions.
- ☐ Masters of Love and Closeness always have the ability to show their true feelings. However, the authentic display of feelings does not imply telling everyone how you feel all the time. Newer trainees tend to mask their feelings or select veiled silence more often than circumstances warrant (often venting them inappropriately at a later date).
- ☐ Masters of Love and Closeness can say what they feel while they are feeling it, to the actual person involved (if there is another person involved), at an intensity appropriate to the moment. Can you summon up the emotion you feel for another right then, while you are eyeball to eyeball, or do your circuit breakers shut off? A good question for loop students to ponder.
- ☐ And finally, emotional completion: if you were leaving the planet in five minutes, is there anybody whom you desperately need to call to free your heart from its turmoil?

The School of Love, like each of the four schools, affords a never-ending series of personal growth opportunities for everyone, but for those who are majoring in the school, the lessons carry extra importance.

Life-Purpose Maps That Exemplify the School of Love

Appendix I: Archetypal Combinations and Case Studies features life stories that exemplify each of the four schools. If your school is love, check the following seven case studies in particular for more information on your school.

- Ms. Steamroller (see page 168)
- The Matriarch or The Patriarch (see page 177)
- The Leader with Heart (see page 182)
- Negative Juliet (see page 206)
- Negative L'Oreal (see page 209)
- Susan B. Anthony (see page 243)
- The Butterfly (see page 263)

THE SCHOOL OF WISDOM

TENTED ARCH

OBJECTIVE: To move from evaluation to action
REQUIREMENT: Two tented arches (one tented arch is borderline)
SKILL NEEDED: Taking the risk of personal exposure

- Wisdom, as discussed here, means being a participant, not just an observer, in life.
- It is the willingness to commit, to bet your marbles, to get off the diving board.
- It includes good judgment without self-righteousness, objectivity without coldness, insight without too much rationalization.

Overview

If you are in the School of Wisdom you inhabit the least common of the four schools (there are fewer tented arches than the other three main fingerprint types in the general population). It is also the one most difficult to recognize if you are in it. As a wisdom trainee, you are challenged to gain insight through experience, to step out of your observer mode, and to risk being alive. Investigate, extrapolate, and strategize; compare, contrast, and evaluate, but be careful not to use your intelligence as a way to insulate yourself from others or from life itself. It is one of the big ironies of soul psychology that in the School of Wisdom you must learn *not* to think when not thinking is the wise thing to do.

Accessing the wisdom promised by the tented arch comes from putting yourself fully at stake, being vulnerable to loss, actually showing up. Flush out that part of you as yet unconscious of its unwillingness to be a full participant in life and join those who are gaining meaning and satisfaction in a variety of wise man / wise woman careers.

At the IIHA, we use a diving board analogy to help put this learning program into perspective. As every person knows, thinking about all the details of your possible leap does not make leaping easier, just the opposite. If you are in the School of Wisdom, every decision, small or large, can become a high-dive situation. Asking for a date; revealing yourself before you can be sure of the response; entering, staying in, or leaving a relationship; changing careers—these are some of the big diving boards people face in life. The tendency for those in this school is to clutter their lives with a series of undived diving boards. Worse, they typically do not recognize any problem: "I am thinking it over . . . give me a few more weeks . . ."

As in all the schools, the Goldilocks Rule says that there will be overleaping and underleaping before Just Right leaping is attained. Do not be deceived into thinking you are past all challenges in this school if you are a wing-walking, sky-diving, scuba-instructing, rodeo bronco buster. The element of risk in this school is the risk of exposure, especially emotional exposure that leaves you no place to hide.

Four Steps to Wisdom through Doing

Of all the topics I talk about with clients, commitment issues seem to elicit the highest number of deer-in-the-headlights looks. Similarly, when we do classes on commitment at the IIHA, we need a phone bank to handle all the last-minute flat tires and my-aunt-Mathilda-is-in-the-hospital excuses as half the class or more bales out. Commitment issues can be so hard to look at. Nevertheless, in the School of Wisdom, commitment defines success or failure.

Step 1: The Setup You have a choice to make, one that requires a commitment on your part.

Step 2A: All Goes Well You decide not to jump off this diving board. Fine. Masters of Wisdom do not overcommit themselves. Or you *do* decide to jump. Life offers no guarantees, but it is your choice and you are glad to make it. You leap directly into the no-man's-land of true commitment. No turning back now. The die is cast. You are exposed. Jeopardy is attached. Sink, swim, or splat, your future is rushing up to meet you.

or

Step 2B: Complications Arise You put off the decision. A million rationalizations rush forward supporting your decision to put off deciding. Make no mistake, if you have even one tented arch in your fingerprint chart, this is not the normal procrastination impulse at work. It is your soul psychology working its way into the everyday affairs of your life. Those struggling with the School of Wisdom will do almost anything to avoid exposure, including spending their entire life in the big gaping hole.

Step 3: Escalation It looks like you committed but you didn't. Getting married certainly looked like a commitment, but was it? Your New Year's resolutions may be a true commitment. We will find out soon enough. Like service and love, commitment is not an action performed, it is a state of consciousness. As such, wisdom through doing is available to anyone at any moment regardless of circumstance.

Take a moment if you will and contemplate what that last sentence means in your life. Have you been taking the path of least resistance? Do you have thoughts of really going for it, but not right now? If so, what is it that is keeping you from putting yourself at stake today? Think of the man who is sure every woman he dates is "the one," only to bail when things get rough, or the woman (like Betty in the story below) who has had five careers in ten years, believing each time that this one is "it," then quitting when it gets too hard to face her stuff. What is the price for living this way?

Contemplating how little his life has amounted to, T. S. Eliot's Prufrock (he who has measured out his life with coffee spoons) despairs: "I have seen the eternal Footman hold my coat, and snicker." To insure your eternal footman does not snicker at you, see what you can learn about the nature of commitment from the following story.

Mars and Venus and Issues of Commitment Whereas it is common knowledge that there are men who won't commit in love, it is not so well known, nor talked about, that some women do the exact same thing (usually about career), missing out in like manner on similar high-payoff possibilities. Betty is a good example. Her hands revealed all the ingredients needed for creative success, yet Betty's career was going nowhere fast.

"Nothing ever works out for me," she reported. "First there was the flower shop. I was actually making good money on that one, but my partner was such a pain, I just had to give it up." After that, there was the art gallery. "That was my favorite, I guess. I was taking watercolor classes and getting quite good at it, if I do say so myself. But you have no idea how hard it is to work with artists. Everyone thinks they are the next incarnation of Picasso and . . ." Betty's story went on for another three businesses. "Maybe I should just stay home and make babies. Forty-two isn't too old to start a family. What do my hands say about children?" she asked, hoping there was some specified future that would finally pull all the threads of her life together.

Instead, Betty heard her hand reader tell her that she had issues of commitment marked in her fingerprints. Betty could see that in the past, perhaps, she used to, maybe, have a commitment issue, maybe in relationships. She did have a history of picking married men as relationship partners. But since her marriage, that was all behind her. "I am constantly putting my whole life at risk," she said. "If I knew for sure what I wanted, I would put it all on the line again."

I agreed that her marriage was a move in the right direction but suggested that her biggest commitment issue, accessing the vast creative potential revealed in her hands, was still in front of her. "Pick your canvas of choice, Betty, and pour yourself completely into your endeavor. Stop piddling around. Burn your bridges. No escape clauses." I went on like this for a bit, despite Betty's stare-out-the-window-and-stop-pestering-me look that indicated how displeased she was with the turn of our conversation.

I decided a gender reversal story was in order. "When you married Maurice, would it have been OK with you if he took his address book, complete with ex-girlfriends' phone numbers, on your honeymoon? After all, with the divorce rate at 50 percent, a man should have some insurance, don't you agree?" Betty did not agree. "Well," I countered, "what if he just saw other women on days that you were busy? Then it wouldn't interfere with your time together." No, Betty had been in relationships like that, and now she wanted someone who was willing to go all the way, someone who wanted to make things work out whether things were going well or not because, well because, that is what she wanted.

"Like the guy who jumps out of the airplane knitting his parachute on the way down—he just has to succeed. There is no other option. Are you saying that is what you want in your marriage, Betty?"

"Yes. Exactly. And Maurice wants the same."

"Good. Here's the point of your hand reading today: your creativity requires the same commitment that you have given your marriage." We sat in silence for a while. "Until you are willing to offer the same level of commitment to your career, all you can possibly hope for are halfway successes and a guarantee of boredom a year or two down the road."

"If I just knew for sure what I wanted to do, I would jump right in," Betty objected.

"When Maurice knows for certain that his marriage to you will work out, that's when he should burn his address book?" I asked.

"I see your point, but how do you do commit like that?" Betty replied.

"How did you commit like that to Maurice?"

"I don't know. I just did."

"Yup, that's how it's done." I concluded.

Step 4: Breakthrough The commitment-phobe thinks he will commit when he meets the right woman. The hideout artist thinks the same about her career. Will either stretch beyond their immediate comfort zone and go for the deeper meaning that commitment allows?

What about you? Maybe you have already achieved commitment in one part of your life but not in all parts. Maybe there is another talent or lurking desire that you have put on hold for the last two decades. Maybe not. Maybe the wise man or wise woman in you has fully emerged and you are currently living in your right life.

Realizing that life offers no guarantees and that you are always at risk anyway, if you are in the School of Wisdom your life purpose requires that you learn by experience what true commitment really means.

Steps to Wisdom Mastery Summary

STEP 1 The Setup: A choice appears that requires a commitment.

STEP 2 Complications Arise: You manage to not make a choice.

STEP 3 Escalation: You look like you committed but you didn't.

STEP 4 Breakthrough: Commitment yields freedom and fulfillment.

Master of Wisdom Checklist

☐ Masters of Wisdom do not use their intellect to insulate themselves from life.

☐ Masters of Wisdom are willing to take chances, but they are far from foolhardy.

☐ Masters of Wisdom know how to commit.

☐ Masters of Wisdom have also been known to change their minds.

Life-Purpose Maps That Exemplify the School of Wisdom

Appendix I: Archetypal Combinations and Case Studies features life stories that exemplify each of the four schools. If your school is wisdom, check the following two case studies in particular for more information on your school.

- Dealing with Disapproval/Caroline (see page 239)
- The Wing Walker (see page 265)

THE SCHOOL OF PEACE

ARCH

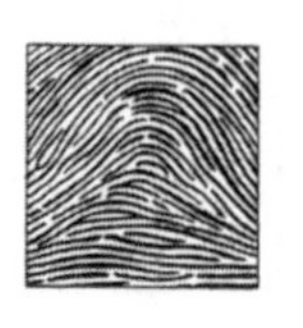

OBJECTIVE: To feel safe in your body and on the planet
REQUIREMENT: Two arches (one arch counts as borderline)
SKILLS NEEDED: Moving through struggle and panic to alert stillness; separating self-esteem from circumstance; body ease, allowing for the possibility of pleasure; balancing inner and outer worlds

- Inner peace implies finding a deep sense of peace within yourself.
- It allows hard work when necessary, but leaves time for family, friends, and play.
- It includes dealing with responsibilities without creating an endless chain of "emergencies."
- Gaining inner peace means enjoying being alive.

Overview

The School of Service is the most paradoxical of the four schools; the School of Love is the most common and misunderstood; the School of Wisdom is famous for its denial factor; but the School of Peace is probably the most uncomfortable. In Archland, fear is the currency and the payment required for graduation is steep.

For candidates in the School of Peace, survival fears already imprinted five months prior to birth project themselves from the unconscious into three-dimensional form. Going directly through this fear tunnel, emerging not unscathed but appropriately experienced, this is the transformational path available to those with two or more arch pattern fingerprints. *Only as your fears take tangible form and are confronted can the soul's intention for this lifetime be realized.* Take a deep breath; reread this paragraph slowly; proceed.

It is one thing to be startled by the howling wind and a creaking door as the heroine walks nervously down the corridor of the haunted house, you chomping away on your popcorn, safe in your theater seat. It is quite another thing to be the heroine herself. As the panic works its way into your bloodstream, say what you will, dealing with fear is, well, it is scary. So scary, in fact, most peaceniks do not even recognize the process. "Me? Scared?" Come to terms with the real fears at the base of your existence and you will access the inner peace your life purpose requires.

Mr. Sticks and Plates

Once I worked out the fingerprints and their implications, it was like being hit on the head by a falling brick. My own life story took on a whole new perspective. I was in the School of Peace, and borderline in the School of Service and the School of Wisdom. Again and again as I read the hands of others in the School of Peace, my own archlike behaviors became clearer to see. What a revelation!

Mr. Sticks and Plates had been driving my car, and I had been his kidnapped passenger in the back seat. If you are not familiar with Mr. S&P, he is the circus performer whose act consists of balancing spinning plates on top of five-foot sticks. As long as the plates spin, they naturally stay on the end of the stick; lose the spin and the plates come tumbling down. Eventually Mr. Sticks and Plates gets sixteen sticks and plates going at once, running frantically from stick to stick, arriving to renew the spin just in the nick of time. Usually.

Truth be told, my entire life had been one continuous S&P affair: always one short step ahead of the advancing avalanche, never enough time to catch my breath—like this memorable day from the third year of my financial planning career (the career I eventually left to become a full-time hand analyst). Client A calls in to transfer some funds, but I am out of transfer forms and so is the Houston office. I spend a hair-pulling hour of frustration on the phone talking to four different people in the Dallas office before one agrees to send me an extra form. I am now late for my appointment with Mr. B, who is nice enough, but we run out of time before we can complete our business. Fighting traffic to get back to the office, I arrive to learn client C wants to accelerate the payment schedule on his IRA, but I cannot find the original payment form that has to be attached to the change of payment form 3625A. Arrgghh!

Three hours of this and I am literally spinning in circles. I have this piece of paper in my left hand, that one in my right, and I have just knocked over a pile of papers on my desk for the third time. With all the strength I can muster, I hold on to my chair and sit still for five minutes. Exhaling, I leave for Galveston Island to walk on the beach and consider my fate.

It was only years later, hearing similar stories from archy hand reading clients in completely different circumstances, that I put two and two together. It was me, not my circumstances, sending my life into a tizzy. Not that this had been the first time or the last. Listen to this one:

I was driving through the Nevada desert. The sign said ninety-two miles to the next gas station and with a bit more than a quarter tank of gas, I decided I could make it. What was going on with me? I did make it (on fumes) only because there was a gas station eighty-four miles ahead. I had to walk into a biker bar and risk my life to avoid running out of gas in the middle of nowhere. Why not just get gas without the melodrama? Well, maybe my adrenaline addiction is stronger than I realized.

"My name is Richard Unger."

"Hi, Richard!"

"I am an adrenal addict and have been from before I was born. The last time I had a hit of adrenal intoxicant was . . ."

Time and again I have selected the harder, more edgy possibility. Of course, it is this part of me that allows me to have found my life's work. What conservative bone in my body would have picked reading hands as a career? Edgy is good. Thank you for being there for me, my edgy self. But conscious edgy is one thing, edgy adrenal addiction is another.

Mr. Mellow and Ms. Lah-Dee-Dah

Most of those enrolled in the School of Peace wrestle with Mr. Sticks and Plates seeking an elusive arrangement of circumstance that will finally allow true relaxation and the smelling of roses. However, the real goal here is the development of a consciousness that allows for alert stillness regardless of circumstance. Mr. Sticks and Plates is too much alert/not enough stillness. Keeping the Goldilocks Rule in mind, let's not overlook Mr. Mellow and Ms. Lah-Dee-Dah: too much stillness/not enough alert.

Those with five or more arches are the likely candidates for this section of the School of Peace. In this category are the druggies and drinkers, excessive meditators, and professional slackers. They have dropped out and retreated into the deep woods. These trainees in the School of Peace (or those in this pendulum swing of the training) are cool. Nothing fazes them. Numbed out instead of arched out, they are the epitome of serene. "You've abducted my child. That's cool."

The challenge here, as in each of the four schools, is to be appropriate to the moment. Bring your superman or superwoman self with you, but be careful you don't overidentify with struggle as the source of your aliveness. Likewise, take it easy, but don't get seduced into narcotic escape for decades at a time.

Four Steps to Peace

Masters of Peace have wrestled with life's biggest questions and achieved a balance point without slipping into Lah-Dee-Dah answers. Meeting their existence head-on, Masters of Peace access a depth of meaning not available to the uninitiated. Here is their training program.

Step 1: The Setup Stuff happens. It doesn't matter what. (Archers are capable of using whatever is available: money problems, family issues, time pressures, anything or nothing, to click into adrenal overdrive or blissed-out underdrive.)

Step 2A: All Goes Well You handle it, then you have lunch. When the next thing happens, you handle that too, the best you can. After all, you're only human. All you can do is all you can do. You put one foot in front of the other, keeping your life in balance as you go.

or

Step 2B: Complications Arise You find yourself overextended for the umpteenth time. The faster you go, the behinder you get. Like the gambler needing just one big score to escape his troubles, the gang member living on borrowed time, the coal miner another day older and deeper in debt—you have landed in Archville all over again (whether you are willing to admit it or not).

Step 3: Escalation Unconsciously careening through your life, the noise gets so loud you can't even hear yourself think. You get more and more out of control as distraction after distraction wrests your attention away from that still voice within.

Step 4: Breakthrough You admit that you have been an adrenal addict, a necessary step in recovering your life. Slowing down enough to pay attention to your inner world, a real, true-to-life, stare-into-the-void-and-still-be-happy-to-be-alive inner peace eventually emerges. Learning to take life in stride, you allow the future to unfold of its own accord in its own time.

Steps to Peace Mastery Summary

STEP 1 The Setup: Something happens, it doesn't matter what.

STEP 2 Complications Arise: You overextend yourself.

STEP 3 Escalation: Handling one emergency after another, you lose contact with your inner self.

STEP 4 Breakthrough: Balancing your inner and outer worlds, you find you enjoy your life as it is.

The Master of Peace Checklist

- ☐ Masters of Peace have time for family, friends, and play. Rest and relaxation are gained without ignoring responsibilities or resorting to illness, injury, or repetitive crises.
- ☐ Masters of Peace smoothly handle life's ups and downs, an ability earned by having survived troubled waters in the past.
- ☐ Masters of Peace have learned to live in "now time" instead of in a future "if only" existence. No more struggling to feel comfortable in their bodies. No more life without pleasure. Childlike without being childish, they find that the natural world speaks to them, providing a shelter from the storms of life and a source of eternal happiness.

Life-Purpose Maps That Exemplify the School of Peace

Appendix I: Archetypal Combinations and Case Studies features life stories that exemplify each of the four schools. If your school is inner peace, check the following three case studies in particular for more information on your school.

- The Loser (see page 173)
- Mr. Not Enough (see page 216)
- Get a Tan (see page 266)

****

A summary of the four schools appears in the chart below. You can refer back to this chart to see what each school's Too Much, Too Little, and Just Right descriptions are, which you will need to know in future chapters. Remember that Just Right represents a consciousness to inhabit as opposed to a set of circumstances to arrive in.

FOUR SCHOOLS SUMMARY

School	Goldilocks Rule: Too Much and Too Little	Just Right
Service	Servitude (too much focus on others) Self-indulgence (too little focus on others)	Joyous Service
Love	Explosion (too much feeling, out of control) Stuffed feelings (too little emotional connection)	Love and Closeness
Wisdom	Stuck on the diving board (too much thinking) Weak, nonlasting commitments (too little thinking)	True Commitment
Peace	Mr. Sticks and Plates, overextension (too much alert) Ms. Lah-Dee-Dah, slacking off (too much stillness)	Alert Stillness

MULTIPLE SCHOOLS

If you find yourself in more than one school, take heart, it's not a rare occurrence. Following is a short description of the most common multiple-school combinations. To get the fullest sense of your schools, it's a good idea to carefully read through the descriptions of each of your schools earlier in this chapter.

School of Service + School of Love

- Fingerprint Profile: Exactly three whorls and seven loops
- At Your Best: Loving service fills your life with happiness.
- At Your Worst: Inappropriate sacrifice and burdensome relationships drain you dry.

If you have exactly three whorls and seven loops, the issue under observation this lifetime is avoiding feelings by doing for others. After all, if you do the laundry, the dishes, the everything, if you become an entire rescue team of one, then you cannot possibly be rejected, right? "They couldn't live without me." At least that is the hope.

The challenge here is *not* avoiding the mistake of doing too much for others; that is a mistake that is sure to occur. The challenge is recognizing the error when it happens and taking corrective measures. Until you can say no to your aunt Mathilda's requests, until you can bear the emotional consequences of her displeasure with you, you are never going to have the emotional presence necessary to unlock your life purpose.

School of Love + School of Wisdom

- Fingerprint Profile: Exactly eight loops and two tented arches
- At Your Best: Emotional risk leads to wisdom from the heart.
- At Your Worst: After playing it safe too long, an unwise choice brings disaster.

With eight loops and two tented arches, the theme of emotional risk is going to be in the middle of all life's ups and downs. Thinking about asking Helen of Troy to the dance while waiting for just the right time, which never quite comes, is one obvious example of emotional risk not taken. But it is the more subtle level of this double school that can be so challenging.

Sharing some of your feelings while hiding others (especially from yourself) is common for those in this training. So is playing it safe in mate selection. Or dealing with a seemingly overemotional spousal partner expressing enough emotion for two people, while you remain the calm one, ever so rational. The possibilities are endless, but the theme is the same: are you still essentially sheltered, even if some feelings are visible?

Further, are you willing to show feelings only after you know it is safe? It is one thing to tell a boyfriend or girlfriend how sad you are when a parent dies. Who would reject you for this type of vulnerability? But can you share jealous feelings without dumping on your partner? What about insecurities that belie your public image? Your life purpose requires the ability to take the emotional risk, a skill you will have to acquire through the experiencing process.

School of Love + School of Peace

- Fingerprint Profile: Exactly eight loops and two arches
- At Your Best: Safety and ease in a relationship bring happiness to your life.
- At Your Worst: Relationship struggles and more relationship struggles exhaust you.

Owners of these prints often set up circumstances so melodramatic that the deeper levels of the emotional self are drowned out by the noise of it all. Fears associated with love and intimacy can be that great. The businessperson so busy that little time can be found for family or friends is an obvious example of this double school. In just a few more days, a couple of weeks, maybe a month or so, then you can relax, as soon as the Smith account is settled. But, if you are not careful, the Smith account is followed by the Jones account, the Johnson account, and so on. By the time you are ready to smell the roses, all the roses may have left town.

Some with this fingerprint combination reverse the pattern. Instead of Mr. Sticks and Plates, Mr. Mellow or Ms. Lah-Dee-Dah takes charge. Everything is calm, *no problems mon*, every day, no matter what. If this is you, do not be misled. It is the same pattern in disguise. The challenge remains: can you trust your feelings sufficiently that the deeper levels of your emotional self rise to the surface, unencumbered by pictures of what your life is supposed to look like?

The more comfortable you get with your emotional self, the deeper the levels of feelings that you allow to surface, the less often you will find that upsetting distractions are keeping you from the love and closeness that are your birthright.

School of Service + School of Peace

- Fingerprint Profile: Four or more whorls plus two or more arches
- At Your Best: Easy service fills your life with joy.
- At Your Worst: Inappropriate overdoing for others leaves little time for your own life.

With this combination, the challenge is to create a life that accomplishes its service intention without leaving you with no life of your own. Ann, a much-beloved therapist who died in her midforties, had these fingerprints. Her memorial service was held in the Golden Pyramid in Houston, Texas, with one thousand people in attendance. I had no idea that she had touched so many lives so deeply. Ann's Famous Healer life purpose had clearly surfaced, but just how tormented she was by struggle and servitude we will never know for sure.

Regardless of the exact locations of the four or more whorls and the two or more arches, all owners of this double school start life with a struggle and servitude mentality. Doing too much for others and doing it the hard way are the traps that must be fallen into and gotten out of before life purpose can bloom. In Ann's case, this meant seeing too many clients for too little money and offering workshops with extensive phone follow-ups that taxed her schedule. Would Ann ever find the time to build a life of her own?

One thousand people attended her memorial service, but her on-again, off-again boyfriend couldn't make it.

School of Wisdom + School of Peace (aka The School of Courage)

- Fingerprint Profile: Two or more tented arches plus two or more arches
- At Your Best: The wisdom gained by jumping off life's diving boards brings inner peace.
- At Your Worst: Procrastination leads to problems, which leads to more procrastination. . . .

This hodgepodge is the most agitating of the dual-school fingerprint charts and for owners of this fingerprint combination, huge pendulum swings are to be expected. Alternately overreacting to mole hills (a tendency for those in the School of Peace) and underclimbing what appears to be insurmountable mountains (the School of Wisdom at its worst), scared to move forward and afraid to stand still, School of Courage candidates often feel as if they have not enough thumbs for the series of leaky dikes that is their life.

Others in the School of Courage try to keep the melodrama under control by distancing themselves from close relationships, like Ennis in *Brokeback Mountain* or the Eagles' song-title character Desperado, who is admonished to "let somebody love you before it's too late." (*Brokeback Mountain* and *Desperado* are required reading for students in the School of Courage.)

If you do well in your studies, you will find that you can both reach out to others and enjoy your own company without becoming a hermit. At this point, supported by those who really care about you, your life takes on a more manageable pace and the wisdom you earned through experience becomes a centerpiece of your new life.

In this chapter, you identified your ten fingerprints and your school. You learned the steps to self-discovery that each of the four schools offer and you found out that some people have more than one school.

In the next chapter, you will learn what role your school plays as part of your life-purpose map, as well as how to identify your life purpose and life lesson.

CHAPTER THREE

DECIPHER YOUR LIFE PURPOSE AND LIFE LESSON

There are three principal ways in which man can find meaning in life. The first is what he gives to the world in terms of his creations; the second is what he takes from the world in terms of encounters and experiences; the third is the stand he takes to his predicament in case he must face a fate he cannot change.

—VIKTOR FRANKL, *THE WILL TO MEANING*

In chapter two you learned to identify and record your fingerprints and to find your school. In this chapter, you will use that information as you identify your life purpose and life lesson, your next two steps in life-purpose map construction. After deepening your understanding of your purpose and lesson in chapter four, you will pull all the parts of your life-purpose map together by creating your life-fulfillment formula in chapter five.

STEP 3: IDENTIFY YOUR LIFE PURPOSE

To identify your life purpose, you will use the fingerprint rankings chart on the next page to locate your highest ranking fingerprint(s). Next you will find the meaning inherent in the location(s) of your highest ranking print(s). And finally, you will combine the Just Right phrase of your school with the highest ranking print meanings to form a life-purpose statement.

But first things first. The chart on the next page applies a rank value to the four main fingerprints and their common variations (see page 22 for more information about fingerprint variations). As you can see, the whorl is the highest ranking print with a value of 4, the arch is the lowest ranking print with a value of 1, and the other prints fall somewhere in between.

FINGERPRINT RANKINGS

Print	Symbol	Rank Value
Whorl		4
Composite Whorl		3.9
Peacock		3.5
Loop		3
Loop/ Tented Arch		2.5
Tented Arch		2
Arch		1

To determine your highest ranking print(s), look up the ranking value for each one of your ten fingerprints. In example 1, the ranking value for each fingerprint is recorded below the fingerprint symbol. As you can see, the right thumb has a loop (ranking value of 3), the right index also has a loop (ranking value of 3), and so on. In this example, only the right ring finger has a whorl (ranking value of 4). None of the other nine fingerprints is ranked as high as the fingerprint on the right ring finger. Thus, the highest ranking fingerprint for this person is the whorl on the right ring finger.

EXAMPLE 1

	Thumb	Index Finger	Middle Finger	Ring Finger	Little Finger
Right	3	3	3	4	3
Left	3	1	3	3	3

In example 2, the right and left thumbs and right and left index fingers have loops (ranking value of 3). The remaining six fingerprints are arches (ranking value of 1). Therefore, the highest ranking prints for this person are the loops on the right and left thumbs and right and left index fingers.

EXAMPLE 2

	Thumb	Index Finger	Middle Finger	Ring Finger	Little Finger
Right	3	3	1	1	1
Left	3	3	1	1	1

In the chart below or in your life-purpose journal, record the symbol for each of your ten fingerprints in the space provided, and add the appropriate ranking value for each fingerprint in the lower right-hand corner.

MY FINGERPRINTS

	Thumb	Index Finger	Middle Finger	Ring Finger	Little Finger
Right					
Left					

Your next step is to find the meaning inherent in the location(s) of your highest ranking print(s). The Ten Locations Overview Chart (opposite) summarizes in short descriptions the meanings that characterize each of the ten places that fingerprints typically appear. (Believe it or not, fingerprints can also appear on the surface of the palm. These less common scenarios are covered at the end of chapter four.) Think of each of these ten locations as a classroom at the Earth University. One (or more than one) of these classes is your major field of study for this lifetime, the zone in which you seek to find your life's fulfillment (your life purpose). Circle your major field of study (or studies, if you have more than one) on the chart (or note them in your life-purpose journal).

Important: If you have seven or more fingerprints with the same *highest ranking* fingerprint, turn to page 60 for special instructions.

TEN LOCATIONS OVERVIEW CHART (LIFE PURPOSE)

	Thumb	Index Finger	Middle Finger	Ring Finger	Little Finger
Right	Success	Power	Responsibility	Creativity	Communi-cations
Left	Family	Passion	Integrity	Innovation	Insight

To create your life-purpose statement, combine the one-word summary of your highest ranking print(s) with the Just-Right statement (chart on page 56) associated with your school(s). For example, if your highest ranking print is on the right ring finger (creativity) and your school is love (love and closeness), then your life-purpose statement is Creativity + Love and Closeness. If you have only one highest ranking print and belong to only one school, this process is pretty simple. Things get more complicated when you have multiple highest ranking prints or you belong to more than one school, or both. We'll address these issues in a moment. First, go ahead and record your key meaning(s) and Just-Right statement(s) below (or in your life-purpose journal).

Key meaning(s) of my highest ranking fingerprint(s)

____

+ Just-Right statement(s) of my school(s)

____

My life purpose is ____

____

JUST-RIGHT STATEMENT CHART

School	Just-Right Statement
Service	Joyous service
Love	Love and closeness
Wisdom	True commitment
Peace	A Life in balance

If you have more than one highest ranking fingerprint, combine the key meanings and then pair them with the Just-Right statement to create your life purpose. For example, if you have highest ranking prints on your right thumb (success) and your right index finger (power) and you are in the School of Service, your life purpose would be: Success and Power + Joyous Service. If you also have more than one school, combine the Just-Right statements of the schools in a similar way.

Extra Guidelines for Life Purpose Identification

Like any coding system, LifePrints needs to be simple enough for ease of use yet complex enough to cover a wide range of possibilities. The four fingerprints and ten locations that you have studied so far provide a forty-letter alphabet to convey the fingerprints' message. Using the fingerprint census to find the school, and the ranking system to delineate your life purpose and life lesson are the first two steps to using this alphabet to decipher your soul psychology. The following guidelines complete your LifePrints training. If you have any of the situations described on the next few pages, follow the instructions in that section to help you further clarify your life purpose.

Your Highest Ranking Prints Appear on the Same Finger of Both Your Left and Right Hands Use this key word in your life-purpose statement:

Left and right thumbs: Success

Left and right index fingers: Power

Left and right middle fingers: Integrity

Left and right ring fingers: Creativity

Left and right little fingers: Insight

Notice what happens here. When the highest ranking prints appear on the same finger of the left and right hands, you use the meaning inherent in the fingers of the right hand for your life purpose, except when the highest rankers are the middle finger or the little finger. In that case, the key meaning to use in your life-purpose statement comes from the meaning inherent in the middle finger or little finger of the left hand.

You Have One of the Many Patterns Made Up of Two or More Highest Ranking Fingerprints Called an Archetypal Combination An *archetypal combination* is a pattern of two or more highest ranking fingerprints that are often found together. Most of the fingerprint combinations that occur with regularity are archetypal combinations and have titles that smoothly combine the qualities represented by the fingers having the highest ranking prints. Identifying archetypal combinations when they occur greatly simplifies life-purpose identification. In example 1, the left index, middle, and ring fingers have the highest ranking prints and form the combination known as The Pioneer.

EXAMPLE 1

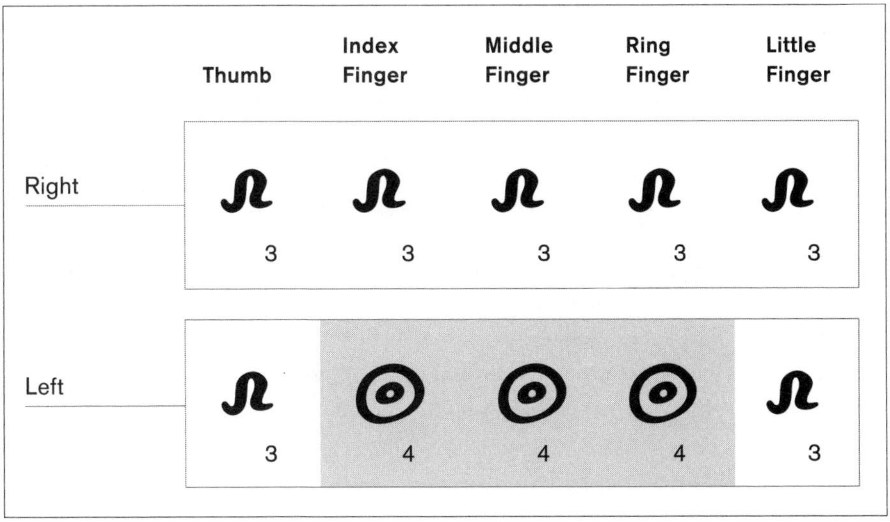

	Thumb	Index Finger	Middle Finger	Ring Finger	Little Finger
Right	3	3	3	3	3
Left	3	4	4	4	3

It is also common for an archetypal combination to be part of a larger set of highest ranking fingerprints. For instance, in example 2, a highest ranking fingerprint on the right thumb joins The Pioneer combination to create The Successful Pioneer life purpose.

EXAMPLE 2

	Thumb	Index Finger	Middle Finger	Ring Finger	Little Finger
Right	4	3	3	3	3
Left	3	4	4	4	3

Had the whorl on the right thumb remained a loop and the right little finger had a whorl instead, you would be looking at The Pioneer in Communications life purpose. The life-purpose permutations are too numerous to list, but using this method will allow you to interpret pretty much all the fingerprint combinations. See Lee Harvey Oswald's fingerprints on page 241 for more information on complex fingerprint charts.

Each of the archetypal combinations is described in chapter four and further explained in Appendix I: Archetypal Combinations and Case Studies. As you read chapter four, make a note of your archetypal combination(s) if you have any. These descriptions will greatly add to the clarity of your life purpose.

You Have One or More of the Three Fingerprint Variations and Your Highest Ranking Fingerprints Are Close in Value If you have one or more of the fingerprint variations (all of which have ranking values to the right of the decimal point), you may end up with close-ranked fingerprints. In example 3, there is a whorl (ranking value of 4) and a composite whorl (ranking value of 3.9). There are two ways to approach this situation.

In a strict interpretation of the ranking system, if one fingerprint is ranked higher than another, the higher of the two becomes part of the life-purpose statement and the lower of the two does not. End of discussion. Thus, in the example below, the life purpose would be Success (highest ranking right thumb) + Love and Closeness (School of Love).

EXAMPLE 3

	Thumb	Index Finger	Middle Finger	Ring Finger	Little Finger
Right	4	3	3	3	3
Left	3	3	3	3	3.9

If your ten fingerprints are very similar, then small variations in ranking become more significant. In example 4 (on the next page), there's one whorl on the right thumb and nine composite whorls on the rest of the fingers. Using a strict interpretation of the ranking system and taking the similarity of the fingerprints into account, you would again consider the right thumb to be the highest ranking print. Thus, this person's life purpose would be Success (highest ranking right thumb) + Joyous Service (School of Service).

In a looser interpretation of the ranking system, whorls (4) and composite whorls (3.9) get bunched together. I often do the same with peacocks (3.5) and whorls (4). In example 3, the life purpose would combine the key meanings for the right thumb and left little finger to create a life purpose of Success and Communications + Love and Closeness. In example 4, I would use a stricter interpretation because one fingerprint is significantly different from the other nine. Thus, the life purpose would be Success + Joyous Service as above. Both methods of interpretation are accurate, but one might feel more accurate right now than the other. If you have this situation, try both approaches and pick the one that feels true to you.

EXAMPLE 4

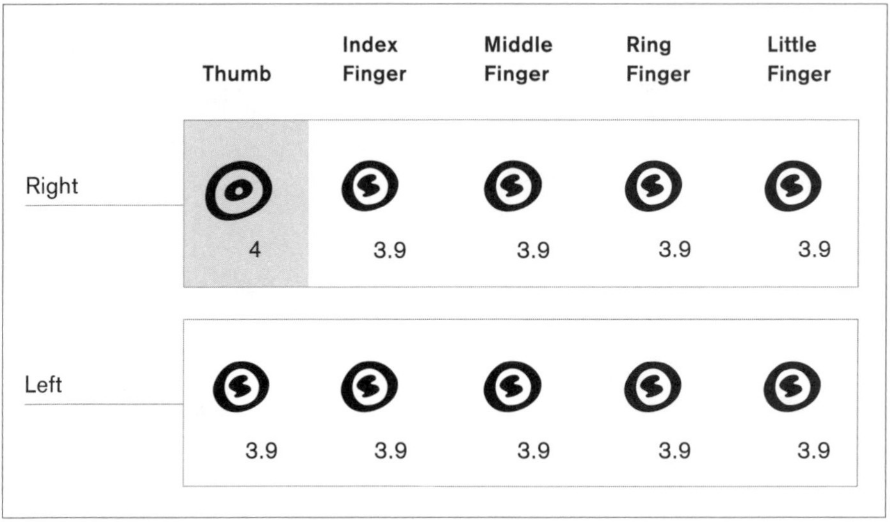

	Thumb	Index Finger	Middle Finger	Ring Finger	Little Finger
Right	4	3.9	3.9	3.9	3.9
Left	3.9	3.9	3.9	3.9	3.9

You Have Radial Loops Radial loops open toward the thumb and are ranked 3.1. Ulnar loops, which open away from the thumb, are ranked 3. Sometimes this small difference in ranking can make all the difference in the world. See the discussion of close-ranked fingerprints above for more information about reading these types of prints.

You Have a Peacock on Your Left Little Finger Peacocks on the left little finger count as the full equivalent to a whorl.

Peacocks and whorls appear on the left little finger much less often than on the other fingers. This statistical differentiation is the rationale for this wrinkle in the ranking system.

Your Highest Ranking Prints Appear in Seven or More of the Ten Fingerprint Locations Use this method to identify your life purpose:

1. Identify the type of the highest ranking fingerprint located in seven or more locations.
2. Identify the school associated with that fingerprint type.
3. Use the Just-Right phrase of *this* school as your entire life-purpose statement.

For example, if the seven or more fingerprints *that tie for the highest ranking* are:

Whorls: Your life purpose is Joyous Service.

Loops: Your life purpose is Love and Closeness.

Tented arches: Your life purpose is True Commitment.

Arches: Your life purpose is a Life in Balance.

Note: In the unlikely event that there is a six-way tie for highest ranking fingerprint and no archetypal life-purpose combination is present, use the above guideline to determine the life purpose.

What about a set of fingerprints with a single radial loop and nine ulnar loops, but the radial loop looks a little bit like a loop/tented arch? Would you count it as higher ranking? If you are clever enough, you can invent an entire series of questions exactly like this one. In cases like these, you are advised to use the rules you have learned plus your intuition and good sense to carry you through the innumerable possibilities. The language of fingerprints is relatively simple and it has its own logic, but the subject matter in question is you and the big questions at the core of your existence. If you find yourself caught between two competing interpretations of your fingerprints, most likely both are correct, one more so at this time of your life than the other.

STEP 4: IDENTIFY YOUR LIFE LESSON

The next step in life-purpose map construction is identifying your life lesson. Your life lesson is the hardest part of yourself to look at straight in the eye, an aspect of you that can keep tripping you up indefinitely. If you haven't yet identified and understood your life lesson, it can be especially problematic. Once you've done so, however, you are on the way to changing it from your nemesis to your ally. The process of identifying your life lesson is very similar to that of identifying your life purpose.

To identify your life lesson, you will use the fingerprint rankings chart (see page 52) to locate your lowest ranking fingerprint(s). Next you will find the meaning inherent in the location(s) of your lowest ranking print(s). And finally, you will combine the Too Much/Too Little statement of your school with the lowest ranking print(s) to form a life-lesson statement.

As before, the chart applies a rank value to the four main fingerprints and their common variations (see page 22 for more information about fingerprint variations). The whorl is the highest ranking print with a value of 4, the arch is the lowest ranking print with a value of 1, and the other prints fall somewhere in between. You use the fingerprint rankings chart to identify your life lesson the same way you identified your life purpose, only now you are looking for your lowest ranking fingerprints.

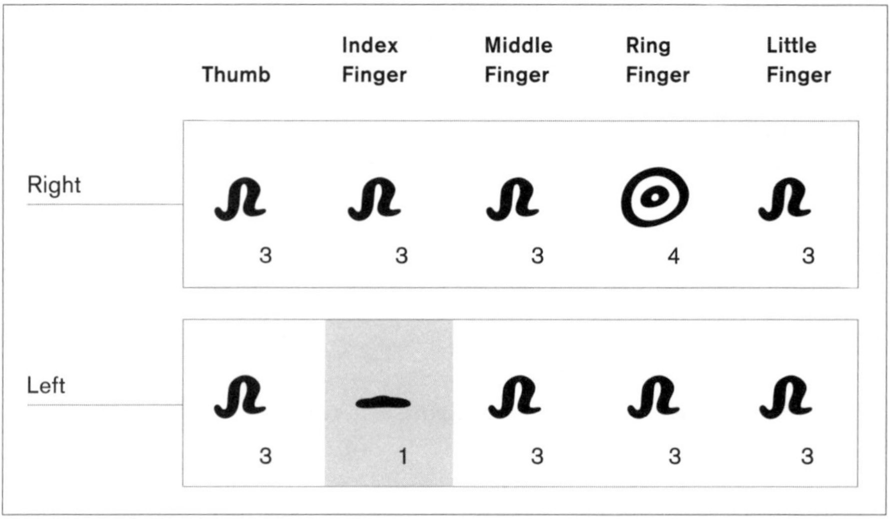

	Thumb	Index Finger	Middle Finger	Ring Finger	Little Finger
Right	3	3	3	4	3
Left	3	1	3	3	3

In the example above, the left index finger has an arch (ranking value of 1). None of the other nine fingerprints is ranked as low. Thus, the lowest ranking fingerprint for this person is on the left index finger.

On the chart opposite or in your life-purpose journal, record the symbol for each of your ten fingerprints in the space provided, and add the appropriate ranking value for each fingerprint in the lower right-hand corner.

To find the meaning inherent in the location(s) of your lowest ranking print(s), review the Ten Locations Overview Chart. This chart summarizes in short descriptions the meanings that characterize the life lessons associated with each of the ten fingers. These meanings describe the inverse of the life purposes for the same fingers; now we are looking at problematic possibilities. Once again, think of each of these ten locations as a classroom at the Earth University. One (or more than one) of these classes requires remedial attention if you are to unlock your life purpose. Circle your major field of study (or studies, if you have more than one) on the chart (or note them in your life-purpose journal).

Important: If you have seven or more fingerprints with the same *lowest ranking* fingerprint, turn to page 66 for special instructions.

MY FINGERPRINTS

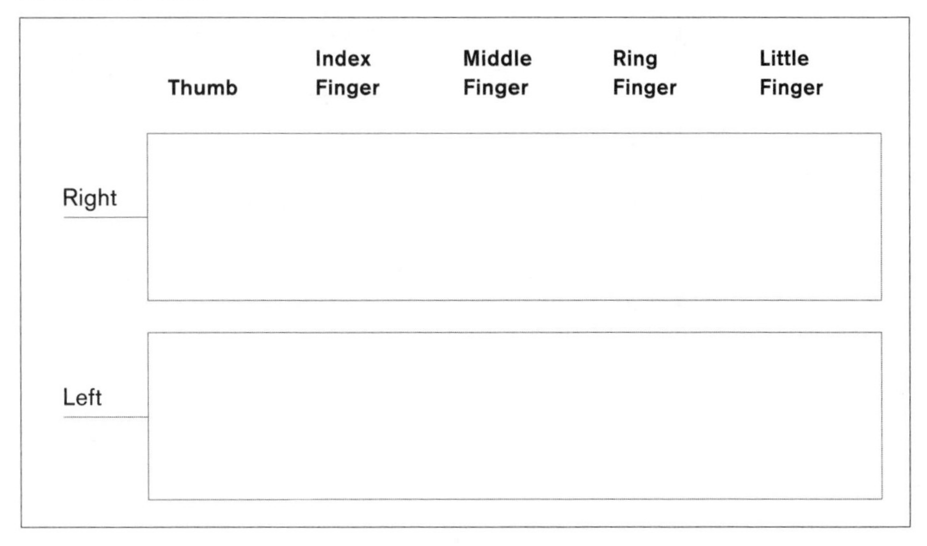

	Thumb	Index Finger	Middle Finger	Ring Finger	Little Finger
Right					
Left					

TEN LOCATIONS OVERVIEW CHART (LIFE LESSONS)

	Thumb	Index Finger	Middle Finger	Ring Finger	Little Finger
Right	Failure	Power-lessness	Irrespon-sibility	Hiding out	Not speaking up
Left	Family issues	Blocked passions	Guilt issues	Disapproval fears	Intimacy issues

To find your life-lesson statement, combine the short description of your lowest ranking print(s) with the Too Much/Too Little statement associated with your school. For example, if your lowest ranking print is on the right index finger (powerlessness) and your school is love (explosion/stuffed feelings), then your life-lesson statement is Powerlessness + Explosion/Stuffed Feelings. As with your life-purpose statement, if you have one lowest ranking print and belong to one school, this process is simple enough. If you have mutiple lowest ranking prints and/or belong to more than one school, your life-lesson statement will be more complicated. For now, record your key meaning(s) and Too Much/Too Little statement(s) below or in your life-purpose journal.

Key meaning(s) of my lowest ranking fingerprint(s)

____

+ Too Much / Too Little statement(s) of my school(s)

____

My life lesson is ______________________________

____

TOO MUCH / TOO LITTLE STATEMENTS CHART

School	Too Much / Too Little Statement
Service	Servitude / Self-Indulgence
Love	Explosion / Stuffed Feelings
Wisdom	Weak Commitments / Indecision
Peace	Overextensions / Slacking Off

If you have more than one lowest ranking fingerprint, combine the key meanings and then pair them with the Too Much/Too Little statement to create your life lesson. For example, if you have lowest ranking prints on your right thumb (failure) and your right index finger (powerlessness) and you are in the School of Service (servitude/self-indulgence), your life lesson would be: Failure and Powerlessness + Servitude/Self-Indulgence. If you also have more than one school, combine the Too Much/Too Little statements of the schools in a similar way.

Extra Guidelines for Life-Lesson Identification

If you have any of the situations below, follow the instructions in that section to help you further clarify your life lesson.

Your Lowest Ranking Prints Appear on the Same Finger on Both Your Left and Right Hands Use this key meaning in your life-lesson statement:

Left and right thumbs: Failure

Left and right index fingers: Powerlessness

Left and right middle fingers: Guilt Issues

Left and right ring fingers: Hiding Out

Left and right little fingers: Intimacy Issues

This is similar to what happens when the highest ranked prints appear on the same fingers on both the left and right hands. With lowest ranking prints, you also use the key meaning inherent in the fingers of the right hand, except when the lowest rankers are the middle finger or the little finger.

You Have One of the Many Patterns Made Up of Two or More Lowest Ranking Fingerprints Called an Archetypal Combination Archetypal combinations are just as likely for life lessons as they are for life purposes. Each of the life-lesson archetypal combinations is described in chapter four and explained in further detail in Appendix I: Archetypal Combinations and Case Studies.

The Exalted Life Lesson Progress on your life lesson unlocks your life purpose and brings life satisfaction. However, in some cases, advanced trainees at the Earth University do more than merely make progress on their life lesson. They master it, turning what was once a weakness into a strength. This is called exalting your life lesson.

In Soap Opera on page 193, the lowest ranking print is on the left index finger, indicating that progress in unblocking passions is required for the owner of these prints to see his Artist life purpose emerge. If he exalts his life lesson, not only will

The Artist emerge, but a Passionate Artist will dominate his life—and that would be a fine life indeed.

You Have a Composite Whorl Composite whorls are the lowest ranking whorls with the unusual capacity of flipping on and off like a light switch. Treat them as a simultaneously highest ranking and lowest ranking fingerprint, therefore making the fingers they occupy part of the life purpose and part of the life lesson. For instance, if the composite whorl is on the right index finger, power is all or part of the life-purpose statement and powerlessness is all or part of the life-lesson statement. For an example of how the composite whorl works, read the case study of Harold the Herald on page 250.

You Have a Lowest Ranking Print on Your Left Ring Finger Experience has shown that when there is a lowest ranking left ring finger as part of a group of lowest ranking prints, it is best to treat it as the most important fingerprint of the group. Lee Harvey Oswald's fingerprints on page 241 are an example of this.

Your Lowest Ranking Prints Appear in Seven or More of the Ten Fingerprint Locations Use this method to identify your life lesson:

1. Identify the type of lowest ranking fingerprint appearing in the seven or more locations.
2. Identify the school associated with that fingerprint type.
3. Use the Too Much / Too Little phrase of *this* school as your entire life-lesson statement.

For example, if the seven or more fingerprints *that tie for lowest ranking* are:

Whorls (School of Service): Your life lesson is servitude/self-indulgence.

Loops (School of Love): Your life lesson is explosion/stuffed feelings.

Tented Arches (School of Wisdom): Your life lesson is weak commitments/ indecision.

Arches (School of Peace): Your life lesson is overextension/slacking off.

Note: In the unlikely event that there is a six-way tie for lowest ranking fingerprint and no archetypal life-lesson combination is present, use the above guideline to determine the life lesson.

You Have a Complex Fingerprint Chart Most people have fingerprint charts that can be interpreted easily enough from the rules you are learning here. However, sometimes fingerprints create complex patterns that are more difficult to interpret. Lee Harvey Oswald's fingerprints on page 241 are an example of this and contain guidelines for interpreting complex charts.

****

So far, you have been learning the mechanical process of life-purpose map construction. To facilitate this process, one-word descriptions—key meanings—were used for each of the ten finger locations. The next chapter will expand on these descriptions, giving you a deeper understanding of your life purpose and life lesson. After reading chapter four, you will be ready to pull your life-purpose map together by creating your life-fulfillment formula in chapter five.

CHAPTER FOUR

DEEPEN YOUR UNDERSTANDING

Thus he that Nature rightly understands,
May from each Line imprinted in his Hands,
His future Fate and Fortune come to know:
And what Path it is his Feet shall go;
His secret Inclination he may see,
And to what Vice he shall addicted be:
To th'End that when he looks into his Hand,
He may upon his Guard the better stand;
And turn his wandering Steps another way,
Whene'er he finds he does from Virtue stray.
—ARISTOTLE

While describing the mechanics of life-purpose map construction in the previous chapter, I used short descriptions of the ten finger locations for both the highest and lowest ranking fingerprints as a shorthand method of understanding each finger location's key meanings. However, the characteristics of the ten fingers are much deeper and more nuanced than these simple descriptions.

In this chapter, I address each of the ten finger locations (followed by some characteristics of the palm) in more detail to give you a better sense of what your life-purpose and life-lesson statements really mean. I start with the right thumb, move to the left thumb, then alternate right and left through the rest of the fingers. Have your fingerprint chart with highest and lowest ranking prints handy so as you read each section you know whether you have a highest, lowest, or non-ranking print in that location.

Each finger location discussion is broken into two sections: section one explains the relevance of having a highest ranking print on that finger and section two explains the relevance of having a lowest ranking print on that finger. However, since the key meanings for highest and lowest ranking prints are inverses of each other, it's helpful to read the entire description for every finger on which you have a highest or lowest ranking print so you can see, for instance, what it looks like if you are exalting your life lesson or falling short of your life purpose. In any case, be sure to follow the cross-references at the end of each section, which will lead you to archetypal combinations and case studies relevant to your fingerprints. If you don't have a highest or lowest ranking print (a non-ranking print) in a particular finger location, then you don't have to read that section (but you can if you want to).

As you read through the detailed descriptions of your highest and lowest ranking fingerprint(s), take notes in your life-purpose journal about anything that feels particularly relevant to your life right now. After you understand your highest and lowest ranking fingerprint(s) more thoroughly, you may amend your life-purpose and life-lesson statements, picking the words or phrases you feel are most pertinent at this time in your life. These notes will help you create your life-fulfillment formula in chapter five, so try to complete this step thoughtfully.

The descriptions of the ten finger locations are organized into the following sections:

For Highest Ranking Prints

- A brief introduction to the characteristics of that finger
- A description of how the characteristics express their highest possibilities as all or part of the life purpose
- A list of typical occupations that bring fulfillment to those with a highest ranking print on this finger
- A list of common obstacles encountered by those with a highest ranking print on this finger
- A list of famous people, both real and fictional, who epitomize the qualities associated with this finger location
- The life-purpose inverse for people with a highest ranking print in this location (or, what it looks like when this life purpose is not blossoming)
- Frequently asked questions by people who have a highest ranking print on this finger
- A checklist to take stock of your current state of progress
- A short guide combining this finger's characteristics with each of the four schools
- A list of the common ways that a highest ranking print on this finger combines with highest ranking prints on other fingers (or, the life-purpose archetypal combinations)

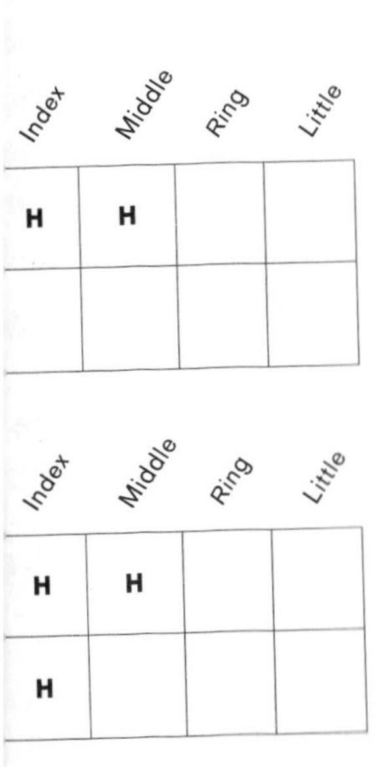

For Lowest Ranking Prints

- A Goldilocks Rule description (Too Much, Too Little, and Just Right) of how this location works as a life lesson
- A list of the common ways that a lowest ranking print on this finger combines with lowest ranking prints on other fingers (or, the life-lesson archetypal combinations)

The information you are about to read is the distillation of the experiences of dozens of fingerprint practitioners in well over 100,000 cases. Read the lists slowly, and take time to integrate these generic descriptions into your own life story.

RIGHT THUMB

LIFE PURPOSE: The Master of Success / The Doer
LIFE LESSON: Breaking the Failure Cycle

Thumbs indicate one's ability to oppose. In the outer world, the ability to oppose refers to humanity's tool-making capacities: building a shelter to oppose the elements, making a weapon to hold off your enemy or to succeed in the hunt. In the inner world, the ability to oppose refers to your ability to impose your will on yourself: to stay up later to study for the exam, for example. We are the descendants of the descendants of those whose thumbs were up to the task.

Thumbs represent humankind's ability to make manifest, to bring into three-dimensional form that which we imagine, to get things under our thumb. A master of thumbness, The Doer knows when to oppose and when not to, when to exert control and when to let go. Here, we look at the right thumb (or both thumbs) life purpose from the soul psychology perspective.

See page 168 for more information about The Doer.

Highest Ranking Print on the Right Thumb: The Master of Success

Masters of Success . . .

- Turn ideas into reality
- Create tangible, measurable results
- Take personal responsibility for seeing things through to completion

Masters of Success Are Happiest When . . .

- Immersed in a project
- Using skills or learning new ones
- Energizing others with a natural enthusiasm

Typical Occupations To find fulfillment in your work, the ke in what you do but in your focus and commitment to proc able results in the world. The actual format you choose is s

- Entrepreneur: Launching a business, or starting up a new existing company
- CEO, company president: Being the one to say how resu
- Sales leader: Making a record number of sales, inspiring surpass the industry standard
- Producer or director of creative projects: Taking somethin from conception to completion
- High achiever in any field, for instance: Singing the lead a up an architectural firm, quarterbacking the football team: on you

Common Obstacles

- Following an unsuitable career path, for instance, attempti else's goals instead of your own
- Relying on unreliable people
- Stopping just short of success
- Becoming ruined by your success

Famous Masters of Success

- The Genie in the Magic Lamp, Seabiscuit, Hercules, Rock
- Helen Keller, Thomas Alva Edison, Muhammad Ali, Martina
- Sir Edmund Hillary and Tenzing Norgay

Life Purpose Blossoming

- Focus, ambition
- Results
- Feelings of accomplishment

Life Purpose Inver

- Scattered direc
- Logistical nightr
- Feelings of failu

What's Up? (Frequently Asked Questions) Following are que by many Doers over the years, followed by my most commo

pouring feelings into each song, a successful entreprene all might qualify as a Doer with Heart.

The Master of Success in the School of Wisdom: Wisdom greatest success. College professors and corporate consu as do second grade teachers and dedicated scientists. A r esting dualistic personality: part civil engineer, part rebe invention languish on his desk or will it reach the marke more tented arches need to put themselves at risk to gai this life purpose.

The Master of Success in the School of Peace: "Succe your motto. Live by this credo and don't let the Sticks Lah-Dee-Dah Lethargy gain control over your life.

The Master of Success: Archetypal Combinations To fig chetypal combinations below, review the fingerprint char lowest ranking prints. If your highest ranking prints ap as denoted by an H below, then the archetypal combin charts, the H stands for highest ranking print, regardless

The Tycoon

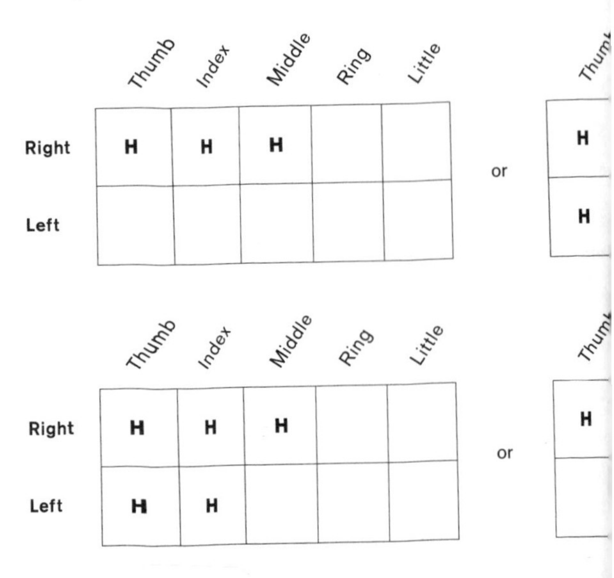

Fingerprint Profile: Right thumb or both thumbs + index fingers + right middle finger as the highest ran Power + Money = The Tycoon)

See page 170 for more information about The Tyc

Masters of Success Are Happiest When . . .

- Immersed in a project
- Using skills or learning new ones
- Energizing others with a natural enthusiasm

Typical Occupations To find fulfillment in your work, the key for you is not so much in what you do but in your focus and commitment to producing tangible, measurable results in the world. The actual format you choose is secondary.

- Entrepreneur: Launching a business, or starting up a new product line within an existing company
- CEO, company president: Being the one to say how results will be produced
- Sales leader: Making a record number of sales, inspiring your sales staff to surpass the industry standard
- Producer or director of creative projects: Taking something like a movie or a play from conception to completion
- High achiever in any field, for instance: Singing the lead at the opera, heading up an architectural firm, quarterbacking the football team: everyone is counting on you

Common Obstacles

- Following an unsuitable career path, for instance, attempting to fulfill someone else's goals instead of your own
- Relying on unreliable people
- Stopping just short of success
- Becoming ruined by your success

Famous Masters of Success

- The Genie in the Magic Lamp, Seabiscuit, Hercules, Rocky I, II, III, IV . . .
- Helen Keller, Thomas Alva Edison, Muhammad Ali, Martina Navratilova
- Sir Edmund Hillary and Tenzing Norgay

Life Purpose Blossoming

- Focus, ambition
- Results
- Feelings of accomplishment

Life Purpose Inverse

- Scattered direction; unclear goals
- Logistical nightmares
- Feelings of failure

What's Up? (Frequently Asked Questions) Following are questions I've been asked by many Doers over the years, followed by my most common answers.

For Lowest Ranking Prints

- A Goldilocks Rule description (Too Much, Too Little, and Just Right) of how this location works as a life lesson
- A list of the common ways that a lowest ranking print on this finger combines with lowest ranking prints on other fingers (or, the life-lesson archetypal combinations)

The information you are about to read is the distillation of the experiences of dozens of fingerprint practitioners in well over 100,000 cases. Read the lists slowly, and take time to integrate these generic descriptions into your own life story.

RIGHT THUMB

LIFE PURPOSE: The Master of Success / The Doer
LIFE LESSON: Breaking the Failure Cycle

Thumbs indicate one's ability to oppose. In the outer world, the ability to oppose refers to humanity's tool-making capacities: building a shelter to oppose the elements, making a weapon to hold off your enemy or to succeed in the hunt. In the inner world, the ability to oppose refers to your ability to impose your will on yourself: to stay up later to study for the exam, for example. We are the descendants of the descendants of those whose thumbs were up to the task.

Thumbs represent humankind's ability to make manifest, to bring into three-dimensional form that which we imagine, to get things under our thumb. A master of thumbness, The Doer knows when to oppose and when not to, when to exert control and when to let go. Here, we look at the right thumb (or both thumbs) life purpose from the soul psychology perspective.

See page 168 for more information about The Doer.

Highest Ranking Print on the Right Thumb: The Master of Success

Masters of Success . . .

- Turn ideas into reality
- Create tangible, measurable results
- Take personal responsibility for seeing things through to completion

I am working hard but the results aren't coming. What's up? Most Doers do not produce results early on that live up to expectations. Maybe all you need is consistency of action over time and not enough time has passed as yet. Maybe your picture of what success looks like is not what *your* success actually looks like. Y'know, life is like a luncheonette. The cosmic cook might still be working on earlier orders. Let me warm up your coffee as we wait for your current order to work its way forward on the spindle.

I am doing well at work, but I don't like the rest of my life. What's up?
Are you sure you are doing what you really want to be doing?

I just had a big (or small) failure. What's up?
Reread the two answers above.

The Master of Success Checklist When you are living your life purpose, you should be able to check off all the items on this list. Make a note of your answers today and compare them to your answers one year from now. (Don't forget, life purpose is a process.)

- ☐ I like my work.
- ☐ I am good at what I do.
- ☐ I take ideas and make them happen.
- ☐ I exercise initiative, reliability, and persistence.
- ☐ My life purpose is at the center of what I do every day.
- ☐ I bring projects to successful completion.
- ☐ I enjoy the fruits of my labors.
- ☐ I am successful on my own terms.
- ☐ I enjoy my leisure time. I know how to have fun.
- ☐ My future looks bright.

The Master of Success in Each of the Four Schools When combined with the four schools, The Doer's life purpose looks like this.

The Master of Success in the School of Service: Satisfaction comes if you can maintain the self-focus to succeed while not losing track of the soul's intention to be of service to others. Attempting to balance your own needs with those of everyone else is sure to bring about thorny complications. Grapple as best you can, learn from your victories and mistakes, and watch as your success grows.

The Master of Success in the School of Love (see also Ms. Steamroller on page 168): At his or her best, this Doer employs the heart as the main result-producing muscle (as opposed to physical or mental exertion). A nurse or social worker, a lead singer pouring feelings into each song, a successful entrepreneur in the day care business, all might qualify as a Doer with Heart.

The Master of Success in the School of Wisdom: Wisdom is the cornerstone of your greatest success. College professors and corporate consultants come easily to mind, as do second grade teachers and dedicated scientists. A recent client had this interesting dualistic personality: part civil engineer, part rebellious radical. Will his new invention languish on his desk or will it reach the marketplace? Doers with two or more tented arches need to put themselves at risk to gain the rewards promised by this life purpose.

The Master of Success in the School of Peace: "Success the Easy Way" becomes your motto. Live by this credo and don't let the Sticks and Plates Spin Cycle or Lah-Dee-Dah Lethargy gain control over your life.

The Master of Success: Archetypal Combinations To figure out if you have the archetypal combinations below, review the fingerprint chart showing your highest and lowest ranking prints. If your highest ranking prints appear in the finger locations as denoted by an H below, then the archetypal combination applies to you. In the charts, the H stands for highest ranking print, regardless of fingerprint type.

The Tycoon

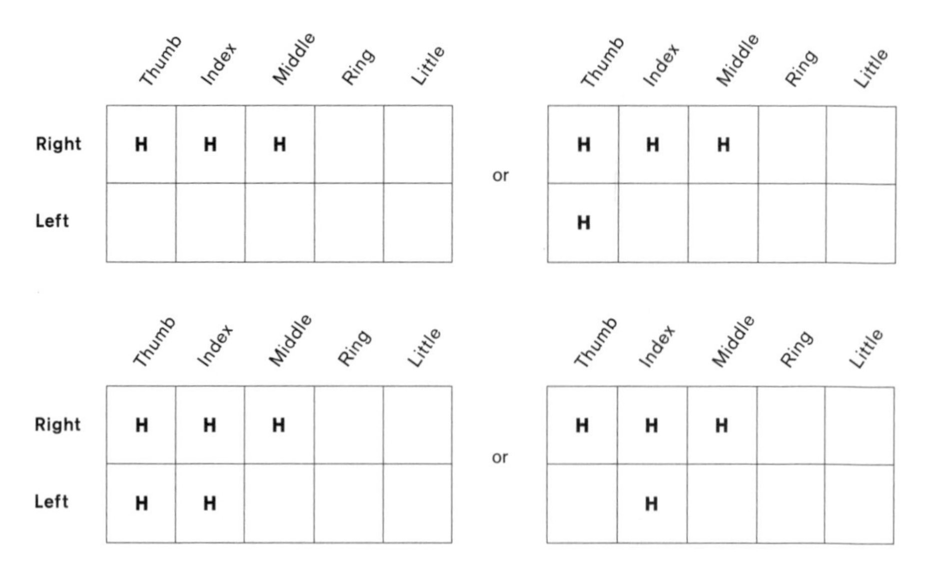

	Thumb	Index	Middle	Ring	Little
Right	H	H	H		
Left					

or

	Thumb	Index	Middle	Ring	Little
Right	H	H	H		
Left	H				

	Thumb	Index	Middle	Ring	Little
Right	H	H	H		
Left	H	H			

or

	Thumb	Index	Middle	Ring	Little
Right	H	H	H		
Left		H			

Fingerprint Profile: Right thumb or both thumbs + right index finger or both index fingers + right middle finger as the highest ranking fingerprints (Success + Power + Money = The Tycoon)

See page 170 for more information about The Tycoon.

The Big Shot

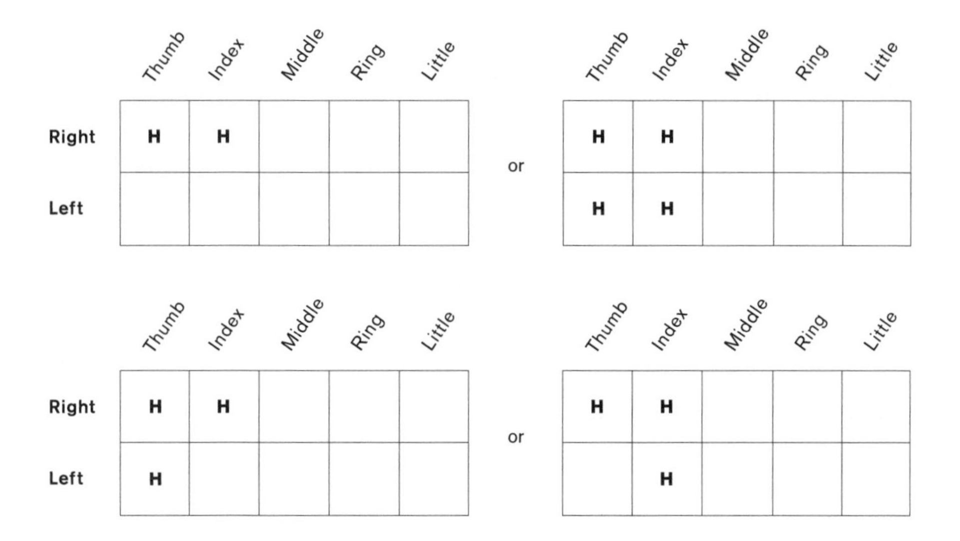

	Thumb	Index	Middle	Ring	Little
Right	H	H			
Left					

or

	Thumb	Index	Middle	Ring	Little
Right	H	H			
Left	H	H			

	Thumb	Index	Middle	Ring	Little
Right	H	H			
Left	H				

or

	Thumb	Index	Middle	Ring	Little
Right	H	H			
Left		H			

Fingerprint Profile: Right thumb or both thumbs + right index finger or both index fingers as the highest ranking fingerprints (Success + Leadership = The Big Shot or Effective Leader)

See page 185 for more information about The Big Shot.

The Prima Donna

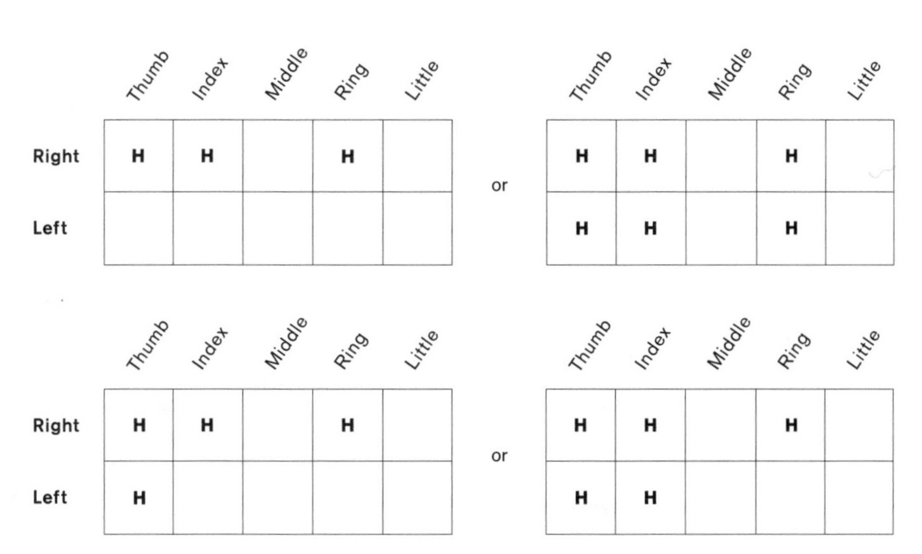

	Thumb	Index	Middle	Ring	Little
Right	H	H		H	
Left					

or

	Thumb	Index	Middle	Ring	Little
Right	H	H		H	
Left	H	H		H	

	Thumb	Index	Middle	Ring	Little
Right	H	H		H	
Left	H				

or

	Thumb	Index	Middle	Ring	Little
Right	H	H		H	
Left	H	H			

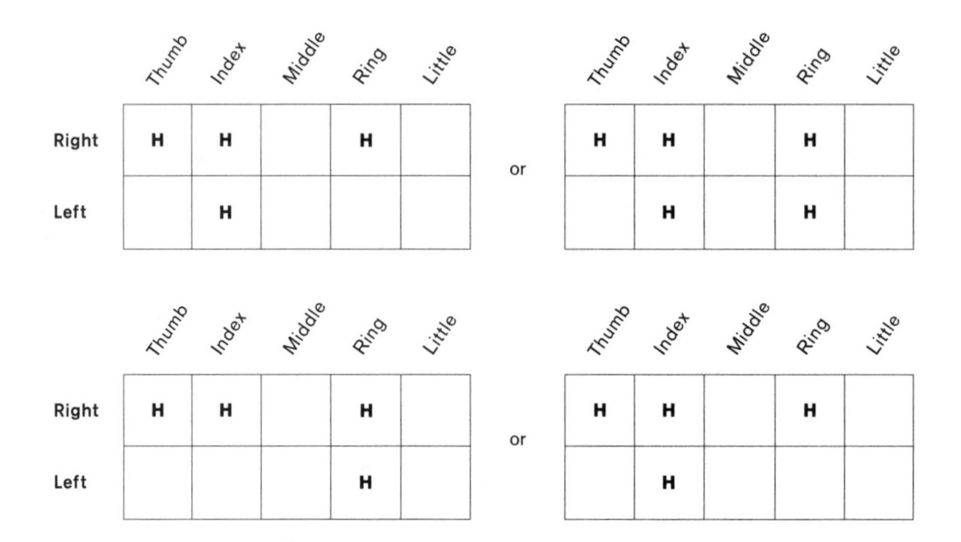

	Thumb	Index	Middle	Ring	Little
Right	H	H		H	
Left		H			

or

	Thumb	Index	Middle	Ring	Little
Right	H	H		H	
Left		H		H	

	Thumb	Index	Middle	Ring	Little
Right	H	H		H	
Left				H	

or

	Thumb	Index	Middle	Ring	Little
Right	H	H		H	
Left		H			

Fingerprint Profile: Right thumb or both thumbs + right index finger or both index fingers + right ring finger or both ring fingers as the highest ranking fingerprints (Success + Power + Creativity = The Prima Donna)

See page 186 for more information about The Prima Donna.

Persuasion

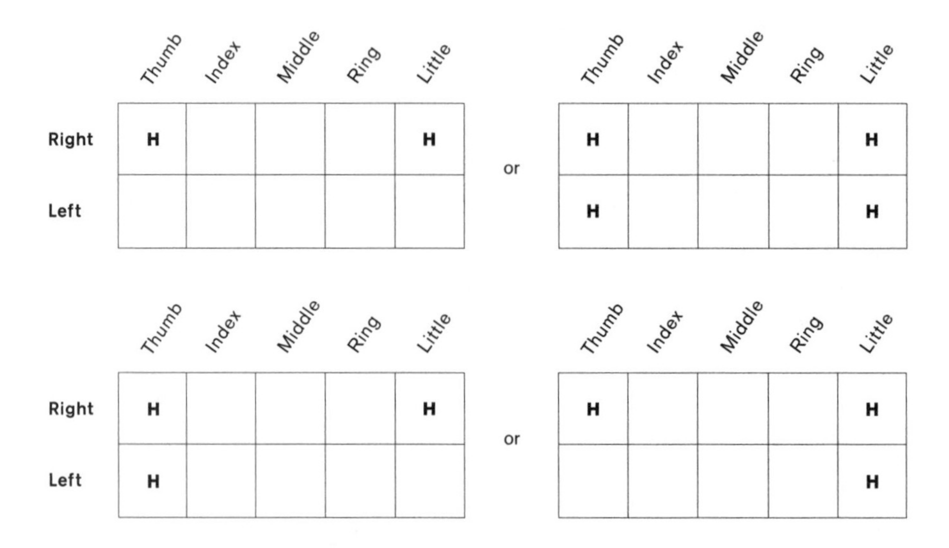

	Thumb	Index	Middle	Ring	Little
Right	H				H
Left					

or

	Thumb	Index	Middle	Ring	Little
Right	H				H
Left	H				H

	Thumb	Index	Middle	Ring	Little
Right	H				H
Left	H				

or

	Thumb	Index	Middle	Ring	Little
Right	H				H
Left					H

Fingerprint Profile: Right thumb or both thumbs + right little finger or both little fingers as the highest ranking prints (Success + Communications = Persuasion)

See page 244 for more information about Persuasion.

Lowest Ranking Print on the Right Thumb: Breaking the Failure Cycle

The right thumb challenges you to maintain awareness regarding producing results in the world. Goldilocks says the most common forms of results unconsciousness are as follows:

Too Much Right Thumb

- You create results, but you don't appreciate them.
- You create results but for the wrong reason or in the wrong field of endeavor.
- You create results but ruin the rest of your life in the process.

Too Little Right Thumb

- Your incomplete efforts yield insufficient outcomes (woulda, coulda, shoulda).
- You count on the big sale, that one big score, the lottery bonanza to pay your rent.
- You blame others for your failures: the government, the weather, your aunt Mathilda.

The Exalted Life Lesson (Just Right)

- You are successful in the world and have just the life you always wanted.
- Oprah is on line 1, she wants to interview you for her upcoming "Success Now" show.

See page 172 for more information about Breaking the Failure Cycle.

Breaking the Failure Cycle: Archetypal Combinations

To figure out if you have the archetypal combination on the next page, review the fingerprint chart showing your highest and lowest ranking prints. If your lowest ranking prints appear in the finger locations as denoted by an L below, then the archetypal combination applies to you. In the charts, the L stands for lowest ranking print, regardless of fingerprint type.

The Loser

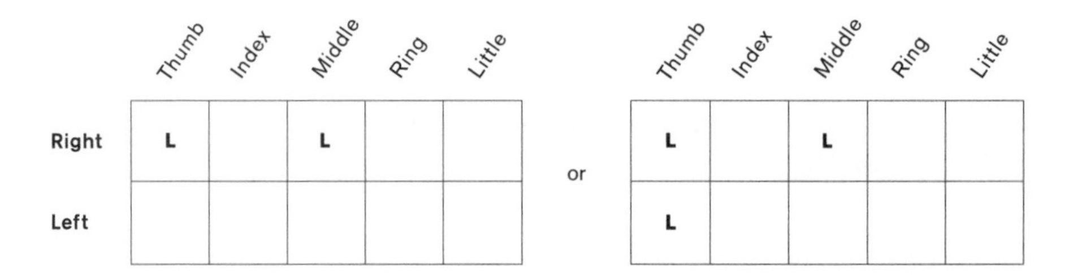

	Thumb	Index	Middle	Ring	Little
Right	L		L		
Left					

or

	Thumb	Index	Middle	Ring	Little
Right	L		L		
Left	L				

Fingerprint Profile: Right thumb or both thumbs + right middle finger as the lowest ranking fingerprints (Failure + Irresponsibility = The Loser)

See page 173 for more information about The Loser.

LEFT THUMB

LIFE PURPOSE: The Master of Family or Community
LIFE LESSON: Family or Community Issues

As we move from the right hand to the left, the focus shifts more inward. For those who have the left thumb as the highest ranking print, fulfillment comes from creating a personal environment that provides a sense of safety, security, and well-being. By and large, this translates into developing a positive family or community consciousness. In this context, family can refer to your blood family or it could also mean your community, clan, tribe, team, coworkers, and so on.

See page 175 for more information about Family Connection in the School of Love.

Highest Ranking Print on the Left Thumb: The Master of Family or Community

Masters of Family or Community . . .

- Are naturally supportive
- Know how to compromise without feeling a loss of personal identity
- Maintain connections through good times and bad

Masters of Family or Community Are Happiest When . . .

- Operating within a well-connected family or community framework
- Teamwork comes before personal accomplishment
- The entire group feels part of your success

Typical Occupations To find fulfillment in your work, the key for you is to participate fully in a family-minded group. The actual format you choose is secondary.

- Father, mother, or step-parent: Important roles for anyone, but when your life purpose is Family, your parenthood becomes *the* key element in your life. You can still pursue personal goals and talents, as long as you remember what is of primary importance.
- Elementary school teacher: Your family now totals thirty or more children.
- Coach for team sports/scoutmaster: Emphasis is on teamwork, cooperation, unified goals.
- Middle level management, small business owner: The work environment becomes the "family" focal point, especially if there is a need for a small number of people working closely together over a lengthy period of time.
- Community spokesperson: You either join an existing community or organize a new one.

Common Obstacles

- Starting out in an abusive family, or picking the wrong family or community when older
- Doing too much to get the family or community to like you
- Staying the lone wolf to avoid family hassles
- Taking care of everyone except yourself

Famous Masters of Family or Community

- The Cleavers, the Cartwrights, the Waltons, the Huxtables, Seinfeld and his pals, the characters of *Friends*
- The Kennedys, the Bushes
- The Hatfields and the McCoys

Life Purpose Blossoming

- Togetherness
- Support
- Cooperation
- Taking care of yourself

Life Purpose Inverse

- Dysfunctional families, isolation
- I'll do it myself
- Resentment, betrayal
- Physical well-being ignored

What's Up? (Frequently Asked Questions) Following are questions I've been asked by budding Masters of Family over the years, followed by my most common answers.

I've tried being a family member, and it was a disaster. What's up?
Perhaps your original family was abusive. Perhaps your friends in high school were busy stealing hubcaps, or worse. In these cases, it was entirely appropriate for you to dismiss yourself from the group. Despite these experiences, the highest meaning and fulfillment available for you will be inside a family or community.

I thought my life purpose would involve my music. What's up?
There is no need to abandon your talent. But if you can pursue your talent inside a deeply connected group, you are much more likely to find the satisfaction you seek.

I just had a big fight with my family. What's up?
Sometimes arguments and even breakdowns are the doorway to appropriate family connection. Perhaps crisis is just what is needed to put this particular family to the test.

The Master of Family or Community Checklist When you are living your life purpose, you should be able to check off all the items on this list. Make a note of your answers today and compare them to your answers one year from now. (Don't forget, life purpose is a process.)

- ☐ I am working out whatever issues I may have had with my mother and father.
- ☐ My chosen circle knows the real me.
- ☐ I can fight or argue inside a group without undue injury.
- ☐ I look forward to the holidays and other family get-together times.
- ☐ I can let go of old resentments.
- ☐ I am more or less the same person inside a group or on my own.
- ☐ My family communications are up-to-date.
- ☐ Family or team obligations do not control my life.
- ☐ I get the alone time I need. I know how to take care of myself.
- ☐ I feel supported by the families or communities of which I am a member.

The Master of Family or Community in Each of the Four Schools When combined with the four schools, The Master of Family or Community life purpose looks like this.

The Master of Family or Community in the School of Service (see also Family Issues in the School of Service on page 179): When your life is filled with family or community service, or both, and you are *so* happy it is, that is when you can truly say you are on purpose here. Conversely, ongoing escalating and inappropriate sacrifice for family would indicate that you are in your life-purpose inverse.

The Master of Family or Community in the School of Love (see also Family Connection in the School of Love on page 175): The School of Love is the natural home for Family as the life purpose. For those with this life-purpose/school combination, creating a comfortable and loving home life is the road to happiness. Straightforward as it may seem, difficult families with difficult family members can turn this life path into an uncomfortable emotional roller coaster.

The Master of Family or Community in the School of Wisdom: Are you the stay-up-late-talking-to-Aunt-Mathilda, designated insightful listener in the family? Be careful that this is not your way of avoiding your rightful wisdom-based career.

The Master of Family or Community in the School of Peace: A short but memorable hand reading appointment comes to mind: Mary arrived ten minutes late, huffing and puffing. She had two young children in tow plus an infant that she immediately sat down to nurse as she entered my office. Before we could begin, her cell phone rang with an emergency regarding her eight-year-old. I never did get to read her hands that day or any other. Apparently, Mary's entire life was one Sticks and Plates experience after another with no letup in sight.

The Master of Family or Community: Archetypal Combinations To figure out if you have the archetypal combination below, review the fingerprint chart showing your highest and lowest ranking prints. If your highest ranking prints appear in the finger locations as denoted by an H below, then the archetypal combination applies to you. In the charts, the H stands for highest ranking print, regardless of fingerprint type.

The Matriarch or The Patriarch

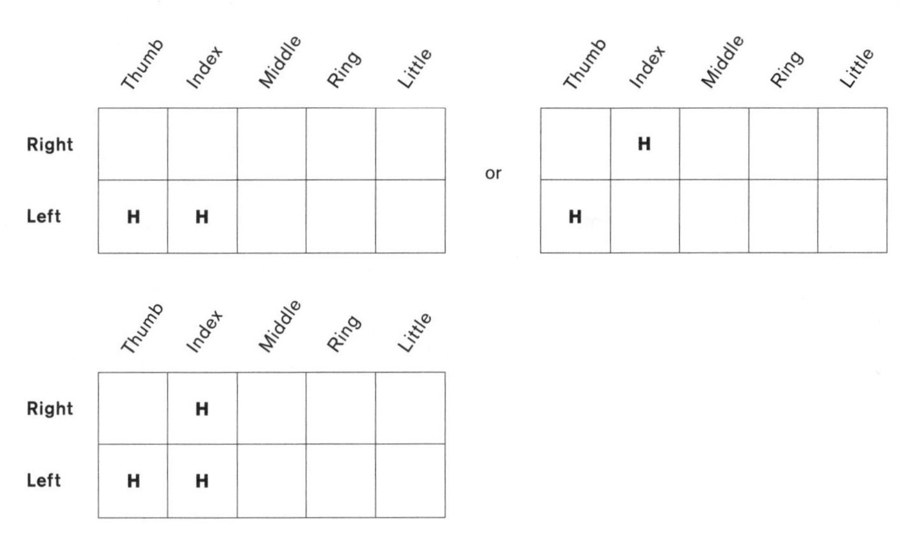

	Thumb	Index	Middle	Ring	Little
Right					
Left	H	H			

or

	Thumb	Index	Middle	Ring	Little
Right		H			
Left	H				

	Thumb	Index	Middle	Ring	Little
Right		H			
Left	H	H			

Fingerprint Profile: Left thumb + one index finger or both index fingers as the highest ranking fingerprints (Family + Power and/or Passions = The Matriarch or The Patriarch)

See page 177 for more information about The Matriarch or The Patriarch.

Lowest Ranking Print on the Left Thumb: Family or Community Issues

The left thumb asks you to create appropriate family and community connection. Goldilocks says the most common forms of family unconsciousness are:

Too Much Left Thumb

- You are still trying to escape an abusive family environment (at home or work).
- A controlling family or community has taken over your life.
- You are constantly sacrificing for the needs of the family or community at your own expense.

Too Little Left Thumb

- You are the lone wolf with no family or community connection at all.
- You have no like-minded, supportive connection.
- You find it hard to remember to take care of yourself.

The Exalted Life Lesson (Just Right)

- You are a marriage and family counselor, using the difficult experiences with your own family to help you understand the problems others face in this part of their lives.
- You love your role as mother (or father, or grandmother, or grandfather). It gives you great joy.

See page 179 for more information about Family Issues in the School of Service.

The Master of Family or Community Issues: Archetypal Combinations To figure out if you have the archetypal combination opposite, review the fingerprint chart showing your highest and lowest ranking prints. If your lowest ranking prints appear in the finger locations as denoted by an L below, then the archetypal combination applies to you. In the charts below, the L stands for lowest ranking print, regardless of fingerprint type.

Guilt in the Family

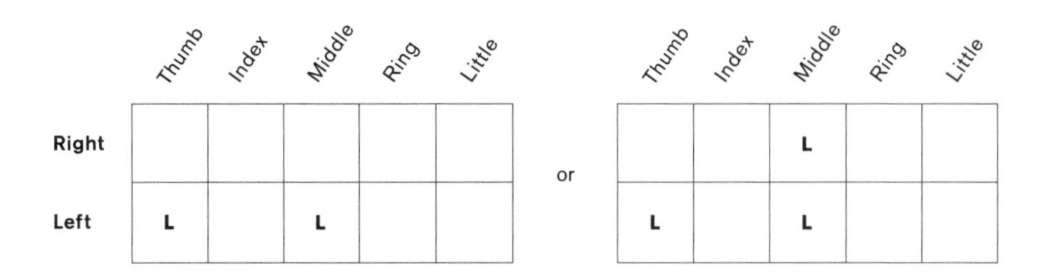

Fingerprint Profile: Left thumb + left middle finger or both middle fingers as the lowest ranking fingerprints (Guilt Issues + Family Issues = Guilt in the Family)

See page 214 for more information about Guilt in the Family.

RIGHT INDEX FINGER

LIFE PURPOSE: The Master of Power / The Leader
LIFE LESSON: Reclaiming Your Power

If the Master of Power is your life purpose, fulfillment comes as you exercise power and influence. Power in this context refers to a consciousness to be inhabited, not a set of circumstances. Using this definition, Tim Robbins in *The Shawshank Redemption* is a man of power even though he is in prison for life. So is Sally Field, an hourly worker turned union organizer in *Norma Rae*. Prisoner or protestor, in soul psychology power is an inner condition forged in the fires of experience.

See page 182 for more information about The Leader with Heart.

Highest Ranking Print on the Right Index Finger: The Master of Power / The Leader

Masters of Power . . .

- Operate with independence of action, initiate new projects, and are confident but not reckless
- Have faith in their abilities, have a vision for the future, and make a difference in the world
- Do not run from confrontation and are glad the buck stops here

Masters of Power Are Happiest When . . .

- Building a new territory or running an existing one
- Reaching for high goals
- Using talents to their fullest

Typical Occupations To find fulfillment in your work, the key for you is *furthering your capabilities of leadership and influence.* The actual format you choose is secondary.

- CEO, company president, manager: Those with this fingerprint chart naturally rise to the top, whatever the profession.
- Entrepreneur, self-employed business owner: Success is completely in your own hands.
- Quarterback of the football team, band director, movie producer: You're in charge, taking the credit for success, the heat for failure.
- Author, painter, architect, doctor, candlestick maker: In any field, you're a high achiever.
- President, governor, senator, mayor: Politics offers the chance to make a difference.
- Union president, PTA spokesperson, influential TV personality: Everyone is turning to you for guidance and direction.

Common Obstacles

- Underselling your talents, reaching for easily attainable goals instead of the brass ring
- Becoming hijacked by other people's agendas
- Fear of failure
- Fear of success

Famous Masters of Power

- George Washington, Eleanor Roosevelt, Ghandi, General Patton
- Oprah Winfrey, Gloria Steinem, Rosa Parks
- Frodo, King Arthur, Ben Cartwright

Life Purpose Blossoming

- Ambition
- Independence of action
- Confidence, potency

Life Purpose Inverse

- Unclear goals
- Dependency, feeling trapped
- Helplessly overwhelmed, I can't, I can't

Himalaya: The Story of a Leader Ironically, the majority of those with The Leader as their life purpose spend the early phases of their lives opposing those in power. The movie *Himalaya* provides a good example. With the world's tallest mountains as the backdrop, a yak-herding tribe faces a power struggle completely familiar to any city council meeting. A young yak herder thinks the older leader too set in his outdated ways. The leader thinks the younger fellow too inexperienced. They argue. Eventually, the young hothead leaves with a small band of followers to take his yaks on a different route through the mountains.

As fate would have it, a storm hits the main herd and the older leader is injured. Only the young rebel has the strength and courage to climb the mountain to try and save the revered tribal chieftain. The young rebel makes it to the ridge, but he is too late. The death scene that follows is the climax of the drama.

The youth apologizes for causing so much trouble. "It was my destiny," the dying man replies. In his remaining moments, he hands over the scepter of power to the rebellious one. The young man objects. "Me, the leader? I am not the type." The old man responds, "You remind me so much of myself at your age. You are the right one for our people." With that the old leader dies and, with the Himalayas glistening in the setting sun, the new leader considers his future.

What's Up? (Frequently Asked Questions) Following are questions I've been asked by many Leaders over the years, followed by my most common answers.

Me, a leader? I am not materialistic, competitive, nor ambitious.
Remember, fingerprints indicate soul psychology, not personality makeup. Your fingerprints do not say leadership is what you want to do. Your fingerprints do say, however, that this is where the highest meaning and fulfillment are available.

This can't be right. I have a hard time seeing myself as part of the power structure.
This is one of the life purposes that often takes four or more decades before coming to the fore. You may wish to look back over your earliest school yard days for perspective. It is likely that at least one of the two characters from *Himalaya* will be obvious on review.

Me a high achiever? I don't even know what I want to do next week.
Good point. I guess you have your work cut out for you, leadership candidate. My advice is to keep saying no to what you don't want to do until the resounding yes that is in there somewhere makes its presence known.

The Master of Power Checklist When you are living your life purpose, you should be able to check off all the items on this list. Make a note of your answers today and compare them to your answers one year from now. (Don't forget, life purpose is a process.)

- ☐ I am in touch with my core values.
- ☐ I am willing to have what I say measured against what I do.
- ☐ I have earned the respect of my peers.
- ☐ I am not too afraid of confrontation, nor do I attract unnecessary conflict.
- ☐ I operate with independence of action.
- ☐ I have a vision for the future. I want to make a difference in the world.
- ☐ I am willing to take the heat of disapproval.
- ☐ I have faith in my abilities.
- ☐ I take pride in my accomplishments.
- ☐ I surround myself with people who are supportive of my life goals.

The Master of Power in Each of the Four Schools When combined with the four schools, The Leader's life purpose looks like this.

The Master of Power in the School of Service: Leaders who exemplify true service have earned the universal respect they so richly deserve. But beware the hidden danger lurking in the leadership + service combination: doing for others as a way to avoid responsibility for living up to *your* potential. Servitude would be the ultimate penalty for not inhabiting your power.

The Master of Power in the School of Love (see also The Leader with Heart on page 182): One man with this fingerprint combination was Lyndon Baines Johnson. Perhaps he saw himself as The Leader with Heart at the outset of his presidency. But as the Vietnam War dragged on, his life-purpose inverse of powerlessness, failed leadership, and a broken heart seem the more likely content of his inner dialogue.

The Master of Power in the School of Wisdom: Wise Leaders gain the main sequence of their life purpose through experience. They can be critical without becoming dogmatic. Rhodes scholars and others who become experts in their fields may qualify for this title, but Laurel and Hardy's wisdom can carry equal influence.

The Master of Power in the School of Peace: Quiet certainty inspires confidence in your leadership. At least, that is the fulfillment possibility for those with this fingerprint combination. To achieve this state, you will have to overcome either insufficient ambition (Ms. Lah-Dee-Dah) or, more commonly, the trap of chronic overwork (Mr. Sticks and Plates). If and when you get your life more or less in balance, your power and influence will shine through, bringing you the life you've always wanted.

The Master of Power: Archetypal Combinations To figure out if you have the archetypal combinations below, review the fingerprint chart showing your highest and lowest ranking prints. If your highest ranking prints appear in the finger locations as denoted by an H below, then the archetypal combination applies to you. In the charts, the H stands for highest ranking print, regardless of fingerprint type.

The Big Shot

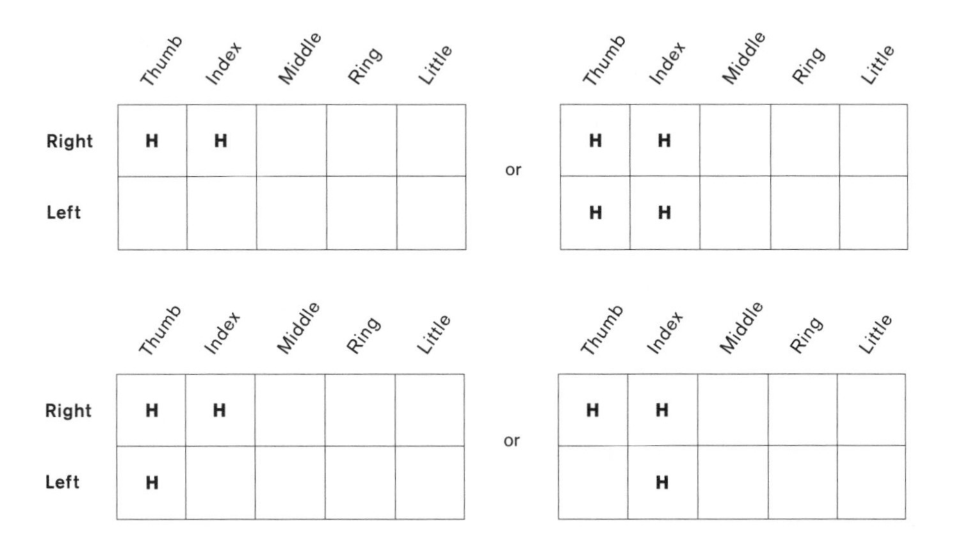

	Thumb	Index	Middle	Ring	Little
Right	H	H			
Left					

or

	Thumb	Index	Middle	Ring	Little
Right	H	H			
Left	H	H			

	Thumb	Index	Middle	Ring	Little
Right	H	H			
Left	H				

or

	Thumb	Index	Middle	Ring	Little
Right	H	H			
Left		H			

Fingerprint Profile: Right thumb or both thumbs + right index finger or both index fingers as the highest ranking fingerprints (Success + Leadership = The Big Shot or Effective Leader)

See page 185 for more information about The Big Shot.

The Prima Donna

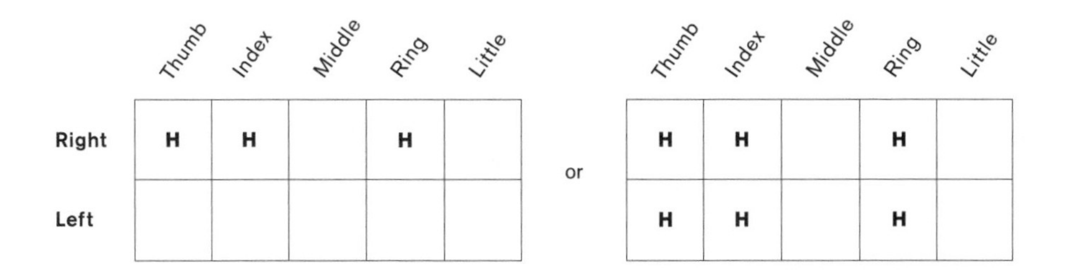

	Thumb	Index	Middle	Ring	Little
Right	H	H		H	
Left					

or

	Thumb	Index	Middle	Ring	Little
Right	H	H		H	
Left	H	H		H	

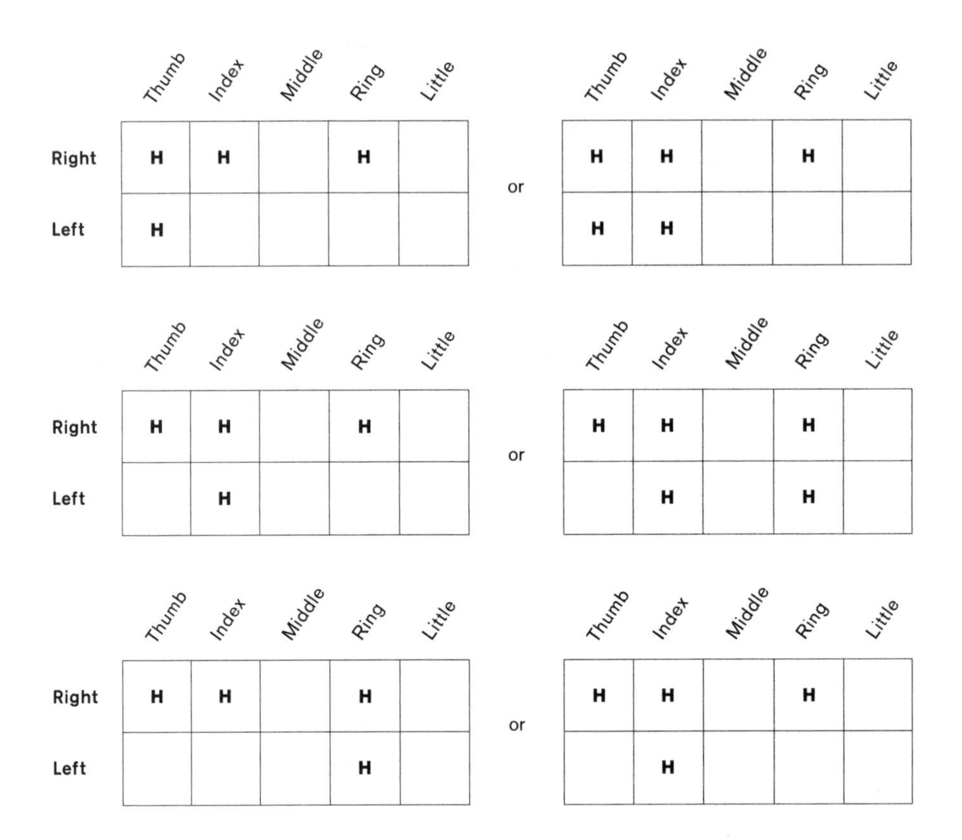

	Thumb	Index	Middle	Ring	Little
Right	H	H		H	
Left	H				

or

	Thumb	Index	Middle	Ring	Little
Right	H	H		H	
Left	H	H			

	Thumb	Index	Middle	Ring	Little
Right	H	H		H	
Left		H			

or

	Thumb	Index	Middle	Ring	Little
Right	H	H		H	
Left		H		H	

	Thumb	Index	Middle	Ring	Little
Right	H	H		H	
Left				H	

or

	Thumb	Index	Middle	Ring	Little
Right	H	H		H	
Left		H			

Fingerprint Profile: Right thumb or both thumbs + right index finger or both index fingers + right ring finger or both ring fingers as the highest ranking fingerprints (Success + Power + Creativity = The Prima Donna)

See page 186 for more information about The Prima Donna.

The Tycoon

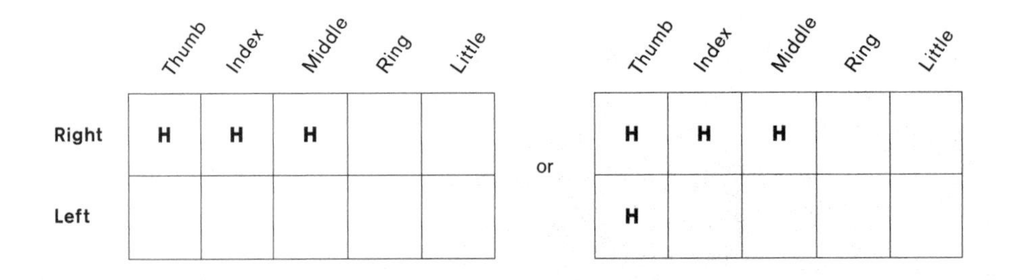

	Thumb	Index	Middle	Ring	Little
Right	H	H	H		
Left					

or

	Thumb	Index	Middle	Ring	Little
Right	H	H	H		
Left	H				

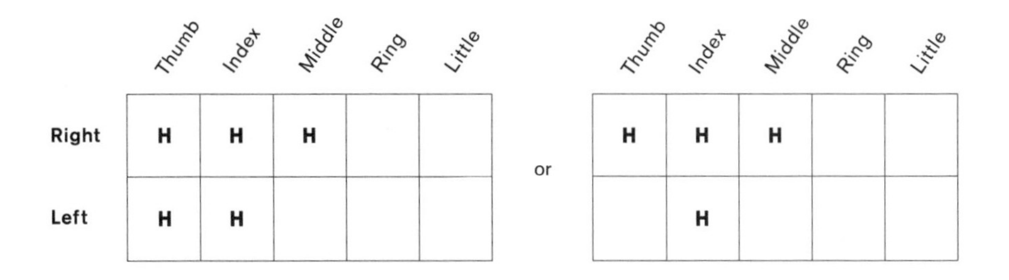

	Thumb	Index	Middle	Ring	Little
Right	H	H	H		
Left	H	H			

or

	Thumb	Index	Middle	Ring	Little
Right	H	H	H		
Left		H			

Fingerprint Profile: Right thumb or both thumbs + right index finger or both index fingers + right middle finger as the highest ranking fingerprints (Success + Power + Money = The Tycoon)

See page 170 for more information about The Tycoon.

The Mentor to Leaders

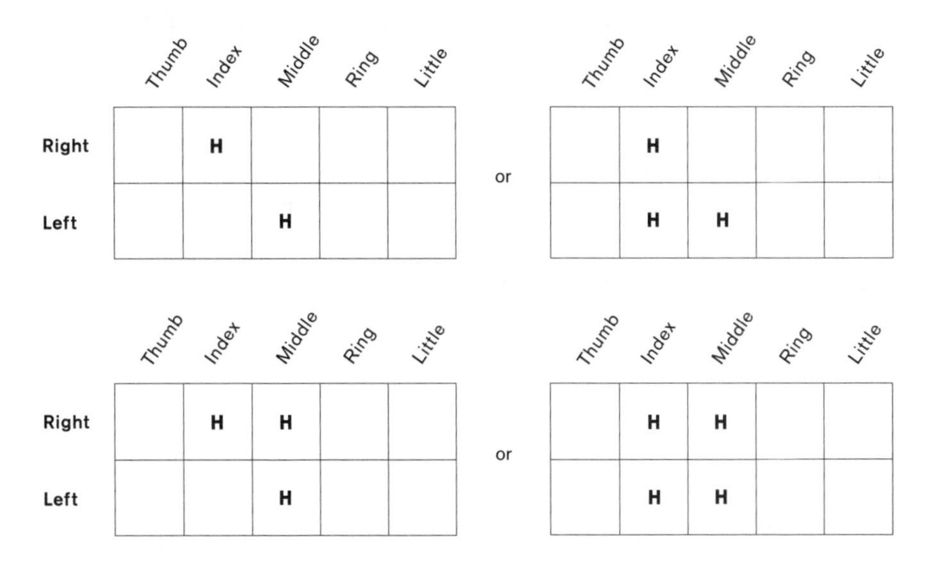

	Thumb	Index	Middle	Ring	Little
Right		H			
Left			H		

or

	Thumb	Index	Middle	Ring	Little
Right		H			
Left		H	H		

	Thumb	Index	Middle	Ring	Little
Right		H	H		
Left			H		

or

	Thumb	Index	Middle	Ring	Little
Right		H	H		
Left		H	H		

Fingerprint Profile: Left middle finger or both middle fingers + right index finger or both index fingers as the highest ranking fingerprints (The Mentor + The Leader = The Mentor to Leaders)

See page 203 for more information about The Mentor to Leaders.

The High-Profile Person

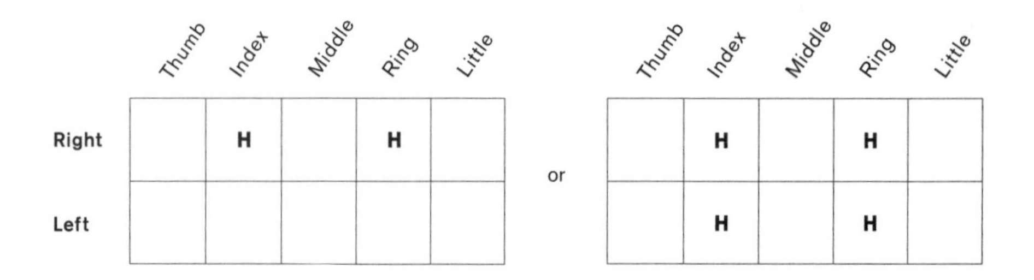

	Thumb	Index	Middle	Ring	Little
Right		H		H	
Left					

or

	Thumb	Index	Middle	Ring	Little
Right		H		H	
Left		H		H	

Fingerprint Profile: Right ring finger or both ring fingers + right index finger or both index fingers as the highest ranking prints (The Leader + The Artist = The High-Profile Person)

See page 231 for more information about The High-Profile Person.

Lowest Ranking Print on the Right Index Finger: Reclaim Your Power

The right index finger challenges you to claim your full power and authority. Goldilocks says the most common Reclaiming Your Power errors are as follows:

Too Much Right Index Finger

- Your independent actions regularly cause problems for other people (or so they say).
- You exercise power without appropriate restraint.
- You pick a fight with your cat when you are actually angry at your dog.

Too Little Right Index Finger

- You are stuck in someone else's life movie.
- You fear that you are insufficient for what life asks of you.
- You are playing it safe, selling out on what you really want.
- You have trouble standing your ground, often running from confrontation.

The Exalted Life Lesson (Just Right)

- I am a man or woman of influence, and I like it.

See page 190 for more information about Reclaiming Your Power.

Reclaim Your Power: Archetypal Combinations To figure out if you have the archetypal combination below, review the fingerprint chart showing your highest and lowest ranking prints. If your lowest ranking prints appear in the finger locations as denoted by an L below, then the archetypal combination applies to you. In the charts, the L stands for lowest ranking print, regardless of fingerprint type.

Mr. Not Enough

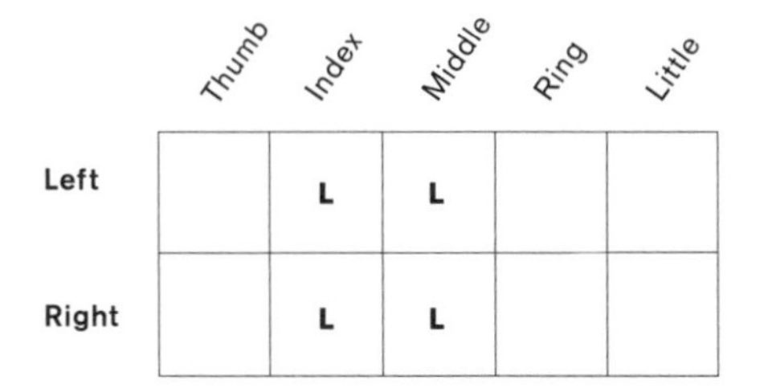

Fingerprint Profile: One middle finger or both middle fingers + one index finger or both index fingers as the lowest ranking fingerprints (Powerlessness + Guilt = Mr. Not Enough)

Mr. Not Enough, the voice of insufficiency, is the most common life-lesson archetypal combination. The standard version above is followed by eight common subtypes below and on the following page, each with its own specific slant.

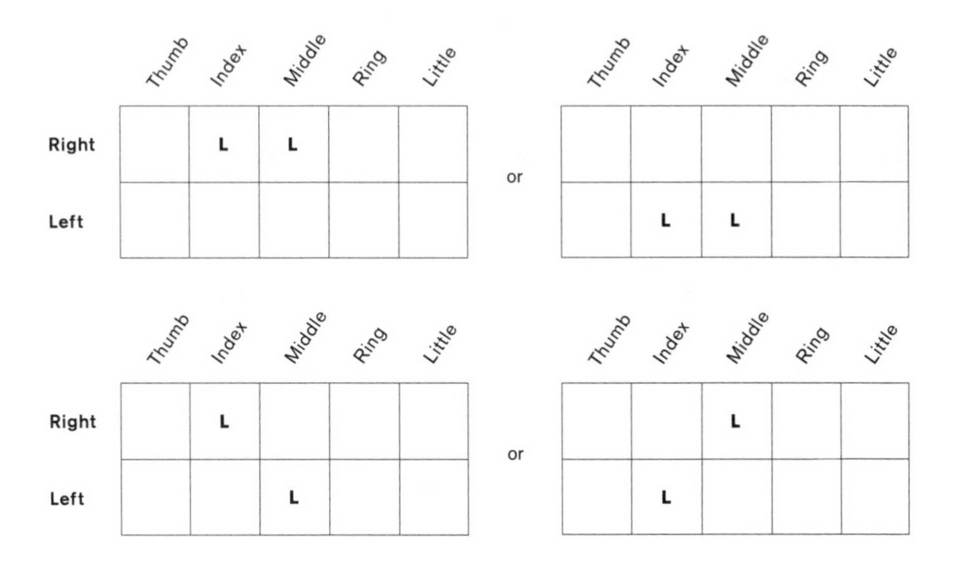

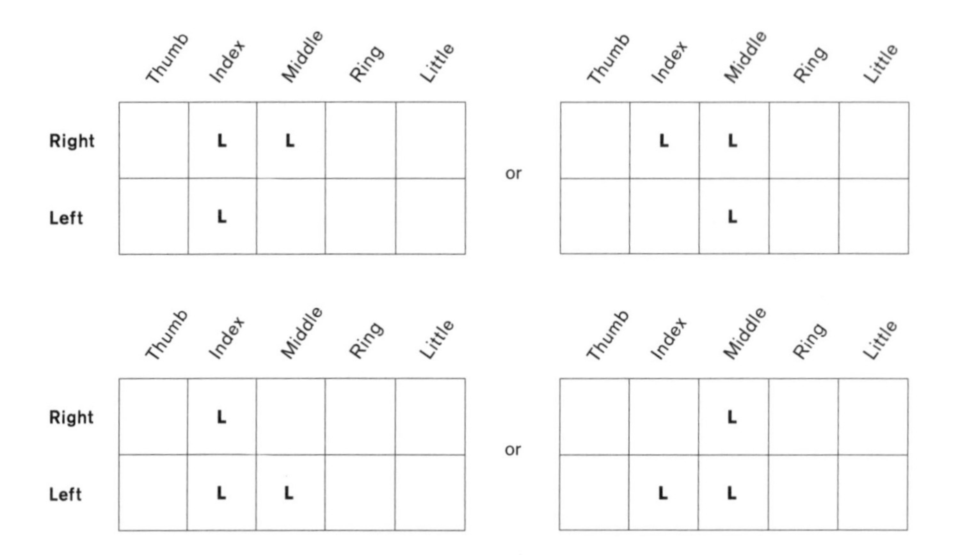

	Thumb	Index	Middle	Ring	Little
Right		L	L		
Left		L			

or

	Thumb	Index	Middle	Ring	Little
Right		L	L		
Left			L		

	Thumb	Index	Middle	Ring	Little
Right		L			
Left		L	L		

or

	Thumb	Index	Middle	Ring	Little
Right			L		
Left		L	L		

See page 216 for more information about Mr. Not Enough.

LEFT INDEX FINGER

LIFE PURPOSE: The Master of Living Your Passions
LIFE LESSON: Blocked Passions

The focus here is on doing what you really want to be doing with your life regardless of, well, regardless of anything. This is one of the non-activity-specific life purposes. This means that, from a soul level, *what you do* in this life *is not nearly as important as how* you do it. In a parallel irony with authority-avoidant right indexers, the majority of left indexers struggle to find that one thing to be passionate about. Those who do, however, are some of the most clear, centered, excited (and exciting) persons whom you will ever meet.

See page 192 for more information about Living Your Passions.

Highest Ranking Print on the Left Index Finger: The Master of Living Your Passions

Masters of Living Your Passions . . .

- Know what they want and have the courage to do something about it
- Are true to their goals, ideals, and values, and do not base their happiness on others' approval
- Are emotionally independent and able to keep from being emotionally blackmailed
- Set clear limits and communicate them cleanly; define boundaries and protect their turf

Masters of Living Your Passions Are Happiest When . . .

- Doing what they really want, pursuing something exciting and important
- Standing up for themselves
- Galvanizing people into joint action by working with them one-to-one

Typical Occupations To find fulfillment in your work, the key for you is not in the *what* but in the *how* you do things. The actual format you choose is secondary.

- Athlete: Committing enough to do all the practice it takes to excel
- Actor, artist, entertainer: Expressing your characters with passion and zest
- Revolutionary philosopher, photographer, author: Burning for social change
- Entrepreneur: Loving the excitement of being immersed in your own business, passionately manifesting something from nothing
- Zealous monk, school teacher in a ghetto, muckraking journalist: Being passionate about spirituality, empowering the children, revealing the truth

Common Obstacles

- Other people's passions
- Not knowing what you want
- Boredom, apathy, desensitization, going numb

Famous Masters of Living Your Passions

- Tiger Woods, John McEnroe, Geronimo
- Katherine Hepburn, Sophia Loren, Antonio Banderas
- Mr. Rogers (You can live your passions and be a quiet type, too.)

Life Purpose Blossoming	***Life Purpose Inverse***
▪ Passion, intensity, strong desires	▪ Numbness, not knowing what you want
▪ Independence	▪ Dependency
▪ Originality	▪ Conformity
▪ Sense of freedom	▪ Feeling trapped

What's Up? (Frequently Asked Questions) Following are questions I've been asked by budding Masters of Living Your Passions over the years, followed by my most common answers.

I already live my passions, but I don't see the meaning in that. What's up?
Eating ten ice cream cones in a row is not the advanced form of this life purpose. Did you really desire that last cone? Learning the difference between real, belongs-deep-down-to-my-essence desires and passing infatuations is at the core of this life path.

Okay. I'll bite. How do you know which passions are real and which are not?
Exactly the reason you are alive, Sir or Madam. Experience will be your best teacher. Make your choices, engender your consequences, repeat as necessary.

But, but, but . . .
There are a million buts: but what about the money, what about the kids, what about global warming? The details don't matter. Living your passions does. Ultimately, living your passions will help with all those other things.

The Master of Living Your Passions Checklist When you are living your life purpose, you should be able to check off all the items on this list. Make a note of your answers today and compare them to your answers one year from now. (Don't forget, life purpose is a process.)

- ☐ Life is an exciting adventure.
- ☐ Basically, I know what I want most of the time.
- ☐ I do not feel boxed in by other people's demands.
- ☐ I know how to stand my ground.
- ☐ I am comfortable with my emotional intensity.
- ☐ I am comfortable making requests.
- ☐ I have emotional independence.
- ☐ I do not have to suppress my appetites to not be controlled by them.
- ☐ I know how to say no.
- ☐ I can express my anger in an appropriate fashion.

The Master of Living Your Passions in Each of the Four Schools When combined with the four schools, the Living Your Passions life purpose looks like this.

The Master of Living Your Passions in the School of Service: This is an interesting dualistic life purpose, one that requires an exquisite balance between the poles of me-ishness and you-ishness. If you can muster the courage to repel those who seek to control your life, you will gain the satisfaction that only true service offers.

The Master of Living Your Passions in the School of Love (see Amelia Earhart, page 192): For some, unlocking the Passions Department is a piece of cake. For these in-touch individuals, the question is: Is your love life more the warm and endearing type, like Tom Hanks and Meg Ryan in *You Have Mail*, *Sleepless in Seattle*, or is it closer to the scream-and-scratch-your-eyes-out version of Elizabeth Taylor and Richard Burton's *Who's Afraid of Virginia Woolf?* For others, the challenge is having any access at all to the Passions Department. If your head is trying to figure out what you desire, odds are your heart will not be in your relationships.

The Master of Living Your Passions in the School of Wisdom: Quite the delicious dilemma, this life purpose: the left index seeks passionate expression and tented arches would be pleased as punch to never leave the library. Find some cause, some wise man/wise woman mission to get all excited about, and you will be living exactly the life you were born to live.

The Master of Living Your Passions in the School of Peace: Beware Mr. Mellow and Ms. Lah-Dee-Dah. They are the roads to ruin with a Live Your Passions life purpose. The life assignment here is to bring out your passionate self and to trial-and-error your way to a life in balance (the Just-Right possibility in the School of Peace).

The Master of Living Your Passions: Archetypal Combinations To figure out if you have the archetypal combinations on the next pages, review the fingerprint chart showing your highest and lowest ranking prints. If your highest ranking prints appear in the finger locations as denoted by an H below, then the archetypal combination applies to you. In the charts, the H stands for highest ranking print, regardless of fingerprint type.

The Matriarch or The Patriarch

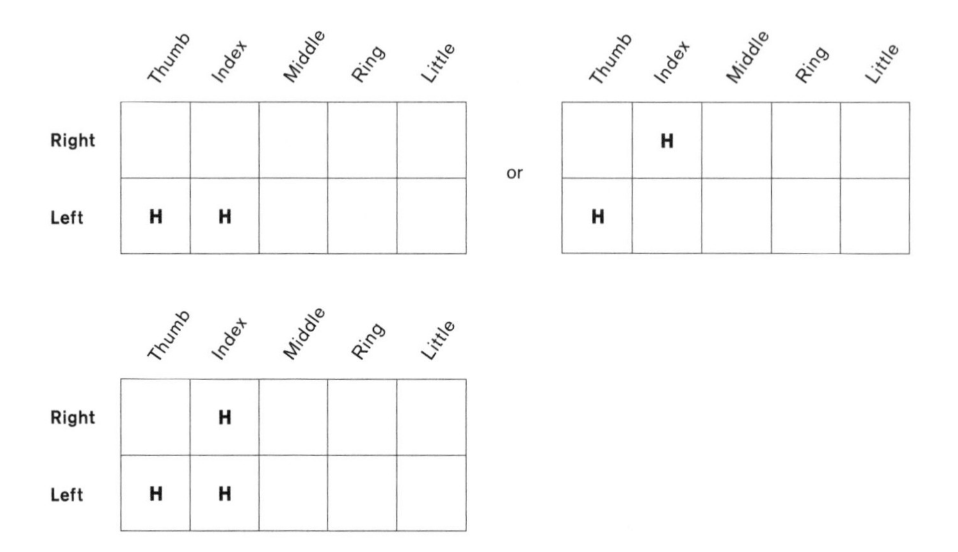

	Thumb	Index	Middle	Ring	Little
Right					
Left	H	H			

or

	Thumb	Index	Middle	Ring	Little
Right		H			
Left	H				

	Thumb	Index	Middle	Ring	Little
Right		H			
Left	H	H			

Fingerprint Profile: Left thumb + one index finger or both index fingers as the highest ranking fingerprints (Family + Power and/or Passions = The Matriarch or The Patriarch)

See page 177 for more information about The Matriarch or The Patriarch.

The Pioneer

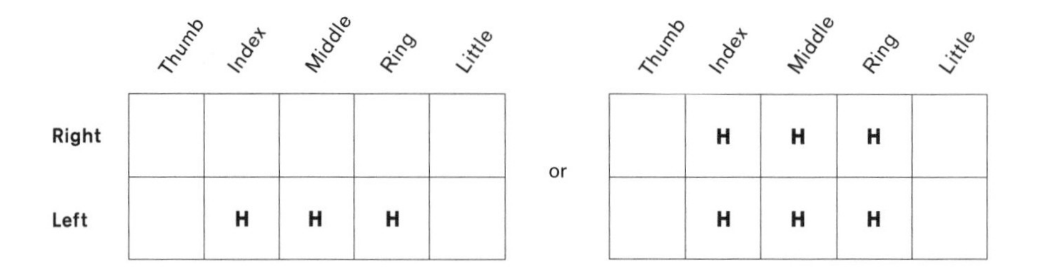

	Thumb	Index	Middle	Ring	Little
Right					
Left		H	H	H	

or

	Thumb	Index	Middle	Ring	Little
Right		H	H	H	
Left		H	H	H	

Fingerprint Profile: Left index finger or both index fingers + left middle finger or both middle fingers + left ring finger or both ring fingers as the highest ranking fingerprints (Passions + Integrity + Innovation = The Pioneer)

See page 236 for more information about The Pioneer.

The Pioneering Leader

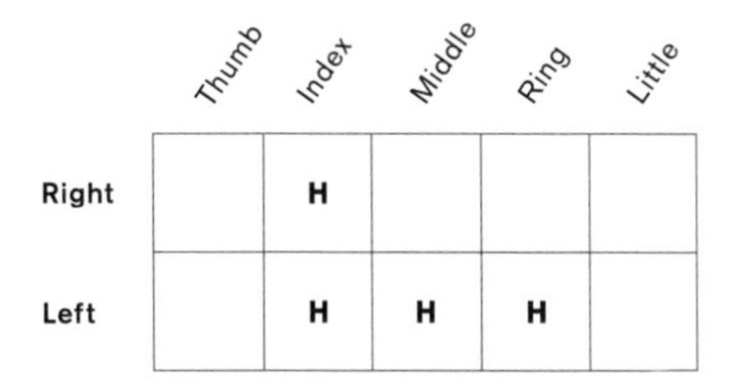

	Thumb	Index	Middle	Ring	Little
Right		H			
Left		H	H	H	

Fingerprint Profile: Left index finger or both index fingers + left middle finger + left ring finger as the highest ranking fingerprints (Leader + Integrity + Innovation = The Pioneering Leader)

See page 236 for more information about The Pioneering Leader.

The Pioneer in Business

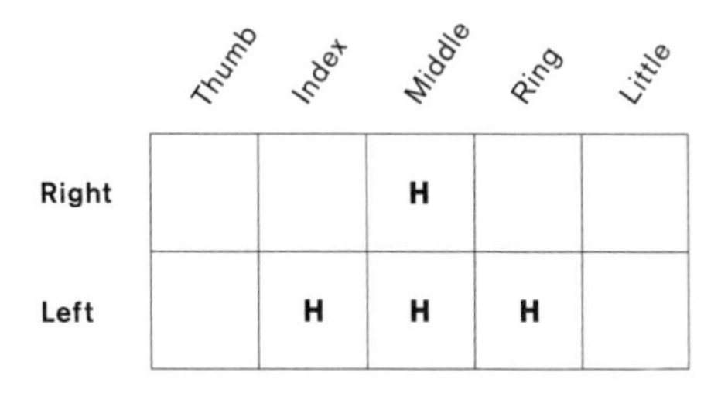

	Thumb	Index	Middle	Ring	Little
Right			H		
Left		H	H	H	

Fingerprint Profile: Left index finger + left middle finger or both middle fingers + left ring finger as the highest ranking fingerprints (Passion + Business Integrity + Innovation = The Pioneer in Business)

See page 237 for more information about The Pioneer in Business.

The Pioneering Artist

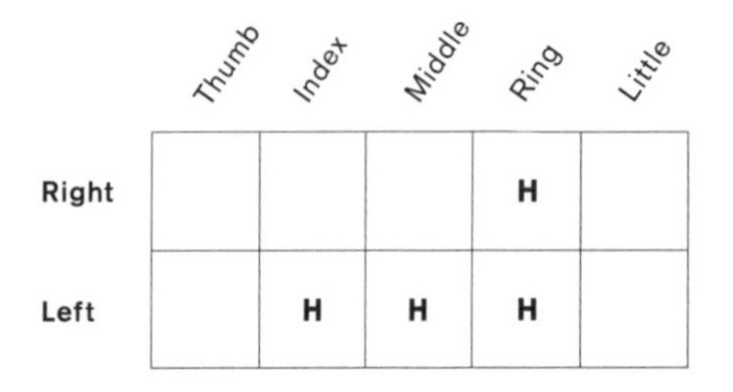

	Thumb	Index	Middle	Ring	Little
Right				H	
Left		H	H	H	

Fingerprint Profile: Left index finger + left middle finger + left ring finger or both ring fingers as the highest ranking fingerprints (Passion + Integrity + Creative Innovation = The Pioneering Artist)

See page 237 for more information about The Pioneering Artist.

Lowest Ranking Print on the Left Index Finger: Blocked Passions

The left index finger challenges you to unearth your passions and express them appropriately. Goldilocks says the most common forms of passions unconsciousness are:

Too Much Left Index Finger

- You do whatever you want whenever you want with no sense of appropriate restraint.
- You take action on your desires, but there is no sense of satisfaction.
- You have trouble noticing when you are stepping on other people's toes.

Too Little Left Index Finger

- You often go numb, not registering your feelings.
- You have trouble knowing what you want.
- You do not set appropriate boundaries; you have trouble asking for what you need.
- You feel trapped by other people's needs.
- You have become a professional victim as a life-scale hiding place.

The Exalted Life Lesson (Just Right)

- I bring a sense of passion and excitement to all that I do.

See page 193 for more information about Blocked Passions.

Blocked Passions: Archetypal Combinations To figure out if you have the archetypal combinations below, review the fingerprint chart showing your highest and lowest ranking prints. If your lowest ranking prints appear in the finger locations as denoted by an L below, then the archetypal combination applies to you. In the charts, the L stands for lowest ranking print, regardless of fingerprint type.

Sexual Violation

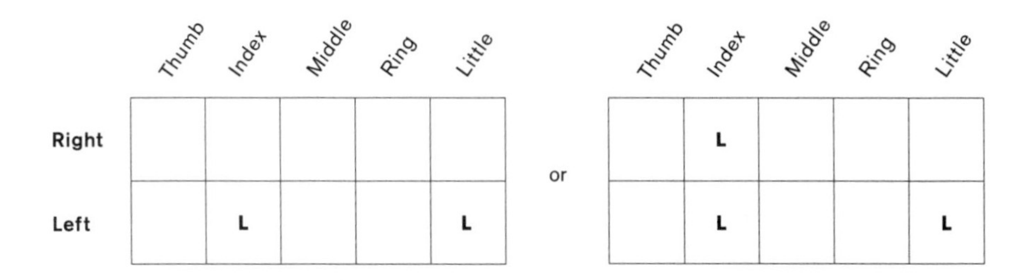

	Thumb	Index	Middle	Ring	Little
Right					
Left		L			L

or

	Thumb	Index	Middle	Ring	Little
Right		L			
Left		L			L

Fingerprint Profile: Left index finger or both index fingers + the left little finger with the lowest ranking fingerprints (Boundary Violation + Intimacy Issues = Sexual Violation)

See page 195 for more information about Sexual Violation.

Mr. Not Enough

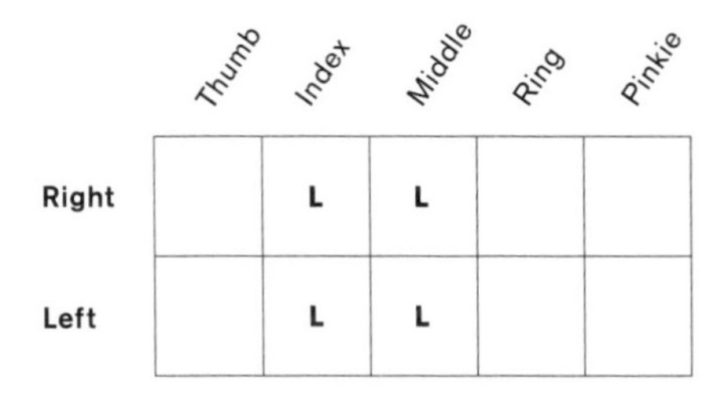

	Thumb	Index	Middle	Ring	Pinkie
Right		L	L		
Left		L	L		

Fingerprint Profile: One middle finger or both middle fingers + one index finger or both index fingers as the lowest ranking fingerprints (Powerlessness + Guilt = Mr. Not Enough)

Mr. Not Enough, the voice of insufficiency, is the most common life-lesson archetypal combination. The standard version above is followed by eight common subtypes (on the following page), each with its own specific slant.

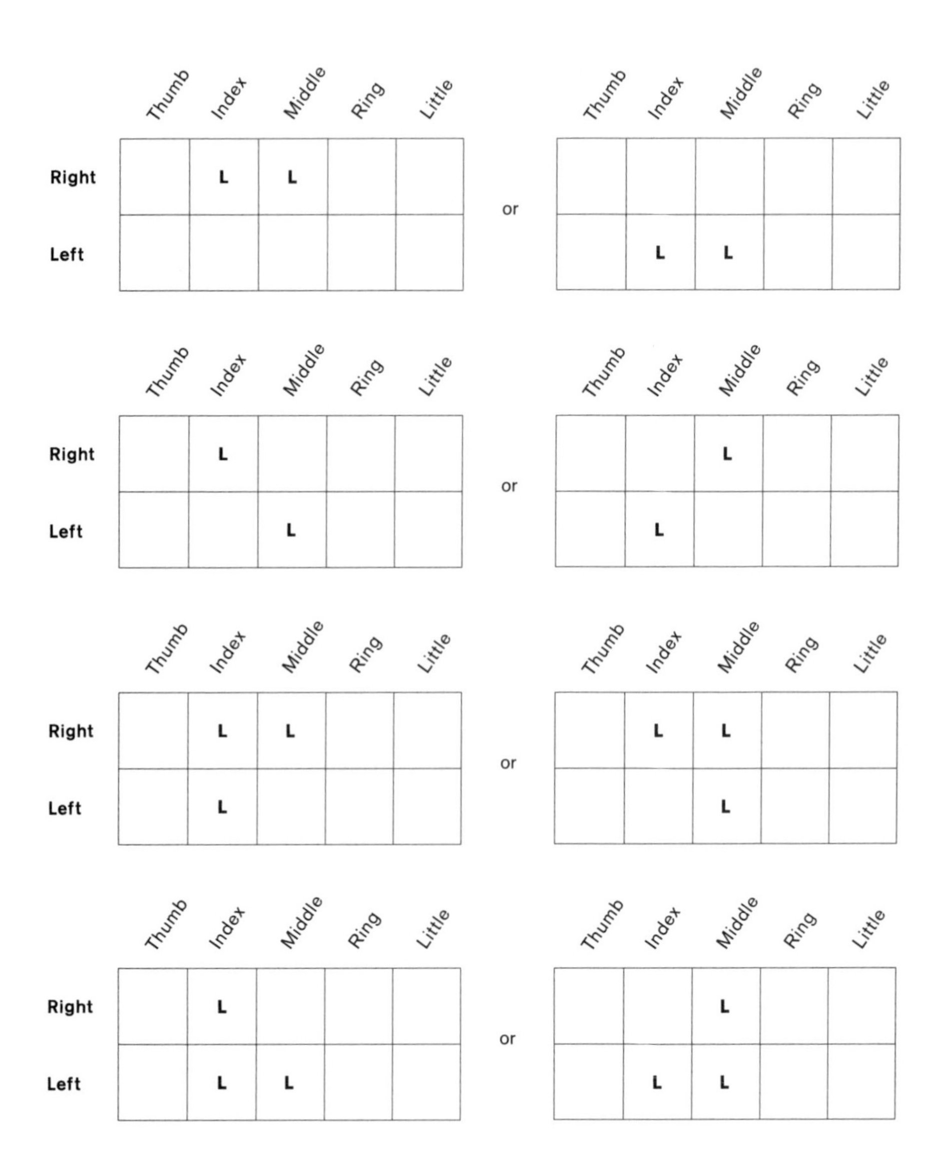

See page 216 for more information about Mr. Not Enough. See page 195 for more information about Left Index Finger archetypes

RIGHT MIDDLE FINGER

LIFE PURPOSE: The Master of Responsibility / The Businessperson
LIFE LESSON: Irresponsibility

If your highest ranking fingerprint is on the right middle finger, your life purpose is to bring the world of business, work, money, and responsibility into balance. You will know you are on the road to mastery when your relationship with money supports your happiness and fulfillment, when you feel worthy and valuable regardless of circumstance, and when you operate responsibly in the world and are treated responsibly by others. If that means learning how to support yourself financially or starting a thriving enterprise, your challenge is to recognize this as the deepest expression of your personal and spiritual growth. Conversely, it may well be your life assignment to let go of an overattachment to security and material affairs.

There must be a million how-to books on money management, but this book takes a soul psychology approach. From this perspective, you can consider handling money (or other responsibilities) to be your daily mantra, challenging you to be fully present and alert. Your spiritual ledger book is not concerned so much with profit and loss as it is with conscious awareness. Constant financial crises or arguments, obsessive concern about money, or avoidance of money issues are all indicators that something is amiss. If you don't know how much you have or how much you spend, if money issues clutter your life (regardless of who seems to be at fault), odds are your internal ledger is out of balance.

Do not be too disappointed if, upon taking a personal inventory, you find yourself short of perfection in this regard. More important: are you moving in the right direction?

See page 196 for more information about Worldly Responsibility.

Highest Ranking Print on the Right Middle Finger: The Master of Responsibility

Masters of Responsibility . . .

- Know their worth, enjoy their work, finish what they begin
- Keep their agreements and contracts, and expect the same from others
- Have a sensitive inner alarm system that informs them if something is out of integrity

Masters of Responsibility Are Happiest When . . .

- Setting things right
- Getting organized, completing a to-do list
- Money flows easily (financial melodrama finally ceases)

Typical Occupations To find fulfillment in your work, the key for you is *operating with integrity in the world of business and contracts.* The actual format you choose is secondary.

- Business owner/manager: Seeing the big picture, keeping it all together, creating financial success
- Scientist, engineer, dentist: Technical expertise meeting the marketplace
- Teacher, educational administrator, publisher: Shaping the minds that shape our future
- Environmental activist, bank inspector, umpire: From EPA watchdog to NFL referee, being on the lookout for violations
- Law enforcer: From police on the street to district attorney or judge, upholding society's rules

Common Obstacles

- Issues of commitment
- Issues of completion
- Irresponsibility, lack of integrity, inappropriate behaviors

Famous Masters of Responsibility

- Abe Lincoln, Simon Wiesenthal, Stephen Covey
- Atticus Finch (Gregory Peck's role in *To Kill a Mockingbird)*
- The entire staff of *Consumer Reports*, the Heritage Society, the EPA

Life Purpose Blossoming

- Contracts kept
- Money ease
- Completion

Life Purpose Inverse

- Contracts broken
- Money upsets, logistical logjams
- Getting 90 percent of the way there

What's Up? (Frequently Asked Questions) Following are questions I've been asked by budding Businesspeople over the years, followed by my most common answers.

I don't care what my fingerprints say, I am not a money-oriented individual. What's up? Sometimes the personality matches the life purpose, other times, it doesn't. I guess the latter is true for you. If you are living off the land on next to no money and your highest ranking print is on the right middle finger, it is still your meaning point to achieve responsibility in the world, whatever that means in your case. Maybe you turn your bee-raising hobby into a successful business and buy the homestead you always wanted.

But I am specifically drawn to a non-business-related career path. What's up?
Maybe you are a lawyer defending indigent clients for a pittance compared to your law school buddies or you feel fortunate to have landed a job as a forest ranger near Big Sur. These and similar low-paying career choices are completely consistent with this life purpose, and as such, are likely to bring a deep sense of satisfaction. Being responsible in the world, and helping others to do the same, does not necessarily mean big bucks.

The Master of Responsibility Checklist When you are living your life purpose, you should be able to check off all the items on this list. Make a note of your answers today and compare them to your answers one year from now. (Don't forget, life purpose is a process.)

- ☐ I hold myself accountable for my actions and hold others accountable as well.
- ☐ I am ethical in my business dealings.
- ☐ I can make a living doing what I really want to do.
- ☐ I value my contribution to the world.
- ☐ I am responsible with time and money.
- ☐ I have confidence in my ability to handle business affairs.
- ☐ I complete my tasks, large and small.
- ☐ I do things the right way because it is the right thing to do.
- ☐ I know my true worth and freely recognize the worth of others.
- ☐ I take time to smell the roses.

The Master of Responsibility in Each of the Four Schools When combined with the four schools, The Businessperson's life purpose looks like this.

The Master of Responsibility in the School of Service: For the worldly responsibility + service life purpose, the likelihood is that one of the two components will emerge first and the other will stay in the background for decades. *Schindler's List*, by Stephen Spielberg, provides an excellent example of this possibility. Schindler, a no-nonsense, me-first businessman, opens a munitions factory in Germany. Just his luck, World War II begins and he is making money hand over fist. By the end of the movie, genuine humanitarian service comes to dominate his every action. Whichever side emerges first in your life, businessperson or joy-in-service person, make sure the other half has sufficient opportunity to make its contribution.

The Master of Responsibility in the School of Love: Good job + good relationship? Good goin'! If you are not there yet, perhaps one of the following two big banana peels is standing between you and this life goal. Big Banana Peel #1:Your heart is not in your work. Big Banana Peel #2:Your heart's in your work, but when's payday? If you love your work, love it so much you would do it for free, that's nice. However, when you get to the Gates of Heaven you will be asked to show your pay stubs to prove you were properly paid for your labors on this planet.Volunteers, social workers, and others in like professions are especially challenged to keep Big Banana Peel #2 in perspective.

The Master of Responsibility in the School of Wisdom: Financial planners, tax attorneys, and fashion designers who become unofficial life coaches for each client: all these are examples of what this life purpose could look like.You have practical experience, give good advice, and you work in a field that holds meaning for you.

The Master of Responsibility in the School of Peace: Money ease or money struggle: which will it be?

Surprise Quiz for The Master of Responsibility Trainees in the School of Peace

Question #1:You are paying off the holiday purchases that you put on your Master Card six months ago. Three more payments and you are out of the hole. Passing Smith's jewelry store, you spot the ring you have been salivating over on sale at half price. For twenty points: should you put the ring on your Master Card? After all, you have been sooo good for soooo long. At half price, how can you afford not to buy now? Or should you martyr yourself by not having what you know you deserve and desire? What good is making yourself feel bad anyway?

Question #2:They need someone to volunteer to go to East Frasalia this weekend to look over the Smith account. You have other plans but the boss says they really need some help on this one and you are the only one in the office without children. Then again, they always expect you to volunteer whenever they have a lousy assignment. Gosh whiz. For twenty points, what do you do?

Answers: It doesn't matter what you *do*. In soul psychology, it is the consciousness with which you do something that counts. In question #1, the challenge is to get out of the money-as-the-source-of-struggle and/or money-as-the-source-of-happiness mentality. It seems that whatever the person in question #1 does, we can expect frustration and pattern repetition to be the inevitable outcome. The person in question #2 seems ready to fall into the same self-loathing pit no matter what choice is made.

The optimal strategy for both of these characters is to develop a more appropriate attitude toward money, work, and responsibility. Perhaps #1 gets a financial planner to help her create a budget in line with her finances. Perhaps #2 gets a coach to help him improve his self-image and improve his sales. Whatever they do, it would be to the advantage of each to not continue as is.

The Master of Responsibility: Archetypal Combinations To figure out if you have the archetypal combination below, review the fingerprint chart showing your highest and lowest ranking prints. If your highest ranking prints appear in the finger locations as denoted by an H below, then the archetypal combination applies to you. In the charts below, the H stands for highest ranking print, regardless of fingerprint type.

The Tycoon

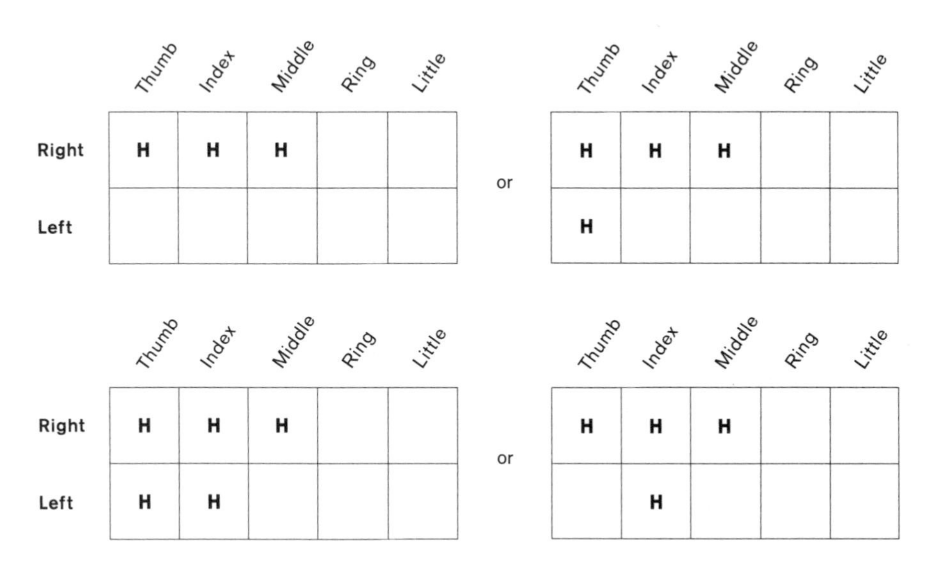

	Thumb	Index	Middle	Ring	Little
Right	**H**	**H**	**H**		
Left					

or

	Thumb	Index	Middle	Ring	Little
Right	**H**	**H**	**H**		
Left	**H**				

	Thumb	Index	Middle	Ring	Little
Right	**H**	**H**	**H**		
Left	**H**	**H**			

or

	Thumb	Index	Middle	Ring	Little
Right	**H**	**H**	**H**		
Left		**H**			

Fingerprint Profile: Right thumb or both thumbs + right index finger or both index fingers + right middle finger as the highest ranking fingerprints (Success + Power + Money = The Tycoon)

See page 170 for more information about The Tycoon.

Lowest Ranking Print on the Right Middle Finger: Irresponsibility

The right middle finger challenges a person to stay awake in the world of responsibility. Goldilocks says the most common forms of responsibility unconsciousness are as follows:

Too Much Right Middle Finger

- You marry for money or stay at a job you hate just for the money.
- You are too responsible for things having nothing to do with your life purpose.
- You allow too many responsibilities to keep you from the life you want.

Too Little Right Middle Finger

- You don't do what you say you are going to do.
- Your behaviors are inappropriate.
- You procrastinate on things that are important.
- You blame others or circumstances for your incomplete efforts.
- You have poor or no records of your finances.
- You do not believe in your own value. You continually find yourself underpaid for your efforts.

The Exalted Life Lesson (Just Right)

- I teach financial planning at the local college and practice what I preach.

See page 198 for more information about Learning to Be Responsible.

Irresponsibility: Archetypal Combinations To figure out if you have the archetypal combinations below, review the fingerprint chart showing your highest and lowest ranking prints. If your lowest ranking prints appear in the finger locations as denoted by an L below, then the archetypal combination applies to you. In the charts, the L stands for lowest ranking print, regardless of fingerprint type.

Learning to Be Responsible

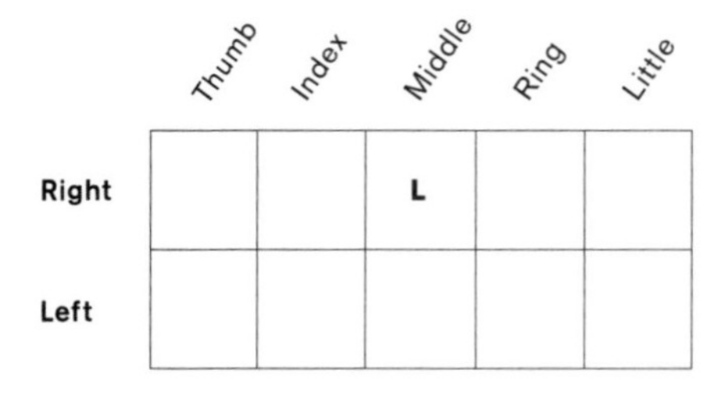

	Thumb	Index	Middle	Ring	Little
Right			**L**		
Left					

Fingerprint Profile: Right middle finger as the lowest ranking fingerprint

See page 198 for more information about Learning to Be Responsible.

The Loser

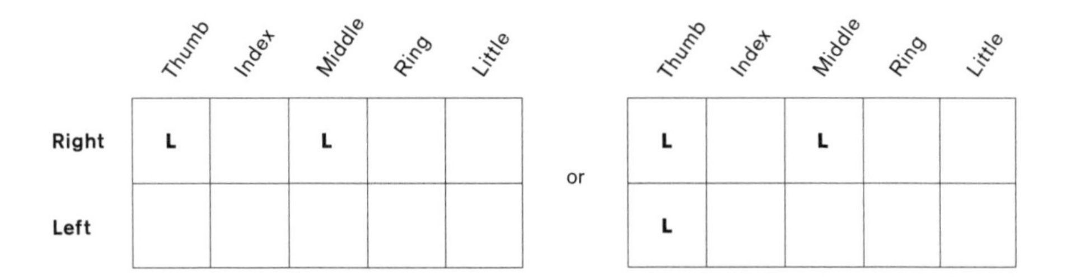

	Thumb	Index	Middle	Ring	Little
Right	L		L		
Left					

or

	Thumb	Index	Middle	Ring	Little
Right	L		L		
Left	L				

Fingerprint Profile: Right thumb or both thumbs + right middle finger as the lowest ranking fingerprints (Failure + Irresponsibility = The Loser)

See page 173 for more information about The Loser.

Worthy of Love

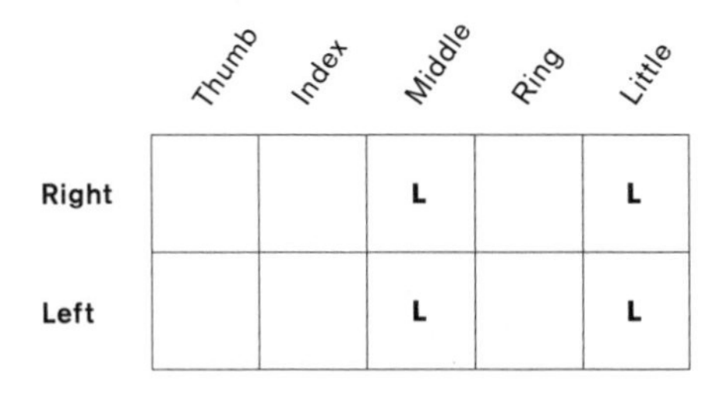

	Thumb	Index	Middle	Ring	Little
Right			L		L
Left			L		L

Fingerprint Profile: Both middle fingers and both little fingers as the lowest ranking fingerprints (Self-Worth + Intimacy Issues = Worthy of Love)

See page 211 for more information about Worthy of Love.

Mr. Not Enough

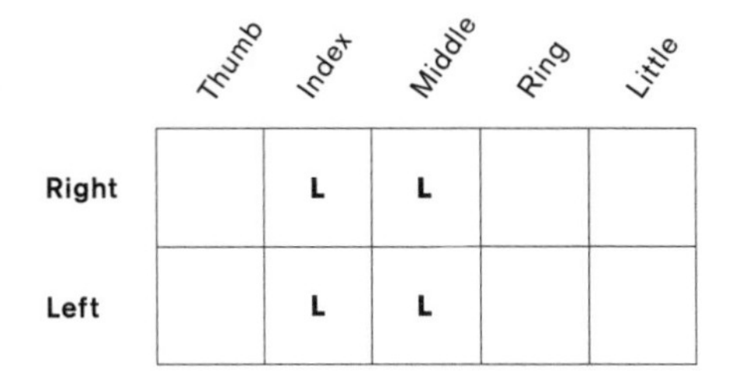

	Thumb	Index	Middle	Ring	Little
Right		L	L		
Left		L	L		

Fingerprint Profile: One middle finger or both middle fingers + one index finger or both index fingers as the lowest ranking fingerprints (Powerlessness + Guilt = Mr. Not Enough)

Mr. Not Enough, the voice of insufficiency, is the most common life-lesson archetypal combination. The standard version on page 107 is followed by eight common subtypes below, each with its own specific slant.

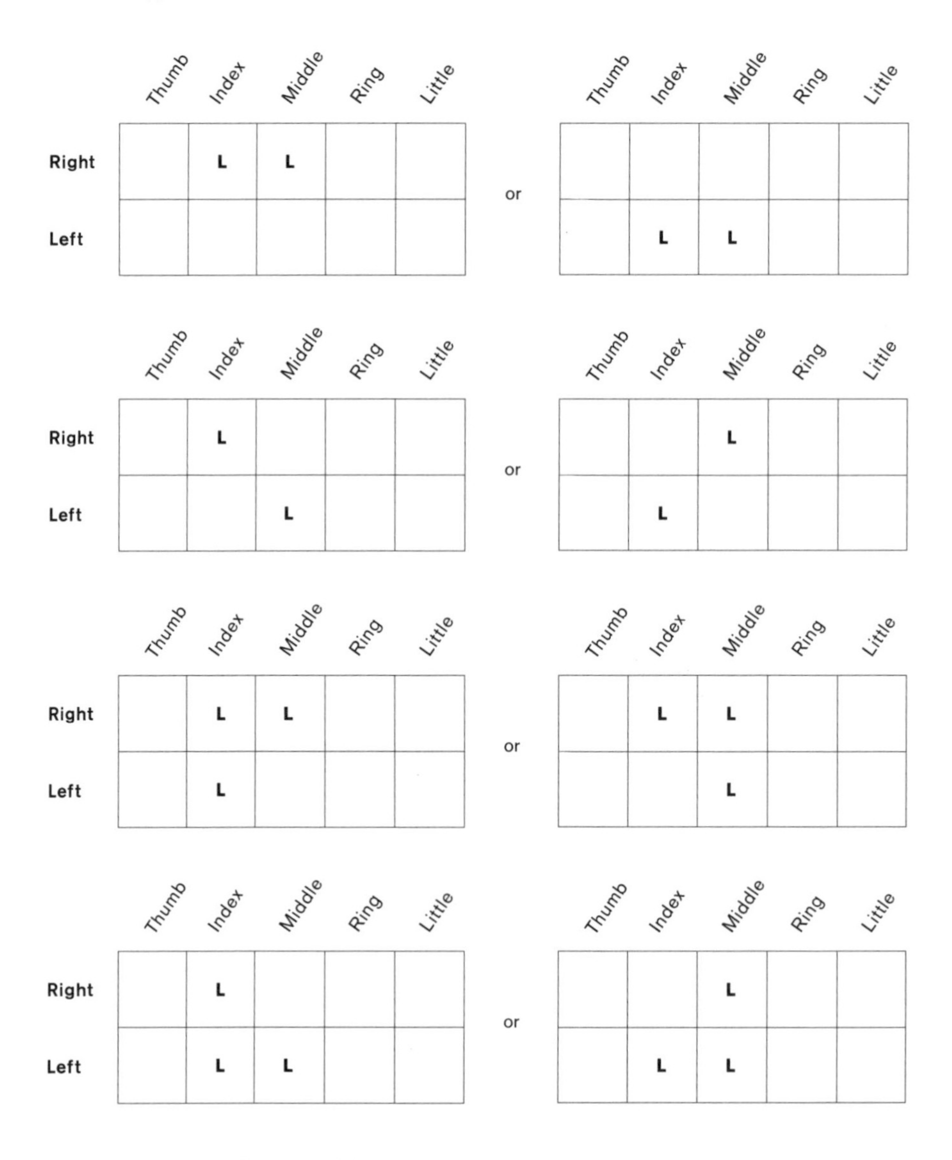

	Thumb	Index	Middle	Ring	Little
Right		L	L		
Left					

or

	Thumb	Index	Middle	Ring	Little
Right					
Left		L	L		

	Thumb	Index	Middle	Ring	Little
Right		L			
Left			L		

or

	Thumb	Index	Middle	Ring	Little
Right			L		
Left		L			

	Thumb	Index	Middle	Ring	Little
Right		L	L		
Left		L			

or

	Thumb	Index	Middle	Ring	Little
Right		L	L		
Left			L		

	Thumb	Index	Middle	Ring	Little
Right		L			
Left		L	L		

or

	Thumb	Index	Middle	Ring	Little
Right			L		
Left		L	L		

See page 216 for more information about Mr. Not Enough.

What I Say Matters

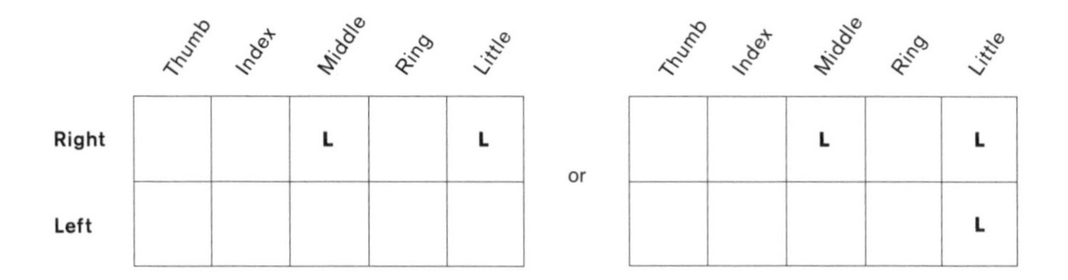

Fingerprint Profile: Right middle finger and right little finger or both little fingers as the lowest ranking fingerprints (Self-Worth + Speaking Up = What I Say Matters)

See page 247 for more information about What I Say Matters.

LEFT MIDDLE FINGER

LIFE PURPOSE: The Master of Integrity / The Mentor
LIFE LESSON: Guilt Issues

With the left middle finger or both middle fingers as the life purpose, it is your challenge to operate at the highest levels of integrity in both your professional and personal worlds, ultimately creating a desire in others to emulate your behavior. This life purpose requires an extremely high personal growth component. For this reason, if The Mentor does come to the fore, it tends to reach its main expression later in life (late forties or early fifties) rather than earlier. This is as it should be. After all, we can't have just anybody setting the standard for others to follow.

Despite its long gestation period, a close inspection is likely to reveal that The Mentor has been in operation as far back as your sandbox days. You probably helped several four-year-olds learn to share their toys and not pull hair when upset. If your own existence seems to be taking too long in coming together, patience is the recommendation. You are probably right on schedule.

For some, The Mentor appears in the workplace (i.e., elementary school teacher, sales trainer). For others, there is no formal title or position: the team member whom everyone looks up to, the caring parent or grandparent, the wise elder statesman. Regardless of the arena of operation, the key ingredient for Mentors is their ability to demonstrate integrity no matter the circumstances.

See page 199 for more information about The Mentor.

Highest Ranking Print on the Left Middle Finger: The Mentor

Masters of Integrity . . .

- Walk the walk, consistently stick to principles
- Do the right thing regardless of pressure from others
- Feel good about themselves even when things are not going their way

Masters of Integrity Are Happiest When . . .

- Speaking up for true feelings (emotional integrity)
- Honestly examining beliefs about themselves and the world (intellectual integrity)
- Creating a life that matches their ideals (spiritual integrity)
- Keeping promises (daily accountability)

Typical Occupations To find fulfillment in your work, the key for you is *keeping your integrity*. The actual format you choose is secondary.

- Montessori schoolteacher, college professor, public school teacher, trades: Teaching is the natural career choice for this life purpose
- Author, public speaker, seminar leader: Teaching people you may never meet
- Scientist, especially research-oriented fields such as medicine, chemistry, biology, psychology, astronomy: Following the data wherever it leads
- Law enforcement, environmental activist, bank inspector, umpire: Being on the lookout for violators
- Wise elder in any field: Being the person everyone looks to for guidance
- Government official: Serving as a role model, as *true* political figures do

Common Obstacles

- Personal accountability can get soooo boring, and what if you aren't perfect in every way?
- In an instant gratification society, your fierce adherence to high principles may not be appreciated
- Persistent self-questioning can exhaust and confuse you

Famous Masters of Integrity

- Martin Luther King, Madame Curie, the Dalai Lama, Jane Goodall
- Michael Jordan ("I wanna be like Mike"), Barbara Jordan, Sally Ride
- *Father Knows Best*, Yoda and Obi-Wan Kenobi

Life Purpose Blossoming	*Life Purpose Inverse*
▪ Strong inner values	▪ Situational ethics
▪ Personal accountability	▪ Low self-esteem
▪ Persistence	▪ Irresponsibility
▪ Discipline	▪ Inconsistency

What's Up? (Frequently Asked Questions) Following are questions I've been asked by many Mentors over the years, followed by my most common answers.

If I am supposed to be such a role model for others, why is my own life such a mess?
Mentor trainees gain mastery by making messes, owning the problem, then fixing it. If your whole life is still a mess, maybe you are in the early phase of your Mentor training.

I used to teach, but I'm glad I don't anymore. What's up?
Teaching is the perfect profession for you. Who knows what hassles caused you to quit, but I wouldn't be surprised if you return someday, perhaps in an unexpected setting.

The Master of Integrity Checklist When you are living your life purpose, you should be able to check off all the items on this list. Make a note of your answers today and compare them to your answers one year from now. (Don't forget, life purpose is a process.)

- ☐ It feels good to know that people say I am someone who can be counted on.
- ☐ I like compliments, but I look to myself as the main source of my esteem.
- ☐ It wouldn't feel good to take advantage of someone's generosity.
- ☐ I renegotiate if I find I cannot do what I said I was going to do.
- ☐ I pay my debts.
- ☐ Even small out-of-integrity behaviors bother me, in myself or in others.
- ☐ If accused of wrongdoing, I listen carefully. I'm willing to admit it if I was wrong.
- ☐ However, I do not apologize unnecessarily.
- ☐ I am often asked for advice.
- ☐ Overall, I am nice to myself.

The Master of Integrity in Each of the Four Schools When combined with the four schools, The Mentor's life purpose looks like this.

The Master of Integrity in the School of Service: Quite a high aspiration, this life purpose. At their best, owners of these fingerprints have learned that they do not have to be perfect and do everything for everybody. In this way, more people receive the services they *actually* need and The Mentor has the free time to pursue a hobby.

The Master of Integrity in the School of Love: Come to terms with your feelings in the most demanding of emotional circumstances and ultimately become the man or woman looked up to by others when their own emotional crises seem beyond hope. Become a social worker specializing in alcoholic rehab or a hospice chaplain. Write books about step-parenting or the power of teamwork. Whatever you do with these fingerprints, your deepest meaning comes from developing an emotional integrity that stands up to the rigors of life's greatest emotional challenges.

The Master of Integrity in the School of Wisdom: This is the life-purpose map of someone born to bring what he or she has learned about life to others. Philosophers, guidance counselors, elementary school teachers, and carpenters teaching the new guy how it is done right are all in line with the intention behind these fingerprints.

The Master of Integrity in the School of Peace: Can you maintain your ethical base as Mr. Sticks and Plates makes his presence felt? Can you believe in yourself as circumstances careen out of your control? Is there a more difficult life purpose than this one? Maybe there is, but The Mentor in the School of Peace makes any soul psychologist's Top Ten Most Demanding Life Purposes list.

The Master of Integrity: Archetypal Combinations To figure out if you have the archetypal combinations below, review the fingerprint chart showing your highest and lowest ranking prints. If your highest ranking prints appear in the finger locations as denoted by an H below, then the archetypal combination applies to you. In the charts below, the H stands for highest ranking print, regardless of fingerprint type.

The Mentor to Artists

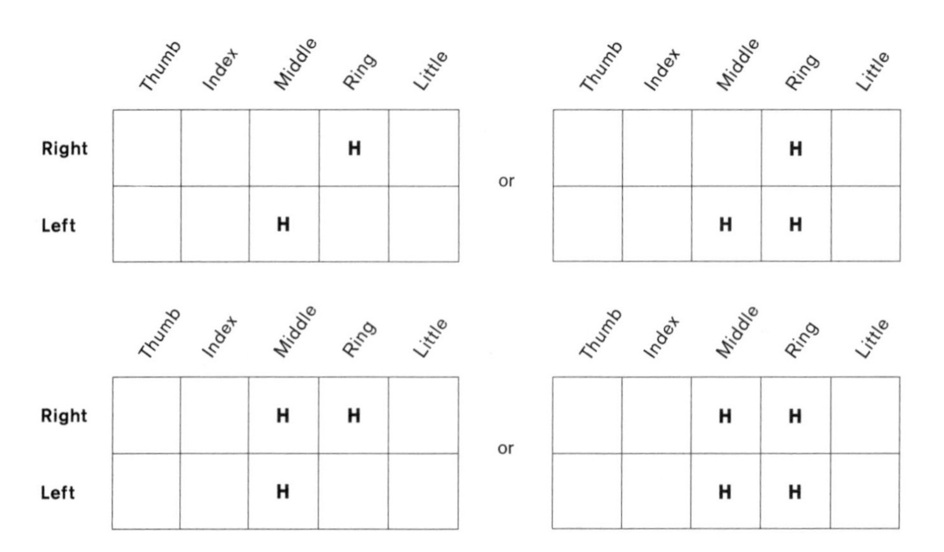

Fingerprint Profile: Left middle finger or both middle fingers + right ring finger or both ring fingers as the highest ranking fingerprints (The Mentor + The Artist = The Mentor to Artists)

See page 203 for more information about The Mentor to Artists.

The Mentor to Leaders

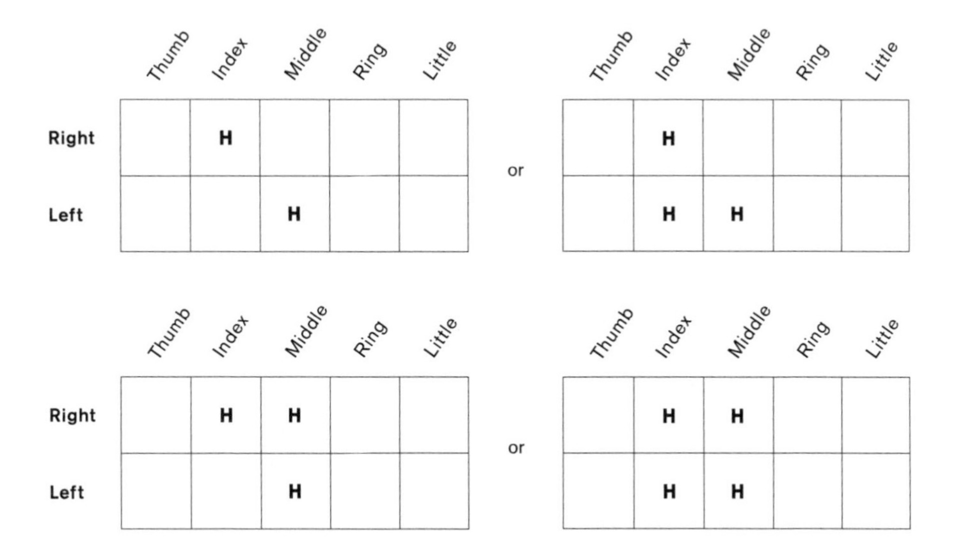

Fingerprint Profile: Left middle finger or both middle fingers + right index finger or both index fingers as the highest ranking fingerprints (The Mentor + The Leader = The Mentor to Leaders)

See page 203 for more information about The Mentor to Leaders.

The Pioneer

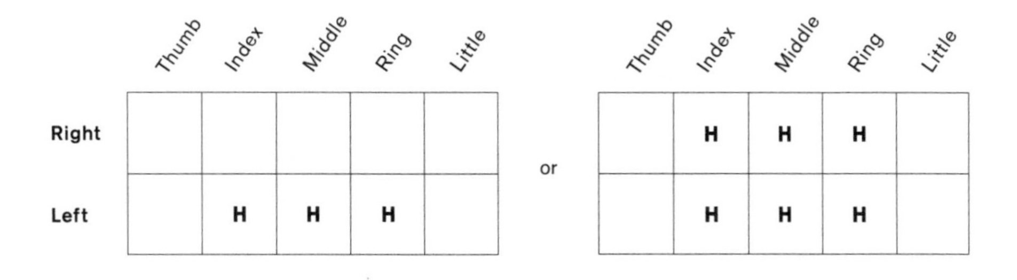

Fingerprint Profile: Left index finger or both index fingers + left middle finger or both middle fingers + left ring finger or both ring fingers as the highest ranking fingerprints (Passion + Integrity + Innovation = The Pioneer)

See page 236 for more information about The Pioneer.

The Pioneering Leader

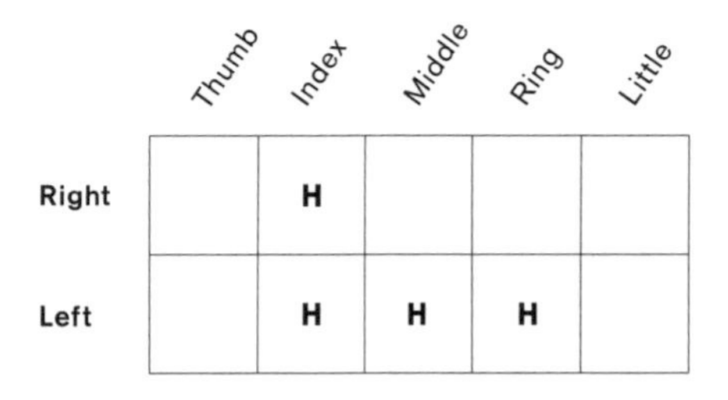

Fingerprint Profile: Left index finger or both index fingers + left middle finger + left ring finger as the highest ranking fingerprints (Leader + Integrity + Innovation = The Pioneering Leader)

See page 236 for more information about The Pioneering Leader.

The Pioneer in Business

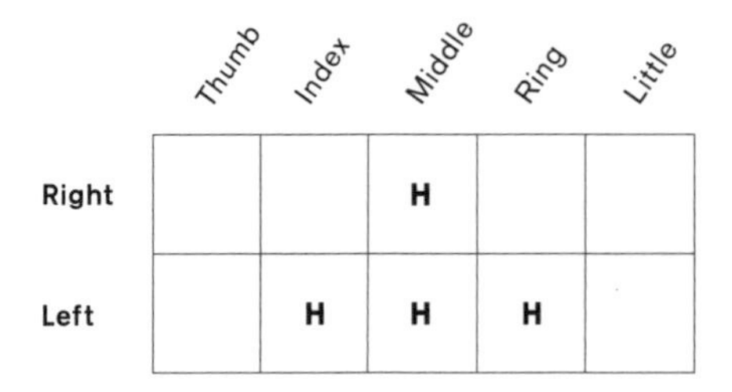

Fingerprint Profile: Left index finger + left middle finger or both middle fingers + left ring finger as the highest ranking fingerprints (Passion + Business Integrity + Innovation = The Pioneer in Business)

See page 237 for more information about The Pioneer in Business.

The Pioneering Artist

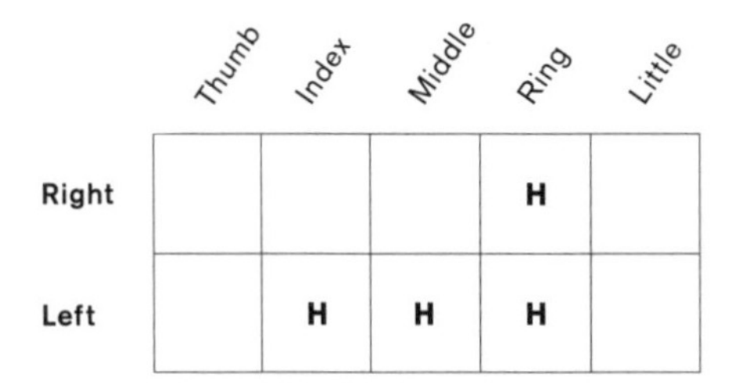

	Thumb	Index	Middle	Ring	Little
Right				H	
Left		H	H	H	

Fingerprint Profile: Left index finger + left middle finger + left ring finger or both ring fingers as the highest ranking fingerprints (Passion + Integrity + Creative Innovation = The Pioneering Artist)

See page 237 for more information about The Pioneering Artist.

The Shaman

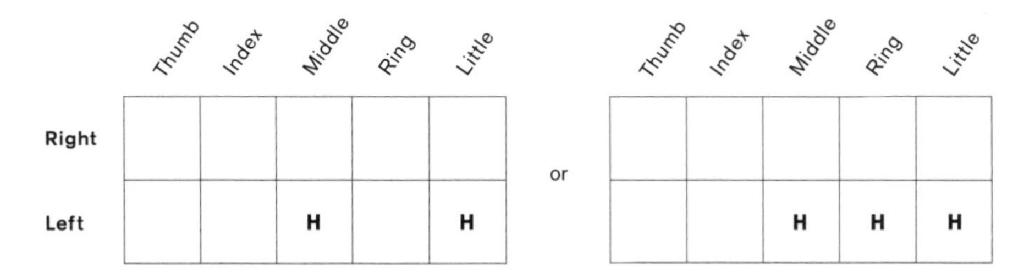

	Thumb	Index	Middle	Ring	Little
Right					
Left			H		H

or

	Thumb	Index	Middle	Ring	Little
Right					
Left			H	H	H

Fingerprint Profile: Left middle finger + left little finger as the highest ranking fingerprints (The Mentor + The Healer = The Shaman); addition of a highest ranking left ring finger = variation of The Shaman (The Mentor + The Innovator + The Healer)

See page 254 for more information about The Shaman.

Lowest Ranking Print on the Left Middle Finger: Guilt Issues

The left middle finger challenges you to develop a consciousness consistent with personal integrity and high self-worth. Goldilocks says the most common forms of integrity unconsciousness are:

Too Much Left Middle Finger

- You never feel guilty even if your guilty behavior is staring you in the face.
- You believe you are right and therefore whatever actions you take are just fine.
- You do not hold yourself accountable for your actions.

Too Little Left Middle Finger

- You apologize way too often.
- You allow others to treat you poorly.
- You change your essential self to meet the expectations of others.
- You agree to do things you don't want to do to avoid feeling guilty.
- You do not hold other people accountable for the promises they make to you.

The Exalted Life Lesson (Just Right)

- I am a mentor and role model. I am delighted that others look at me this way.

See pages 206 and 214 for more information about Guilt Issues.

Guilt Issues: Archetypal Combinations To figure out if you have the archetypal combination below, review the fingerprint chart showing your highest and lowest ranking prints. If your lowest ranking prints appear in the finger locations as denoted by an L below, then the archetypal combination applies to you. In the charts, the L stands for lowest ranking print, regardless of fingerprint type.

Negative L'Oreal

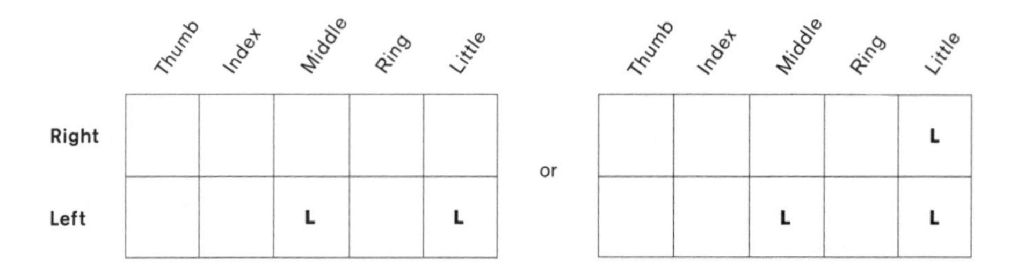

Fingerprint Profile: Left little finger or both little fingers + left middle finger as the lowest ranking fingerprints (Guilt + Intimacy Issues = Negative L'Oreal)

See page 209 for more information about Negative L'Oreal.

Worthy of Love

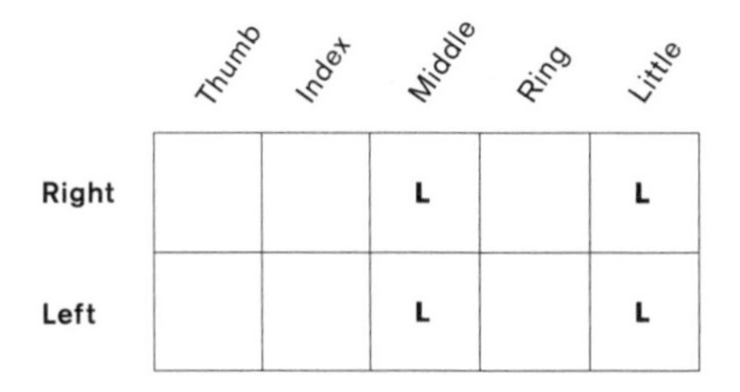

	Thumb	Index	Middle	Ring	Little
Right			L		L
Left			L		L

Fingerprint Profile: Both middle fingers and both little fingers as the lowest ranking fingerprints (Self-Worth + Intimacy Issues = Worthy of Love)

See page 211 for more information about Worthy of Love.

Guilt in the Family

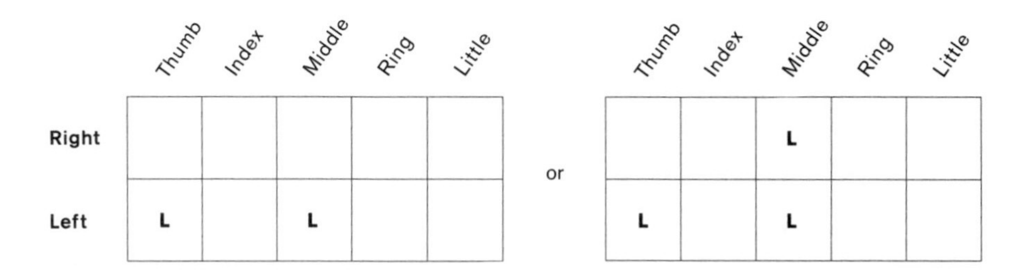

	Thumb	Index	Middle	Ring	Little
Right					
Left	L		L		

or

	Thumb	Index	Middle	Ring	Little
Right			L		
Left	L		L		

Fingerprint Profile: Left middle finger or both middle fingers and left thumb as the lowest ranking fingerprints (Self-Worth + Family Issues = Guilt in the Family)

See page 214 for more information about Guilt in the Family.

Mr. Not Enough

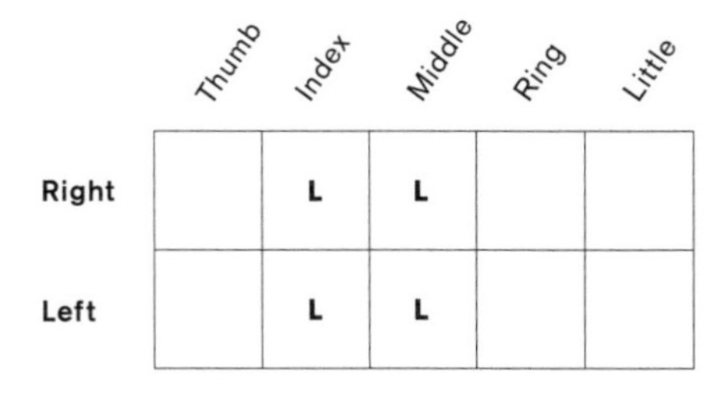

	Thumb	Index	Middle	Ring	Little
Right		L	L		
Left		L	L		

Fingerprint Profile: One middle finger or both middle fingers + one index finger or both index fingers as the lowest ranking fingerprints (Powerlessness + Guilt = Mr. Not Enough)

Mr. Not Enough, the voice of insufficiency, is the most common life-lesson archetypal combination. The standard version on page 117 is followed by eight common subtypes below, each with its own specific slant.

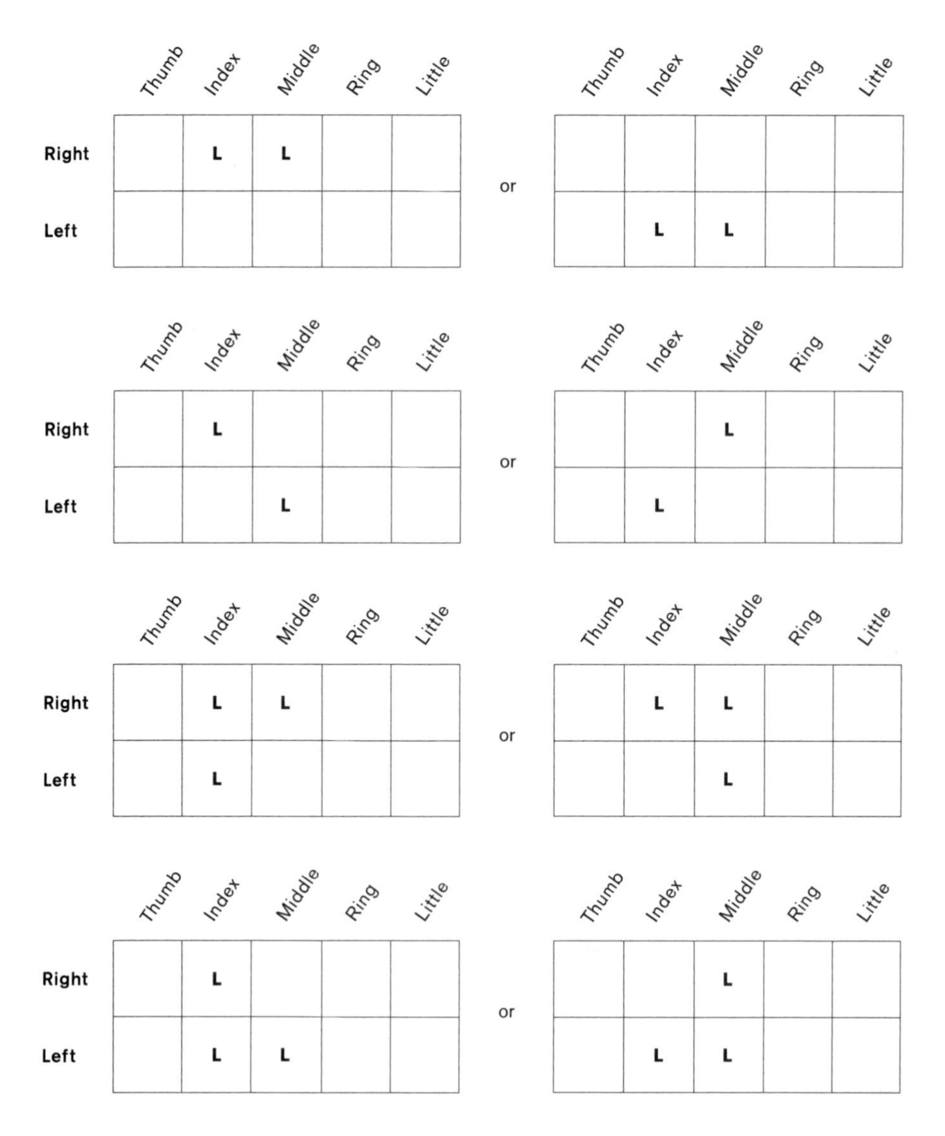

	Thumb	Index	Middle	Ring	Little
Right		L	L		
Left					

or

	Thumb	Index	Middle	Ring	Little
Right					
Left		L	L		

	Thumb	Index	Middle	Ring	Little
Right		L			
Left			L		

or

	Thumb	Index	Middle	Ring	Little
Right			L		
Left		L			

	Thumb	Index	Middle	Ring	Little
Right		L	L		
Left		L			

or

	Thumb	Index	Middle	Ring	Little
Right		L	L		
Left			L		

	Thumb	Index	Middle	Ring	Little
Right		L			
Left		L	L		

or

	Thumb	Index	Middle	Ring	Little
Right			L		
Left		L	L		

See page 216 for more information about Mr. Not Enough.

RIGHT RING FINGER

LIFE PURPOSE: The Master of Creativity/The Artist
LIFE LESSON: Hiding Out

If the right ring finger is your highest ranking fingerprint, or both ring fingers are your highest ranking fingerprints, creative emergence is the most likely life theme. No matter the format, from the traditional arts to Model T restoration, the challenge here is to go beyond technical proficiency to true artistry. Fulfillment comes when you have poured your unique self onto your canvas of choice and you can stand back and say, "Yes: that is me."

Other times, the central focus is on appearance, applause, and approval. If this sounds superficial to you, remember the Goldilocks Rule: Too Much, Too Little, and Just Right. With the ring finger as your highest ranked fingerprint, your goal is to find the appropriate measure of display that gives your true inner nature a chance to shine.

For some, this means coming out of the closet and dealing with public disapproval, like a homosexual football player talking to the press, or a scientist defending his or her controversial research in a peer reviewed journal. Not everyone has this type of searing spotlight to deal with. Some are just spending this lifetime learning how to be themselves without putting on airs, like the main characters in the story below.

See page 229 for more information about The Artist with Heart.

Highest Ranking Print on the Right Ring Finger: The Master of Creativity

Appearance and Reality—Taxi Stories For two years in the early seventies, I drove a taxi in America's biggest city and met some very interesting people. I remember sitting in the unheated taxi office fascinated as some of the older drivers held court. There was an old guy who had driven during the Great Depression. There was an even older fellow who had driven a horse-drawn taxi before World War I. They had seen it all.

Leroy was the most colorful of the experienced drivers and had the best biggest-tip story. Early in his taxi days, Leroy picked up a fare at the Waldorf-Astoria hotel. The fare needed to go to the airport, and since it was raining and traffic was heavy they were together for quite a while. The fare started talking about this big business that he ran in Atlanta and how much trouble his vice president of sales was giving him. Leroy listened quietly at first, nodding at the appropriate intervals, but as time passed, Leroy started to be more forthcoming until the businessman was laying out his entire business and taking notes as Leroy offered his sage advice.

"Taking notes?" someone asked as another taxi returned to the garage. I was glad it wasn't mine so I could hear how it all turned out for Leroy. "Yup. He was taking notes." As they got to the airport, the businessman said he wanted to hire Leroy as his VP. Leroy was sharper than any of the other replacement candidates and would he consider relocating? Leroy was coy but said he would consider it. As he got out of the cab, the fare said he wanted to pay Leroy for his advice. If he had hired a consultant, he would have paid at least one hundred dollars an hour for advice that wouldn't have been one-tenth as valuable, he said, as he handed Leroy a thousand-dollar check to cover the fare and tip. "Consider this a down payment on your new job."

"I was spending all my new money already when I started to wonder: so what if he was well dressed and got in at the Waldorf? How do I know he didn't walk up with his luggage after staying at some fleabag hotel downtown? Here I was trying to be somebody I wasn't, and I got taken in by a guy who wasn't what he appeared to be either. Then again, maybe it was all true."

"So, tell us, what happened? Did the check clear? Did you ever fly down to Atlanta?"

"I'm still driving taxi, ain't I?"

Masters of Creativity . . .

- Are one of a kind
- Are not phony
- Enjoy the spotlight (Dislike the spotlight? Check What's Up? below)

Masters of Creativity Are Happiest When . . .

- Expressing their individuality in all parts of their lives
- Taking their creativity to the next level
- Receiving the recognition of their peers

Typical Occupations To find fulfillment in your work, the key for you is not so much in what you do but in *bringing out your creative, individualistic side.* The actual format you choose is secondary.

- Performer or traditional artist: Dancer, singer, actor, stand-up comedian, painter, author, poet; practice, practice, practice, then let go and see what surfaces
- Artisan: Woodworker, jeweler, glassblower; the wood lathe is an extension of your hand and mind

- Practical artist: Architect, graphic designer, interior decorator; going beyond technical ability into free creative expression
- Cutting-edge person: Computer programmer for virtual reality systems
- Anyone who makes a living in the spotlight: Tour guide or radio personality, for example
- Technical professionals: Strong pressure to conform to standardized norms often spawns creative individualists, usually finding their niche on the "radical" fringe
- Bringing forth an unusual talent or vision: George Lucas, Walt Disney

Common Obstacles

- Living in disguise, hiding out
- Tomato fears (boo, hiss, the audience throws rotten tomatoes); fear of ridicule, rejection
- Choosing a stage too small for your capabilities

Famous Masters of Creativity

- Liberace, Magic Johnson, Dancing Barry, Dr. Phil, Dr. Ruth, Princess Diana
- Frank Lloyd Wright, Evel Knievel, Andy Goldsworthy

Life Purpose Blossoming

- Creativity flows
- Applause, appreciation, approval
- I found my niche

Life Purpose Inverse

- Writer's block
- Tomatoes, tomatoes, tomatoes
- I don't belong

What's Up? (Frequently Asked Questions) Following are questions I've been asked by many Artists over the years, followed by my most common answers.

Do I have to seek the spotlight to find satisfaction with this life purpose? What's up?
Be flamboyant or be humble. Be who you are. But as your true talents emerge, surprise, you may find that the spotlight actually may seem attractive to you.

Creativity as my life purpose? I'm an eye doctor. What's up?
Technical professions usually spawn a small number of creative individualists, in other words, Artists. I know an eye doctor who lectures on nutrition as a way to reduce glaucoma surgery. The audience applauds and asks meaningful questions or they criticize him and walk out. Sounds like a right ring finger life purpose to me.

The Master of Creativity Checklist When you are living your life purpose, you should be able to check off all the items on this list. Make a note of your answers today and compare them to your answers one year from now. (Don't forget, life purpose is a process.)

- ☐ I make time and have an appropriate place for my creative endeavors.
- ☐ My creativity reveals the real me, to others and myself.
- ☐ I am always fine-tuning my craft.
- ☐ I am willing to be seen.
- ☐ I have created appropriate alone time and sanctuary for myself.
- ☐ I step back and look at my creation(s) and overall, I am pleased.
- ☐ When I receive a compliment, I look the giver in the eye and say thank you.
- ☐ I have found my appropriate niche.
- ☐ I do not let performance anxiety keep me from doing my own thing.
- ☐ I am not held hostage by my own image.

The Master of Creativity in Each of the Four Schools When combined with the four schools, The Artist's life purpose looks like this.

The Master of Creativity in the School of Service: The Artist in the School of Service is another dualistic life purpose. Can you allow your ego its spotlight and yet not lose track of the soul's intention to be of service? Consider Liz Taylor's life story. If she were not a media magnet, how much AIDS awareness could she muster? Imagine what forces of circumstance and inner gyroscope were required in synchronized order to yield her current life path. And Audrey Hepburn and Jerry Lewis and Bono and. . . .

The Master of Creativity in the School of Love (see Soap Opera on page 193 and The Artist with Heart on page 229): Emotional exploration and vulnerability are the keys to unlocking your creative talent. This is a common life purpose, expressing itself in a variety of ways, two of which are covered in the stories listed above.

The Master of Creativity in the School of Wisdom: Risking tomatoes, your ideas finally reach your appropriate audience. TA DAH! Make sure you seize the moment, Oh Wise One. Have you written your book yet? Finished your thesis? Does next year seem like a better time?

The Master of Creativity in the School of Peace: On this life path, grand humiliation is to be sought and found, embraced and overcome as the arches exponentially amplify normal social jitters into mortifying social terror. What was adolescence like for these intrepid journeymen and women? Prom night? What schoolyard pranks must they have endured? The stories I have heard exceed my worst embarrassing moments by a factor of one hundred. Yet here they be, breathing the same air as you and I. In the long run, handling the big tomatoes that infiltrate your personal life becomes the key that unlocks your creative success. Having gone through the difficulties life has sent your way, how could the possibility of others' negative opinions keep you from your right life?

The Master of Creativity: Archetypal Combinations To figure out if you have the archetypal combinations below, review the fingerprint chart showing your highest and lowest ranking prints. If your highest ranking prints appear in the finger locations as denoted by an H below, then the archetypal combination applies to you. In the charts below, the H stands for highest ranking print, regardless of fingerprint type.

The Mentor to Artists

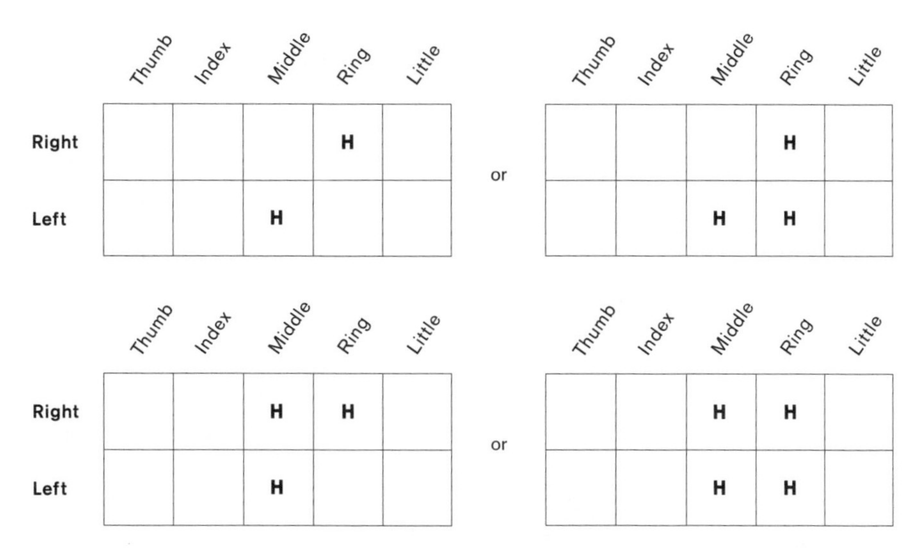

Fingerprint Profile: Left middle finger or both middle fingers + right ring finger or both ring fingers as the highest ranking fingerprints (The Mentor + The Artist = The Mentor to Artists)

See page 203 for more information about The Mentor to Artists.

The High-Profile Person

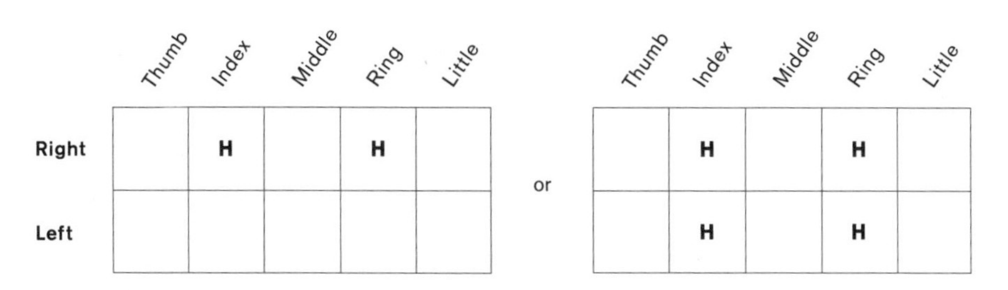

Fingerprint Profile: Right ring finger or both ring fingers + right index finger or both index fingers as the highest ranking prints (The Leader + The Artist = The High-Profile Person)

See page 231 for more information about The High-Profile Person.

Public Impact in the Healing Arts

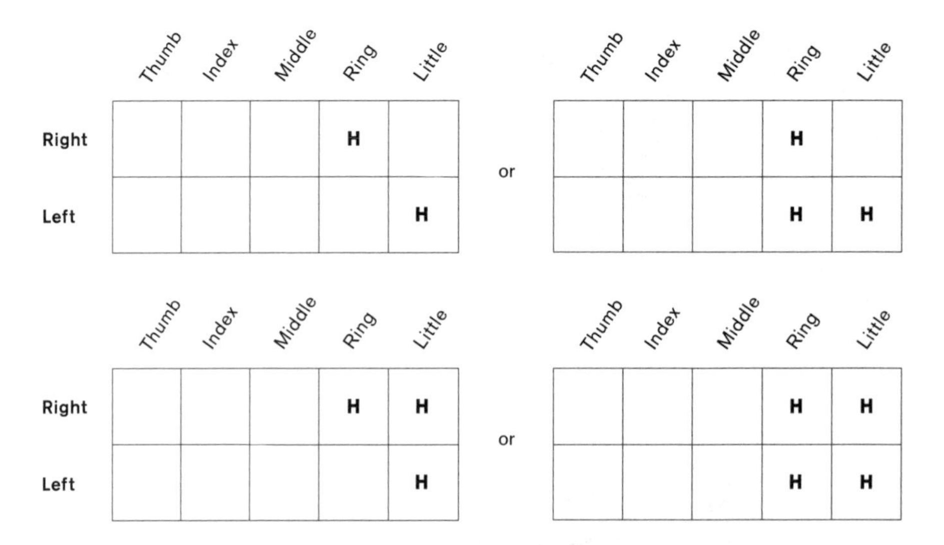

Fingerprint Profile: Right ring finger or both ring fingers + left little finger or both little fingers as the highest ranking prints (Living in the Spotlight + The Healer = Public Impact in the Healing Arts)

See page 252 for more information about Public Impact in the Healing Arts.See also pages 186 and 203 for more information about Right Ring Finger archetypes.

Lowest Ranking Print on the Right Ring Finger: Hiding Out

The right ring finger challenges you to come to grips with your tomato fear so that it cannot run your life. Goldilocks says the most common forms of tomato fear unconsciousness are:

Too Much Right Ring Finger

- You overdramatize everything to avoid actually being seen.
- You take on an exaggerated persona as a hiding place.
- You act too defensive much more often than circumstances warrant.

Too Little Right Ring Finger

- You live in disguise, not showing up as the real you; you hide out.
- Your performance anxiety and excessive shyness have you by the throat.
- You play it safe, hiding out as a big fish in a small pond.
- You dilute your talent so as to not generate any attention.

The Exalted Life Lesson (Just Right)

- TA DAH! Standing ovations

See page 232 for more information about Dealing with Disapproval/Esther.

LEFT RING FINGER

LIFE PURPOSE: The Master of Self-Approval / The Innovator
LIFE LESSON: Disapproval Fears

The constant in any left ring finger–based life purpose is learning to stick to your own way of doing things regardless of the attitudes and comments of everybody else. You are at your best when, having wrestled with the expectations of others, the constraints of the marketplace, and the pressure of your peers, you have carved your own niche *and* found support for having done so.

To accomplish this, you will need to develop a strong sense of self-approval. So have your feelings hurt, suffer the humiliation, recover. Hurt someone else's feelings, recognize what you have done, fix things up. Repeat these and a thousand other reveal yourself/don't reveal yourself experiences until you learn to develop a genuine interaction style that honestly reflects your inner nature. Then, when your social mask is neither too loud nor too quiet, when your life is no longer based upon a series of pretenses, major and minor, your life purpose will emerge and blossom.

See page 234 for more information about The Innovator.

Highest Ranking Print on the Left Ring Finger: The Innovator

Masters of Innovation . . .

- Are experimental
- Need freedom and are willing to pay the price to get it
- Are not controlled by the opinions (and potential disapproval) of society

Masters of Innovation Are Happiest When . . .

- All masks are finally removed
- Self-acceptance increases, disapproval loses its deadly sting
- The biggest skeptics change their tune

Typical Occupations (Note the overlap with the right ring finger.) To find fulfillment in your work, the key for you is *to do your own thing.* The actual format you choose is secondary. In each of these cases, the emphasis is on finding a unique approach and eventually gaining the acceptance that is your birthright.

- Entrepreneur, consultant, or businessperson with a new product or service
- Scientist, engineer, or any similar field: Taking a new approach, dealing with controversy

- Advertising, sales: Converting the skeptics is how you get paid
- Arts and crafts: Musician, sculptor, woodworker, jeweler; your unique style sets you apart
- Entertainment: Talk show host, stand-up comedian; you wear your public persona with ease
- Architect, interior designer, computer games inventor, chef: Any profession in which personal style and innovation are at a premium

Common Obstacles

- Becoming a hermit to avoid rejection and ridicule
- Becoming a pleaser person to avoid rejection and ridicule
- An overly harsh inner critic turns all outcomes into self-rejection and ridicule

Famous Masters of Innovation

- Jackie Robinson, Orson Welles, Nelson Mandela
- Galileo, Leonardo da Vinci, Louis Pasteur, Charles Darwin, Buckminster Fuller
- The young man in front of the tank in Tiananmen Square

Life Purpose Blossoming

- Standing up to peer pressure
- Breaking new ground
- Purity of your craft
- High levels of support
- Acceptance
- I found my niche

Life Purpose Inverse

- Caving in to peer pressure
- Conformity
- Selling out
- Lack of support
- Betrayal
- I don't belong

What's Up? (Frequently Asked Questions) Following are questions I've been asked by budding Innovators over the years, followed by my most common answers.

I don't seek confrontation. As a matter of fact, I am quite conservative. What's up?
Are you saying you would go along with the crowd even if you disagreed with it?

I didn't say that. I just mean that I am not the kind of person to cause a stir. What's up?
Neil Diamond's character in *The Jazz Singer* (see page 128) was not interested in causing a stir either. He just wanted to do his own thing. If his father hadn't made such a fuss, and his wife hadn't sided with his father, and, and, and . . .

With a left ring finger as highest ranking print, stirs get caused, whether you try to create them or not. At your best, you learn to know your own true self in the midst of all the noise of other people's opinions of who you should be and how you should live your life.

The Master of Innovation Checklist When you are living your life purpose, you should be able to check off all the items on this list. Make a note of your answers today and compare them to your answers one year from now. (Don't forget, life purpose is a process.)

- ☐ I have made peace with my past.
- ☐ I can accept myself, warts and all.
- ☐ I choose and keep friends who value me for who I really am.
- ☐ I am not too self-conscious.
- ☐ I have learned what my tastes are: what I like and what I don't like.
- ☐ I don't try as hard to get liked as I used to, though I am far from indifferent.
- ☐ No matter who I am with, I can still be me.
- ☐ I have found my appropriate niche.
- ☐ I do not let performance anxiety keep me from doing my own thing.
- ☐ I am not held hostage by my own image.

The Jazz Singer *Challenge (Tomato Fear Again)* If the left ring finger is your highest ranking print, no matter which school it combines with to form your life purpose, it is your life challenge to be true to yourself over the opposition of those who matter most. Under such pressure, the challenge is twofold: (a) don't prostitute your essential nature, and (b) don't turn your back on your group (or, if you must, don't lock the door).

The Jazz Singer with Laurence Olivier and Neil Diamond illustrates this issue. Neil wants to sing his own type of music, while his father wants him to follow in the family footsteps. They argue. Eventually Neil becomes a rock star, having had no contact with his father for several years. The highlight of the film is when Laurence Olivier shows up, unannounced, at his son's concert and to his own surprise winds up leading the applause. No personal success could match the reward of his father's approval, yet it had to be on the son's own terms.

All the ingredients of your life are here: the desire to be individualistically creative, the pressure to conform. Your challenge is to be true to yourself and eventually convert the skeptics. If you are watching this movie with friends who do not have a left ring finger life purpose, do not be surprised if they cannot understand why you are crying over some silly old grade B movie. Make sure you are ready with your own tissues, however.

Notice, if you will, the narrative's requirement of the father's disapproval. In your own life, you face the same type of battle against some apparently outside force. Yes, *apparently* outside force. Imagine, if you can, that the entire drama is actually taking place inside you and has been from before you were born. When you can view the disapproving voice as an ally of your own design, helping you to grow and develop, shaping the circumstances that reveal your true innovative nature, you will have come a long way on this life path.

The Master of Innovation in Each of the Four Schools When combined with the four schools, The Innovator's life purpose looks like this.

The Master of Innovation in the School of Service: Innovators in the School of Service often face a period of nonappreciation for all their good works. Sometimes, the nonappreciation phase never ends. Sometimes it never existed (it was all a figment of your imagination). Sometimes your biggest skeptic reluctantly becomes your biggest booster. (How sweet it is!) Any and all of these scenarios are likely events if these are your prints.

The Master of Innovation in the School of Love: How many people still have their emotional hooks into you? Is anyone pressuring you to become something or somebody that definitely is not you? Is *The Jazz Singer* your favorite movie?

The Master of Innovation in the School of Wisdom: Werner Heisenberg was a world-class scientist who turned his back on almost every colleague to stay in Germany and work on Hitler's atomic bomb project. Some say he sold out on his principles, others claim he used delaying tactics to save the world from unimaginable horrors. Your choices may not mean life or death for millions, but if the left ring finger is your highest ranking fingerprint, you were born to explore this issue in whatever permutations your circumstances allow. As you learn from your everyday experiences, you gain the tomatoes-are-okay-with-me confidence this life purpose requires.

The Master of Innovation in the School of Peace: You are a general contractor and you are behind on payroll (not to mention your own rent). Should you use substandard materials that you know won't be discovered until years later? At what point are you irredeemably compromised? There is no one correct answer that solves all left-ring-finger-slippery-slope dilemmas, but this can be stated with certainty: those doing well on this life path have learned where in the sand to draw the line. Those doing extremely well can draw such a line even in the Sahara. In a storm.

The Master of Innovation: Archetypal Combinations To figure out if you have the archetypal combinations on the next pages, review the fingerprint chart showing your highest and lowest ranking prints. If your highest ranking prints appear in the finger locations as denoted by an H below, then the archetypal combination applies to you. In the charts below, the H stands for highest ranking print, regardless of fingerprint type.

The Pioneer

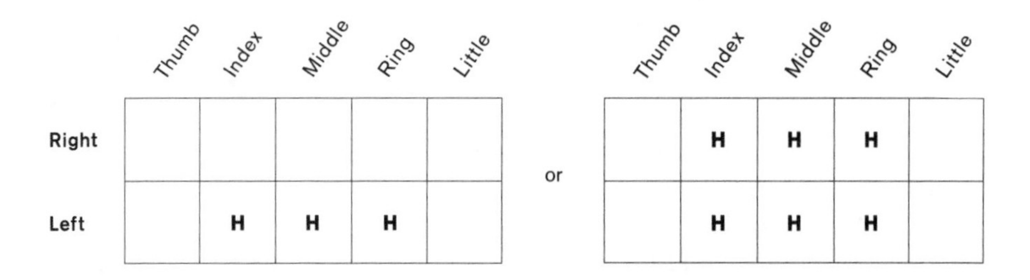

	Thumb	Index	Middle	Ring	Little
Right					
Left		**H**	**H**	**H**	

or

	Thumb	Index	Middle	Ring	Little
Right		**H**	**H**	**H**	
Left		**H**	**H**	**H**	

Fingerprint Profile: Left index finger or both index fingers + left middle finger or both middle fingers + left ring finger or both ring fingers as the highest ranking fingerprints (Passion + Integrity + Innovation = The Pioneer)

See page 236 for more information about The Pioneer.

The Pioneering Leader

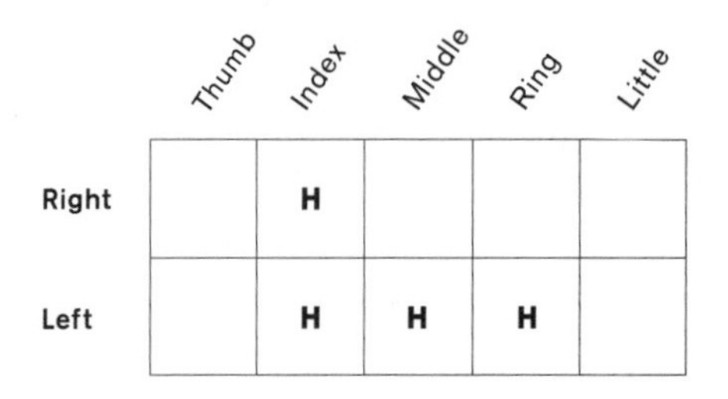

	Thumb	Index	Middle	Ring	Little
Right		**H**			
Left		**H**	**H**	**H**	

Fingerprint Profile: Left index finger or both index fingers + left middle finger + left ring finger as the highest ranking fingerprints (Leader + Integrity + Innovation = The Pioneering Leader)

See page 236 for more information about The Pioneering Leader.

The Pioneer in Business

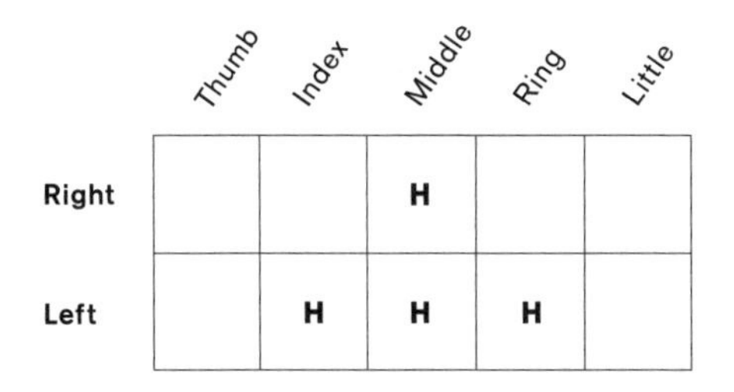

	Thumb	Index	Middle	Ring	Little
Right			H		
Left		H	H	H	

Fingerprint Profile: Left index finger + left middle finger or both middle fingers + left ring finger as the highest ranking fingerprints (Passion + Business Integrity + Innovation = The Pioneer in Business)

See page 237 for more information about The Pioneer in Business.

The Pioneering Artist

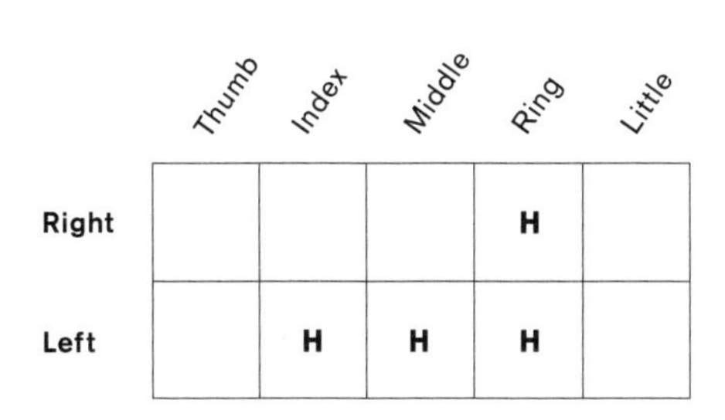

	Thumb	Index	Middle	Ring	Little
Right				H	
Left		H	H	H	

Fingerprint Profile: Left index finger + left middle finger + left ring finger or both ring fingers as the highest ranking fingerprints (Passion + Integrity + Creative Innovation = The Pioneering Artist)

See page 237 for more information about The Pioneering Artist.

Lowest Ranking Print on the Left Ring Finger: Disapproval Fears

Humans crave acceptance and approval, but at what point does this need cross the line of human foible and become a person's defining characteristic? Goldilocks says the most common forms of approval unconsciousness are as follows:

Too Much Left Ring Finger

- You ignore all social mores.
- You exclude yourself before others can reject you.
- You reject others, turning the tables on them and diverting the attention away from you.

Too Little Left Ring Finger

- You try too hard to get everyone to like you.
- Too many people have their hooks into you.
- You often feel like you don't belong.

The Exalted Life Lesson (Just Right)

- Other people want to join *your* club.

See page 239 for more information about Dealing with Disapproval.

RIGHT LITTLE FINGER

LIFE PURPOSE: The Master of Communications/The Author
LIFE LESSON: Not Speaking Up

With the right little finger as your highest ranking fingerprint, your life purpose is to find your message and deliver it to the public. Neither the vehicle nor the content of your message is revealed by this configuration; both of those are for you to fathom through life experience, introspection, and revelation. Only you can perceive the world as you do. Tell us what you see and hear; what you think; how you feel; what has changed you. Make *us* think, feel, and change and in so doing come to *your* right life.

This is a life purpose that often sneaks up on a person. Take Ansel Adams. He didn't start out with the idea of becoming a man with a message, but like a photograph slowly coming into focus in its emulsion, Adams's entire life gradually became an environmental statement. Or consider Candy Lightner, founder of Mothers Against Drunk Driving. She had no designs on public discourse prior to the untimely death of her child, yet that is where she found her meaning.

Regardless of whether you seek public communications as your life's work or it seeks you, satisfaction on this life path comes when your core truth is presented to and received by the general public. Meanwhile, unpublished poetry, holiday lectures to family members, or e-mails to co-workers about politics are not the ultimate expressions to which you aspire. Masters of Communications succeed in bringing their very personal message to the very impersonal public.

Highest Ranking Print on the Right Little Finger: The Author

Masters of Communications . . .

- Know themselves well
- Are willing to speak up and are equally willing to listen
- Have found their proper forum for self-expression

Masters of Communications Are Happiest When . . .

- Words flow easily
- Everyone feels fully heard
- Understanding amongst all parties shifts the dynamics to a win-win situation

Typical Occupations To find fulfillment in your work, the key is *finding your message and making yourself heard*. The format you choose is secondary.

- Author, public speaker, journalist, seminar leader: These are the most frequently selected occupations for this life purpose.
- Sales career: This is the second most common occupation associated with this life purpose—moving people to action through your spoken word.
- Songwriter, painter, comedian, storyteller, fingerprint analyst, athlete: Communication can come in many forms.
- Counselor, therapist, psychiatrist, social worker: Professional listeners help people to understand themselves better.
- TV personality, talk show host, radio disc jockey: Professional talkers and listeners communicate with an enormous public audience.
- Minister, priest, rabbi: Your communications can provide the moral glue for an entire community.

- Former addict, bank robber, sinner (any type): The reformed are on a mission to help others turn to something constructive.
- Labor negotiator, divorce mediator, diplomatic ambassador: These communicators work under difficult conditions.

Common Obstacles

- Seemingly random career path, no message is apparent
- Preaching to the choir, not finding your right audience
- Poor listening skills

Famous Masters of Communications

- Woody Guthrie, Edward R. Murrow, Neil Simon, Neil Armstrong, Emily Dickinson
- Clarence Darrow and William Jennings Bryant; Abe Lincoln and Frederick Douglass
- Smokey the Bear, Kermit the Frog, Mr. Ed, Homer Simpson

Life Purpose Blossoming

- Communications
- Clarity, insight
- Eloquence

Life Purpose Inverse

- Withdrawal
- Confusion, misunderstanding
- Talk too much, say too little

What's Up? (Frequently Asked Questions) Following are questions I've been asked by many Authors over the years, followed by my most common answers.

The very idea of public speaking makes my teeth rattle. What's up?
Your fingerprints (if you have a highest ranking right little finger) say your highest fulfillment is available through public communications. Your fingerprints do not say whether this is through public speaking or some other medium, whether you are ready yet to take on such a role, nor whether this will be easy for you.

I don't feel I have a particular message to bring to the world. What's up?
Reread the answer above.

Are you sure about this? I am really the quiet type. What's up?
Reread the answer above.

The Master of Communications Checklist When you are living your life purpose, you should be able to check off all the items on this list. Make a note of your answers today and compare them to your answers one year from now. (Don't forget, life purpose is a process.)

- ☐ I listen to other points of view.
- ☐ I cultivate my own interests and beliefs.
- ☐ I am willing to speak out for what I believe in.
- ☐ I ask for what I want.
- ☐ My word is my oath.
- ☐ There is a clear theme in my life that I can call my message.
- ☐ I find effective ways to make my message heard and understood.
- ☐ I have learned to handle criticism effectively.
- ☐ People often say that I have given them good ideas.
- ☐ I find my audience wherever I go.

The Master of Communications in Each of the Four Schools When combined with the four schools, The Author's life purpose looks like this.

The Master of Communications in the School of Service: The communications life purpose often emerges in three phases: find your message, hone it, bring it to the public. Successfully navigating these three phases often means overcoming the inclination to use servitude as a hiding place. If you are so busy doing for others that you have no time for your communications purpose, it is worth asking yourself if the tasks you are doing are the true service available to you in this lifetime.

The Master of Communications in the School of Love (see Susan B. Anthony on page 243): Sally Field's character in the movie *Punchline* must have had these fingerprints. Caught between her role as wife and mother and her desire to become a comedian, the more she reached for one, the more the other seemed to disappear. You will have to rent the video to see how she gets out of her delicious dilemma. PS: Susan B. Anthony, famous for her speeches on women's rights and the abolition of slavery, *did* have these fingerprints.

The Master of Communications in the School of Wisdom: This is the realm of many professional communicators. Leave your ivory tower, wisdom messenger, go beyond your technical expertise, and bring your wisdom to the world.

The Master of Communications in the School of Peace: Serious trauma is a common theme with these fingerprints: child abuse, the early death of a parent, debilitating injury, take your pick. In this case, a combination of life lesson and School of Peace issues is likely to dominate for a number of years. Yet your own transformation, if you can manage it, is designed to yield a message of inner peace to an embattled audience. The challenge here, beyond simple survival, is to keep in mind that there is a life purpose for you in the potential message that you carry.

The Master of Communications: Archetypal Combinations To figure out if you have the archetypal combination on the next page, review the fingerprint chart showing your highest and lowest ranking prints. If your highest ranking prints appear in the finger locations as denoted by an H below, then the archetypal combination applies to you. In the charts below, the H stands for highest ranking print, regardless of fingerprint type.

Persuasion

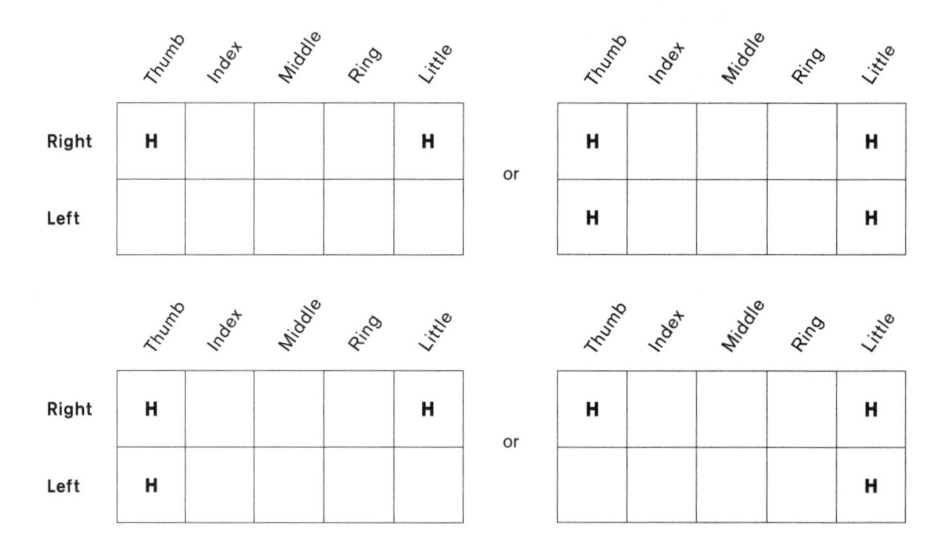

	Thumb	Index	Middle	Ring	Little
Right	H				H
Left					

or

	Thumb	Index	Middle	Ring	Little
Right	H				H
Left	H				H

	Thumb	Index	Middle	Ring	Little
Right	H				H
Left	H				

or

	Thumb	Index	Middle	Ring	Little
Right	H				H
Left					H

Fingerprint Profile: Right thumb or both thumbs + right little finger or both little fingers as the highest ranking prints (Success + Communications = Persuasion)

See page 244 for more information about Persuasion.

Lowest Ranking Print on the Right Little Finger: Not Speaking Up

The right little finger challenges you to get clear regarding your communications. Goldilocks says the most common forms of communications unconsciousness are:

Too Much Right Little Finger

- You talk way more than circumstances warrant.
- You are not aware of the messages you are putting out.
- People claim that you are not listening to them; misunderstandings are common.

Too Little Right Little Finger

- You have a hard time speaking up on your own behalf.
- You do not promote your own agenda.
- You withdraw if you don't immediately get your way.

The Exalted Life Lesson (Just Right)

- You are a paid public speaker.

See page 245 for more information about True Communications.

Not Speaking Up: Archetypal Combinations To figure out if you have the archetypal combinations below, review the fingerprint chart showing your highest and lowest ranking prints. If your lowest ranking prints appear in the finger locations as denoted by an L below, then the archetypal combination applies to you. In the charts, the L stands for lowest ranking print, regardless of fingerprint type.

Worthy of Love

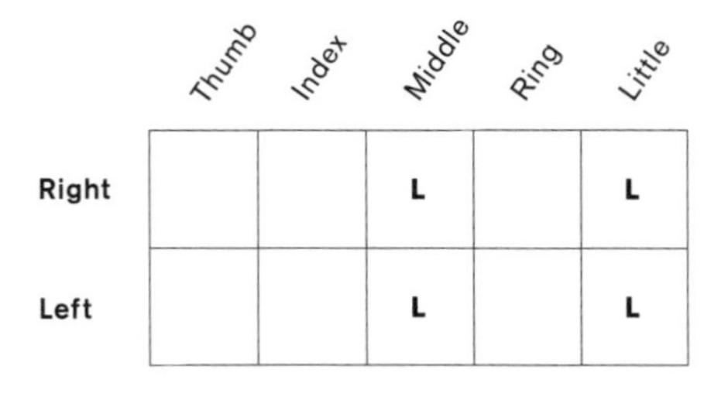

	Thumb	Index	Middle	Ring	Little
Right			L		L
Left			L		L

Fingerprint Profile: Both middle fingers + both little fingers as the lowest ranking fingerprints (Self-Worth + Intimacy Issues = Worthy of Love)

See page 211 for more information about Worthy of Love.

What I Say Matters

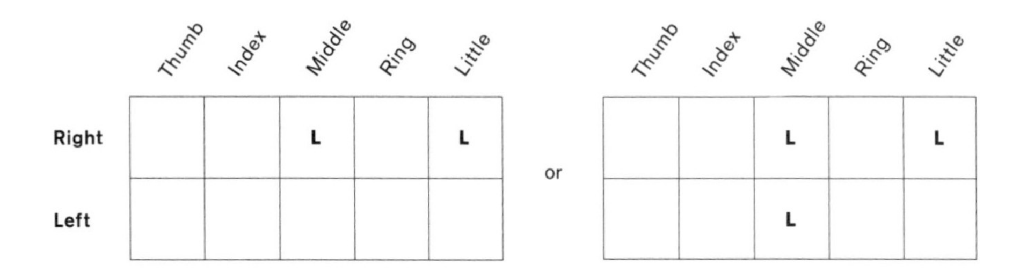

	Thumb	Index	Middle	Ring	Little
Right			L		L
Left					

or

	Thumb	Index	Middle	Ring	Little
Right			L		L
Left			L		

Fingerprint Profile: Right middle finger or both middle fingers + right little finger as the lowest ranking fingerprints (Guilt + Speaking Out = What I Say Matters)

See page 247 for more information about What I Say Matters.

LEFT LITTLE FINGER

LIFE PURPOSE: The Master of Insight / The Healer
LIFE LESSON: Intimacy Issues

With the left little finger or both little fingers as your highest ranking fingerprint(s), your greatest fulfillment comes when you see your insightful communications helping others. The key factor for you is maintaining a connection to *your own* inner knowledge regardless of external circumstance—then somehow promoting this process in others.

Being the counselor to your family or circle of friends will, in the long run, fail to fulfill this life purpose. In most cases, you can reach *your* highest potential only when you have become a professional growth catalyst available to the public. It is interesting to note that on The Healer's path, many emerge out of daunting personal and family circumstances. Events may conspire to bring you repeatedly to the brink where only a full leap of faith has any chance of pulling you through. Recognizing that this is part of your training program may help you persevere.

Deanna's story is typical for many who have a left little finger life purpose. Deanna's title at work was "secretary," but she spent more time counseling her co-workers and boss than typing or filing. It was as if she had a sign on her desk: "Counselor Is In." Talk to Deanna about any problem for only a few minutes and she would see the hidden dynamics at work. However, Deanna's own life was a mess. She felt trapped both at work and at home, unable to find her way to take any action on her own behalf. Truth be told, with the left little finger as her highest ranking fingerprint, Deanna will not find what she is searching for until she moves the counselor/therapist role, a role for which she is exquisitely well suited, from the periphery of her life to its center.

See page 249 for information about The Healer.

Highest Ranking Print on the Left Little Finger: The Master of Insight

Masters of Insight . . .

- Are committed to their own personal growth
- Are committed to the truth in all aspects of their lives
- Trust their inner voice, wherever it may lead

Masters of Insight Are Happiest When . . .

- Learning new tools for self-discovery
- Discussing personal matters of deep meaning
- Assisting others in becoming more self-aware

Typical Occupations To find fulfillment in your work, the key for you is to be *inspired and inspiring.* The actual format you choose is secondary.

- Counselor, therapist, social worker: Helping people to grow, psychologically and emotionally
- Football coach, personal trainer, drill sergeant: Inspiring people to "be all you can be"
- Minister, priest, rabbi, shaman: Providing a spiritual perspective
- Doctor, nurse, holistic health practitioner, body worker, acupuncturist: Using knowledge, wisdom, and insight to assist people in healing their bodies
- Seminar leader, sales trainer, public speaker: Inspiring large numbers of people, and providing tools to improve their lives
- Middle level manager: Team building based on personal empowerment and shared goals
- Inspirational author, songwriter, painter, filmmaker: Illuminating, empowering, and inspiring through creativity
- Professional psychic, hand analyst, graphologist, astrologer: Bringing legitimacy to what may be considered a pseudoscience

Common Obstacles

- Doubting your inner guidance
- Healer heal thyself: personal crises take up all your time and energy
- Burnout: other people's crises take up all your time and energy

Famous Masters of Insight

- Sigmund Freud, Carl Jung, Irwin Yalom, Wayne Dyer
- Og Mandino's *Greatest Salesman in the World*, Napoleon Hill's *Think and Grow Rich*
- Deepak Chopra, John Gray, Swami Beyondananda

Life Purpose Blossoming

- Clarity
- Communications
- Spiritual values
- Inspiration, faith

Life Purpose Inverse

- Confusion
- Withdrawal
- Borrowed values
- Self-absorption, mistrust

What's Up? (Frequently Asked Questions) Following are questions I've been asked by budding Healers over the years, followed by my most common answers.

I am interested in personal growth but have no professional ambitions. What's up?
Is your name Deanna (see page 138)?

OK, I see your point. But what am I to do, go back to college and get another degree?
I am not sure what you are to do. I can say, however, that if you have a highest ranking fingerprint on your left little finger, it is very much in your interest to create an insightful communicator career for yourself, whether as a therapist or in some other capacity. If this means starting over from scratch, I would certainly give it a lot of thought if I were you. Consider this: if you are Deanna, how long have you been unhappy and what are your other plans for creating the life you really want?

The Master of Insight Checklist When you are living your life purpose, you should be able to check off all the items on this list. Make a note of your answers today and compare them to your answers one year from now. (Don't forget, life purpose is a process.)

- ☐ I have learned to trust my inner voice.
- ☐ I am willing to invest time and money on my own development.
- ☐ Others often seek me out for advice. I am willing to take advice as well.
- ☐ I know and live my life purpose.
- ☐ I have had my ups and downs and can appreciate other people's dilemmas.
- ☐ I reflect on things without getting paralyzed by indecision.
- ☐ My career and lifestyle reflect my spiritual values.
- ☐ I am humbly but sincerely inspired by my own words and deeds.
- ☐ I honor my relationship partner and he or she honors me as well.
- ☐ What a life!

The Master of Insight in Each of the Four Schools When combined with the four schools, The Healer's life purpose looks like this.

The Master of Insight in the School of Service: If you have found a career in the healing arts, you are right on target, but be careful you do not encourage an overdependency on the part of your clients. Servitude would surely ensue.

The Master of Insight in the School of Love: With this fingerprint combination, fulfillment comes when you are working in the healing arts *and* enjoying a good love life, both at the same time. You would think this would not be such a problem. International spy, bank robber, merchant marine at sea six months at a time, these seem like more difficult professions to blend with a happy marriage. Yet this life purpose option has a higher-than-average relationship casualty index. At your best, you bring emotional insight to your professional *and* personal life.

The Master of Insight in the School of Wisdom: Satisfied-with-my-own-life psychology professors, personal development authors, and sales trainers teaching the ten rules of true success are likely candidates for these fingerprints. If this is you, be sure to pay attention to the following question: is your teacher self the natural synergistic expression of your life's work or your way of hiding from the real world? With these fingerprints, either or both states of being is possible.

The Master of Insight in the School of Peace: Multiple arches often signal preoccupation with life circumstances. Can you find enough quiet in the midst of your personal obstacle course to pay attention to your inner voice? If so, it will lead you all the way to a healing arts career and, beyond that, all the way to a healing arts career *plus* a happy life. No law of physics says you cannot; in fact, you were made for it.

The Master of Insight: Archetypal Combinations To figure out if you have the archetypal combinations below, review the fingerprint chart showing your highest and lowest ranking prints. If your highest ranking prints appear in the finger locations as denoted by an H below, then the archetypal combination applies to you. In the charts below, the H stands for highest ranking print, regardless of fingerprint type.

Public Impact in the Healing Arts

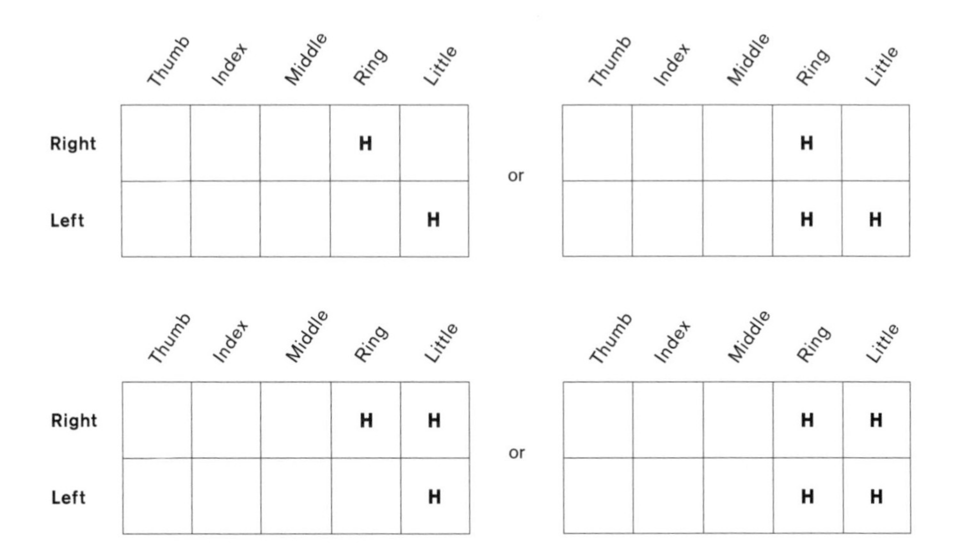

	Thumb	Index	Middle	Ring	Little
Right				H	
Left					H

or

	Thumb	Index	Middle	Ring	Little
Right				H	
Left				H	H

	Thumb	Index	Middle	Ring	Little
Right				H	H
Left					H

or

	Thumb	Index	Middle	Ring	Little
Right				H	H
Left				H	H

Fingerprint Profile: Left little finger or both little fingers + right ring finger or both ring fingers as the highest ranking prints (Insight + The Spotlight = Public Impact in the Healing Arts); highest ranking ring finger or both ring fingers as highest ranking indicating that the person with insightful communications wishes to reach a large audience

See page 252 for more information about Public Impact in the Healing Arts.

The Shaman

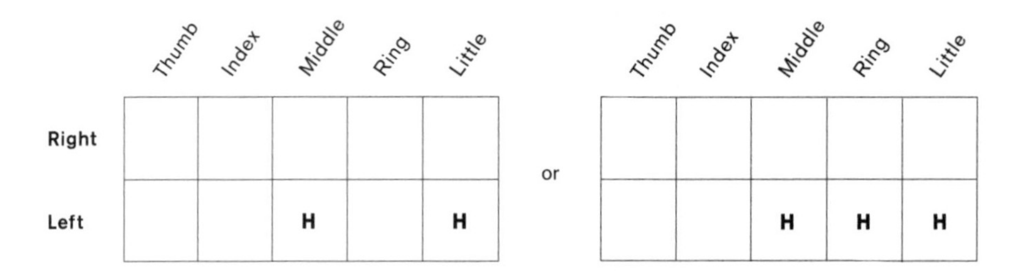

Fingerprint Profile: Left middle finger + left little finger as the highest ranking fingerprints (The Mentor + The Healer = The Shaman); addition of a highest ranking left ring finger is another variation of The Shaman (The Mentor + The Innovator = The Healer)

See page 254 for more information about The Shaman.

Lowest Ranking Print on the Left Little Finger: Intimacy Issues

The left little finger as the life lesson challenges you to surrender to your inner truth and/or surrender to intimacy. Goldilocks says the most common left little finger errors are:

Too Much Left Little Finger

- You are too mistrustful, especially in relationship matters.
- You manipulate people to get your way.
- You have to win every argument.

Too Little Left Little Finger

- You ignore your inner alarm when it warns you that someone should not be trusted.
- You withdraw if you don't immediately get your way.
- You tend to abandon yourself in personal relationships.

The Exalted Life Lesson (Just Right)

- You are a well-respected therapist or counselor.

See page 256 for more information about Intimacy Issues, Trust, and Surrender.

Intimacy Issues: Archetypal Combinations To figure out if you have the archetypal combinations below, review the fingerprint chart showing your highest and lowest ranking prints. If your lowest ranking prints appear in the finger locations as denoted by an L below, then the archetypal combination applies to you. In the charts, the L stands for lowest ranking print, regardless of fingerprint type.

Sexual Violation

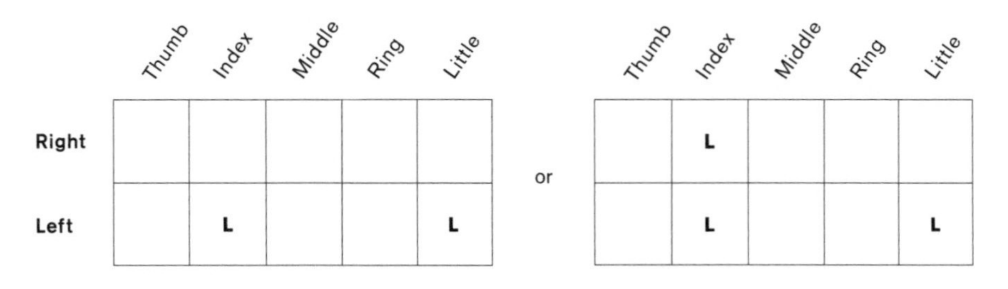

Fingerprint Profile: Left index finger or both index fingers + left little finger with the lowest ranking fingerprints (Boundary Violation + Intimacy Issues = Sexual Violation)

See page 195 for more information about Sexual Violation.

Negative L'Oreal

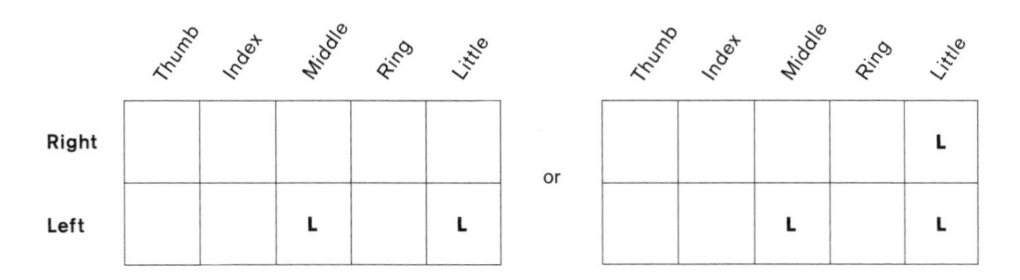

Fingerprint Profile: Left little finger or both little fingers + left middle finger with the lowest ranking fingerprints (Guilt + Intimacy Issues = Negative L'Oreal)

See page 209 for more information about Negative L'Oreal.

Worthy of Love

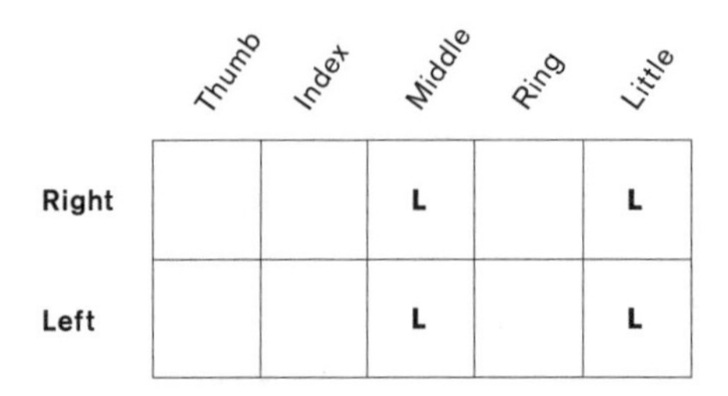

	Thumb	Index	Middle	Ring	Little
Right			L		L
Left			L		L

Fingerprint Profile: Both middle fingers + both little fingers as the lowest ranking fingerprints (Self-Worth + Intimacy Issues = Worthy of Love)

See page 211 for more information about Worthy of Love.

What I Say Matters

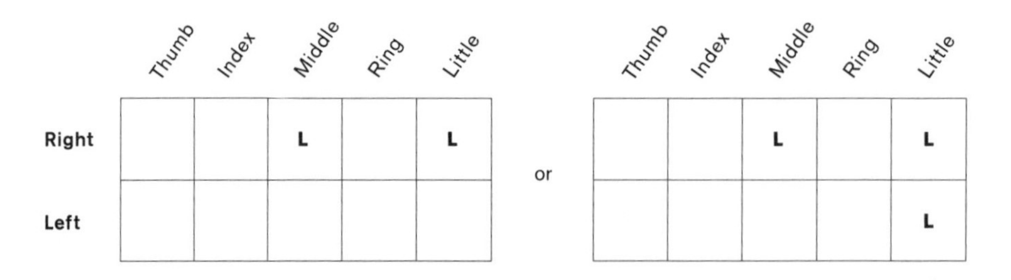

	Thumb	Index	Middle	Ring	Little
Right			L		L
Left					

or

	Thumb	Index	Middle	Ring	Little
Right			L		L
Left					L

Fingerprint Profile: Right middle finger + right little finger or both little fingers as the lowest ranking fingerprint (Value in the World + Communications = What I Say Matters)

See page 247 for more information about What I Say Matters.

THE PALMAR LOCATIONS

MARS, VENUS, AND THE MOON

Besides the ten fingerprint zones under discussion so far, dermatoglyphic (fingerprint) markers appear all over the finger and palmar surface. Many of these markers are commonly used for medical diagnoses or population studies and can be useful in a hand analysis as well. However, for life-purpose analysis, the palmar whorl is the key fingerprint to keep in mind.

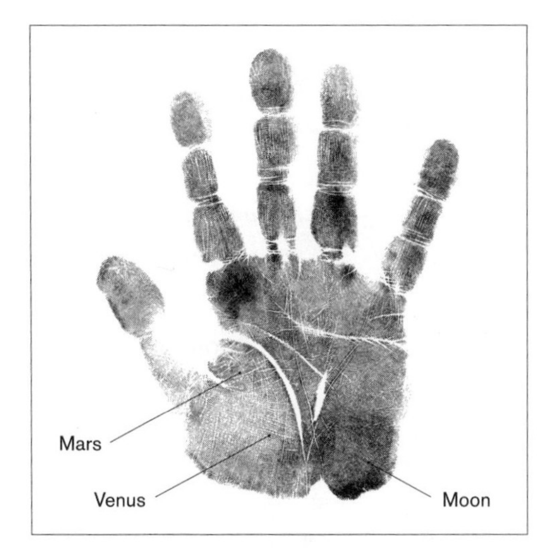

The above handprint shows the mythological names from standard hand analysis for the different regions of the palmar surface. Whorls appearing on the Mars and Venus areas are quite rare. Moon whorls, while uncommon, are more likely, occurring in a bit less than 1 percent of hands. If you encounter any of these palmar whorls, the procedure is to elevate the zone with the whorl to highest ranked status (making it the life purpose for the owner). This does not mean the ten usual fingerprints get ignored. For one, you still need to determine the life lesson and the school. Secondly, the other highest ranking fingerprints should be considered as modifying the Moon, Venus, or Mars whorl, offering a more complete picture of the owner's soul psychology. Still, the appearance of a whorl (or even a peacock) anywhere on the palmar surface immediately becomes the center of the person's life-purpose story.

Note: Loops, tented arches, and arches in the palmar locations do not usually work their way into the life-purpose story and are therefore not covered here.

Palmar Whorl on Venus

Life Purpose Blossoming

- Sensuality, delight
- Warmth, kindness, generosity
- Play, love of life

Life Purpose Inverse

- No romance, icy coldness
- Little or no giving or receiving
- Hard edges, no fun

Palmar Whorl on Mars

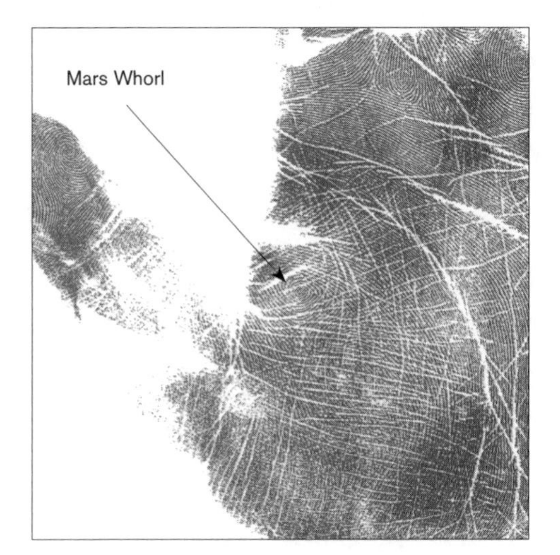

Life Purpose Blossoming

- The Warrior
- Strength, bravery, honor

Life Purpose Inverse

- No dragons to slay or damsels to save
- Cowardice, belligerence

Palmar Whorl on the Moon

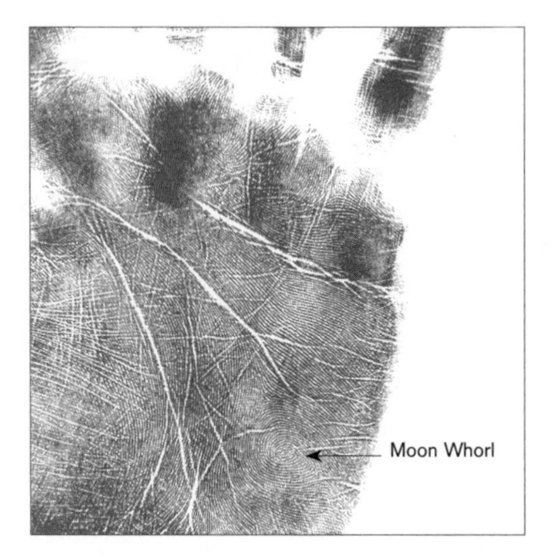

The Moon is the part of the hand least accessible to the thumb. As such, it is associated with the passive principle, including the worlds of imagination and spirituality. In ancient days, the king would call in the moon man to throw the bones and interpret their seemingly random pattern into a prophetic story. Others would see the skeletal remains of a goat thrown on the floor as meaningless, but the Moon expert sees meanings where others do not. For the Moon-based individual, everything is connected; the universe is God's message board.

Like the Native American tracker reading the hidden symbolism in the seemingly invisible markings on the ground, Moonies see hidden signs in life's every detail. It is the ultimate challenge for such individuals to learn to trust this voice within themselves and, over time, make it the centerpiece of a fulfilling lifestyle and career.

See page 259 for more information about the Moon as Life Purpose.

Life Purpose Blossoming

- Spirituality in action
- Seer of deep meanings
- Holistic psychologist, life coach
- Professional intuitive
- Insight into life's mysteries
- Imagination, intuition

Life Purpose Inverse

- Alienation, stagnation
- The Big Gaping Hole
- Stuck in the void
- Delusional behaviors
- Disillusionment, depression
- Lack of contact with the inner world

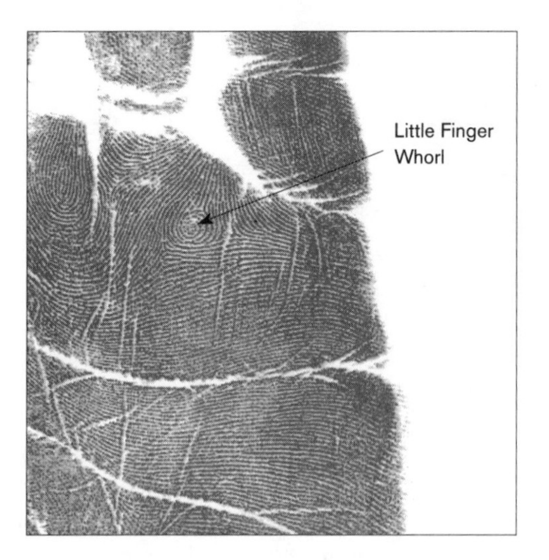

Palmar Little Finger Whorl: Reluctant Communications

Less common than the Moon whorl but more likely than the Venus or Mars whorls, the palmar little finger whorl has the same meaning as a single whorl appearing on the little finger. Right little finger palmar whorls indicate a life purpose of communications; left little finger palmar whorls indicate the presence of The Healer. The difference between a normal little finger whorl and one that is embedded in the palm is the amount of resistance involved in getting to your appropriate voice. This palm-based whorl represents a heavily reluctant communicator regardless of which hand it inhabits.

I have seen owners of this marking promote the writing and speaking of others while secretly harboring the desire for a like career for themselves. Buried in the palm rather than being on the fingertip, such a person has more work to do to bring the whorl into the light of day. This is not an impossible task, but in my experience it is safe to add an extra decade or two to the expected life experience required for the life purpose to flower.

The arrow denotes the palmar little finger whorl, the indicator of a Reluctant Communicator or Reluctant Healer. Whorls can also appear another half inch toward the thumb side of the palm (also just below the top of the palmar surface), and in cases like these you are looking at The Reluctant Artist (right hand) or The Reluctant Innovator (left hand).

****

Before you move on to the next step in understanding your soul psychology—creating your life-fulfillment formula—let's review what you have learned:

You now know how to identify your life purpose by locating your highest ranking fingerprint(s). You then take the meaning inherent in the location(s) of your highest ranking print(s) and combine it with the Just-Right phrase of your school to create your life-purpose statement.

You now know how to identify your life lesson by locating your lowest ranking fingerprint(s). You then take the meaning inherent in the location(s) of your lowest ranking print(s) and combine it with the Too Much/Too Little phrase of your school to create your life-lesson statement.

You have reviewed the fuller explanation of the finger(s) with your highest ranking fingerprint(s) to get a more in-depth understanding of your life purpose.

You have reviewed the fuller explanation of the finger(s) with your lowest ranking fingerprint(s) to get a more in-depth understanding of your life lesson.

Hang in there. The big payoff is just around the corner.

CHAPTER FIVE

CREATE YOUR LIFE-FULFILLMENT FORMULA AND LIVE A LIFE ON PURPOSE

As a man's real power grows and his knowledge widens, ever the way he can follow grows narrower; until at last he chooses nothing, but does only and wholly what he must do.

— URSULA K. LE GUIN, *A WIZARD OF EARTHSEA*

Nature forms us for ourselves, not for others; to be, not to seem.

— ANONYMOUS

You now know which school you belong to in the Earth University, and you have created life-purpose and life-lesson statements. It is time to pull it all together to create your life-fulfillment formula. The quick description of this formula is: *Progress on your life lesson unlocks your life purpose.* It sounds simple enough, yet the implications can be profound.

CREATING YOUR LIFE-FULFILLMENT FORMULA

Let's practice with a few examples before working with your own fingerprints.

In example 1 on the following page, the highest ranking fingerprint is on the right ring finger: The Artist. The lowest ranking fingerprint is on the left index finger: Blocked Passions. There are eight loops, so this person is in the School of Love.

EXAMPLE 1

	Thumb	Index Finger	Middle Finger	Ring Finger	Little Finger
Right	3	3	3	4	3
Left	3	1	3	3	3

Life-purpose statement: The Artist + Love and Closeness
Life-lesson statement: Blocked Passions + Explosion / Stuffed Feelings

These statements are the raw materials we have to work with. However, before we create a life-fulfillment formula for this person, we need to convert the life-purpose statement and life-lesson statement into a more personal format. This is where the notes you took from the last chapter will come in handy.

Life-Purpose Statement

Let's start with the life-purpose statement: The Artist + Love and Closeness. Now that you know more about what it means to belong to the School of Love and to have a highest ranking fingerprint on the right ring finger, you do not have to limit yourself to the one-word descriptions and Just-Right phrases I came up with to create a life-purpose statement.

For instance, if the above fingerprints were yours, perhaps now you would describe the key meaning of your highest ranking fingerprint on your right ring finger as The Individualist or Creativity or any other word or phrase you identify with from the right ring finger description in chapter three (refer to the notes you took while reading the details about each finger location). Similarly, knowing the themes of the School of Love, perhaps you would characterize your Just-Right statement as "using vulnerability skills." Perhaps your more personalized life-purpose statement would be "creativity with vulnerability" or The Artist with Heart. Refer to page 122 (The Artist in Each of the Four Schools section) for more ideas on combining the highest ranking right ring finger with the School of Love.

Life-Lesson Statement

The same concept applies to the life-lesson statement. In the above example, the lowest ranking print on the left index finger indicates that blocked passions is the big hurdle for this person's life, but you could also use any of the challenges listed for the left index finger, like "knowing what you want" or "developing boundary skills." You are also no longer limited to the exact Too Much/Too Little phrase in constructing your life-lesson statement. A new life-lesson statement for this person could be "Acknowledge and express your feelings and find your true passion."

Let's put this concept to work in a real-life example. The fingerprints discussed on these last two pages belong to a friend of mine. I know enough about her life history to be able to see the fingerprint theme in several manifestations at different times in her life. Twenty years ago, she was struggling with relationship issues that had her squeezed into a corner. It was not until two years after her divorce that the creative side of her nature became visible enough to offer a clear picture of what her new life could be. Now, several years later, she owns her own design business.

I do not know every detail of my friend's prior marriage difficulties, but the entire left index finger list of problematic possibilities received nodding agreement when I told her about her fingerprints. Conversely, I can assume she is better at left index finger skills and School of Love skills today or she would not be happy with the life she is living.

No matter what happens next for my friend, her life will continue to follow the formula laid out in her fingerprints before she was born. She may continue to live a rewarding life or revert to the constant frustrations of earlier times, but the life-purpose map she carries on her fingertips will always be available as a guide to her right life. Her life-fulfillment formula reads: Express your feelings, unleash your passions, and find The Artist with Heart.

Let's move on to another example. In the chart on the following page, the highest ranking fingerprints are on two fingers: the right index finger and the left ring finger, The Leader and The Innovator. The lowest ranking fingerprints are also on two fingers: the right little finger and the left thumb, whose key words are Not Speaking Up and Family. There are two arches: the school is the School of Peace.

EXAMPLE 2

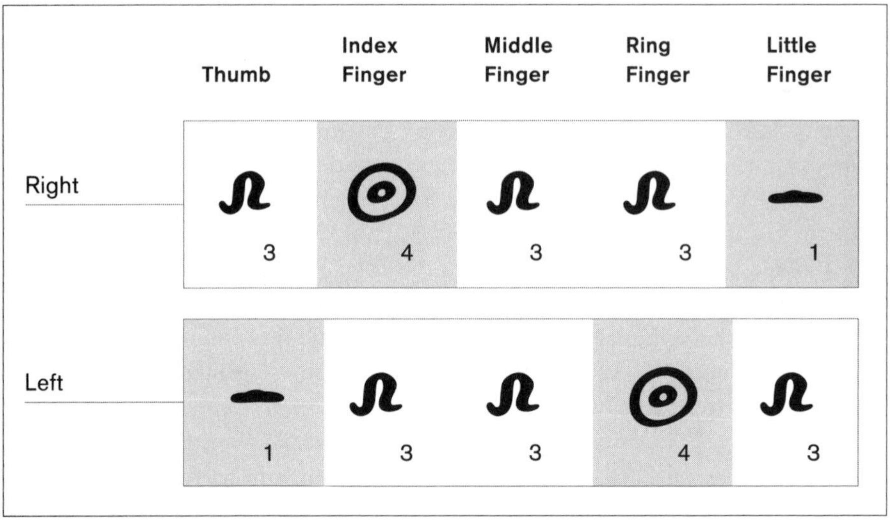

	Thumb	Index Finger	Middle Finger	Ring Finger	Little Finger
Right	3	4	3	3	1
Left	1	3	3	4	3

Life-purpose statement: The Leader and The Innovator + Life in Balance
Life-lesson statement: Not Speaking Up and Family + Overextension/Slacking Off

Repeating the same process used on the prior page, we could rework the two statements as follows:

The life purpose is: The Innovative Leader, Living Life in Balance
The life lesson is: Not Speaking up in the Family, Causing Chronic Overextension

These fingerprints belong to another person whose life history is familiar to me, allowing me to choose from the different choices the fingerprints present. Unable to ask his staff to do what needed to be done, this man often worked a sixty-hour week (or more). Knowing this, I could safely ignore the Ms. Lah-Dee-Dah possibilities of the School of Peace and focus on Mr. Sticks and Plates. As he learned to speak up, the more rewarding possibilities of Innovative Leadership emerged. This culminated in his successfully lobbying the local college into starting a program to teach restaurant skills to retarded kids. Now scores of formerly unemployable youths are earning a living.

He could have spent his entire life in the big gaping hole, overworked and underappreciated. It was up to him to learn from the experiences generated by his life lesson in order to bring his life purpose forward. This highly rewarding possibility exists at any time in any person's life.

Now, it's time to turn your attention back to your own life-fulfillment formula. Fill in the chart opposite or refer to your life-purpose journal to find your original life-purpose and life-lesson statements. Based on the information you learned in chapter four, do you want to rework either of your statements? If you feel the original statement is accurate for you, then by all means, don't change it. Knowing that progress toward your life lesson unlocks your life purpose, write down your life-fulfillment formula on the following page or in your life-purpose journal.

To truly live your life purpose, the decisions you make now and in the future should be informed by this formula whenever possible. If this sounds like a difficult goal, read on. The next section features journaling exercises that will help you integrate the information you've learned into your everyday life.

MY FINGERPRINTS

	Thumb	Index Finger	Middle Finger	Ring Finger	Little Finger
Right					
Left					

My original life-purpose statement (page 55) ________________________________

____

My original life-lesson statement (page 64) ________________________________

____

My reworked life-purpose statement ________________________________

____

My reworked life-lesson statement ______________________________

____

My life-fulfillment formula (life lesson progress unlocks life purpose) __________

____

USING YOUR LIFE-PURPOSE MAP

It is one thing to name your life purpose. The real power of fingerprint analysis happens when you can bring your life purpose directly into your life and use it as a daily compass to meaning and fulfillment. When the life purpose that has been yours from before your birth becomes obvious to you in its ever-changing, everyday disguises, a renewed sense of direction and mission will energize you as never before.

Fingerprint analysis is both as direct as a sledgehammer and as subtle as anything can be. Students often come up to me and tell me that since they have been actively looking at their life-purpose map for several years, it is finally starting to sink in. With this in mind, it is worthwhile to read the archetypal combinations and case studies associated with your fingerprints very carefully and attempt to connect their messages to *your* past and current circumstances.

The intent of these stories was to give you an opportunity to see you own life purpose and life lesson playing out in real-world terms. As should be clear, the difficulties initiated by your life lesson are perfectly suited to bring you the experiences you need to successfully bring your life purpose forward. If you can keep this perspective in mind while wrestling with the recurring and frustrating themes that never seem to reduce to zero in your life, you are already more than halfway there. Turning your life lesson from nemesis to ally will get you the rest of the way into your right life.

THE LIVING-ON-PURPOSE EXERCISE

The following written exercises are designed to help you better apply what you have learned about your life purpose and your life lesson. You can do the exercises right in the book or write them in your life-purpose journal. You may wish to share your answers with someone you trust such as a therapist, a best friend, or your spouse to get more feedback on these issues. Before we get to your journal exercises, let's look at a sample journal to give you a sense of how to work through the questions.

Sample Journal

Start by writing down your life-purpose statement(s), life-lesson statement(s), and life-fulfillment formula.

My life purpose is:
Public Impact in the Healing Arts + A Life in Balance

My life lesson is:
Right Work for Right Pay + Mr. Sticks and Plates

My life-fulfillment formula is:
Find the right job in the healing arts and stop the chronic overextension that has kept my life off balance.

Describe three major events in your life and identify how your life purpose(s) and life lesson(s) were present then. The more you can identify your life purpose and life lesson acting in their more obvious forms during events from your past, the easier it will be to recognize current versions that may not be so obvious.

1. *At the XYZ Company, I did all the training for the new staff. I loved the work, but I was never actually paid for all the extra time I put in.*

2.

3.

List three ways you see your life purpose unfolding today. For instance, if your life purpose is The Leader and you have your own business, record that here. Similarly, if your life purpose is The Leader and you work in the mail room, but you organized some friends to vacation together, record that here. Your life purpose is visible (either obviously or less obviously) at all times in your life if you look for it.

1. *At the ABC Company, I lead a monthly in-house workshop on teamwork.*

2.

3.

List three ways you see your life lesson manifesting itself in your current circumstances. Your life lesson is also present at all times in your life. Certainly, it was more obvious ten or twenty years ago. Certainly, you would no longer get yourself into such a tough set of circumstances as you did back then. No doubt, you are older and wiser. But you have the same fingerprints you've always had, and you can be sure your life lesson is still around today.

1. *I am still not getting paid directly for the work that I find most rewarding. Eighty percent of what I do at work has nothing to do with what really inspires me.*

2.

3.

List three actions you can start now that are consistent with Living on Purpose. If none come to mind, take some time to think it over. The actions need not be gigantic. As a matter of fact, small steps are recommended. For instance, if your life purpose is Responsibility in the World, maybe cleaning up your attic or getting your financial records up to date are good starting points.

It is also important that you choose an action that is measurable. For instance, my goal for finishing this book was to write twenty pages a month. At the end of each month, it would be easy enough to tell whether I had written twenty pages. Saying, for instance, "I will write more often" is not specific enough for this step of the Living-on-Purpose process.

1. *I will write a proposal by the end of this month to show my boss how it would benefit the company to expand the teamwork workshops and put me in charge of them.*

2.

3.

Based on past experiences, the following obstacles will likely show up when I try to institute the three actions listed above (be as specific as possible). Limit yourself to no more than three expected obstacles and, most important, be specific. "Wasting time" as an expected obstacle is not specific enough. "Too many hours watching television" is. If your expected obstacles are specific, your counterstrategies will also be specific.

1. *I don't have enough time to write the proposal because I am already working a fifty-hour week.*

2.

3.

I will use these countermeasures to stay on purpose. Saying you will really buckle down is not a counterstrategy. Every counterstrategy needs a plan B. My plan B for finishing this book was to keep all day Wednesday open on my agenda. If I was on schedule with my writing, I could take Wednesday off or fill it with clients.

1. *I will ask Fred to help me with the financial reports this month, freeing up the time I need to create the proposal. If Fred can't help me, I'll ask Marty or Bob.*

2.

3.

To verify and support myself as I bring my life purpose forward, I commit to the following. The verification and support aspect of the Living-on-Purpose process is important. Do not skip past it. Hire a coach, go into therapy, join a support group, get three friends to join you in the Living-on-Purpose process and meet with them on Tuesday nights. Do whatever it takes. Experience has shown that you will get better results when you link your behavior to a specific and regular infrastructure of support.

I will create a life-purpose support group with four members. We will check in with each other once a week to make sure we are on task. I will ask Arlene first, then . . .

Journal Exercise

Now it's your turn. Start by writing down your life purpose, life lesson, and life-fulfillment formula.

My life purpose is ______________________________

____

My life lesson is ______________________________

____

My life-fulfillment formula is ______________________________

____

Describe three major events in your life and identify how your life purpose(s) and life lesson(s) were present then. The more you can identify your life purpose and life lesson acting in their more obvious forms during events from your past, the easier it will be to recognize current versions that may not be so obvious.

1. ______________________________

____

2. ______________________________

____

3. ______________________________

____

List three ways you see your life purpose unfolding today. For instance, if your life purpose is The Leader and you have your own business, record that here. Similarly, if your life purpose is The Leader and you work in the mail room, but you organized some friends to vacation together, record that here. Your life purpose is visible (either obviously or less obviously) at all times in your life if you look for it.

1. ______________________________

____

2. ______________________________

____

3. ______________________________

____

List three ways you see your life lesson manifesting itself in your current circumstances. Your life lesson is also present at all times in your life. Certainly, it was more obvious ten or twenty years ago. Certainly, you would no longer get yourself into such a tough set of circumstances as you did back then. No doubt, you are older and wiser. But you have the same fingerprints you've always had, and you can be sure your life lesson is still around today.

1. ______________________________

____

2. ______________________________

____

3. ______________________________

____

List three actions you can start now that are consistent with Living on Purpose. If none come to mind, take some time to think it over. The actions need not be gigantic. As a matter of fact, small steps are recommended. For instance, if your life purpose is Responsibility in the World, maybe cleaning up your attic or getting your financial records up to date are good starting points.

1. ______________________________

I will start on this action on [date]. ______________________________

2. ___

I will start on this action on [date]. ___

3. ___

I will start on this action on [date]. ___

Based on past experiences, the following obstacles will likely show up when I try to institute the three actions listed above (be as specific as possible).

1. ___

___

2. ___

___

3. ___

___

I will use these countermeasures to stay on purpose:

1. ___

___

2. ___

___

3. ___

___

To verify and support myself as I bring my life purpose forward, I commit to the following:

The Living-on-Purpose process is a real eye-opener. Most people who go through this process are highly motivated, and chances are you are, too. You either want to get out of the big gaping hole or you want to bring your life-purpose to the next level. Yet at some point along the way, all of us will run into the biggest obstacle there is between living your life purpose and living your life-purpose inverse. And that obstacle is you.

The Living-on-Purpose process is designed to expose you to yourself. The specific outcome you manage to create with your selected action steps is not nearly so important as the recognition you gain regarding how you keep getting in your own way and how you get yourself out of it. Expected obstacles that have tripped you up for decades may disappear almost immediately. Or maybe the counterstrategies you've come up with need to be augmented considerably. Perhaps unexpected obstacles have surfaced. In this case, add the unexpected obstacle to the expected obstacle list and create a new set of counterstrategies.

You may decide to scuttle your action plans almost immediately as it becomes clear that what is listed is not something you actually want to do. This is not a failure. It is an excellent outcome. Getting clear on what you really want to do regarding your life purpose is at least as important as actually doing something about it. In the end, what you learn about yourself is the biggest reward this process affords.

Final Thoughts

Remember those puzzles from childhood that asked you to find George Washington's face hidden in the picture? Once it was pointed out, you couldn't look at the picture without seeing it. Life purposes and life lessons work the same way. Once you start to look for them, they are everywhere to be found. Training your attention to recognize this aspect of yourself is your first step in creating the wonderful life it was always in you to live.

Being a witness to people's awakening to their life purpose and life lesson has been a privilege I hold sacred. Each day as I watch people gain a deeper sense of meaning in their lives, I am grateful to be alive.

Thank you for being you, and thank you for reading *LifePrints*.

APPENDIX I

ARCHETYPAL COMBINATIONS AND CASE STUDIES

Those lines on your palm, they can be read for a hidden part of your life that only those links can say—nobody's voice can find so tiny a message as comes across your hand. Forbidden to complain, you have tried to be like somebody else, and only this fine record you examine sometimes like this can remember where you were going before that long silent evasion that your life became.

—WILLIAM SAFFORD, "TURN OVER YOUR HAND"

All of the material in this appendix is cross-referenced from the finger location descriptions in chapter four. However, if you would like to turn directly to relevant archetypal combinations or case studies, use the following directory to help you find your way.

LIFE-PURPOSE DIRECTORY

Read the information on the pages referenced for each location on which you have highest ranking fingerprints. For each finger location, start by reading the first entry, then work your way to the end to discover which archetypal combinations and case studies apply to you.

Right Middle Finger (Responsibility): Worldly Responsibility (page 196), The Tycoon (page 170)

Left Middle Finger (Integrity): The Mentor (page 199), The Mentor to Artists (page 203), The Mentor to Leaders (page 203), The Pioneer (page 236), The Shaman (page 254)

Right Ring Finger (Creativity): The Artist with Heart (page 229), Dwight D. Eisenhower (page 188), Charles Manson (page 189), Albert Einstein (page 190), The Mentor to Artists (page 203), The High-Profile Person (page 231), Public Impact in the Healing Arts (page 252)

Left Ring Finger (Innovation): The Innovator (page 234), The Pioneer (page 236)

Right Little Finger (Communications): Susan B. Anthony (page 243), Persuasion (page 244)

Left Little Finger (Insight): The On-Again, Off-Again Healer (page 249), Public Impact in the Healing Arts (page 252), The Shaman (page 254)

All highest ranking fingerprints: Palmar Whorls on the Moon (page 259)

LIFE-LESSON DIRECTORY

Read the information on the pages referenced for each location on which you have lowest ranking fingerprints. For each finger location, start by reading the first entry, then work your way to the end to discover which archetypal combinations and case studies apply to you.

Right Thumb (Failure): Breaking the Failure Cycle (page 172), The Loser (page 173)

Left Thumb (Family Issues): Family Issues in the School of Service (page 179), Guilt in the Family (page 214)

Right Index Finger (Powerlessness): Mr. Not Enough (page 216)

Left Index Finger (Blocked Passions): Soap Opera (page 193), Sexual Violation (page 195), Mr. Not Enough (page 216)

Right Middle Finger (Irresponsibility): Learning to Be Responsible (page 198), The Loser (page 173), Worthy of Love (page 211), Mr. Not Enough (page 216), What I Say Matters (page 247)

Left Middle Finger (Guilt Issues): Crumb Work (page 205), Negative Juliet (page 206), Negative L'Oreal (page 209), Worthy of Love (page 211), Guilt in the Family (page 214), Mr. Not Enough (page 216)

Right Ring Finger (Hiding Out): Dealing with Disapproval (page 232)

Left Ring Finger (Disapproval Fears): Dealing with Disapproval (page 232), Lee Harvey Oswald (page 241)

Right Little Finger (Not Speaking Up): True Communications (page 245), Worthy of Love (page 211)

Left Little Finger (Intimacy Issues): Intimacy Issues, Trust, and Surrender (page 256), Sexual Violation (page 195), Negative L'Oreal (page 209), Worthy of Love (page 211), What I Say Matters (page 247)

SCHOOL DIRECTORY

The references listed below are to case studies associated with each school.

The School of Service: Lone Tree on the Plain (page 261), Family Issues in the School of Service/Emily (page 179), Crumb Work (page 205)

The School of Love: Ms. Steamroller (page 168), The Matriarch or The Patriarch (page 177), The Leader with Heart (page 182), Negative Juliet (page 206), Negative L'Oreal (page 209), Susan B. Anthony (page 243), The Butterfly (page 263)

The School of Wisdom: The Wing Walker (page 265), Dealing with Disapproval/ Caroline (page 239)

The School of Peace: Get a Tan (page 266), The Loser (page 173), Mr. Not Enough (see page 216)

ARCHETYPAL COMBINATIONS AND CASE STUDIES

The Doer

The Right Thumb or Both Thumbs as the Life Purpose in an Archetypal Combination

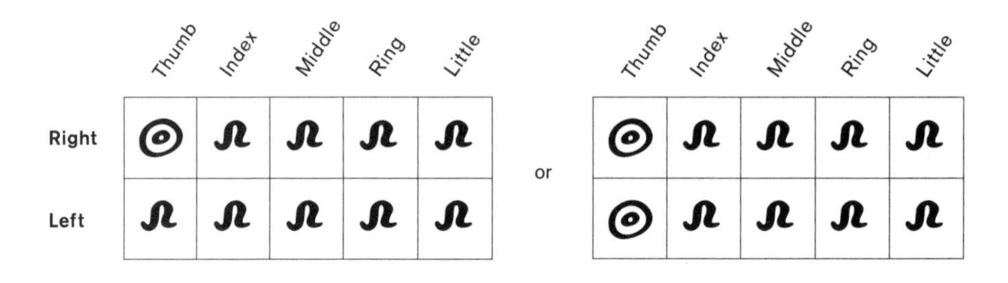

Fingerprint Profile: Whorl on right thumb or both thumbs + eight or nine loops

Life Purpose: Success in the World

Life Lesson: Emotional Connection, Vulnerability Skills

School: Love

Life-Fulfillment Formula: Open your heart and learn the true meaning of success.

Often, when the school is love, the focus of life is relationships: family, friends, spouse. But for Ms. Steamroller, with her Success in the World life purpose, this couldn't be further from the truth. She, like others with similar fingerprints, is challenged to open her heart so that a particular activity-based life purpose may properly emerge.

Ms. Steamroller A full day of reading hands in the sunroom and I was pleasantly tuckered out. Ready for dinner, I was considering my options when SHE marched in. SHE was an extravagantly attired, rather large-ish woman in her midforties with a manner so direct as to shock me back to full attention. "I am the youngest woman ever to graduate from Harvard Law School," she announced in a booming voice. "By the age of thirteen, I had read every book in the main library in Peoria, had climbed El Capitan alone, and by sixteen I had mastered six languages, including Mandarin."

She proceeded to bring her curriculum vitae closer to the current decade as I wondered where all this was headed. "They said out front that you are the resident hand reader here. Well, read these!" And with that, she took the empty seat in front of mine and thrust her two hands, palms up, in my face. Regaining my balance, I repositioned her hands and dove right in.

Ms. Steamroller had hands that very much matched her stated achievements. If I was only partially impressed with her accomplishments, I was truly impressed with her hands. But all was not rosy in her queendom.

Ms. Steamroller told me she had been starting to miss appointments, two in the last three months she said. Her concentration, always impeccable, was leaving her. Was she losing her mind? I could find no indications of neurological problems in her hands, but I did see a series of markers that ancient palmists would have said represented periods of incarceration.

Instead of being hung by her thumbs in some medieval dungeon, my twentieth-century client was feeling boxed in, thwarted by circumstances seemingly beyond her control. "Nincompoop Prison," I declared. "Your mind is fine, but it is getting worn to a nub trying to escape Nincompoop Prison."

"What do you mean?" she asked, no longer employing the five-star general's tone she had brought with her into my office.

"Nincompoop Prison: here you are, working on whatever you are working on, and inevitably you find yourself dependent upon total fools who cannot seem to do anything right. 'Is the whole world filled with nothing but nincompoops?' I can hear you yelling out loud each day, as idiot after darn idiot messes everything up. Now you must use twice as much of your own time to fix the mess as it would have taken you to do the job yourself in the first place."

Ms. Steamroller relaxed her shoulders a bit, Atlas temporarily relieved of her load, as we compared stories of inexcusable incompetence in our employees. We laughed together at the person whom I had asked to make some copies for me. She had copied the blank side of the pages as well as the printed side, *not* by accident. "I didn't know which side you wanted me to copy," she had told me, "so I copied both sides to be safe." She had a better one, Ms. S. said, trumping my tale of woe with a more grand, more unbelievable episode. We were pals now, Ms. Steamroller and I, five-star colleagues surrounded by fools, and I hoped that connection would ease my delicate task of explaining her life-lesson dilemma and its choices.

"All is as it should be," I suggested. "If everyone had your capabilities and determination, they would all be generals and there would be no privates in your army." My client chuckled. "As time moves on, however, your garden keeps growing in size, and no amount of exertion on your part will ever be enough to bring in the entire harvest yourself. It is a healthy fact of your life that at some point you will outgrow your ability to take care of everything you have built. At this point of inevitability lies your moment of truth. To get your garden to grow to its full majesty you must somehow get those with half your initiative to do most of the actual labor.

"How will you do it? Not by intimidation, not by sheer effort of will. Somehow you must get your serfs to care about *your* garden, and to do this your serfs must feel an emotional connection with you. No wonder your head swirls and loses clarity. The challenge is one of heart, not head."

It took a while for Ms. Steamroller to digest the idea of her heart as the key to her happiness, but true to her nature, she buckled down and did a great job integrating the concept. Ms. Steamroller had a lot to do if she was going to connect enough to gain the support she needed to build the queendom she had in mind. But a lot to do is not too much to ask of hands like hers.

Summary Ms. Steamroller needed to open her heart or her worldly success, no matter how large, would represent only a hollow victory. Like Scrooge, money and power would not satisfy the soul's need. Most people with these fingerprints do not have Ms. S.'s ambition (who does?), and as they struggle against the loops life lesson, the life-purpose inverse (failure, bankruptcy) becomes their jailer. Others with these fingerprints flip-flop: years of work without relationship, years of relationship without work. But for owners of this life-purpose map, it is the simultaneous expression of heart *and* results in the world that is the prize being sought.

The Tycoon

The Right Thumb as the Life Purpose in an Archetypal Combination

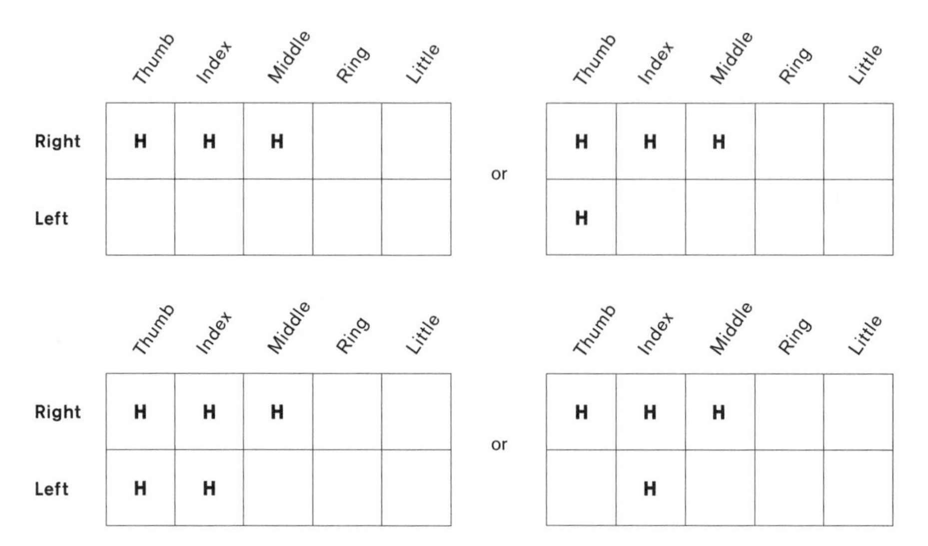

Fingerprint Profile: Right thumb or both thumbs + right index finger or both index fingers + right middle finger as highest ranking prints

Life Purpose: Success + Power + Business = The Tycoon

Life-Fulfillment Formula: Tycoons are designed for exceptionally high achievement.

Tycoons come in a wide range of personality types, from those with a personality naturally inclined toward high achievement (high school valedictorian, president of the student council in college) to the shy, retiring type with no particular ambition. Regardless, all those with Tycoon fingerprints will find their highest sense of personal fulfillment in exceptional achievement. The following story could apply to a Tycoon in any of the four schools and with any life lesson.

Lowenstein and Hart Hart: "Some people think gin is a game of chance. Maybe it is, for them. But for me, I make my income exclusively from gin rummy and there is no chance that I will lose. Oh, I may lose a match, but I have never met another player who has more of my money than I have of his."

Lowenstein: "Gin rummy is a miraculous microcosm of life and the Universe. When things are going right, I can tell you all ten cards my opponent has and what the next three cards of the deck will be. When I have that groove, I am unbeatable and life is grand."

People would crowd around Lowenstein and Hart to watch two consummate masters compete. Lowenstein, the flamboyant genius, would inevitably have the grandest, most satisfying victories over the course of a match. The crowd would be talking about his brilliant maneuvers for hours. However it was Hart, the quiet plodder, who came out on top in the money column. Why am I telling you this, Tycoon candidate? Am I suggesting that plodding beats flamboyance? No.

Here is the secret that hardly anyone noticed at the gin rummy championship: Hart always kept score. Hart's goal was to win money, and as such, he was more interested in the score than Lowenstein was. Lowenstein's goal was to play great gin. Each succeeded at what he was trying to do.

I am not advocating either style of play or life. Be a Hart, be a Lowenstein. Be who you are. But at gin rummy, the money winners are usually the ones who keep score. Useful to know.

Summary In any Tycoon lifetime, no matter the personality type, winners have learned to properly define what success really means.

Breaking the Failure Cycle

The Right Thumb or Both Thumbs as the Life Lesson in an Archetypal Combination

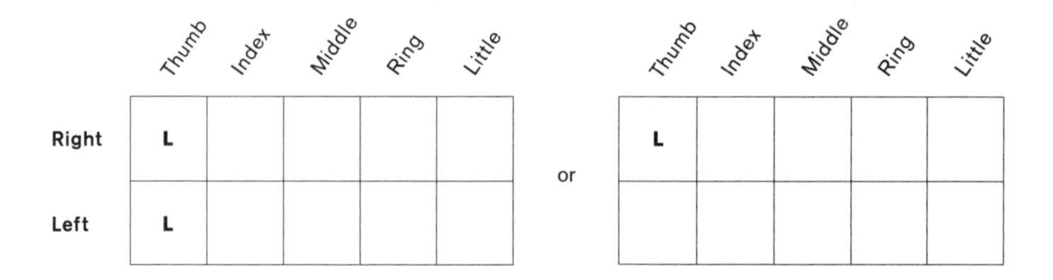

Fingerprint Profile: Right thumb or both thumbs with the lowest ranking print(s)

Life Lesson: Results in the World

Life-Fulfillment Formula: Learn to take projects to completion and your right life appears.

If your lowest ranking fingerprint is on the right thumb or both thumbs, your life assignment is to break out of a pattern of repeated failure and find your true measure of success. For some, this means successfully turning a hobby into a working enterprise (like Tracey's attempt in the story below). For others, the challenge is to appreciate the success they have already achieved. In its more strenuous variation, those with a right thumb life lesson face what seems to be a never-ending supply of insurmountable obstacles (the Will Smith movie *Happyness* is one such story), success being so much sweeter because of the effort it took to get there.

La Fuente "This is it," my friend Tracey announced proudly as I stepped over some broken chairs in the bottom floor of an abandoned apartment complex. Tracey's life dream was to become a restaurant owner, and her eyes beamed as she outlined her vision. Each of the six upstairs apartments would be gutted and turned into individually decorated dining rooms that could be rented by private parties. Downstairs, eighteen tables would be arranged in a circle around the huge fountain that was currently inoperable but could easily be fixed. The restaurant would be called "La Fuente" (The Fountain) with a Mexican/La Playa theme.

We sat down on the edge of the empty fountain, and Tracey shared some stories of prior projects that had not quite succeeded. This time, she assured me, everything was perfect. The building had been a steal at only thirty thousand dollars. Her brother would do all the construction, and Tracey would do the cooking herself. Tracey was a great cook, and I promised to arrive hungry on opening night.

Tracey called that night, near tears. It turned out the city was building a new sewer system on that street. That is why the apartment building was so cheap and had not sold for so long. Everything was being held up in litigation, and it could have been years before water was available.

Tracey never did get to open her Mexican restaurant. She died suddenly less than two years later and is badly missed by her family and friends.

Summary It is not uncommon for those with a right thumb life lesson to get frustrated with the time lag between the success desired and the time required. If this is your life lesson, it is worthwhile to pay close attention to each and every step your projects need for successful completion. The right thumb as the life lesson has thwarted many a talented person, yet I also know those with the same fingerprints who have built something in the world and sustained it over time. Usually they have gone through the same failure cycle as Tracey and simply persevered one step further. Or they found a business partner or mentor along the way who helped them through the hard times. If this is your life lesson, my advice is to hang in there. Get help if you need it. Take small steps that you know you can finish. And keep your eye on the prize.

The Loser

The Right Thumb as the Life Lesson in an Archetypal Combination

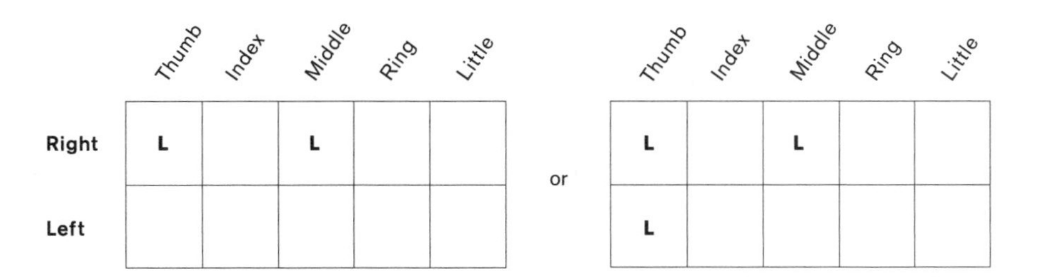

Fingerprint Profile: Lowest ranking prints on right thumb or both thumbs + right middle finger

Life Lesson: Failure + Money Problems = The Loser

School: No school is shown, but the School of Peace is the most common one for The Loser

Life-Fulfillment Formula: Root out that part of you that is convinced you cannot and should not win and become the person it was always in you to become.

The Loser is one of the most fearsome life lessons available. "I never get things right" (right thumb fears) + inappropriate behaviors (the right middle finger life lesson at its worst) combine to give this dragon its fiery breath. Most people have bumped into Loser-like thought streams at one point or another without going down the existential drain. Who among us has never been spotted at The Loser's Lounge, crying in our beer? However, ducking legitimate responsibilities and repeated sabotaging of your success, along with other Loser-as-the-life-lesson reactions, can be more problematic.

Mary Ann Mary Ann got her first credit card and immediately spent way over her credit limit. When the bills arrived, she ignored them. Eventually, a clerk scissored Mary Ann's card in half when she tried to buy some school supplies for her daughter and Mary Ann wrote a bad check to cover the purchase. No health insurance, no auto insurance, no proper tags on her car, late for work, behind on her rent, Mary Ann just hopes she can get through today without running into her former roommate, whose calls she has been ducking.

Given what you have read so far, it may not seem likely that Mary Ann could ever get to the exalted form of her life lesson (The Winner). But she did, and as such she is enjoying a high measure of life-purpose fulfillment. If you have the same life lesson and are residing in the same Loser dungeon, you will probably be interested to find out how Mary Ann managed her escape.

Under pressure from the court to join a twelve-step program or lose custody of her child, Mary Ann took a stringent self-inventory and, looking in the truth mirror, saw the sad eyes of Mary Ann The Loser looking back. Instead of running off or blaming the world, Mary Ann somehow found the courage to maintain eye contact (I contact) and reached out to the desperate side of herself that didn't know how to do anything right. Using support group techniques as a model, big Mary Ann let little Mary Ann know she was not alone. "I won't abandon you. I am right here. It must be hard to feel so frightened. I love you Mary Ann. It is OK." God bless twelve-step programs.

Some people fall right back into their old behaviors five minutes later, but Mary Ann's conversion was real and long lasting. At first, changes were small and incremental. Mary Ann cleaned her apartment. She stopped stealing pennies from the Take-a-Penny, Leave-a-Penny thing at the 7-Eleven. She started to show up for work on time. I would love to tell you that Mary Ann instantly found her pot of gold at the end of the rainbow but . . . actually, I wouldn't want to tell you that because it would be misleading. The truth is, things did not get better right away for Mary Ann. As a matter of fact, The Loser, irritated that its role in her life was being threatened, tried mightily to make a comeback.

Just when Mary Ann was being considered for a higher position with more responsibility, a sheriff came to her workplace and hauled her off downtown for six unpaid parking tickets. Co-workers had to bail her out. How embarrassing. But Mary Ann paid her friends back, even though it took almost a year. The positive feelings generated by living in integrity multiplied themselves over time and eventually Mary Ann started to create a real pot of gold for herself. It wasn't the queen's ransom she had dreamt of in the past, an illusory treasure that would have magically solved all her problems, but she is making a living, supporting herself and her child as a sales trainer. Her success feels all the better because of what she had to go through to earn it.

Summary When the right thumb and the right middle finger are all or part of your life lesson, blind spots tend to skewer your self-evaluation. Early Mary Ann ignored her irresponsibility, never admitting any mistake regardless of the evidence. Some with these fingerprints do just the opposite, falling into pleaser behaviors, seeking validation from others when they can't get it from themselves. The Goldilocks Rule says to expect Too Much and Too Little errors of this kind. Responding to the consequences you've created, learning about yourself as you search for Just-Right solutions—that is the path to The Winner.

Family Connection in the School of Love

The Left Thumb as the Life Purpose in an Archetypal Combination

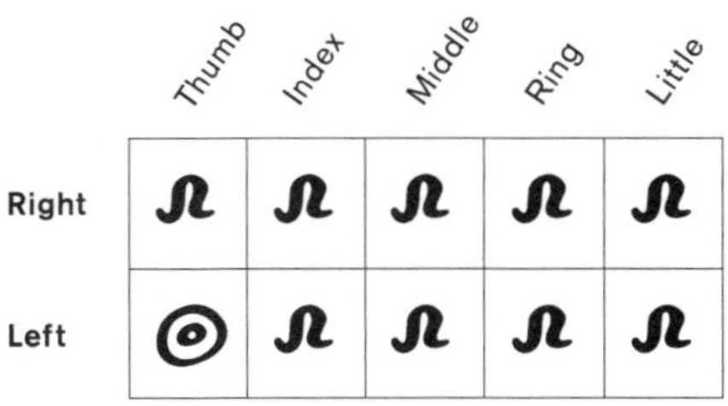

	Thumb	Index	Middle	Ring	Little
Right					
Left					

Fingerprint Profile: Whorl on left thumb + nine loops

Life Purpose: Family Connection

Life Lesson: Vulnerability Skills

School: School of Love (the School of Love is the natural home for a left thumb life purpose)

Life-Fulfillment Formula: Be yourself and find the family connection that you long for.

All students at the Earth University are concerned with family issues, but for those with fingerprints like the ones on the previous page, the ache to gain the inner circle carries extra destruction and resurrection possibilities. With these fingerprints, emotional authenticity developed over time is the only passage to life-purpose satisfaction. Take a ride with me to central Texas, if you will, and let's watch one family doing its thing.

A Wild Evening in Central Texas A hand reading circle, forty-five minutes from Austin, out in the hill country—it had been a beautiful ride, and I was in a particularly mellow mood as I entered a rural ranch house to read another dozen or so hands. As is the custom, I knew nothing of the group I was to read. They could be close friends, total strangers, a men's support group, whatever. In general, the more everyone knows each other the better. Tonight's group knew each other real well; they were three generations of one family. In this case, however, group familiarity was not necessarily in my favor.

First up was grandma—eighty-four and as hard as last Christmas's leftover Corsicana fruitcake. She could be generous when generosity suited her, would not take favors from anyone over twelve years old, and was about as suggestible as hail. Grandma said nothing and showed nothing during her reading. Afterward, she returned to her rocking chair in the circle and warned me to keep telling the truth because "this family needs to hear the gospel and some damn Yankee might be the only person stupid enough to try and smart enough to get it right." I wasn't sure if I was being insulted or praised, but no time to tarry. It was time to read for Miles.

Miles had been openly antagonistic all evening. He took the reading chair, arms folded across his chest, and announced that what was important to him was not in his hands. Besides, Miles went on, he knew whatever he needed to know without some carpetbagger telling him what to think. Did I know how to spell carpetbagger?

Before I could reply, his wife, Judy, and his sister Bertha told him to shut up and leave or shut up and stay. He told them to shut up and do something that is not worth repeating here. Grandma smiled, staring straight ahead without comment as I considered my best exit strategy. Various other family members stood up and expressed their opinions in no uncertain terms. It took several minutes for the furor to die down.

The Jerry Springer Show having subsided, I figured it was my turn to speak. I told Miles that if all these stubborn women wouldn't listen to him maybe he wasn't shouting loud enough. I half shouted, half in fun, "Mind your own beeswax, Bertha!" Miles wasn't sure whether he was being insulted or praised, but, with a sarcastic grin, he ceremoniously placed his hands palms up on his lap, revealing a left-thumb whorl and nine loops. That makes sense, I thought, as I went on.

"Miles, this life of yours is a search for the real meaning of the word 'family.' Fighting for connection in a complex emotional environment where everyone remembers everything forever is exactly what brings you the greatest pleasure as well as the greatest frustration in life. That's where the meaning is for you. Join the club Miles; learn the secret handshake, but don't give in just for the price of admission. Truth be known, the only important thing in your world is the love of your family."

The room had gone quiet. Bertha tried to fill the silence with a bad joke but got shushed. Miles said nothing for a few moments, then extended his hand to shake mine. I extended my hand and Miles pulled his up just as my hand got there. Everyone laughed out loud. I guess I was one of the family now. I continued my readings in the most raucous environment I have ever worked in.

Summary When Miles's game with me was over, it was still the same old Miles seeking love and acceptance from the same old family—and not sure he deserved it. When the life purpose is Family in the School of Love, genuine vulnerability is the only way to get what you need and Miles seemed halfway there, halfway not. As such, his life purpose was halfway awake.

On the other side of this life purpose are those who belong to so-called normal families (whatever that means) and who have developed their vulnerability skills sufficiently to make the Family life purpose shine. Wilma is one. She delights in her role as mother of three and grandmother of six. It is not as if her family never has any problems, but somehow each family problem pulls them closer together. Both of her daughters have Family as their life purpose as well, as do four of her grandkids. With such a good foundation, each of them has a high prognosis for life-purpose satisfaction.

The Matriarch or The Patriarch

The Left Thumb as the Life Purpose in an Archetypal Combination

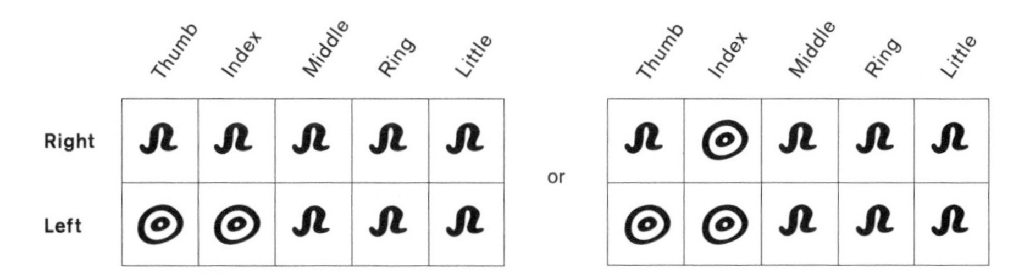

Fingerprint Profile: Highest ranking prints on left thumb + one index finger or both index fingers

Life Purpose: The Matriarch or The Patriarch

Life Lesson: Emotional Authenticity Skills, Vulnerability

School: Love (the most common school for The Matriarch or The Patriarch life purpose)

Life-Fulfillment Formula: Open your heart and unlock the positive Matriarch or Patriarch living inside you.

A positive Matriarch or Patriarch operates as the emotional glue holding a family or community together. The captain of the softball team calling a team meeting, the Scout leader out on a hike with the kids, Mrs. Walton having Thanksgiving dinner on Walton's Mountain, all may be harvesting meaning and fulfillment as The Matriarch or The Patriarch. Or maybe they aren't. Maybe Mrs. Walton feels underappreciated and is secretly planning to run off to Fiji with her tennis instructor. Maybe the Scout leader feels bogged down by parental meddling. Finding and living your life purpose can be tricky business, as this next story demonstrates.

Looking in Unlikely Places Rita's mom had been a negative matriarch extraordinaire, and Rita nearly fell off her chair when I told her The Matriarch was her life purpose. "Don't tell me to get married and have kids," she snapped. The idea of becoming a family-glue person gave Rita the willies. She was forty and a therapist and enjoyed being single.

I told her that maybe The Matriarch in her fingerprints didn't want children. Maybe she wanted a healing center with Rita at its center. Maybe she wanted to start a therapists' organization. The Matriarch often bubbles up to the surface in a person's forties after a certain career level has been established, and it can take any number of forms. One thing was clear: if Rita were the centerpiece of some community she would not make the same mistakes that her mother had made with her. Having considered umpteen possibilities as to what was missing in her life, the fact that Rita had never considered what I was suggesting was an extra clue that it might be her answer.

Summary The early experience of a negative matriarchal figure is common for women with these fingerprints (it is usually their mother) as is a negative early version of the patriarch for men with these fingerprints (usually the man's father). As a matter of fact, it is almost a rarity for this to be otherwise.

It is easy to understand someone's reluctance to become something that is resented so strongly, yet ironically, that is where the meaning is for those on this life path. Being able to look beyond your programming to consider The Matriarch or The Patriarch in a different setting than originally experienced often allows those with these fingerprints to feel good about where their life wants to go.

Family Issues in the School of Service

The Left Thumb as the Life Lesson in an Archetypal Combination

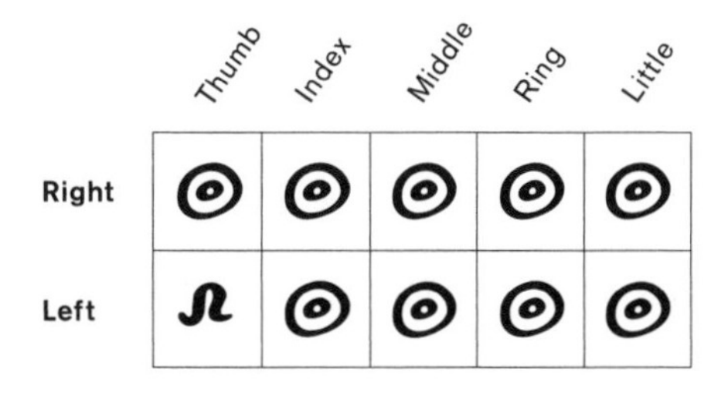

Fingerprint Profile: Lowest ranking print on left thumb, whorls elsewhere

Life Purpose: Service

Life Lesson: Family Connection

School: Service

Life-Fulfillment Formula: How much should you do for family and friends before a healthy concern turns into grossly inappropriate self-sacrifice? The proper answer to this question will lead you to your right life.

With these fingerprints, the fulfillment possibility requires escaping the Too Much trap of living out your family's vision of you (instead of living out your own) without resorting to the Too Little defense of becoming a lone wolf. Almost everyone with these fingerprints falls into both traps. The idea is to catch yourself in the act of falling and correct yourself before a decade or two has slipped through your fingers. This is easier said than done, as this next story illustrates.

Emily The piney woods of east Texas are greener than hardscrabble west Texas, more solid than mossy-mysterious Louisiana just to the east. They have an inclusive embrace, a genuine, not-trying-too-hard beauty all their own. It was here, an hour outside of Nacogdoches, that I read for Emily and her circle of friends.

Emily's home sat at the end of a half-mile dirt road, more an extended driveway really, surprisingly unrutted, almost carpetlike. I parked behind a dozen cars and pickups and followed a path of gardenias toward the front door. There, a porch swing with a commanding view of a distant tree line swayed slightly in the breeze, too new to creak. I half expected to see an apple pie cooling on the window sill and Lassie coming out to greet me. Instead, a note taped to the front door told me to just come in without knocking. I did and took in my surroundings.

The ranch house was simple, refined, spacious, and cozy all at the same time. Though only a few years old, it felt lovingly lived in, as if it had been in the family for generations. Emily's husband had built it himself, I was later to learn. Hospitable, with a firm handshake and clear eyes, Carl quickly excused himself to go upstairs to be with his two young daughters.

Entering the living room, I scanned the wood-paneled walls and looked into the proud faces of great-grandmas and great-grandpas, photos that must have been at least one hundred years old. I felt an ache come over me, a longing for stability over time. Emily offered me one of the two mahogany rocking chairs in front of the fireplace, and I nestled in to read the hands of twelve strangers.

The reading circle proceeded as usual. Tonight's group was all women, and we were bonding and connecting, sharing and laughing together. Emily was the last to be read, and when she opened her hands I quickly realized she had some big decisions to make. Emily loved her family, but it was time to expand her role as spiritual guide and facilitator beyond her close circle of friends to the public at large, the public outside the comfortable confines of the piney woods of east Texas.

Could Carl handle being married to such a woman, or would Emily have to sacrifice her expanding spiritual activities for the sake of family peace? Looking into Emily's hands and back up to her blue eyes, I wondered how best to proceed with her reading. I decided to talk about how meaningful a contribution she was making to an ever-growing community. After everyone had gone, I told Emily about the relationship dilemma that I had seen in her hands.

Emily confided that she had been celibate for over a year. Carl was disgruntled but still affectionate. Emily went on: "I was at a workshop in Dallas last month. Late Sunday night, after most of the others had left, I found myself baring my soul to this young man whose eyes opened up and engulfed me. I felt so fully seen, I wanted to dive in and be embraced forever—until I caught myself mid-dive. I hurriedly made my retreat and drove guiltily home, confused but somehow elated as well, as if sneaking home from my secret lover."

"It is only going to get worse," I suggested. "You can do what you want but you glimpsed your new life, wanted it, and I doubt you are going to get it out of your mind. Not this particular man mind you—your new life."

"Are you saying I should tear up my family over some vague desire for who knows what? My girlfriends say they have desires that they don't act on. So what? That's life."

"Emily, you love Carl and he loves you, right?"

"Yes, but that man last month . . . I can't explain it. He was offering something Carl can't. If I had stayed two more seconds, I don't think I could have stopped myself. Then I come home to my handsome husband, a wonderful man with whom I've built this wonderful life, and nothing. No response at all. What's wrong with me?"

"Have you told any of this to your husband? I have seen this before. Usually, the man or woman is considering leaving a good job or dropping some long-held habit in order to free up more time for spiritual pursuits. In your case, the focus is on your marriage."

"I do not intend to break up my family for anything."

"Good. But if your husband knew how important it was to share what is happening with you—that your life together depended on it—who knows what he would do?"

"But he's not into any of this stuff."

"I know. But listen. Let's say you had this rare disease: kryptonitis. I'll bet Carl would drive to the ends of the earth to help you. He'd read up on kryptonitis, accompany you to kryptonitis support groups, and so on. He didn't pick this as something to be interested in, but that's life. He married you for better or worse, and kryptonitis is just what happens to be the truth of things.

"Emily, you have a form of kryptonitis. It is not a disease and it is not fatal but it is not going away either. If it were clear to your husband that the future of his family depended upon his ability to learn and participate in your rapidly expanding spiritual pursuits, I would not be surprised if he shifted gears. I would bet almost anything he doesn't get that his marriage is at stake—because I am guessing you've never actually told him. That guy last month (a stranger really), do you think he or someone like him is going away? Are you willing to scuttle your spiritual growth activities to keep a lid on it? Is that what either of you actually wants?"

Summary Emily needed Carl to see her as the mystery man had, and for that to happen she needed to reveal more of herself than she had so far. More commonly, people with these fingerprints face dysfunctional family issues in their birth families, in their marriages, and in their community life as well. Abuse, codependency, lives of silent desperation—these themes often crop up when the fingerprints reveal Family as the life lesson. The goal here is to come to terms with your need for connection without becoming a slave to expectations. Some with this chart do just that, balancing family with personal needs. For these fortunate individuals, life purpose blossoms. But in most cases, some epic battle precedes such outcomes.

The Leader with Heart

The Right Index Finger or Both Index Fingers as the Life Purpose in an Archetypal Combination

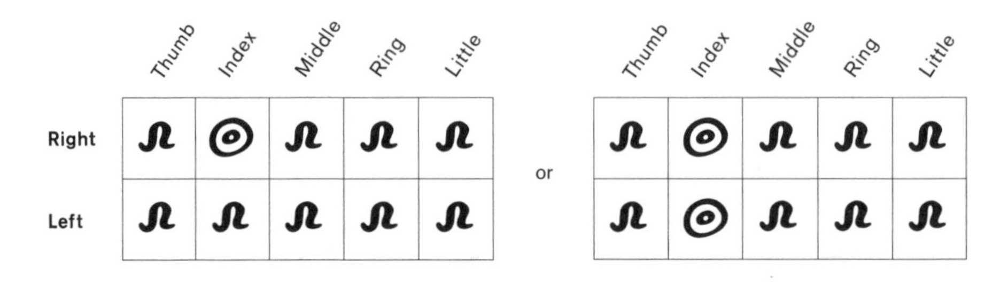

Fingerprint Profile: Highest ranking prints on right index finger or both index fingers, eight or nine loops

Life Purpose: The Leader with Heart

Life Lesson: Emotional Authenticity Skills, Vulnerability

School: Love

Life-Fulfillment Formula: Become the type of person others want to care about and you will find your right life.

Sex, love, and power—wow, what a powder keg! Mastering the combination of heart issues and power issues is quite the challenge, one of the more common challenges that I see in multiple permutations in my practice in California. Partly this is a point of pure arithmetic: the index finger shows the highest fingerprint variance of all digits. This arrangement means that issues of power have an easier time showing up as the life purpose or the life lesson. Is this a long-established truth, a statement of humanity's current state of development, or just a blip on the screen? I wish I knew.

Marion: The Leader with Heart Marion sat down, looked me straight in the eyes, and announced herself ready for the reading. Her hands appeared capable, intelligent, and ambitious, one of the most capable pairs of hands I have ever seen. Although well paid as an executive secretary, she told me, she had no idea what to do with her life. She hoped her reading would give her some sense of direction.

As is so often the case, simply to announce the life purpose would accomplish nothing. "Find love and closeness, Marion, unlock the emotional power you need to become The Leader with Heart." This statement would just be words at this point. For the words to come alive they needed to relate more specifically to the world in which Marion lived.

"Your life purpose involves certain issues of power," I began, "but to understand just what is indicated, we need to talk about the type of men you have selected for relationships. From what I can see, you are attracted only to men who know exactly what they want and go directly after it. No internal debate. A man's gotta do what a man's gotta do. Do you recognize the type?"

"Absolutely. I have married three of these. On closer inspection, they turned out not to be the men of principle I once believed them to be. By the same token, in the last three years I have dated several men who weren't strong enough for me. I am wondering if men can really handle my power. That is what I am working on in therapy."

"Marion, here is part one of the key to finding your life purpose: when you feel insecure about your life choices, you tend to become attracted to men who seem to possess the sense of certainty you wish you had for your own life. When you follow this urge, you become a caboose on his train with outcomes not in your favor. Other times, you pick men weaker than yourself to deflect attention away from your own uncertainty. This is not to indict you for bad deeds, Marion. I have similar markings in my own hands. It is just that until you can contend with your helpless side in a more authentic way, your life purpose will continue to elude you."

"Are you saying I should introduce myself to men as helpless?"

"Yes, Marion. I like it! Hi, I am Marion. I've dropped my hankie and can't seem to find it. Hi, I'm Marion and I can't screw in my own light bulb, you big strong man you."

"You're kidding."

"Yes, I am kidding. But only partially. I am suggesting that until you can get in touch with the helpless Marion, the powerful Marion will be hamstrung. Of course, you are not *only* helpless Marion. You are 98 percent competent, capable Marion. This 98 percent is easy enough to get to; you do it every day. But somehow she cannot, by herself, unlock the door to your life purpose.

"See if you can follow the soul psychology algebra here, Marion. One: you are a Leader with Heart and have been from before your birth. Living this life purpose means bringing The Leader with Heart into your awareness, allowing her to make the life-scale choices, using her as your daily compass. Two: to get to The Leader with Heart, you need a heart capable of walking such a path, a good-at-emotional-connections heart. For you, this means wrestling with the disowned side of your emotional nature: the helpless, needy Marion. If you can do so, you will no longer appear so invulnerable. For a Leader with Heart, this is crucial. Further, this emotionally expanded you is not afraid to meet available men of equal passion and power. Only this you is ready to live your life purpose, and for this you, almost any career you pick would turn out fine.

"Say this Marion becomes a soccer coach. Your team would gladly run through a brick wall for you. Why? Because they feel close enough to you to care enough to do so. *And it is this effort, put forth in response to your emotional connection to your team, that makes the outcome so rewarding—not the score of the game.* Here is your big payoff in life, Marion—what makes it all worthwhile. Your life goal is to become powerful without giving up your heart in the process. In effect, your job is to find the capacity to love and be loved first, hence our visit to your relationship history. Only afterward can the high achiever in you find true success."

"OK, I can agree with that. But what should I do? I can't just pick up and walk out, put a sign on a storefront that says 'Leader with Heart,' and expect to be in business this Friday."

"Good point, Marion. As a matter of fact, if you give it some more thought, as I expect you will in the coming days, you will probably think of several more obstacles to overcome before your Leader with Heart is fully operational in your career. My suggestions are twofold. First: start where you are. Tomorrow, go to work and pretend that you are The Leader with Heart. See how it feels to be wearing this invisible hat. Don't do anything in particular, just try on the hat and see if it feels right. If it does, start sounding and looking more like someone who is wearing this hat and see what comes your way.

"Second, pay more attention to the 2 percent damsel Marion and hear her voice as well. You may want to keep a journal for a few weeks or draw her or talk to your therapist about her and see what she may offer. I do believe she is your ally in disguise.

"I could probably offer a dozen more suggestions, but why bother? Why tell Beethoven how to compose music? You are a problem solver extraordinaire. When you get moving consciously toward your life purpose, there is no end to the good ideas you are likely to have. Look at those capable thumbs. I have thumb envy sitting here in your presence. I am not worried about you, Marion. I am sure you can accomplish anything you put your whole being into."

Summary Marion's story highlights the issue inherent in any achievement-based life purpose that has a life lesson composed of seven or more lowest ranking loops. Before the talents available to this person can bring the meaning that the achiever seeks, the loops life lesson demands attention. Open your heart, Leaders in the School of Love, and find yourself in the life you always wanted.

The Big Shot

The Right Index Finger as the Life Purpose in an Archetypal Combination

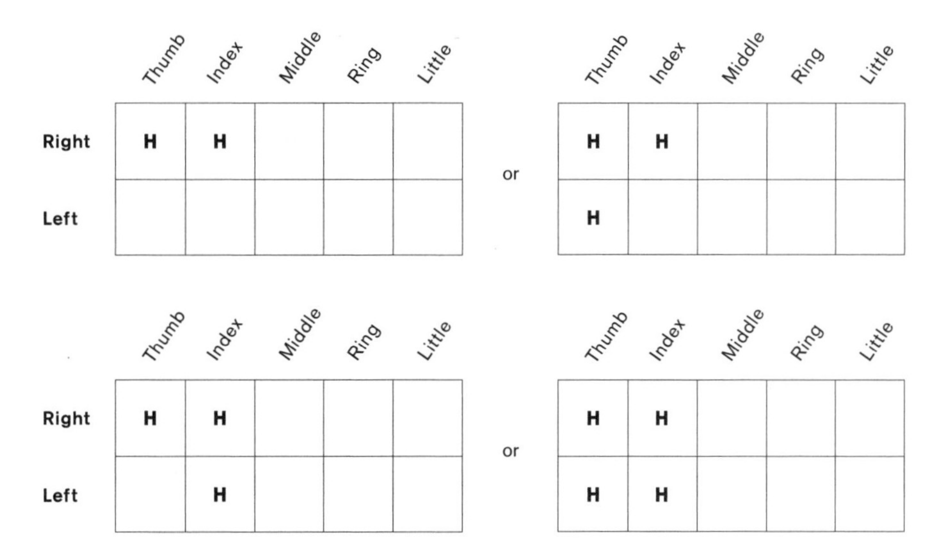

Fingerprint Profile: Right thumb or both thumbs + right index finger or both index fingers as the highest ranking fingerprints (The Doer + The Leader = The Big Shot)

Life-Fulfillment Formula: Are you willing to believe that you are a high achiever?

Calling someone a big shot usually carries a pejorative inflection: "Who do you think you are anyway?" However, at the IIHA we use The Big Shot in the most positive light. To succeed at The Big Shot life purpose means becoming self-focused, setting high standards, and risking failure by putting yourself at stake in meeting those standards. Rising to prominence in their field, Big Shots gain satisfaction by creating results that make a difference in the world.

Ironically, the majority of Big Shots do all they can to avoid positions of authority well into their forties, so if you have these fingerprints and you are younger than forty-five, you are more than likely in the early phases of this life purpose. Make sure you are not sabotaging your own success. If you are forty-five or older, the question becomes: will you accept your appropriate role as a man or woman of influence or will you abdicate your authority?

The Prima Donna

The Big Shot + The Artist as the Life Purpose in an Archetypal Combination

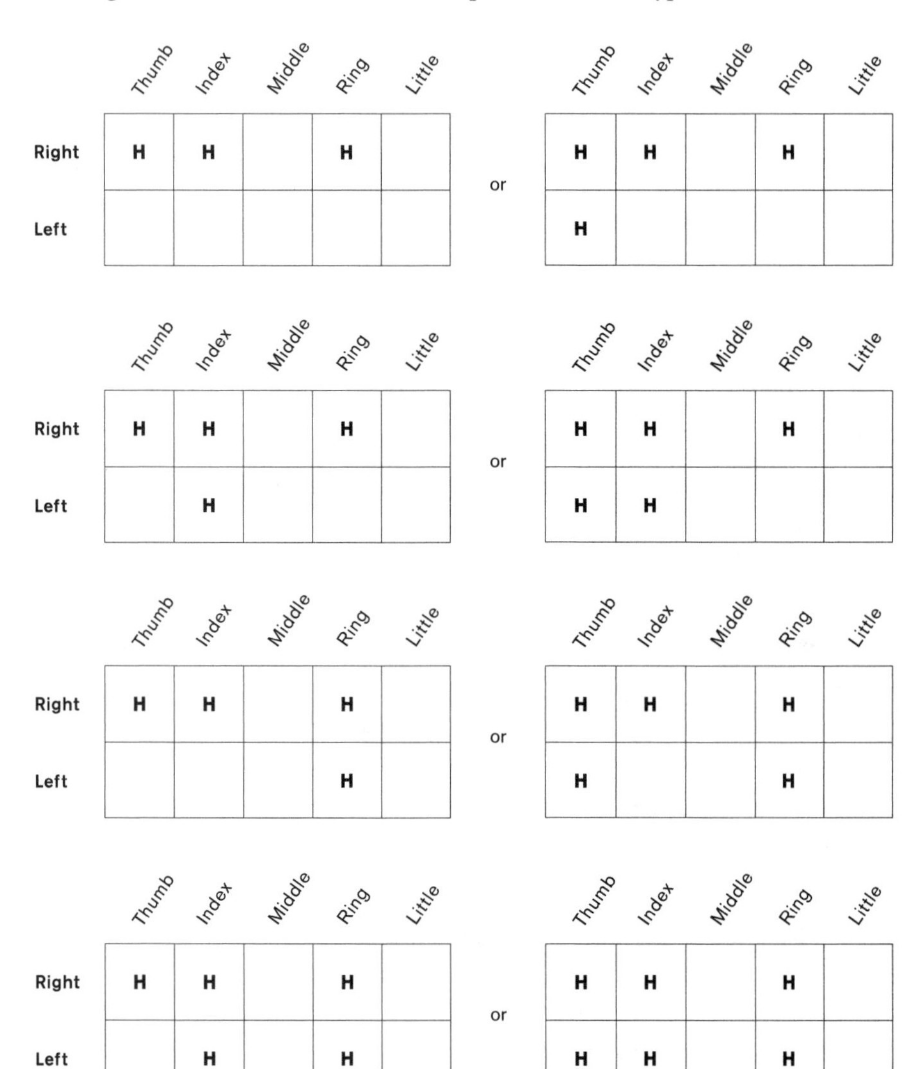

	Thumb	Index	Middle	Ring	Little
Right	H	H		H	
Left					

or

	Thumb	Index	Middle	Ring	Little
Right	H	H		H	
Left	H				

	Thumb	Index	Middle	Ring	Little
Right	H	H		H	
Left		H			

or

	Thumb	Index	Middle	Ring	Little
Right	H	H		H	
Left	H	H			

	Thumb	Index	Middle	Ring	Little
Right	H	H		H	
Left				H	

or

	Thumb	Index	Middle	Ring	Little
Right	H	H		H	
Left	H			H	

	Thumb	Index	Middle	Ring	Little
Right	H	H		H	
Left		H		H	

or

	Thumb	Index	Middle	Ring	Little
Right	H	H		H	
Left	H	H		H	

Fingerprint Profile: Right thumb or both thumbs + right index finger or both index fingers + right ring finger or both ring fingers as highest ranking fingerprints (The Big Shot + The Artist, or The Big Shot in the Spotlight)

Life-Fulfillment Formula: Find the appropriate stage for your talents and you will be happy.

The Big Shot life purpose often combines with other prints to form a more complex life purpose like the eight Prima Donna charts shown opposite. Artistry at a high level of success or succeeding in the spotlight is the meaningful achievement available to owners of such fingerprints. This is one of the more common archetypal combinations. A recent class with two very different personality types having more or less the same fingerprints comes instantly to mind.

Thelma and Louise Thelma was six feet tall and seemed bigger than that. She had a persona that dominated any room. Any room? I mean any airplane hangar. Thelma was an actress but hadn't worked at her chosen profession for several years. The first day of class, Thelma asked if we could change one of the class dates to conform better to her husband's work schedule. The class found an alternative date. But that was not the end of Thelma's requests. Thelma needed the starting time to change and could we take our lunch break a little earlier? Thelma also needed to revamp her payment schedule and, and, and. . . .

After a while it became clear that Thelma was a Prima Donna in search of an audience and the class had been kidnapped for the role. Somehow, someway, one hour of each class seemed to become entirely about Thelma's special requirements. Had she an appropriate stage for her talents, she would not have found the need to dominate class time so completely. Eventually, Thelma took a part at a local playhouse, and her behavior in class shifted—but not completely. Her rightful stage was much bigger than the one she had found, though she was definitely moving in the right direction.

Louise had the same fingerprints but a completely different personality. She never raised her hand in class and was barely audible when she did speak. Her challenge was to get over her shyness sufficiently for her Prima Donna to see the light of day.

Summary If you are a Prima Donna and you are like Louise, you would do well to check your out-there-in-the-spotlight thermostat to see if it needs to be tweaked a wee bit. If your personality is closer to Thelma's, the question is: do you need a bigger stage to showcase your talents?

Three Prima Donnas

Now here is an interesting threesome: Dwight D. Eisenhower, Charles Manson, and Albert Einstein.* Imagine being on a deserted island with these three fellows. All three have fingerprint patterns that, although not identical, have more in common than you might have guessed.

Dwight D. Eisenhower

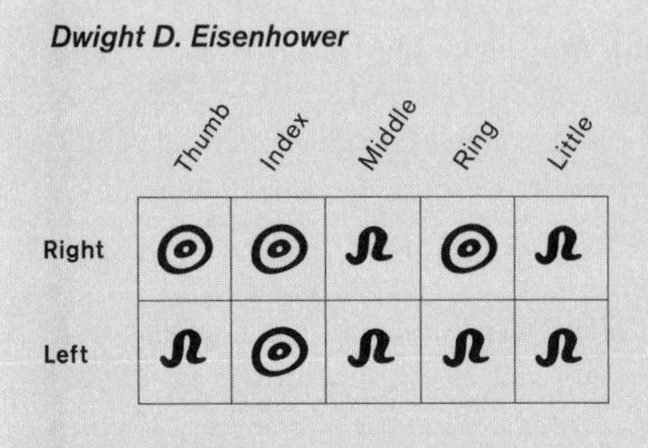

Life Purpose: The Famous Big Shot, The Effective Leader in the Spotlight

Life Lesson: Emotional Connection (Six loops tie for the lowest ranking print.)

School: Service

Life-Fulfillment Formula: Your heart is the key to unlocking big success.

Ike has a standard Prima Donna life purpose with whorls on both index fingers favoring the leadership side of the equation. Had the fingerprints been reversed, whorls on both ring fingers and a single whorl on the right index, the interpretation would be The Influential Artist as the life purpose and, no doubt, someone else would have been in charge of D-day.

Here, the ring finger whorl is more of an indication of the size of the stage that Eisenhower's leadership required. Famous, In the Spotlight, Effective Leadership is his fulfillment point. Effective Leaders have learned to delegate responsibility. Even if Ike were the best cannon cleaner in the whole darn army, even if clean cannons save lives, the free world could not afford to have the head of all European operations exposed on the front lines. If you have fingerprints like Eisenhower's, you too will have to find the appropriate application of your true talents.

* I got Eisenhower's fingerprints from Andre Washington, Manson's (and Ted Bundy's; see page 227) from *Crime and Mental Disease in the Hand* by Paul Gabriel Tesla, and Albert Einstein's came via K. Foong in Malaysia.

Charles Manson

	Thumb	Index	Middle	Ring	Little
Right	Loop	Whorl	Loop	Whorl	Loop
Left	Loop	Radial loop	Loop	Loop	Loop

Note: The loop with the arrow is the symbol used to denote the radial loop.

Life Purpose: The Famous Leader (doing his own thing)

Life Lesson: Emotional Connection

School: Love

Life-Fulfillment Formula: Your heart is the key to unlocking The Famous Leader.

Here's a look at someone who may have lived his life-purpose inverse. Charles Manson's fingerprints, though not exactly a Prima Donna combination, are those of a Famous Leader and not all that different from Ike's. The usual life-purpose inverse for Famous Leaders would be feelings of powerlessness combined with a sense of I-don't-belong. Given the circumstances of Manson's life, it would not be a great leap to conclude that such was the crux of his psychology. Of course, he did achieve a form of leadership. He became the leader of the cult he'd created, a role he no doubt enjoyed immensely. But it is hard to imagine the Sharon Tate murders being the ultimate fulfillment of his true life purpose.

Albert Einstein

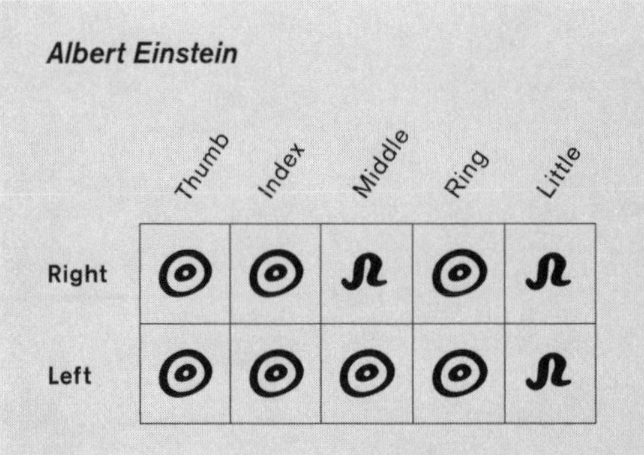

Life Purpose: The Prima Donna + The Mentor

Life Lesson: What I Have To Say Is Important

School: Service

Life-Fulfillment Formula: Can you speak and be heard? If you can, good things are bound to happen.

Albert Einstein's fingerprints include whorls in all the same places as Eisenhower's plus a few extra, the important addition being the whorl on the left middle finger, the mark of The Mentor. Put it all together and you get Prima Donna + The Mentor. The Mentor is someone other people look up to because of the obvious integrity he displays. I would say that Albert Einstein lived up to his life purpose.

Einstein's life lesson is about speaking out. Did you know that he wrote to President Roosevelt encouraging the building of the atom bomb despite his reservations about using it? Or that in the 1950s he spoke out in favor of civil rights? Apparently, at some point, Einstein found his voice and brought his life purpose forward. (See also page 248 for more information about Albert Einstein's fingerprints.)

Reclaim Your Power

The Right Index Finger or Both Index Fingers as the Life Lesson in an Archetypal Combination

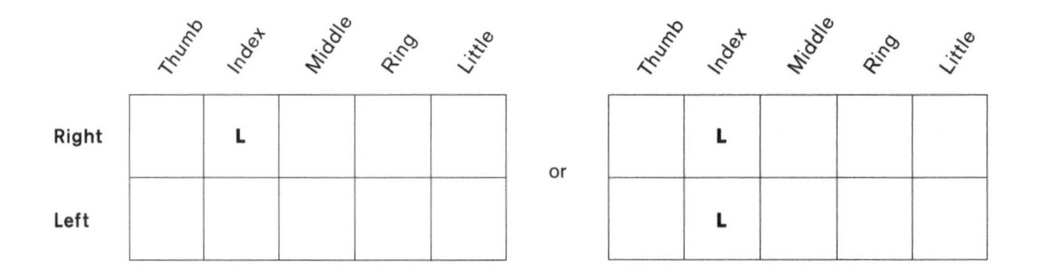

Fingerprint Profile: Lowest ranking fingerprints on right index finger or both index fingers

Life Lesson: Reclaim Your Power

Life-Fulfillment Formula: Reclaim your power and become the person you wish to be.

The right index finger as the lowest ranking print or both index fingers as the lowest ranking print is a common life lesson. For people with these fingerprints, the range of experiences is wide, from those working hard to clarify their desires to people in total life crisis due to repeated violation, up to and including physical abuse. In each case, no matter the highest ranking fingerprint(s) or the school involved, owners of these prints are challenged to ask what would it look like to really be in their power and compare that picture to current circumstances.

The Sheriff We are in the Old West. A sheriff is on patrol. Seeing a gun pointing at him from a dark alley, he pulls his own revolver and shoots the bad guy dead. Only it turns out there was no bad guy. It was a kid with a toy gun. The sheriff's mistaken identification has resulted in tragedy. Feeling terrible, the sheriff decides to hang up his guns. Hearing that the Dodge City sheriff does not wear a gun, every bad guy in the Old West moves into town. They rob the bank three times a day, but the sheriff will not resort to violence. They shoot hats off old ladies' heads just for sport and the sheriff stoically looks on. But when the bad guys start shooting at the feet of the blind man, yelling "Dance! Dance!" well, that's too much.

The sheriff goes upstairs, opens the chest where he has placed his pearl-handled revolvers (the right heroic theme song plays in the background), and once again armed, he strides into the saloon to the jeers and guffaws of the men in black hats. Bang, bang. When the smoke clears, the bad guys are all gone, Dodge City is safe again, and the blind guy goes on to invent the Internet.

Summary The Dodge City sheriff was not a coward. He put his guns away in an attempt to be honorable, but it was a mistaken attempt. Only repeated and escalating violations of his territory convinced him to strap his guns back on. Whenever there is a Reclaim Your Power life lesson, there is always some power giveaway perpetrated with honorable intent. Whether the guns represent a particular talent put on hold because of financial necessity or some lifestyle choice abandoned due to family needs, or something else, all reclaim-your-power persons are challenged to recognize the error of their ways and strap their guns back on.

Living Your Passions/Amelia Earhart

The Left Index Finger as the Life Purpose in an Archetypal Combination

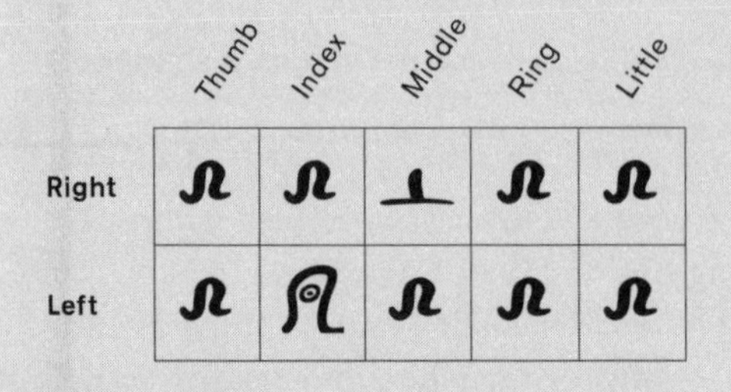

Fingerprint Profile: Highest ranking fingerprint on the left index finger (the peacock)

Life Purpose: LiveYour Passions

Life Lesson: Dot your i's, cross your t's (right middle finger is the lowest ranking print)

School: Love

Life-Fulfillment Formula: Do what your heart tells you to do, but don't forget to check your gas gauge.

The fingerprints above belong to the famous aviator Amelia Earhart.* It is difficult to appreciate the utter fascination and hero worship associated with the aviation pioneers of the early twentieth century, but send your imagination back in time and picture the newsreel and newspaper accounts of a lone female adventurer going where no woman had gone before.

Amelia's handprints revealed the line formations of one with a strong exploratory nature. In combination with her Live Your Passions life purpose, her career choice is less than shocking. But add a large dose of extra pride, also visible in her hands, to a right middle finger life lesson, and we have all the ingredients we need for a tragic fate reminiscent of Icarus.

At her best, Amelia would courageously step outside the normal boundaries, escaping societal pressures that would unfairly restrict her freedom. But her own best friend (her willingness to bend the rules) could also be her worst enemy. As I saw her handprints for the first time and read her fingerprints, I realized that Amelia was just the type of woman to go outside the lines one time too often.

Her ultimate destiny remains a mystery to this day, but her hands bear testimony to a fatal flaw strong enough to bring her down: Amelia—please—check your gas gauge. It may be too far to the next fill-up, and the price for running on empty may be more than you can afford.

* I got Amelia Earhart's fingerprints (and Susan B. Anthony's; see page 243) from *Lion's Paws* by Nellie Simmons Meier.

Summary Those with Live Your Passions as the life purpose are an interesting group. For some, just knowing what they want can be the hardest thing in the world. Others are clear about what they want, it is just that so many obstacles seem to stand in the way.

If you have the Live Your Passions life purpose, the best advice is to do whatever you choose to do for your life's work, but make sure *you* really want to be doing it. In the long run, this is all that really matters. At least Amelia died doing her own thing. There is no better consolation for someone with her fingerprints.

Soap Opera

The Left Index Finger as the Life Lesson in an Archetypal Combination

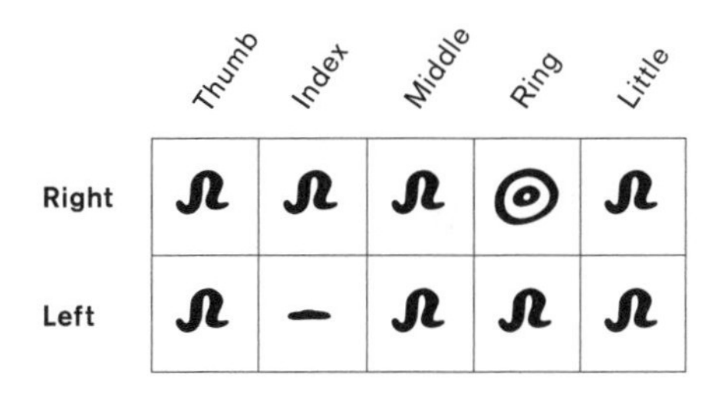

Fingerprint Profile: Whorl on the right ring finger, arch on left index finger, eight loops

Life Purpose: The Artist, The Individualist

Life Lesson: Living Your Passions, Protecting Your Boundaries, Preventing Violation

School: Love

Life-Fulfillment Formula: Put an end to emotional violations and fuel your creativity.

This exact fingerprint combination is another common one. At their best, Soap Opera persons find their passion and unlock their creativity. At their worst, power battles and issues of violation keep the neighbors up at night and leave creativity short of the fuel it needs for ignition.

With the left index finger as the life lesson, your challenge is to protect your boundaries and reclaim your passions or you face the possibility of falling into The Violation Trap—the ongoing systematic disregard of your wants, desires, needs, or rights. This may include:

- Going along with others' agendas to fill the void of not having your own
- Leaving relationships as a form of confrontation avoidance

- Agreement at any cost (or its opposite, constant relationship battles that drain you dry)
- Outright invasion, emotional or physical abuse or both, codependency

Let's see how this theme plays out in the following story.

Gina Sexy Gina, a passionate redhead, married the captain of the football team, only to find herself a football coach's wife. Every time he moved up his career ladder, Gina had to move to a new college town and start her own life all over again. Gina was definitely *not* living *her* passions. Worse, it had been so long since she had made a life choice for herself, she didn't even know anymore how to know what she wanted. The big gaping hole had Gina in its grip.

All that changed one afternoon. Gina was walking across the campus on her way to the football field. They must still be in the locker room, she thought to herself, as she took a seat on the empty bleachers. Gina was in a bubble of her own dark thoughts when she noticed that she was not the only person in the stadium. A lone runner slowly came into view, limping around the track. He struggled to cover the last fifty yards and sat down in the stands, not realizing he had company. Seeing the braces on his legs for the first time, for some unknown reason, Gina found herself going over to talk to him, and so began the end of Gina's big gaping hole. One thing led to another, and Gina eventually became a physical therapist. All she really needed, it turned out, was to step outside her own I-Don't-Know-What-I-Want soap opera for a little while.

Summary The Validity of the Personality says that to be the advanced version of your emotional archetype, you must (1) be your type, and (2) integrate your opposite archetype. For this unhappy live-your-passions type, a boost of genuine consideration for another person was just the medicine she needed to find out what her own desires *really* were.

Sexual Violation

The Left Index Finger as the Life Lesson in an Archetypal Combination

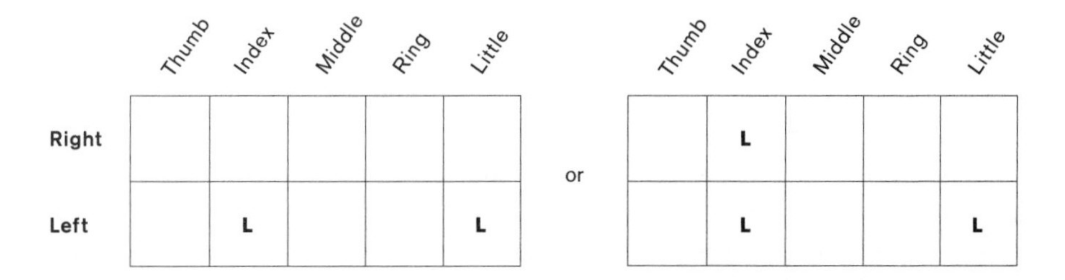

Fingerprint Profile: Lowest ranking prints on left index finger or both index fingers + left little finger

Life Lesson: Boundary Issues + Intimacy Issues

Life-Fulfillment Formula: Recover from sexual violation and reclaim your life.

I see clients with fingerprint combinations like these more often nowadays than I did when I started to read fingerprints. They come in with life stories ranging from the mild (not owning your power in a marriage) to the gory (sexual and emotional abuse), from the victim role to that of the perpetrator, sometimes taking both roles at different stages of their lives.

One man I read for recently had an interesting version of this life lesson. A teacher for over thirty years, he had been accused of sexual improprieties (falsely, he told me) by a twelve-year-old girl. He was on forced leave and was at a loss as to how to prove he didn't do what the girl claimed. If you have this life lesson, sexual violation will work its way into your life sooner or later, one way or another. Nothing can be done to keep this from happening. The idea is to face the challenge head-on and learn what you can from the experience.

Carey Carey's father began abusing her sexually before she was two years old. Carey's mother would hold her down, her father would do his thing, and Carey was left with the shock and trauma. When Carey was seven, her father abandoned the family (by then there were two more children) and Carey's grandmother moved in, ostensibly to help with the housework. Instead, Carey's grandmother turned out to be at least as cruel as Carey's father had been. She browbeat and physically beat Carey, making her do all the cooking and housework for the patchwork family of five. Carey's life was a living hell, but she was just a kid and it was the only life she knew.

Occasionally, Carey was allowed to watch thirty minutes of television, and at Christmas, Carey always got a present (although it was usually an apron or some kitchen appliance). By the time Carey was old enough to figure out that this was not how everyone else lived, her brain had scrambled all the messages it had received, and for Carey, love and abuse were stored in the same set of neurons. She couldn't feel one without the other response being part of the package.

You can guess that her first serious relationship did not go smoothly. Nor her second. But today, Carey is happily married. She is a therapist, specializing in helping abused women. Carey went through hell (and still does to some degree) to pull herself together. Years of therapy, a dozen intense workshop programs, more therapy. Carey needed to get through the shock that had numbed her out to find the Carey that was fully alive one layer below. And she has. I am absolutely inspired by Carey's courage and determination.

Summary One of the toughest life lessons available at the Earth University, this hidden wound emanates from the soul level and was actually present before the terrible events that came afterward. Accepting this, maybe the healing process can be accelerated and the wound, now sufficiently exposed (and one hopes, now healed), can somehow, some way, be a doorway into whatever life purpose is indicated by the highest ranking fingerprints.

Worldly Responsibility

The Right Middle Finger as the Life Purpose

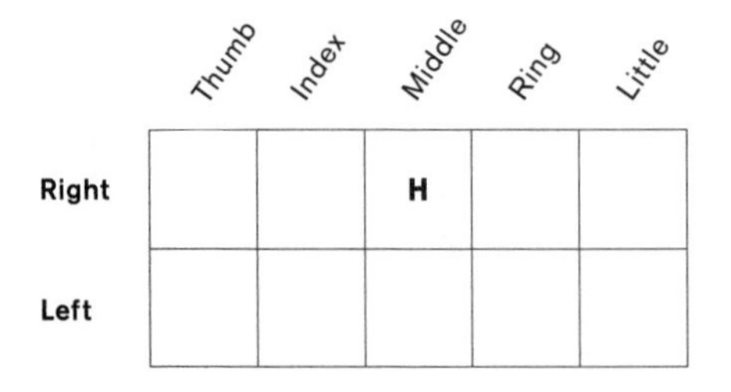

Fingerprint Profile: Highest ranking fingerprint on right middle finger

Life Purpose: Responsibility in the World, The Businessperson

Life-Fulfillment Formula: Bring integrity into your life and find the financial success you seek.

Responsibility, integrity, and accountability are all key attributes for a right middle finger life purpose. On a more philosophic level, the right middle finger is symbolic of any process whereby pain and limitation yield growth and awareness. The educational possibility inherent in suffering and loss is highlighted in the glove compartment story that follows. The right middle finger can also be seen as representing the difference between external values learned from others and internal values based upon personal reflection. The void story that follows illustrates this other right-middle principle.

The Glove Compartment Exercise Think you have a long commute? For a little over a year, I commuted from Houston, Texas, to San Francisco. By car. After one particularly long trip, eager to get home, I crossed the Texas border somewhere in the middle of flat, desert nowhere and, upping my speed to ninety, arrived home at 5 A.M. Too wired to sleep, I sorted through the stack of mail sitting on my desk. One envelope had the new sticker for my license plate. I tossed it through the passenger side window and got into my car, trying to think of a restaurant open at 5:30 A.M. Sunday morning. Concentrating hard to stay within the speed limit, the only vehicle on the road in all of west Houston, I got pulled over. My sticker was three days overdue. "Here is your citation, sir." The state police can be maddeningly polite. Showing the proper sticker, which I swore I would affix momentarily, cut no ice whatsoever. Ouch, an expensive breakfast.

The sun was up as I returned home, the house still quiet. A sticker ticket? Half the cars in Texas have no license plates and gun racks holding automatic weapons, but here I am at the speed limit getting a ticket for a three-days-too-late sticker (two days, five hours, and thirty minutes late, to be precise). Unbelievable. In my most "What-is-the-universe-trying-to-tell-me?" mode, I tried to take my life apart, seeking deeper meaning, but my life was too big to look at. Instead, I opened my glove compartment and started going through the accumulated clutter. Some worn-out batteries, a flashlight with more worn-out batteries, hmmm, what could that mean? Maps. One glove. Oh, look at this. I turned some shade of purple as I came across a paper with various notes reminding me of something I had been trying to forget. My super-guilty reaction informed me that this was the clue I had been searching for. I took a deep breath and resolved to clear up my mess first thing after I slept—all of a sudden I was incredibly tired.

I had almost completely erased my irresponsibility from my mind until the ridiculous ticket and a glove compartment check aroused my attention. After a nap, I cleared up the piece of old business (it wasn't nearly as bad as I feared), put some new batteries in the flashlight, folded the maps properly, and bought a new set of calfskin gloves that felt really good when I put them on. Though it was only a glove compartment, at least one part of my life was in exactly the condition I wanted it to be. It felt good to know that.

The Void Sylvia was a handsome woman, professional, late twenties I guessed. As she came in for her reading, I thought she seemed very present and yet somehow far away, a woman wrestling with a mystery. No doubt it would all come together when I saw her hands. We proceeded to my office.

Various markings led me to conclude that Sylvia was going through a kind of spring cleaning. The problem was that when she eliminated all that did not belong in her life, there seemed to be nothing left. Sylvia filled me in on the details. A lawyer by profession, Sylvia was feeling uncomfortably insecure, without reference points. Her current job was completely untenable, her boyfriend of three years had left her, and her dad, also a lawyer, had died a year ago.

I told Sylvia she had entered The Void. "After all your hard work to become a lawyer and move up the organizational ladder, you are lost. There are no signposts, yet you must go on. Perhaps, in your soul's wisdom, you have entered The Void to challenge each assumption that has shaped your life to date. Who knows what you will eventually decide, but one thing is clear: you have been living your life based upon criteria that are no longer your own. It is time to find out what you truly value."

Summary Each of us is challenged to learn from adversity. Since her dad's death, Sylvia had become more and more aware that her life was built on her family's values, not her own. Her opportunity was to turn her discomfort into an ally, to stare into the truth mirror of personal accountability, and slowly allow this increased self-awareness to inevitably uncover more information about her life purpose.

Learning to Be Responsible

The Right Middle Finger as the Life Lesson

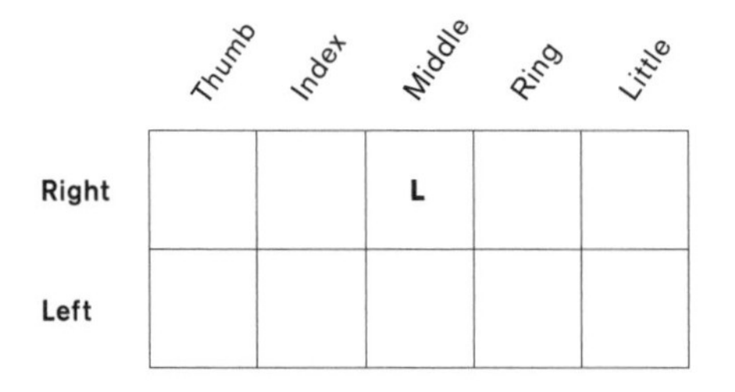

Fingerprint Profile: Lowest ranking fingerprint on right middle finger

Life Purpose: Worldly Responsibilities

Life-Fulfillment Formula: You must take responsibility in all areas of your life, or all is lost.

When the right middle finger becomes the lowest ranking print, expect irresponsibility to creep into a person's life and expect that person not to notice it. Those doing well with this life lesson learn from this mistake, and the emergence of their life purpose is the blessed outcome.

Paul and Paula Paul wants to become a pharmacist, Paula a veterinarian. They are both still in line late Friday afternoon as the college registration office closes. Coming back on Monday morning, they are each informed that there is no late registration in their program and the next opportunity is not until the following September. "September!" Pleading and histrionics fall on deaf bureaucratic ears.

Ten years later: Paul eventually dropped out and never finished college. His right middle finger life lesson is no more advanced than it was during his college years. Paula is a different story. The registration debacle shifted her entire relationship with the world of responsibility. Hard as it was to admit, Paula realized that if she was going to get where she wanted to go, it was ultimately *her* responsibility to get there. After all, whose life was it? She switched her major to political science and is now an assistant professor at the university. She finally paid off her student loans this year. Life-lesson progress is never easy, but the payoff is well worth the effort.

Summary Any lowest ranking fingerprint on the right middle finger creates this life lesson. If the lowest ranking print turns out to be a tented arch, expect irresponsibility to be greatly increased. Tented arches have the highest denial factor of the four schools, and the right middle finger holds the same dubious distinction among the ten fingers. Put the two together and the possibility for unconscious inappropriate behaviors goes through the roof. If *you* have a tented arch here as your lowest-ranking fingerprint, you probably borrowed this book from a friend and will never return it, getting uppity if your friend asks for it back at some later point. Or maybe that is the old version of you, one that you have worked diligently to put behind you. What do you think?

The Mentor

The Left Middle Finger or Both Middle Fingers as the Life Purpose in an Archetypal Combination

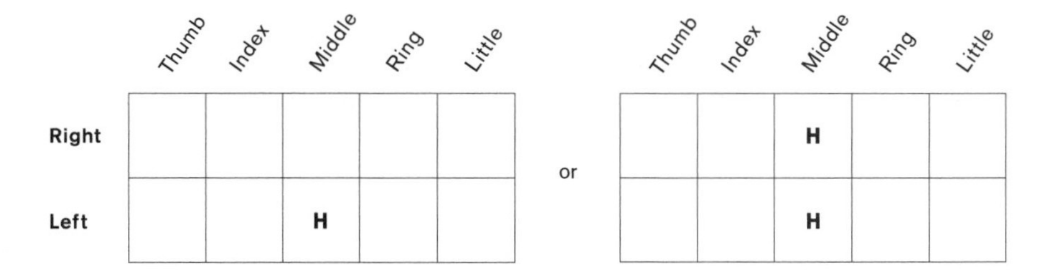

Fingerprint Profile: Highest ranking fingerprint(s) on left middle finger or both middle fingers

Life Purpose: The Mentor

Life-Fulfillment Formula: Become the person others wish to emulate and you are on your true path.

The left middle finger as the highest ranking fingerprint offers a highly rewarding life-purpose possibility: becoming a role model/mentor/teacher. The feeling of satisfaction reported by those living this life purpose is one of the most heartwarming stories I get to hear.

The Chauffeur Steve's plan was to become wealthy, very wealthy. While other kids were playing with dolls and baseballs, Steve was making money mowing lawns and selling lemonade on the golf course. At ten years old, he wasn't allowed on the golf course, naturally, but Steve was ambitious and charming. He often made more in tips than in lemonade sales before being escorted off by the powers that be. As he went through school, he kept to his vision and, as he explained in the life-purpose workshop, he had become wealthier than even he had imagined. Now fifty-two, Steve was looking for his next challenge.

Most of the students in Steve's life-purpose class were looking for a change of life as well. Take Sally. Sally was smart, single, and on the way up. As she explained, she had left the small town she had grown up in—in disgrace—because of her "failure" to marry The One her parents had their hearts set on. Now, gainfully employed but still childless at the advanced age of twenty-five, she finally felt in control of her life. Sort of. As the workshop unfolded, it became clear that Sally was slipping into the same predicament with her current boss that she had been in with her parents. Caught between her need for family connection and her need for freedom, Sally was getting sucked into her boss's expectation machinery just as assuredly as she had with her parents' expectations.

Sally was the youngest in the workshop, and Steve seemed to take her under his wing. He put Sally's dilemma this way: "Do what someone else wants or get out of town." He warned her, "Be careful you don't repeat the same pattern all over again." Sally nodded her understanding, thanking Steve for summing things up in such an easy-to-remember phrase.

Steve became Sally's main supporter throughout the workshop, but he couldn't seem to get a handle on his own goals. As much as he enjoyed the weekend and had been an asset for all in attendance, we were getting near the close and Steve was still without a plan for his own future. Then it hit him like a ton of bricks.

"Something has been stirring around inside, and I couldn't get my finger on it until right now. It had been staring me in the face all weekend and, I guess, all year since I sold my company, but it only came together this instant. Is it all right if I tell a little story?"

I wanted to hear Steve's story as much as everyone else in the room. He went on, "When I was twenty-two I worked as a chauffeur for a wealthy and difficult elderly man. I was young, my wife was pregnant, and this was the only job I could find. My boss was irritating, but he grew on me over time, and after a while I became his personal assistant at his brokerage business." "Sort of Driving Miss Daisy goes to Wall Street," chimed in Sally. Everyone laughed, including Steve.

"You've got the picture. In two years, he taught me everything he knew, and that was how I made my fortune. But here is the part that just came to me today. As he was dying, he asked if I would do him one favor. He had given me everything he had to give, and I told him I would do whatever he asked. He asked me to do the same for someone else that he had done for me. I agreed. He made me promise, and I did so gladly, but until this morning that promise had been lost in my memory somewhere. Earlier this weekend, you told me that my fingerprints had The Mentor in them. I thought that sounded nice, but it didn't really click until this moment. Thank you all for listening. Now I know what I want to do with the rest of my life."

Summary Many Mentors take a long time before the main sequence of their life purpose rises to conscious awareness. For some, this means dedicating themselves to a career path that ultimately shifts of its own accord into the fulfilling role of elder statesman. Others select teaching roles early on, get frustrated, then surprise themselves by returning to a teaching role in a new and unexpected form. If your life purpose is The Mentor, it is recommended that you guard your personal integrity as if your whole life depends upon it. On this life path, it does.

Martin Luther King

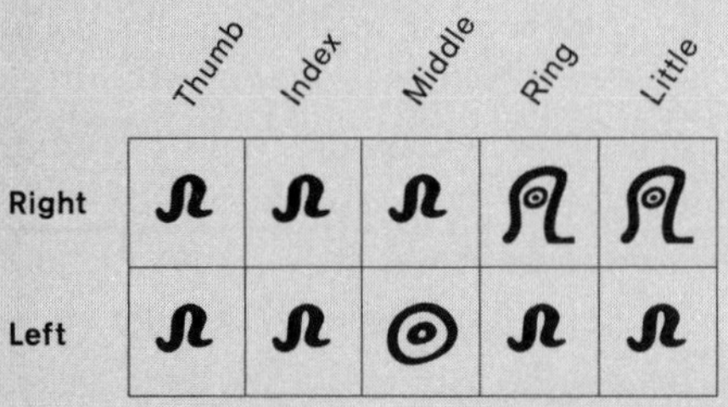

	Thumb	Index	Middle	Ring	Little
Right					
Left					

Fingerprint Profile: Highest ranking fingerprint on left middle finger, followed closely by two peacocks on right ring finger and right little finger

Life Purpose: The Mentor with a Message for the Masses

Life Lesson: Emotional Clarity and Honesty, Closeness, Vulnerability

School: Love

Life-Fulfillment Formula: Unburden your heart and tell the world what it needs to hear.

Martin Luther King's hands reveal an interesting and dualistic personality profile. Visible in numerous newspaper and magazine articles, King's hand shape is a cross between that of a philosopher and a Hollywood starlet. Apparently, the man who made the immortal "I Have a Dream" speech needed both qualities to fulfill his destiny.

King's life purpose asks him to unlock his emotional power sufficiently to enable The Mentor with a Message to emerge. It seems he must have done so—not without wounds, however. Repeated extramarital liaisons, his marriage in a shambles—all while he was at the center of a cyclone of exaltation and hatred—the emotional turmoil must have reached epic proportions.

No other speaker, before or since, reaches as deep into my heart as Martin Luther King. The day before his assassination, King seems eerily prophetic as he speaks:

> *Like anybody, I would like to live a long life. Longevity has its place, but I'm not concerned about that now. I just want to do God's will. And He's* allowed *me to go up to the mountain! And I've looked over, and I've seen the Promised Land. I may not get there with you. But I want you to know tonight, that we, as a people, will get to the Promised Land. And so I'm happy tonight. I'm not worried about anything. I'm not fearing any man. Mine eyes have seen the Glory of the coming of the Lord!*

We each face demons only we have seen; we each struggle to unlock the destiny available for this lifetime. What a privilege to be allowed a closer look at one famous person's struggle to live the life he came to live.

The Mentor to Artists

The Left or Both Middle Fingers as the Life Purpose in an Archetypal Combination

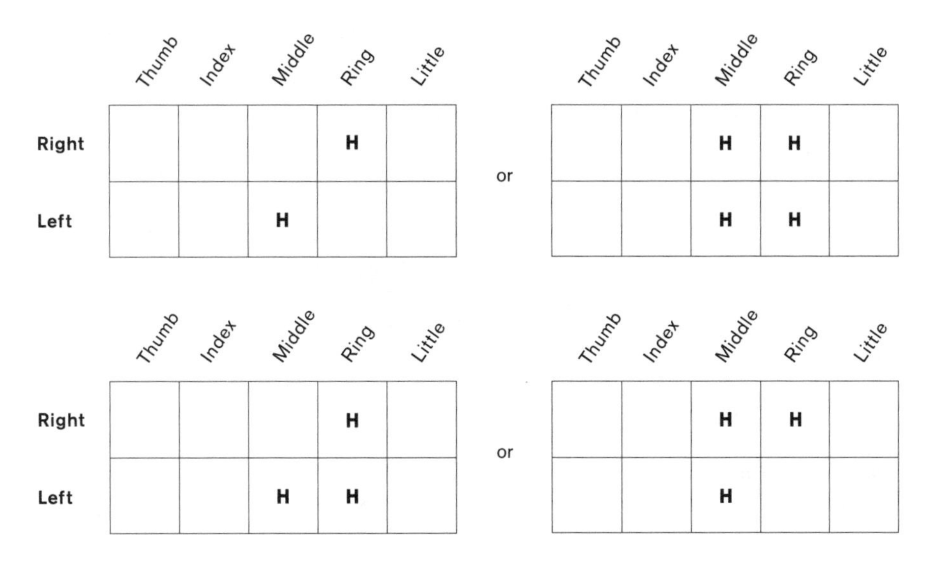

	Thumb	Index	Middle	Ring	Little
Right				H	
Left			H		

or

	Thumb	Index	Middle	Ring	Little
Right			H	H	
Left			H	H	

	Thumb	Index	Middle	Ring	Little
Right				H	
Left			H	H	

or

	Thumb	Index	Middle	Ring	Little
Right			H	H	
Left			H		

The Mentor to Leaders

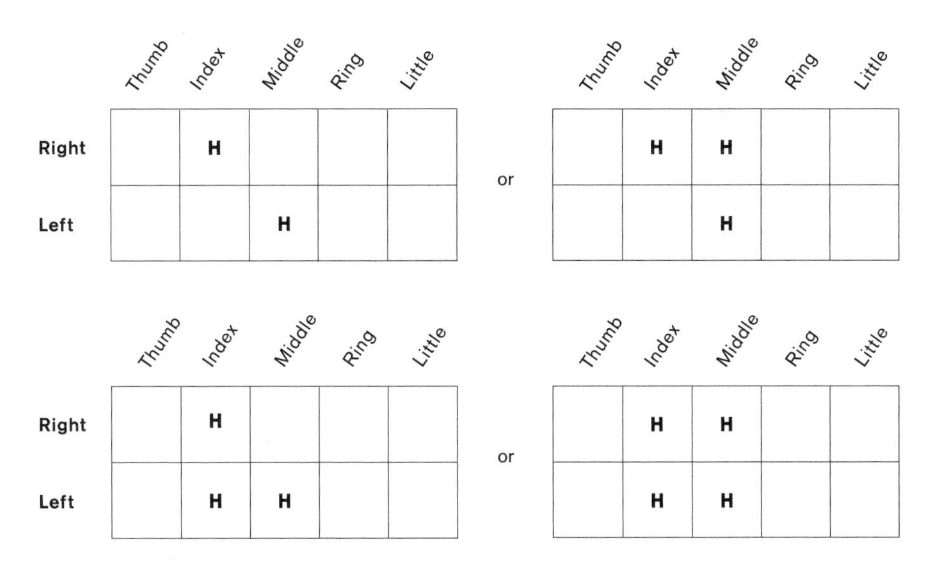

	Thumb	Index	Middle	Ring	Little
Right		H			
Left			H		

or

	Thumb	Index	Middle	Ring	Little
Right		H	H		
Left			H		

	Thumb	Index	Middle	Ring	Little
Right		H			
Left		H	H		

or

	Thumb	Index	Middle	Ring	Little
Right		H	H		
Left		H	H		

Fingerprint Profile: Left middle finger or both middle fingers as the highest ranking fingerprint(s) + right ring finger or both ring fingers (upper charts) or right index finger or both index fingers (lower charts)

Life Purpose: The Mentor to Artists (upper charts), The Mentor to Leaders (lower charts)

Life-Fulfillment Formula: Access your own creative integrity (or leadership integrity), then help others do the same.

The two main archetypal combinations that include a highest ranking left middle finger are pictured on the previous page. After years of wrestling with the integrity of your own process, your greatest fulfillment ultimately comes from consciously redirecting your focus from yourself to helping others to benefit from your years of experience. By this time in your life, there is no effort involved in being the living embodiment of your most deeply held principles.

Madame Souzatska The movie *Madame Souzatska* gives a clear illustration of this life path. In this motion picture from 1988, Shirley MacLaine plays a cranky old lady who teaches piano to young boys. Excuse me. As she says, "I don't teach piano. They already know how to play or they would not become my students." She teaches life, she says, and how a person lives comes through their fingers onto the piano keys. Not every boy is forever grateful to Shirley as she attempts to teach responsibility for actions; not every lesson of personal accountability is received with grace and appreciation. As Shirley holds the truth mirror for her students, she is challenged to turn it around on herself and come to terms with her own shortcomings.

Summary This movie does such a good job of capturing the highs and lows associated with this life purpose that we at the IIHA call all eight of the fingerprint maps from the prior page Souzatska life purposes. Advanced Souzatskas:

- Have gone beyond their own limits, found and expressed their unique capabilities
- Thrive on seeing their "students" come into their own
- Are sought after for direction and counsel

At some point, most Souzatskas face rebellion and mutiny from those in their circle of influence. If you are a Souzatska in this phase of your life purpose, remember to focus on the integrity of your own process. In the long run, you will find your "classroom" fills up again as those who seek shortcuts to success learn by their own experiences how expensive those shortcuts can be.

Crumb Work

The Left Middle Finger as the Life Lesson in an Archetypal Combination

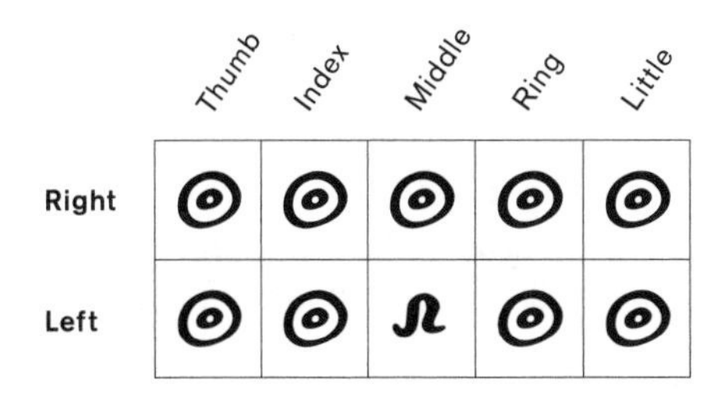

Fingerprint Profile: Lowest ranking fingerprint on left middle finger, whorls elsewhere

Life Purpose: Service

Life Lesson: Self-Worth, Guilt Issues

School: Service

Life-Fulfillment Formula: High self-worth is required to identify true service.

In soul psychology, guilt has a variety of implications. The Crumb Work story below offers a School of Service version. Negative Juliet, the next section, discusses the issue from the School of Love perspective. These two basic guilt-oriented life lessons have several common variations that are highlighted in the stories that follow Negative Juliet.

Crumb Work Another hand reading circle, this time in Marin—I have done over two thousand of these events. Mostly they are pure magic: challenging, fun, life altering. This night, I got to be the alteree.

Early in the lecture portion of the evening, the hostess raised her hand. I thought she was going to ask about thumbs; instead she launched into a line-by-line rendering of her date the night before. "Well, he said this, and I said that and . . ." "Excuse me," I interrupted at what I considered an appropriate interval. "Is this about thumbs?" "No. I'm sorry. Go on with your lecture, young man." I went on. Three minutes later she raised her hand again. "Well, he said this, and I said that and . . ." I must say, she told a good story, but I couldn't let her go on forever. I stopped her and she apologized. "I'll be quiet," she promised. Two minutes later, without awaiting permission, she began to critique her date's dancing skills. "*Stop!*" I insisted, my voice louder than I wished. The room was silent. She made a lock-and-throw-away-the-key gesture toward her lips, folded her hands in her lap, and sat quietly through the remainder of the lecture.

On the break, I went over to help myself to tea and cookies while people happily chatted away. Glancing down, I noticed hands wiping the table clean of cookie crumbs: my hands. I hadn't remembered telling them to do so, but it was hard to dispute the facts. Those were definitely my hands cleaning up the crumbs. "What are you doing?" I thought to myself. The answer came back immediately. "Apologizing."

I realized then that I felt guilty for raising my voice. The fact that my hostess needed snapping at was beside the point. I walked over and said my apologies. "It's a good thing you stopped me, young man. I would have gone on forever." She laughed at herself and quickly resumed talking to her friends. I went over to the snack table and put back the crumbs I had been carrying around. "So Richard," a voice inside asked, "how much of your life is crumb work?"

Summary I had tried to alleviate an uncomfortable feeling by unconsciously offering what I deemed a service. Only after I'd started did I realize what I was doing and the reason for it. My clients report whole careers and marriages based on crumb work. Better to take inventory now before the price gets too high.

Negative Juliet

The Left Middle Finger as the Life Lesson in an Archetypal Combination

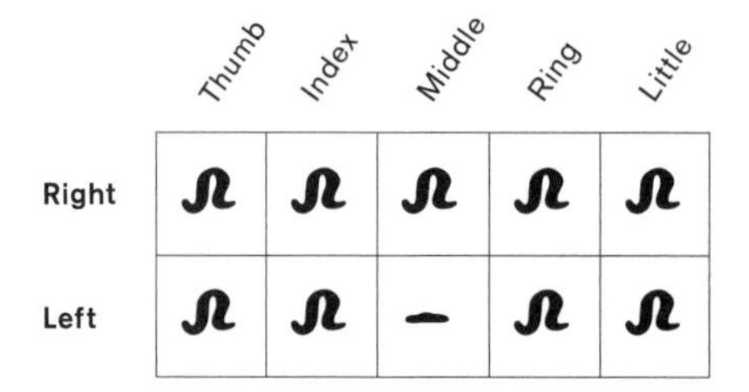

Fingerprint Profile: Lowest ranking fingerprint on left middle finger + School of Love

Life Purpose: Emotional Connection

Life Lesson: Self-Worth, Guilt Issues (Note: Shakespeare's Juliet never doubts her feelings.)

School: Love

Life-Fulfillment Formula: Emotional self-worth is required to gain the closeness you seek.

Crumb Work (see page 205) was about the left middle finger as the life lesson in the School of Service. For Negative Juliet, with the same life lesson in the School of Love, the battle for self-esteem switches to the emotional arena. If this is your life lesson, the I'm-not-okay feeling exists inside you, ready for activation at the slightest cue, even if you haven't done anything to feel guilty about. Let's watch this theme play out in one midtown Manhattan office.

Deon Deon met me at reception and led me to the conference room on the thirty-seventh floor. I liked him right away. Friendly and solid, that's what I decided; a belt *and* suspenders man but not too serious. I got myself situated, Deon did the same, and as I looked at his hands and took some notes, he told me his story.

Deon had moved to New York from Boston three years ago to become the program director for a midsize telecommunications company. His job was to oversee seven employees who basically handled problems that no one else in the company knew what to do with. Deon's problem was handling his seven employees. Marva told Deon she wanted to work three days a week, so Deon rearranged things accordingly. Gail told Deon she couldn't get to the office before 11 A.M., so Deon shifted office meetings to fit her schedule. You get the idea. Deon was a nice guy, but could Deon check in with Deon to see what Deon wanted and needed?

At this point in the reading, Deon's beeper went off. He excused himself to answer it while I checked out the New York City skyline and considered just how I was going to explain the various ramifications of Negative Juliet to this straitlaced New Englander.

Juliet is the IIHA's champion of self-referential emotionality. Juliet never asks her friends what they think about Romeo. She doesn't ask her parents. Not needing confirmation from any source outside herself, there is not one soliloquy in which she doubts her feelings. Of course, Juliet does not have a lowest ranking fingerprint on her left middle finger like Deon. If she reacted Deon-style, she would sound more like: "I love Romeo. At least I think I do. What is love anyway? Last year I thought I loved Mercutio, but you remember how that turned out? Up to her balcony in guilt, if confronted by Mr. and Mrs. Capulet, this Juliet caves in and stops seeing Romeo. With her emotional integrity shot, William Shakespeare finds a more interesting young woman to write about.

Emotional integrity has big implications for Deon's love life too (Love and Closeness is his life purpose after all), but that was not the subject at hand on this particular day. If Deon was ever to get his department to bond together and work as a team, he would have to put his own true feelings into the mix. Without Juliet's self-referential confidence, without her unapologetic emotional certainty, Deon faced the likelihood that sooner or later someone wouldn't like what he has done and he would feel guilty about it.

If he had a surplus of positive Juliet skills it wouldn't be a problem. "How was work today honey?" "Had to take Mathilda off the Smith account. I feel bad, but what could I do?" That is what an advanced Deon might say, but this Deon was in Juliet deficit. Faced with guilt possibilities, this Deon wanted nothing more than to run and hide.

In movies and literature, we admire the hero who demonstrates bravery in the face of danger. Bravo. But in all classic tales the inner demons are always the more dangerous. In the case of Deon and all his left middle finger life-lesson counterparts, when faced with a terrifying potential for guilt, the temptation to go unconscious is overwhelming. The two most common tactics employed are doing what the other person wants or shutting down emotional awareness to keep uncomfortable feelings at bay (like in the Crumb Work story), or both. Either way, life-purpose satisfaction shrinks and the big gaping hole expands. A hero, even one shaking in his boots, who chooses not to run from the Godzilla-size guilt gremlin is a hero indeed.

When I explained his fingerprint chart, Deon knew at once what I was talking about. "You just described my first marriage," he said. "Things are much better now." I wasn't sure at the time whether Deon got the work connection. Could he see that he needed to bring what he had learned at home to his office relationships as well? As I read for the rest of his team, however, things became considerably clearer.

Claire Claire worked for Deon and also had Negative Juliet as her life lesson. This is not uncommon. Whenever I read for work teams, I look for life-purpose and life-lesson parallels, and they are not usually hard to find. Three of Deon's team had the left middle finger as all or part of their life lesson, and each had their own style of dealing with it.

Whereas Deon's Negative Juliet expressed itself mainly in unspoken form, Claire's came pouring out in a ready stream under the slightest provocation. She said "I'm sorry" at least once every five minutes regardless of what was happening. Though attractive, she regularly downgraded her appearance. In her upside-down world, Claire acted guilty for things that weren't broken or didn't matter, while at the same time denying legitimate responsibilities or attention to her life purpose. What a mess.

Deon and Claire both felt guilty at the drop of a hat. Both hated the feeling so much they would do almost anything not to feel it. It was easier for Deon to do too much than to risk feeling guilty if someone didn't like him, even for a moment. It was easier for Claire to pretend to be puny than to actually risk failure or rejection. To gain life-purpose satisfaction, they would have to face their guilt demon on its own terms and turn it into an ally.

Summary The guilt demon is an ally when it functions as an early warning system. When the warning buzzer sounds, Claire or Deon could check to see if something needs fixing. If it did, they could fix it. If not, then they could move on. In this way, Claire and Deon could access a higher sense of personal responsibility (the exalted aspect of the left middle finger) and other team members would be challenged to live up to this standard. Now that was something Deon could get behind.

Negative L'Oreal

The Left Middle Finger as the Life Lesson in an Archetypal Combination

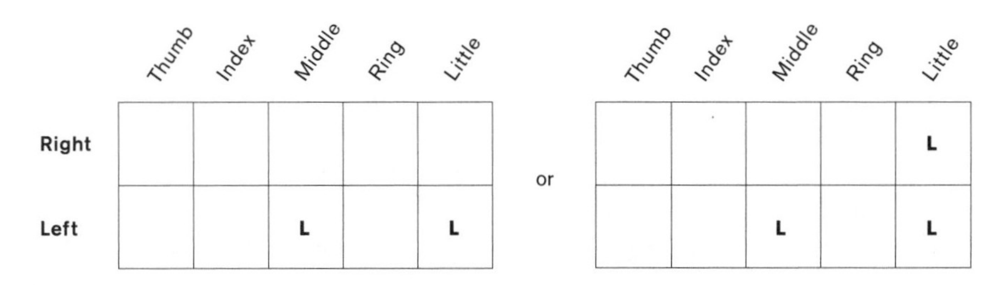

Fingerprint Profile: Lowest ranking fingerprints on left middle finger + left little finger or both little fingers + the School of Love

Life Lesson: Self-Worth, Guilt Issues—Especially in Intimacy

School: Love (there need to be at least seven loops for Negative L'Oreal)

Life-Fulfillment Formula: Emotional self-worth is required to gain the closeness you seek.

Note: Please read the prior story, Negative Juliet (see page 206), *first* if you have these fingerprints. Deon and Claire's Negative Juliet worked its way into a business setting, but more often than not when Negative Juliet shows up, the conversation turns to matters more personal, especially when you add a lowest ranking left little finger (turning the life lesson into Negative L'Oreal). Such was the case for Ms. Argentina.

Ms. Argentina Ms. Argentina came in for her reading a bit unsteadily. At five feet ten inches plus heels, she made a stunning entrance, but one of her high heels was damaged. It made a kind of tin-tin sound as she walked and caused her to tilt ever so slightly to one side. Not that it ruined the show. Ms. Argentina was a knockout. She arranged herself into the chair, and I found myself falling into her deep brown eyes, somewhat tipsy myself. However, interposed with her breathtaking beauty, as if flashing every thirtieth of a second, was a caught-in-the-act expression, like a little girl who has been surprised while trying on her mother's lipstick. The innocent/not so innocent wink on that fleeting face held a question that made me check the fingerprints before any other marking in her hands. That's where I found Negative L'Oreal.

Negative L'Oreal expresses itself in any number of creative ways, the combination of guilt and sexuality providing ample story lines for the student body of Earth University. Sometimes owners of this fingerprint chart take actions that create a lifetime of sexual regret. Others farm out the role, their spouses doing the bad deeds that start the melodrama going. Most commonly however, this chart is associated with diminished sexual self-esteem.

I named these fingerprints over two decades ago after seeing the L'Oreal commercials on TV for the millionth time. If you watch any TV at all you know the commercial: the beautiful supermodel croons, "I use L'Oreal hair color. It costs twice as much, but I'm worth it." And who can doubt her, gloriously beautiful as she is? Does the L'Oreal woman have trouble getting a date for the prom? No problem; she gets her pick. "Let's see: captain of the football team, rich kid with the Porsche, or maybe I'd prefer the smart kid already accepted to Princeton. So many to choose from; life can be sooo hard." And if Mr. Princeton, let's say, does not treat her in the style to which she has become accustomed, how long would the L'Oreal woman put up with such abuse? Two nanoseconds, that's how long. "I am L'Oreal. Hear me roar." Gee, how much does that stuff cost? I want some, too.

Ms. Argentina might have been the most beautiful woman in her native land, but that does not change her fingerprints. No amount of societal recognition will eliminate the L'Oreal deficit that was already present before her birth. That is work that must be done from the inside out, and hard labor it is.

Incredible. Here is the face that graces every magazine cover, smiles from every billboard, and yet Ms. Argentina's history with men is to pick losers who treat her like dirt. Remember, the fingerprints were formed before she was born. A pattern of low relationship worthiness invades this lifetime, and no fact of circumstance can rid the soul psychology of its wound. Identifying the issue (bringing the wound to conscious awareness), expressing her way through the experiencing process, getting to incremental release point breakthroughs—that can shift the energy better than five beauty pageant trophies. Ah, but the process can be so long and painful.

I suggested to Ms. Argentina that to become a later Cinderella, one who dances with a prince instead of sweeping up the floors, she would have to provide her own magic wand and give herself a positive L'Oreal implant. Though her Negative L'Oreal would never go away completely, it could become an ally. "As a proper counterbalance to your beauty-queen good looks, a disarming and charming insecurity, it could be just the element of true vulnerability," I suggested, "that might get you a real prince of a man. You fear no good man would want you. Okay. That is your fear. Can you risk love with a loving man anyway? Take the chance and claim the birthright of love and closeness that is your life purpose."

Ms. Argentina walked out of my office brimming with confidence. "Now I know what I have to do next," she said. But that is not the end of the story. Read Liar's Poker (the next set of fingerprints) and see how the rest of Ms. Argentina's story might play out.

Summary Crumb Work, Negative Juliet, Ms. Argentina, and Liar's Poker form a family of life lessons that revolve around soul psychology's version of guilt issues. If you have any of these, reading the whole lot will give you a better idea of your own life lesson.

Worthy of Love

The Left Middle Finger or Both Middle Fingers as the Life Lesson in an Archetypal Combination

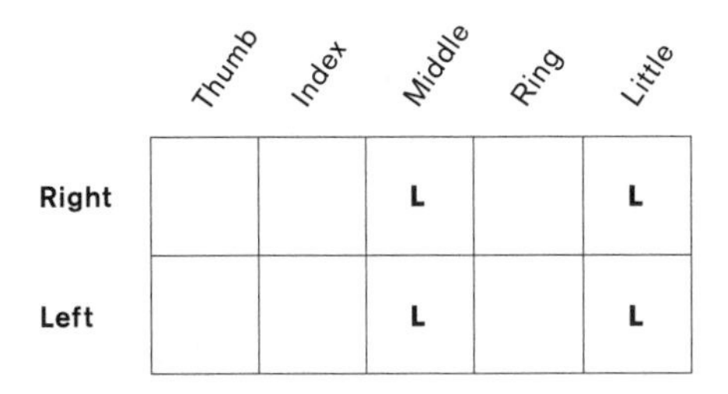

Fingerprint Profile: Lowest ranking fingerprints on both middle fingers + both little fingers

Life Lesson: I Am Worthy of Love

Life-Fulfillment Formula: Develop the emotional self-worth you need to live the life you want.

Here is still another fingerprint chart that highlights guilt issues. It is very similar to Negative L'Oreal (see page 209), but in this case the worthiness issue, although definitely pertaining to intimacy, pervades the owner's entire life experience. While Negative L'Oreal occurs in a hand with seven or more loops, Worthy of Love can occur in a hand with any combination of fingerprint types.

Liar's Poker One of my brothers is a psychotherapist in New York City. He has a theory about love and dating that he calls the Lover's Version of Liar's Poker. Do you know how liar's poker works? Each person picks one card from the deck and holds it face forward on their forehead. In an ironic twist on normal poker, everyone can now see everyone else's card—you are the only player who cannot see your own. The idea of the game is to figure out your own card and its relative strength by the betting behaviors and veiled glances of the other players. Try it sometime. It is a hoot.

Brother Larry says we each go to high school with a liar's poker card on our forehead. In this version of the game, however, the card announces your sexual desirability rating. The captain of the cheerleaders scores one hundred, total nerd creeps score in the minus column, and everyone else is somewhere in between, fifty being average. Larry says that if you guess your own number within twenty points and date others in that range, your love life works out more or less okay. Badly over- or underestimate your number and you can expect disaster. Unequal relationships—wanting too much to be loved by a partner who knows all too well the leverage he or she has over you—who amongst us has never been party to such an unrewarding exercise? Listen to any country music CD if you haven't; it is sure to have a song that covers the topic thoroughly.

Ms. Argentina's liar's poker rating was a ninety-nine. She thought she was a fifty, dated twenties and below, and got treated accordingly. When she came in for her reading, her current boyfriend was at least an eighty, so her prospects were looking up. Peter, whom we will be discussing next, was a fifty, but he thought his wife over eighty, and their relationship was in trouble.

Peter wanted to talk about his current circumstances and talk he did, nonstop for most of the first thirty minutes of our session. His wife and kids were treating him as if he were a twenty-four hour ATM machine. Nothing about his life mattered to them, and everything in their lives was Peter's emergency to be handled. Or so it seemed to Peter. Peter finally stopped to take a breath, and I joined the conversation. After a bit, I asked Peter to tell me something that happened in high school. I was seeking to get him off the treadmill he was on, to look at his current life through a different window.

"Well, okay, I am in high school, and my friend Bill and I meet two girls at the ice skating rink. Bill is way cooler than I am so he starts up with the prettier of the two, and I feel awkward trying to make conversation with the other one. Eventually, I teach her how to skate backward, and that breaks the ice, so to speak. I buy her a hot chocolate, and that night I get my first kiss. I was up all night replaying the whole evening."

"Good. Let's use that evening to look at your way of doing things. Can you see anything going on today that looks the same?"

"Well, one thing is clear. When I don't know what to do, I either buy something for someone or try to help them. That is more or less the wooing style I used with my wife, so how can I blame her for responding so well to it and asking for more? I guess that is how I buy affection."

It sounded to me like Peter had a good understanding of his Worthy of Love life lesson. He knew its meaning, had charted its course. But could he break the cycle? "What can I do?" he asked. "It is totally out of control."

"Peter. Take a breath. Good. It sounds to me like you didn't do too badly. You bought a girl a hot chocolate and got kissed good-night. The problem occurs only if this becomes your exclusive relationship option. You wouldn't want *not* to buy your daughter a gift for her birthday, for instance, but you don't have to take her to Disneyland every weekend. The trick is to not wind up with a 'YES' on your forehead for every request your family can think of."

We talked about how even a small dose of me-firsting could shift the picture. Of course, to use this side of his emotional nature, Peter would inevitably bump into the underlying guilt visible in his fingerprints. But at this point, Peter was in so much pain that the fear generated by making requests and holding to boundaries (standard me-first behaviors) could not possibly be any worse than his current life.

I suggested me-first rehab was in order. For the rest of his session, Peter and I did some role playing exercises. In some I played the exaggerated me-firster, demanding more and more no matter what was offered, and Peter was forced to fend me off. In others he me-firsted me with greater or lesser credibility. Our session was nearing an end, and I sought a final take-home, some me-first barometer he could use on any occasion to monitor his improving skills. The dog and couch story came to mind.

"Peter, visualize a dog on a couch. You tell the dog to get off the couch, and the dog looks you over, doing his canine calculations, deciding if he really needs to vacate his comfortable spot. Then your wife walks in, and Fido leaps off the couch in an instant. What's going on here?"

"I don't know."

"I think you could figure it out if you tried. You plead with Fido and finally scooch beside him, or maybe you find yourself a chair or sit on the floor. Your wife, on the other hand, bops Fido on the head with a newspaper if he doesn't move quickly enough. With you there is no danger, no consequence. Fido knows it, you know it, your wife knows it.

"Here is what I want you to do Peter. I want you to buy a stuffed dog and bop it on the head with a newspaper exactly eleven times a day for eleven days. You'll need a chart to keep track of this. You can't miss one Fido bop, or you have to start all over again. Will you do this and call me on the twelfth day?" Peter agreed.

Peter never did call me on the twelfth day, but soon after I got a card in the mail. Inside was a picture of Peter, his wife and daughter, and a beagle, plus a one hundred dollar bill. All the note said was "Thanks."

Summary Deon, Claire, Ms. Argentina, Peter, and everyone else dealing with uncaused underlying guilt in one form or another have a tough row to hoe. The challenge is not just to get out of whatever oversize predicament has been created, as all important as that may be. The real challenge is to turn this guilt into an ally, an integrity-heightening device that can lead to greater meaning in life.

For example, Ms. Argentina is already doing much better than she was in her biker dudes phase, and she and her new boyfriend seem on solid ground. But Negative L'Oreal has not run its full course. Sooner or later Ms. A. will feel that something is all her fault, and she will want to pull away from whatever intimacy has been attained. At that point, Ms. Argentina will have arrived at another of life's crossroads. The best thing she could do would be to admit to whatever guilt gyrations are passing through her, communicate them (sooner or later) to her partner, and bring a new, heightened sense of closeness to their relationship.

Neither abandoning herself nor her lover, more real and with more emotional integrity than before, Ms. Argentina will have taken another big step forward on her life-purpose path. Or she will be too scared to reveal her insecurities. How much of yourself are you willing to share with another, Ms. A.?

Guilt in the Family

The Left Middle Finger or Both Middle Fingers as the Life Lesson in an Archetypal Combination

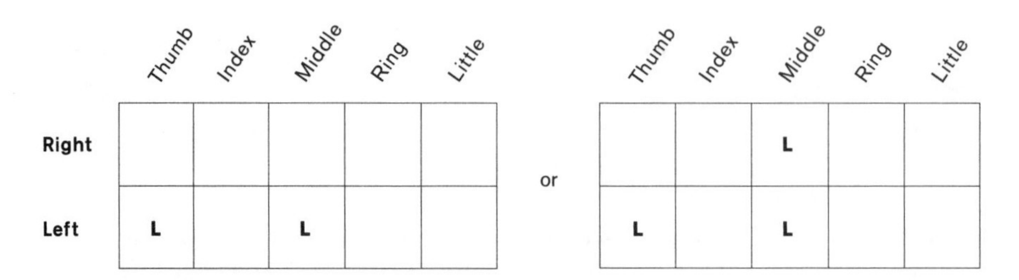

	Thumb	Index	Middle	Ring	Little
Right					
Left	L		L		

or

	Thumb	Index	Middle	Ring	Little
Right			L		
Left	L		L		

Fingerprint Profile: Lowest ranking fingerprints on left middle finger or both middle fingers + left thumb

Life Lesson: Family/Community Issues + Guilt Issues

Life-Fulfillment Formula: Get over your family paranoia and find what makes you happy.

Guilt in the family—have you ever heard of such a thing? Better to ask if you've heard of a family without guilt. Whenever I encounter these fingerprints and begin to discuss their implications, the usual response is: "Well, of course, I come from a

Catholic family." Or, "Well, of course, I come from a Jewish family." Or, "Well, of course, I come from a ______ family." It seems so universal as to be redundant. It's a family—guilt must be involved.

This is not necessarily a bad thing. A healthy dose of guilt neurons can help a person develop integrity (the exalted form of the left middle finger life lesson). Take my late-arriving student for example. Mr. Late interrupts class to find his chair. After he drops a book or two and nods hello to each and every friend in attendance, his cell phone rings. Feigning sheepishness ("What can a person as busy and popular as I do?"), he takes the call. The class waits another minute as he announces he is in a class and cannot take this call. Show over, maybe the rest of the class can resume its normal course.

I am hoping Mr. Late feels a shred of guilt so as to be motivated a bit more to arrive on time for the next class. But those beyond guilt couldn't care less. Living in a bubble, they careen through life blithely making messes for others to clean up, serenely unconcerned about the havoc they create. Society needs guilt to operate and families (minisocieties) would quickly become inoperable without it.

That is not to say that guilt cannot be overdone. As a matter of fact, the Goldilocks Rule insists that it will, especially for those with these fingerprints. Let's take a closer look.

Can We Talk Turkey? In the Barry Levinson film *Avalon*, there is a classic family guilt scene that is just too good to pass up here. Two brothers have a long-standing series of grievances with each other that culminates one Thanksgiving. Brother A and the rest of the family are gathered for the traditional feast. Dinner is delayed, awaiting the inevitably late arrival of brother B. The family waits for hours, but eventually they cut the turkey and begin. Brother B arrives moments later. Aghast at the incredible insensitivity of everyone, especially brother A, he storms out shrieking, "They cut the toikey! They cut the toikey! How could they cut the toikey without me?"

From our comfortable movie-going seat, we can laugh out loud as brother B goes through his gyrations. Who amongst us cannot identify with brother A, the good brother? This is the brother who, after shopping for the food and cooking the dinner, still had the forbearance to wait for hours. All this, only to get dumped on by the irreconcilably obnoxious brother B. Vicariously, popcorn in lap, we get to drain out some of our own family *mischigas* watching the exaggerated scenario on the big screen.

The family guilt theme can also apply in a larger community setting, as with Richard Nixon. Service was the life purpose shown in Nixon's fingerprints, with Family/Community Guilt as the life lesson. Those old enough to remember can review his "Checkers" speech and his "You Won't Have Richard Nixon to Kick Around Anymore" speech in a new light. To me, Nixon always seemed to exude why-am-I-still-being-made-to-sit-at-the-children's-table? vibes, even when he was at the pinnacle of his political power. And his enemies list—here is the president of the United States of America plotting revenge against all his brothers and sisters who cut the turkey without him! Of course it all boomeranged. Nixon's paranoid insecurity culminated in his resignation—the ultimate community guilt.

Summary Because the guilt life lesson is such a common denominator in life lessons, we have visited it in different schools and examined it in combination with other lowest ranking fingerprints. In each case, the exalted possibility is the development of high integrity earned by experience. With family guilt as the life lesson, the usual pattern is to overadjust to family pressures and feel squeezed, then underadjust and feel isolated. Eventually, you hope to find the Just-Right relationship to your family and community at large that provides the proper foundation for your life purpose to come into full expression.

Mr. Not Enough

Both Middle Fingers and Both Index Fingers as the Life Lesson in an Archetypal Combination

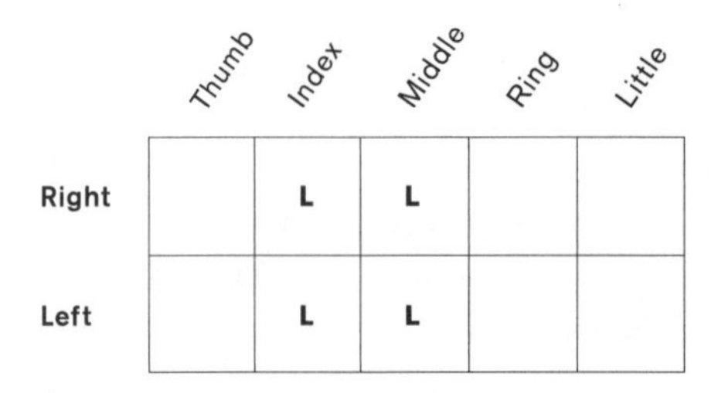

Fingerprint Profile: Lowest ranking fingerprints on both index fingers + both middle fingers

Life Lesson: Mr. Not Enough

Life-Fulfillment Formula: Turn Mr. Not Enough into your ally by learning to develop self-esteem that is independent of circumstance. When you can accomplish this, you can accomplish anything.

Welcome to the mysterious world of Mr. Not Enough, the voice of insufficiency. Always looking for that elusive something that will signal the final victory, feeling somehow short of what life requires—that is Mr. Not Enough. Not having enough money to do what one wants, not having enough time to get the job done, not having enough smarts, good looks, lucky breaks—that is the Mr. Not Enough voice in action.

In the classic Mr. Not Enough chart shown opposite, both index fingers and middle fingers have the lowest ranking fingerprints, but any combination of index finger and middle finger lowest ranking prints qualifies. We will explore several different versions of Mr. Not Enough in the pages ahead, but for now let's look at the basics.

Mr. Not Enough is a dual life lesson based on the combined elements of the index finger and the middle finger. Index finger issues center on power, middle finger issues center on self-worth. The Paradox Principle states that to access your power and self-worth you must visit that aspect of self that feels powerless and worthless, an aspect of self willing to abdicate the responsibility of living your life purpose. Let's examine this more fully.

Being powerful means:

- Exercising independence of action, setting your own life agenda
- Having confidence in your abilities, bringing your talents out into the world
- Standing up for yourself, saying no to violation

Having self-worth means:

- Knowing you are okay even if your circumstances aren't
- Valuing yourself, not apologizing for who you are, not being manipulated by guilt
- Adhering to your ethical and moral code, even if it means risking disapproval

When your power department and self-worth department both go haywire at the same time, when you feel trapped and helpless, insufficient, hopelessly lacking in some essential way—that is Mr. Not Enough. Mr. Not Enough is the voice inside telling you that you are bad, not okay. You will never measure up. Excellent performance or fortunate outcomes cannot deter this section of your consciousness. Climb Mount Everest and Mr. Not Enough says, "Two days?" Work harder, climb Mount Everest in one day, and Mr. Not Enough responds, "South face?" So you climb the north face in the winter in half a day. Does this stop the Mr. Not Enough voice? Hardly. "What about your spouse and kids? How much time have you spent with them lately?"

Most people can relate in some way to Mr. Not Enough. Who among us is 100 percent without self-doubt? At its best, our hesitancy causes us to look before we leap, to properly assess our capabilities. Grappling with uncertainty is part of reaching out to your fullest potential. But for those with these fingerprints, Mr. Not Enough is a recurring life theme of major proportions.

Those with tented arch versions tend to procrastinate, Mr. Not Enough joining forces with Mr. Next Year to become a fearsome double-headed dragon. "I will do it when everything is just right. Then (any time other than now) I will. . . ." Those with arches usually take the opposite tack, rushing around with Mr. Sticks and Plates trying to get everything done perfectly. Still others hide out in Mr. Mellow or Ms. Lah-Dee-Dah. "If I don't do nothin', I can't get it wrong."

"There are so many Mr. Not Enough possibilities, Richard, you'll never be able to tell your readers each one." My gosh. That's right. Since I can't describe each one, maybe I should try to pick a representative sample group. That would be better. Thanks, Mr. Not Enough. Good Idea.

John was afraid that if he attempted something big and succeeded, people would find out just what a fraud he really was—so he committed himself to never succeeding past the point that would get him noticed. Marcie was so busy taking care of everyone else, she had no time to find and express her own considerable talents. Gil's body language shouted, "You wouldn't want to dance with me," as one girl after another turned him down at the dance. Gil decided he could live just fine without a relationship.

John, Marcie, and Gil were each in the clutches of Mr. Not Enough, even if they didn't realize it. Mr. Not Enough has a wide range of disguises, as the following pages will demonstrate.

Other Mr. Not Enoughs

Look at two dozen hands and you will run into Mr. Not Enough several times. He is the most popular archetypal life-lesson combination by a large margin. With that in mind, it is worthwhile to look at a few variations on the theme. Please note, however, that each type of Mr. Not Enough can vary widely in the way it expresses itself, depending upon other factors such as family background and inherent talents, to name just two. It is awe inspiring to consider the infinite scope of human possibilities. Yet, at the core of each Mr. Not Enough life story lies a similar black hole, following the same inexorable law of fingerprint physics.

The following fingerprint charts display the four main Mr. Not Enough subsets in pure form. Each is composed of two lowest ranking prints and shows up either isolated or in combination with other lowest ranking prints. Let's peek in at the life-scale havoc Mr. Not Enough is capable of creating.

Desire Guilt

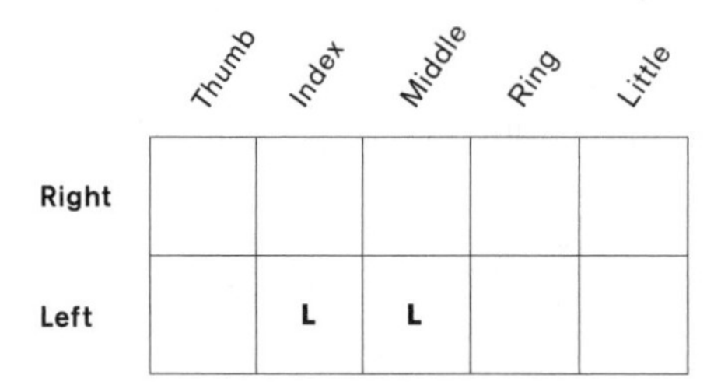

Desire Guilt

In this fingerprint chart, the focus is on learning to accept your desires, including desires you wish you did not have. The goal here is not to act out every desire that comes into your head. The Goldilocks Rule says that would be too much. However, with these prints, the statistically more common error is to lose track of what you actually do want. If you don't know what to do with your life, the possibility of being hijacked into someone else's life movie increases exponentially. The Desire Guilt life lesson is a potentially debilitating condition as indicated by the following two stories.

Young Girl in the Attic "Here's the problem," she announced as I began to examine her hands. "I am forty-eight years old and still don't know what I want to be when I grow up." She smiled at me, attractive, well dressed. But behind her eyes was a frustrated quizzical sadness that seemed on the verge of a waterfall of tears. She pulled herself back together. The nanosecond appearance on her face of a frightfully overwhelmed little girl disappeared, and I was left to wonder if I had imagined it all. No, I decided as I looked back at her hands again.

She had gone from high school to college to marriage to motherhood to empty nest all in a neat row, she told me, always following the path of least resistance. "I know there is someone else in here, but I don't know who she is or how to find her."

A movie picture sequence appeared in my mind's eye. I saw a five- or six-year-old girl in an attic with a dozen or so other people, like Anne Frank's family in the Nazi era. The girl is crying, and her mother asks what's wrong. "I miss my dolly," is the reply. The mother consoles her daughter. At nightfall, daddy sneaks out of the attic and retrieves the missing doll, but he's followed back and they are all captured. The little girl is beside herself with grief and guilt. "It is all my fault. I love my mommy. I love my daddy. I'll never want anything again, ever." My client is crying freely as I tell her the story. "That could have been my story," she tells me.

She sobs for a few minutes, then composes herself. "Is that why I am afraid to have any desire for myself? My whole life has been about what everybody else wants. I don't even know how to know what I want."

We talk for a while, and I suggest some baby-step exercises. She can start by not blaming herself so badly for everything. After all, anyone whose desire system was as frozen as hers would need a lengthy rehab program, and here she is part way into it. We talk about what she doesn't want. She seems good at identifying that. A good beginning, I assure her; we are already past square one. I suggest keeping an "I want . . ." journal where she can take a few minutes to write down any wants or desires that came up during the day and any feelings she has about the entire process. We are making some progress here. She seems more in her body.

Some with Desire Guilt spend decades sacrificing for family or spouse only to wind up surprisingly alone, their efforts unappreciated. "But I did it all for you," they groan as the door slams shut on the house-of-cards life they have built. Others with Desire Guilt float aimlessly from job to job, numbed out, not hearing or paying attention to life purpose's call. Still others have a problem that appears to come from the outside, a spouse who cheats, a child in trouble with the law: illicit desires played out by someone else. In each case, the challenge is to bring out the desires that you *can* access until you finally work your way to the deep-down-true-to-me desires at the center of your being. Depending on your life history, this can be easier said than done.

The Lonely Dominatrix The Young Girl in the Attic represents the standard expression for this life lesson. With so many guilt globules circulating in the bloodstream, personal desires become something to be avoided at almost any cost. But the next story turns the Desire Guilt theme upside down.

Reading hands in the Tribeca section of New York City gave me the opportunity to read for Misty. Misty was tall and wore striking high-heeled leather boots that laced all the way up to her knees. Matching laces almost contained her breasts, which seemed a size too big for her small leather bodice. She crossed her legs seductively and showed me her hands. With the fingerprints shown above and line formations that were a textbook version of every power giveaway marker we list at the IIHA, it was clear that Misty had a stormy relationship history. I started the reading.

"Misty, are you currently in a relationship?"

"Sort of," she replied. "I am seeing a married man, and we plan to start living together as soon as he gets his divorce."

"How old are you?"

"Thirty-one."

I asked if she had ever had a relationship lasting over two years. She told me she had not.

"Your fingerprints are all about the search for love, Misty. (Misty had eight loops to go with arches on the left index and middle fingers.) You seek emotional connection more than anything else, the challenge being to get the love and closeness you seek without having to give away your power or integrity in order to get them."

It was then I learned of Misty's unusual occupation. Men paid her (extremely well, she told me) to dominate them emotionally and (usually) sexually. It was in her personal life she couldn't seem to get on top of things. In her role as dominatrix she knew just what to say and do, but in her own love life she inevitably wound up the victim.

"I became a dominatrix after a six-month trip to Amsterdam when I was nineteen," she explained. "Everything was so open over there. American men and women seem so hung up in comparison. Sex shouldn't be something we are ashamed of. As long as two (or more) adults are doing what they agree to do and no one gets hurt (too much), why should anyone care? I also do workshops for women about enjoying their sexuality." Misty went on to tell me how bad it was to stifle your normal desires because of outdated sexual norms.

Desire integrity is the exalted possibility for Misty, and she was walking a fine line around it. Perhaps she was completely correct. Perhaps her job helped others to find their true sexual identities and desires, to overcome inordinate sexual guilt. What is wrong with that? I asked myself. But if this is desire with integrity, where is the loving connection that her fingerprints promised? Why did she appear stuck in her life-purpose inverse (emotional disconnect)?

Unlike the Young Girl in the Attic, who was afraid to register any desire for fear of its terrible consequences, Misty was on the other side of this fence, reaching deep into the fear pool and encouraging desire's full expression. Whereas Attic Girl had too much guilt, Misty's guilt alarm had been turned off (or at least it was set very low), with results not that different from Attic Girl. Both were struggling with bringing desires into appropriate conscious expression. Would Attic Girl ever know her passions? Would the Lonely Dominatrix ever develop boundary skills sufficient for her love life to blossom?

Some with this life lesson have visited Too Much and Too Little and have developed a Just-Right desire integrity that allows their life purpose to flower. Neither Attic Girl nor Misty had accomplished this, but neither seemed so far away that this possibility was beyond hope. Of course, at the core of this life lesson is the Mr. Not Enough question: am I okay enough for anyone to love me as I am? The starting point is in believing that you are, right now, today.

I Can't Make Any Money

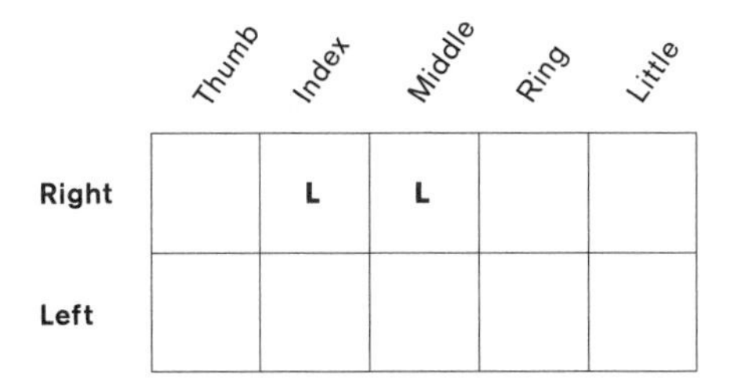

I Can't Make Any Money

With both lowest ranking fingerprints on the left hand, Desire Guilt emphasizes inner growth. It's direct opposite is the I Can't Make Any Money version of Mr. Not Enough. The right index finger as the life lesson says, "I can't, I can't," and the right middle finger deals with your sense of value in the world (Money Issues). The combination produces a life lesson that, at its worst, is capable of overwhelming even the strongest personality.

Owners of these fingerprints start life convinced they are not good enough to earn a decent living. Who would want to pay me? What can I do that is worth anything? In general, I Can't Make Any Money comes in two styles: the overachiever and the underachiever. Overachievers actually earn good money in the world; they just *feel* unsuccessful. Ironically, at their worst, those in this category feel even more like frauds as their success increases. Remember, Mr. Not Enough is not affected by circumstance or outcomes.

The alternate and more common version of this life lesson is the underachiever type. Often, these are the most talent-laden hands I get to see. In a parallel irony, the higher the talent potential, the more difficult it is for the owner of the hands to believe that he or she has any value at all to offer. Again, no amount of success can dissuade the Mr. Not Enough voice until the owner of these prints begins to establish self-esteem from the inside out.

One variation worth noting is that of those who attempt to marry their way out of this life lesson. Feeling they cannot make any money themselves, they hope to land a rich spouse as their meal ticket. Although it may be true that it is just as easy to fall in love with a rich man or woman as a poor one, beware of this trap. The price to be paid can be your aliveness, a stiff price indeed.

Of course there is always another option: make progress, grapple with Mr. Not Enough as best you can, learn from your errors, and watch your life purpose emerge and blossom. Take Veronica. Veronica may be the best example I have of someone turning a life lesson from nemesis to ally. Single mother, no marketable skills, she struggled for years just to squeeze by. But Veronica was smart, talented, and stubborn. Years of juggling responsibilities with little time for play eventually gave way to an easier path.

"I remember my big breakthrough." she told me. "I was rushing around looking for a birthday present for my oldest. I was between work and the university and had just enough time if I could find the right gift quickly enough. Going through the used CD rack at Blockbuster, I came across an old favorite of mine that I used to have in vinyl. A wistful nostalgia engulfed me for half a second as I sped ahead, my immediate purchase goal in mind. Then I stopped in my tracks. An album I loved was staring me in the face, its cost was under five dollars, and I had apparently decided in less than a second that I couldn't allow myself such a luxury. With all the effort I was expending, I couldn't afford five dollars for me, just this once? I started to cry. I bought the CD (plus one for my daughter) and drove the longer, prettier way to class. Somehow, that day shifted my entire life."

Veronica is a highly successful business consultant today with a six-figure income. Her kids are grown, and she is in a good marriage. Her specialty is training executives to smell the roses.

Veronica escaped the Mr. Not Enough trap by recognizing her own value as a human being, a recognition not based on outer-world criteria. Interestingly, when she did so, her outer world circumstances (including her money) went through a remarkable shift.

Wrong Work, No Passion

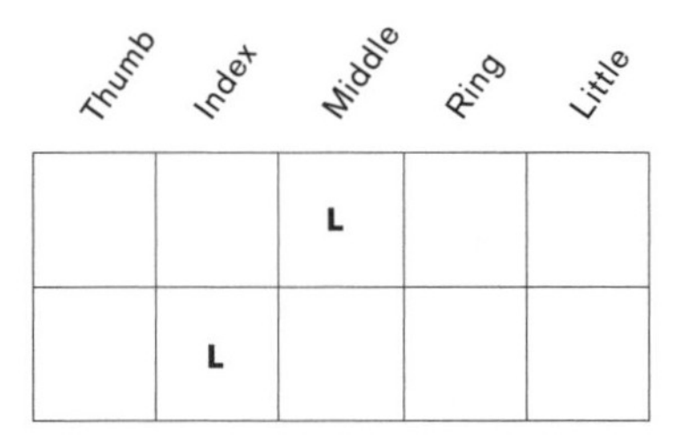

Wrong Work, No Passion

Dear Diary: Went to work again yesterday, just like the day before and the day before that. Ugh. It's just too much, man. I can't stand it anymore. I hate driving to work. I hate walking from the parking lot into this horrible jail of an office building. Ugh. Did I mention ugh yet? My boss is an idiot, my co-workers are idiots, I'm an idiot. Ugh. Gotta go. More exciting notes tomorrow. Ugh.

Dear Diary: Got a hand reading yesterday. The hand reader told me it was not the stupid job. I have to find the place in me that has passion and bring it to my work. I have to believe in myself, believe that I can actually get paid for doing what I want. He's gotta be kidding. Has he even seen the place I work? Has he met my idiot boss? What does he know? Nobody gets paid for what they want to do. I want to go to sleep; who's gonna pay me for that? Gotta go.

Dear Diary: Listened to the tape of my reading again as I drove to work. Hmmm. He said it was not the stupid job. He said to look at how I made up a story in my brain in which everybody is stuck at stupid jobs they hate. Look how I've tried to prove my theory by taking jobs I hate, one after another, and hanging out with people who have done the same. How it was the way I was setting things up in my life and it didn't have to be that way forever even though a part of me thinks I don't deserve any better because, well, because I am me. He said he liked his job a lot, so apparently not everybody hates his or her job, just everybody I think about when I want to prove my theory to myself. Maybe he has a small point. Maybe. But does he realize how tight the job market is? Everybody is downsizing. Oh yeah, he said that didn't matter. When the economy was booming and unemployment was minus 5 percent, I still found a job I hated. He said that was very creative. He said I am very creative. What does he know?

Dear Diary: Put a resume together. Not a bad start, but who knows if it will get me anywhere? I've gotten my hopes up before only to fall on my face, disappointed. Can't hurt though.

Dear Diary represents the most common version of this life lesson: a person with no passion for work. You can guess that passion has left the rest of Dear Diary's life as well. In other versions, passion is present everywhere *except* work. The old adage: "Do what you love and the money will follow" seems a hollow cliché to someone struggling to meet financial obligations. True, money does not automatically accrue just because you love your job. But with these fingerprints, you must find your passion for work or you will find yourself living in the big gaping hole.

Power without Apology

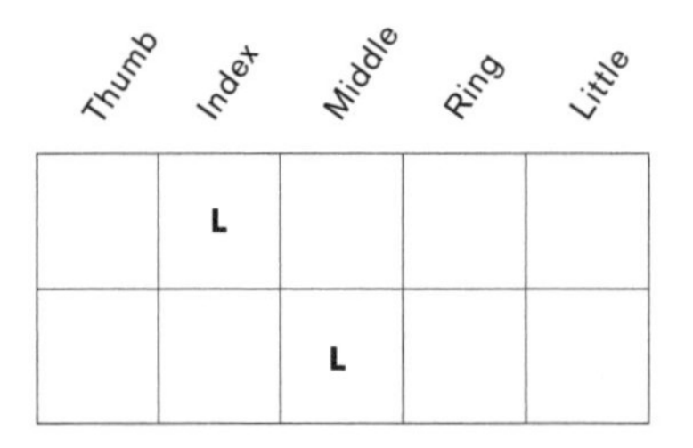

Power without Apology

This Mr. Not Enough, my own life lesson, has been my constant companion for as long as I can recall. In one aspect of its learning program, I am challenged to do what I want despite guilt feelings that threaten to cause me to agree to things I don't want to do at all. Can I tell someone I cannot read their hands early Sunday morning if they insist they must have their hands read and Sunday morning is the only possibility? Do I have the right to fire someone who is incompetent? When I think of handing out the pink slip, I am so nervous I try almost anything to avoid the moment. At times like these, it is good for me to remember I am not in knots over their dilemma. I am in knots because I fear the prospect of someone being upset with me, and I'm afraid of feeling guilty about it. I hate that feeling.

My wife, Alana, shivers as I open the car window, so I roll up the window and perspire. Alana doesn't like Sinatra so I turn the radio off. Alana can't eat for another two hours so I go hungry. What can I do? Diabetics need to keep to their schedules. I go out to buy myself a new basketball and return with flowers for Alana instead. What are you doing to me Alana? Nothing. No one is doing anything to me. I am painting myself into another Mr. Not Enough corner, selling off my independence so as to preempt any possible guilt feelings.

But what can I do?

I can do what I want and feel guilty, if that's what comes up—that's what I can do. Really? I can do what I want to do? But what if Alana doesn't like the song on the radio? She'll tell me she doesn't like it and ask me to change, or maybe it grows on her just like some of her music has rubbed off on me. More likely, she is in her own world somewhere and didn't even notice Sinatra came on. Or she'll get angry—why must I always insist on having everything my way, she may ask. Okay. Is that your biggest fear here, Richard? What if she tells me five other ways in which I am selfish and self-centered? Ten? What if she never wants to talk to me again? What if no woman ever will speak to me, no man or woman? Have I left anyone out? Richard, calm down. It's only a song on the radio. You'll be okay.

If listening to Alana's classical music station half the time is the worst penalty I ever had to pay for being born with these fingerprints, I would gladly pay the fine and be over with it. If only. Truth be known, Mr. Not Enough has bigger fish to fry in my life.

Key words here are *power* and *authority* for the right index finger and *integrity* for the left middle. Since I need to learn to use power with integrity for my life purpose to flower, the Paradox Principle states that I must root out the power abuser aspect of my conscious and unconscious selves. No wonder I am scared of the process.

According to the Goldilocks Rule, power abuse will take two forms. One: I use too much power applied in the wrong way at the wrong time. I blare the radio, overriding Alana's desperate pleas for relief. I overreact to employee errors. I insist on my way only. Can I receive the feedback the world is giving me, apologize if apologies are in order, and return to integrity? This is a skill to be practiced. When I make errors, I will have to correct them if my life purpose is to flourish. Two: I use too little power, inappropriately letting others impose their agendas on me. Can I receive the feedback my inner turmoil is giving me and take a stand, if one is needed, or let things pass, if that is my choice? Good question. What if power abuse is happening in both ways at the same time, if choices are so complicated that I cannot tell for sure whether I am overdoing it to others or they are overdoing it to me? Arrgghh. Well, it is worth remembering, Richard, that this is your life lesson. It is not supposed to be easy for you.

Masters of Power without Apology retain a full range of options in each circumstance that life presents. Responding to the moment as best they can, they adjust their behaviors to fit what is actually going on. Less skillful players get stuck in a rut, replaying a role out of sync with current events. As I can testify in open court, Power without Apology can severely test your mettle.

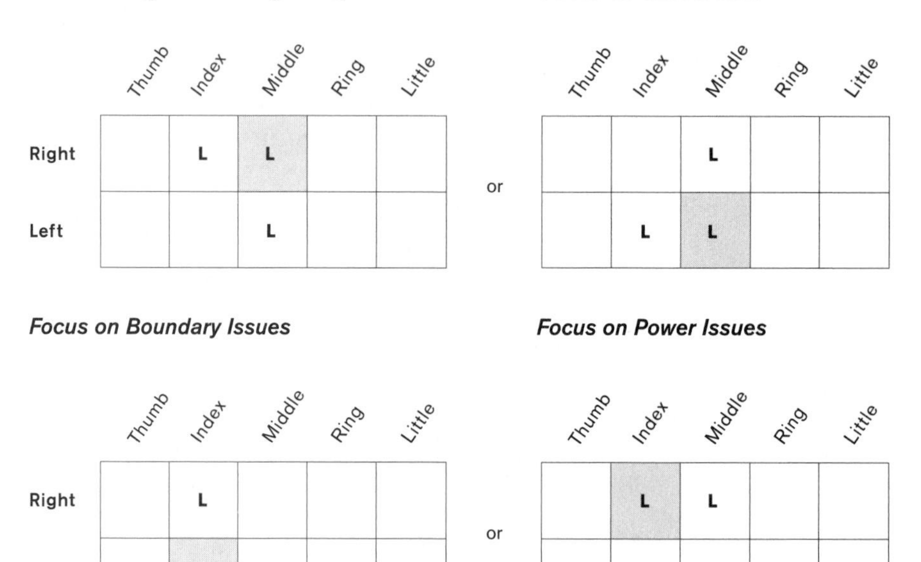

Just as common as the standard version of Mr. Not Enough (four lowest ranking prints), and the four Mr. Not Enoughs made up of two lowest ranking prints, are the Mr. Not Enoughs that have three lowest ranking prints. In cases such as these, the focus is on the elbow print (the lowest ranking fingerprint contiguous to both of the other two lowest ranking prints, the shaded L in the fingerprint charts above). In the first example (upper left), the lowest ranking print on the right middle finger is the elbow print, so the focus is on proper work for proper pay, the usual suspect when the right middle finger is the life lesson. In the lower left example, the main life theme will focus on the left index (the elbow print), with its issues of poor boundaries and personal violation.

Two Famous Mr. Not Enoughs

The two following fingerprint charts present two famous men who resp
ferently to the Mr. Not Enough visible in their fingerprints.

Ted Bundy

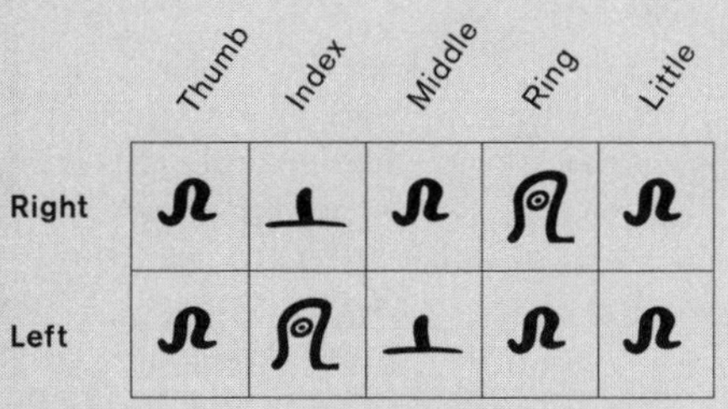

	Thumb	Index	Middle	Ring	Little
Right					
Left					

Fingerprint Profile: Peacocks on right ring finger and left index finger are the highest ranking prints, and Mr. Not Enough (right index finger and left middle finger as the lowest ranking prints) is the life lesson

Life Purpose: The Passionate Artist, The Passionate Individualist

Life Lesson: Power without Apology

School: Wisdom

Life-Fulfillment Formula: Power with integrity unlocks the creativity that is the key to your happiness.

Ted Bundy, owner of the fingerprint chart above, is the famous serial killer who admitted to over thirty gruesome killings. For those seeking Power without Apology, Goldilocks will insist that the journey include a visit to Power Underdeployed (too much apology) or Power Overdeployed (power without conscious restraint). The exalted possibility here is Power with Integrity. As this is my own life lesson, I found it particularly compelling to look into the hands of someone who wrestled with the same gremlin and did so poorly. Unwise power without restraint was the unfortunate outcome.

I am not concerned that if I do not keep an eye on my life lesson I will turn into a serial killer. But Ted Bundy's life story, along with John F. Kennedy's, which follows, shows just how far a human can go in one direction or the other.

John F. Kennedy

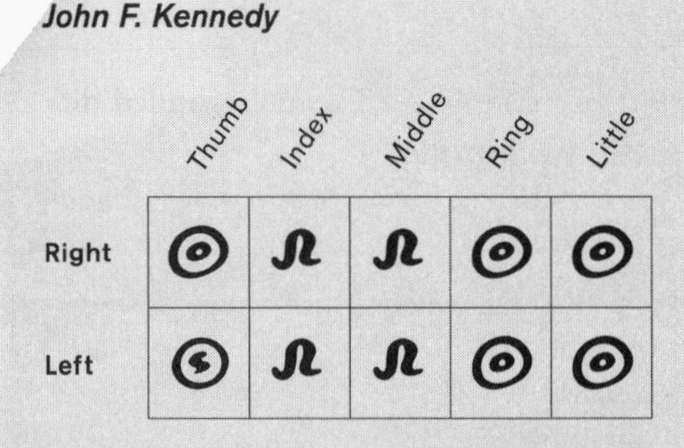

Fingerprint Profile: Whorls on both ring fingers and both little fingers and right thumb are the highest ranking prints, loops on both index fingers and both middle fingers are the lowest ranking prints

Life Purpose: Worldly Success + Public Impact in the Healing Arts = Inspire the Masses

Life Lesson: Mr. Not Enough

School: Service

Life-Fulfillment Formula: Do I have what it takes to inspire the masses? You better believe it.

Most people know that JFK's older brother, Joseph, killed in World War II, was the original focus of their father's political ambitions. Was President Kennedy actually living *his* life dream, or was he flogging himself daily, trying to live up to some impossible standard? Was Mr. Not Enough pushing him up the ladder of success, or was he tearing Kennedy's insides all to pieces? And what about all that Marilyn Monroe stuff? The most powerful person on the planet just had sex with the Eve of the twentieth century. Did he finally feel complete? Or did he immediately get up and look for something to do, something to eat, something else; anything, as opposed to being at home with himself? Since JFK did significant Inspiring of the Masses, we can assume he must have made some progress on his life lesson.

The fate of all humanity may not be hanging in the balance in your life, and Marilyn Monroe may not be coming over shortly for a nightcap, but JFK's story is a good illustration of how your nemesis (life lesson) can become your greatest ally. Ted Bundy's fingerprints make it clear that the reverse is also true: your life lesson can remain your nemesis forever and block your life purpose from ever seeing the light of day.

The Artist with Heart

The Right Ring Finger or Both Ring Fingers as the Life Purpose in an Archetypal Combination

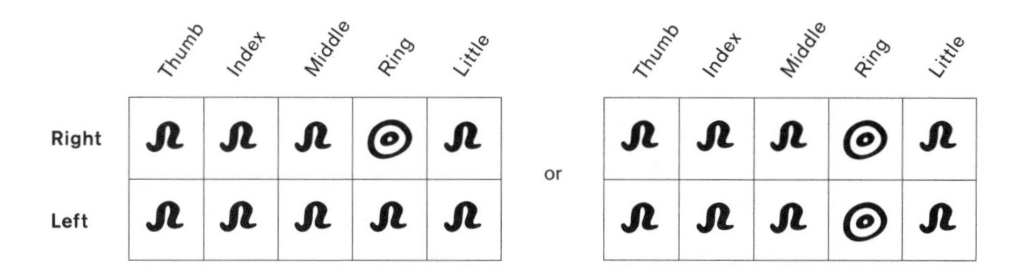

Fingerprint Profile: Right ring finger or both ring fingers with the highest ranking print, loops elsewhere

Life Purpose: The Artist with Heart

Life Lesson: Emotional Authenticity, Vulnerability Skills

School: Love

Life-Fulfillment Formula: Be true to your feelings and your artistry emerges.

Some with The Artist with Heart life-purpose map have a straightforward life story: find your talent, develop it, mature, and see your evolving self reflected back on the canvas of your choice. However, there are quite a few variations on this theme. The most common one is the person struggling to find their niche. If this is the case for you, the challenge is to develop emotional vulnerability through experience. Finding your niche will not come until you do so.

Lemumba and the Nice Garden Syndrome Lemumba had beautiful hands. Lemumba also had beautiful eyes, clothes, and a shiny new car that was a shade of green whose name was something like Jungle Mint. As a matter of fact, that was what struck me about Lemumba: everything about her seemed too perfect. The Nice Garden Syndrome is what we call it at the IIHA when people have hands shaped exactly like a perfect diagram in a palmistry book. For owners of the NGS, all looks fine, all the time. Experts at making a nice impression, even if they have full-scale havoc going on indoors, at least the garden always looks neat and well trimmed (hence the name).

I began Lemumba's reading. "It seems you know how to get people to like you, Lemumba, no matter who they are. If I were taking you home to mother to introduce her to my new bride, I am positive you would have mom eating right out of your hands. In fact, if I were to introduce you to ten different moms, each one a unique and difficult customer, I am sure you could have all ten mothers at your beck and call. What a talent you possess. But as for everyone else, there is always a challenge, and for you, Lemumba, the challenge is finding your proper niche.

"I can just imagine you coming out of the cafeteria with your lunch tray, a transfer student on your first day at your new school, scanning the tables for a place to sit. 'Let's see, should I sit with the nerds, the cheerleaders, the future Jaycees?' I would have only a few tables to pick from, but you are able to create a welcome from each and every table in the lunch room. You are so good at belonging, you actually wind up feeling that you don't really belong anywhere. That must be tough." Lemumba assured me it was.

"What a paradox. Your life purpose is to be The Individualist (another version of The Artist). When the last mask is removed, which is the true face at the bottom of things? Good question for a master chameleon.

"Bottom line for you, Lemumba: your challenge is to get permission from yourself to let others see into your two-way mirror. Here is my homework assignment for you. Do this for three days in a row and I guarantee your whole life will turn around. Tomorrow, I want you to wear a striped shirt with plaid pants.

"Take it easy, Lemumba, I am not serious about the stripes and plaids. I was only sticking a Post-It note in your mind, a reminder designed to pop up whenever you catch yourself making a nice impression when you really would rather be elsewhere. The more you can notice your behaviors in this regard, picking when and where to impress instead of impressing always, you will find, bit by bit, that another part of you will emerge, a part that you have barely met. It is *this* you that knows where your niche is, Lemumba. Follow her and you will find your life purpose."

Summary By sidestepping all rejection possibilities, Lemumba's chameleon self was also denying her life purpose the experiences it needed to round itself into proper shape. If your life purpose is The Artist, you too will have to face the possibility of audience tomatoes if your full, individualistic nature is to find its ultimate form. When the tomatoes come your way, can you see them as your ally, an indicator to double-check yourself and adjust if adjustment is required? Lemumba's life was tomato free, but without a tomato-based feedback loop to guide her, Lemumba's life was also without direction.

The High-Profile Person

The Right Ring Finger or Both Ring Fingers as the Life Purpose in an Archetypal Combination

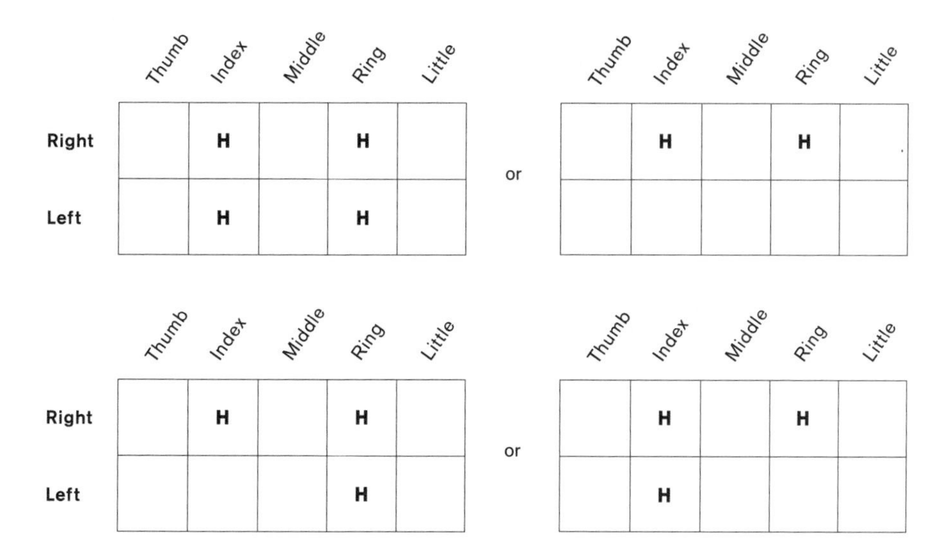

	Thumb	Index	Middle	Ring	Little
Right		**H**		**H**	
Left		**H**		**H**	

or

	Thumb	Index	Middle	Ring	Little
Right		**H**		**H**	
Left					

	Thumb	Index	Middle	Ring	Little
Right		**H**		**H**	
Left				**H**	

or

	Thumb	Index	Middle	Ring	Little
Right		**H**		**H**	
Left		**H**			

Fingerprint Profile: Right index finger or both index fingers + right ring finger or both ring fingers as the highest ranking prints

Life Purpose: The High-Profile Person

Life-Fulfillment Formula: Find your spotlight and show yourself to the world.

Standing alone as the highest ranking print, the right ring finger emphasizes bringing forth your creative potential, taking off the mask, living in the spotlight. When it combines with the right index finger or both index fingers as the other highest ranking print(s), then one of two themes is highlighted:

- The Influential, High Achieving Artist (like Walt Disney, who had the fingerprints in the top right chart above)
- The Famous Leader (like Charles Manson, see page 189)

I have seen many hands with more talent markers than the hands of Walt Disney, yet Disney's impact on the world was more profound than any but the merest few. Like other successful creative types, he had an inner imperative to reach a large audience no matter what obstacles stood in his way. If you have these fingerprints, accepting your soul's legitimate need to gain the spotlight may be a breakthrough point on the way to finding and living your life purpose.

"I don't need to blow my horn," some High-Profile clients tell me. "My creativity is for myself, mainly." I would agree with anyone saying this whose life purpose was the right ring finger in isolation. However, when it is combined with a right index finger highest ranking print, a certain egocentrism that demands attention is part of the soul's formula for life fulfillment.

Dealing with Disapproval

The Right Ring Finger or Both Ring Fingers as the Life Lesson in an Archetypal Combination

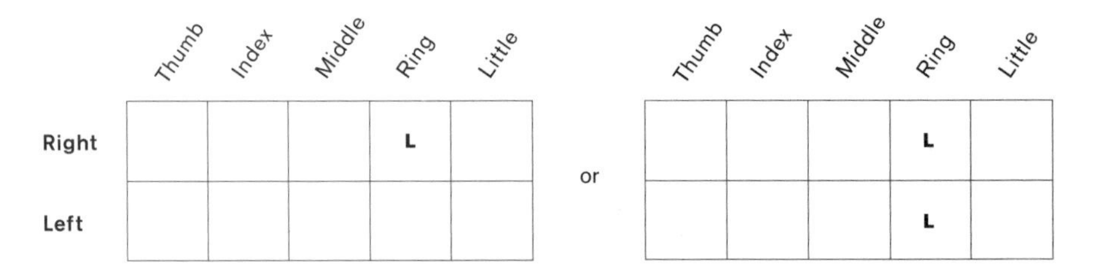

Fingerprint Profile: Right ring finger or both ring fingers as the lowest ranking print(s)

Life Lesson: Hiding Out, Dealing with Tomato Fears (This is the IIHA nickname for the paralyzing fear that if you stand out in any way, people with throw tomatoes at you.)

Life-Fulfillment Formula: Come out of the closet and become the person you really are.

Everybody wants to be cool, not to be controlled by what other people think. Easier said than done. I recall how I felt when I slipped on the microphone cord and fell off the stage during a lecture in San Francisco. I have no trouble bringing to mind the man who walked out of a lecture in 1986. There I was at the podium, 299 souls listening in rapt fascination; one man walked into the atrium to have a cigarette, and my eyes followed him the entire way. Maybe I should include the lecture ten years earlier when absolutely no one showed up—just me and the chairs. The guy who was supposed to collect the money at the door even forgot to show. "Sorry, something came up. I just forgot." How many public speakers have dreams that they are on stage and forget to put on their pants or can't remember what to say or have gone strangely mute? I have. (At least I hope I was dreaming.)

No way around it: rejection, ridicule, social embarrassment—none are high on my list of fun activities. Yet for those with these fingerprints, the life path runs right smack dab in the middle of that mess. Let's take a look at this life lesson from two different angles.

Esther Esther was a life coach, spiritual teacher, marriage and family counselor, and all-around wise woman. At least her hands said she was. When I questioned her, she did admit to being the person people came to all the time when advice was needed. Her actual job title was administrative assistant at ABC Conglomerates, so she had to do her amateur psychiatrist thing at the watercooler and at home on the phone with friends and family.

"You are as qualified to be a personal growth consultant as a person can be," I said in her reading. "It is like looking at Beethoven's hands, seeing the gifted composer there, and finding out he composes only occasionally because he drives a bus for a living. Of course, when it rains, he hears the windshield wipers go da da da dum—but what of it? He has to make a living, and music must take a back seat. My point is this: why not make wise woman your actual job? You do it all the time anyway."

"I can't do that," she said. "I'm too shy."

As much as Esther was built to be the wise advice giver, she had a stay-in-the-closet department of equal proportion. No matter what she did as a profession, this tug-of-war (show yourself vs. hide out) would be central to her life story.

Knowing the cure (feel the fear, do it anyway) is small consolation when you are paralyzed by an entire Greek chorus of everyone you have ever known observing you through a microscope in the theater of your mind. Esther knew what she wanted to do with her life. She just hadn't gotten around to doing it yet.

There seemed no reason to badger her on the point. The reading needed a change of pace, so I told her a musical story. "I was on the program at a weeklong retreat," I began. "About a dozen women had been examining their lives and I was to read their hands. Arriving an hour early, I got to be in the audience for a performance I remember to this day.

"The women had divided themselves into teams, each team demonstrating what they had learned during the week by doing a skit in front of the group. One stands out in my memory. Three women, done up vaudeville style, performed the 'Disapproval Rag.'

"They sang and danced: 'Disapproval . . . disapproval . . . disapproval is okay with me.'" I gave Esther my best vaudevillian voice. "Then one of the three came forward as the other two leaned on their canes. 'So, my father said I had to . . .' 'Really,' the other two countered, gloved palms up to their tilted faces in exaggerated surprise. 'What did you say to him?' 'I said, Disapproval . . . disapproval . . . disapproval is okay with me—dah dah.'

"They sang together, legs kicking Rockette style. They continued until all three had told their stories of disapproval. Apparently, for these women, the big lesson of the whole retreat was learning that they could live with disapproval. Painful as it was, they weren't going to let fear of disapproval run their lives. They were a big hit," I concluded.

That evening I got a call from Esther. She had come home and found, unsolicited in her mailbox, a Burpee seed catalog with a free packet of "The World's Best Tomatoes" attached. She was making a collage to hang over her mantel piece, a reminder that tomatoes would not run her life.

I like it when I hear a happy ending.

Charles Charles was a dandy: a riverboat-gambler peacock, hard-rock version. Wearing tattoos, various rings that punctuated every visible body part, and a costume worthy of Halloween, he pranced into my office to discuss the meaning of life and his career possibilities. I was only slightly surprised to find the same fingerprints as shy Esther's. Charles's hiding place seemed to be in his exaggerated persona. "You can't disapprove of me," he seemed to be saying, "I've already disapproved of you. Either you applaud me or I will declare that you are too establishment and yellow-bellied to handle all that I am."

Charles had been a rave DJ for the last decade. Things were getting stale, he shared; it was all so formulaic. "Time to risk new degrees of disapproval," I offered.

"You mean like doing the next rave in a business suit? Cool."

Summary When the right ring finger is the lowest ranking fingerprint, rejection is not merely uncomfortable, it feels life threatening. Charles's answer to this life lesson was to create an oversize persona as his hiding place. Esther was in hiding. Too Much, Too Little—both were seeking Just Right so that their life purposes could find the light of day.

The Innovator

The Left Ring Finger as the Life Purpose

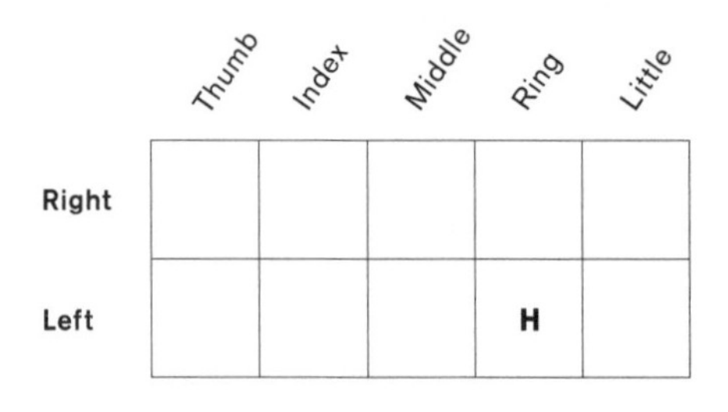

Fingerprint Profile: Left ring finger as the highest ranking print

Life Purpose: The Innovator

Life-Fulfillment Formula: Don't sell out, but don't hide out either.

When the left ring finger becomes the life purpose, satisfaction is greatest when you have stood your ground in the face of opposition, managing not to sell out to pressures to conform, yet not running away to your own island. Finding the balance between what is expected of you vs. what your heart tells you to do is the essence of this life path.

The Plague Convention Six foot five, angular, sun-caked, leather-vested—he could be a cowboy sauntering up to the saloon bar for a whiskey. He has been wearing a distracted grin all night, so I have no idea what he is thinking as he makes his way into the reading chair. His salt and pepper hair, sticking straight up, adds to the effect. I half expect him to spit into the imaginary spittoon beside the reading lamp. He lays his hands down with excessive ceremony, almost daring me to make sense out of his unconventional self. I begin the reading.

"You have Eureka! hands, the hands of someone bent on discovery. I have no doubt that your brain is full of clever new ideas. Let me tell you a story. It is the fourteenth century and a young fellow with a bunch of papers rolled up under his arm travels a long way to the big university. He wants to speak to the man in charge because he has the cure for the plague. He is ushered into an important meeting hall, where a dozen or so important-looking men look up from their important discussion. Without invitation, he launches into a description of his plague cure.

"The Committee listens for about twenty seconds before the head guy interrupts the lad and makes a crude joke at his expense. 'You expect us, the top minds of the kingdom, to believe that a little shaver like yourself has discovered the cure for the plague? What are your credentials? Who is your benefactor? What universities have you attended? I thought so. Don't bother us with your idiotic speculations. Can't you see we have important work to do?'

"'Well then, die without it!' shouts the boy, wincing at the rejection as he runs from the proceedings. And many of them did. He had the plague cure and not one life was saved.

"It's just a story my imagination created looking at your hands, but it captures your life challenge: are you or are you not going to bring your discoveries to the world? Maybe you even act a bit extra-eccentric at the committee meetings, the better to not be taken seriously? After all, if you played the game just a bit, you might have to join the very club you resent so much. Then again, you can't just let your work go down the drain, or can you?" The tall cowboy stood up. "Got me pegged," he laughed, and he moseyed his way back to his original chair in the circle.

Summary If this is your life purpose, you face the same life question: will you bring your unique whatever-it-is to the world? Expect to run into some flak, including the possibility of ad hominem attacks that obscure the real issue, but this is what Innovators often face if they do what they came to do.

The Pioneer

The Left Ring Finger as the Life Purpose in an Archetypal Combination

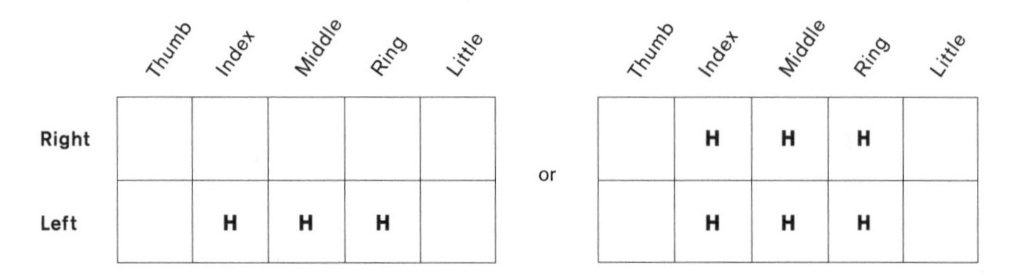

	Thumb	Index	Middle	Ring	Little
Right					
Left		H	H	H	

or

	Thumb	Index	Middle	Ring	Little
Right		H	H	H	
Left		H	H	H	

Fingerprint Profile: Left index finger or both index fingers + left middle finger or both middle fingers + left ring finger or both ring fingers as the highest ranking prints (Passions + Integrity + The Innovator = The Pioneer)

Life Purpose: The Pioneer

Life-Fulfillment Formula: Be true to yourself and your craft and ultimately convert the skeptics.

The Pioneering Leader

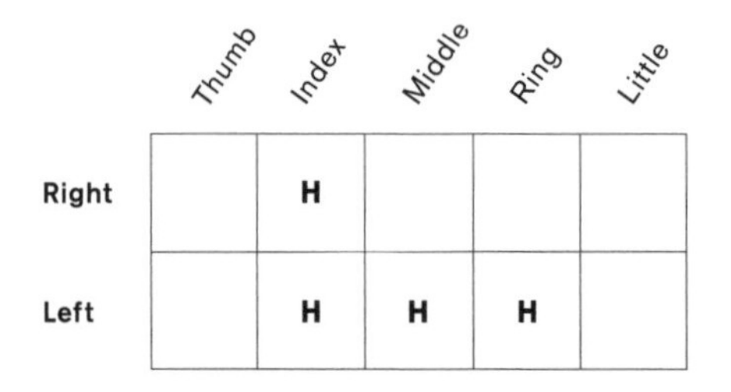

	Thumb	Index	Middle	Ring	Little
Right		H			
Left		H	H	H	

Fingerprint Profile: Left index finger or both index fingers + left middle finger + left ring finger as the highest ranking fingerprints (Leader + Integrity + Innovation = The Pioneering Leader)

The Pioneer in Business

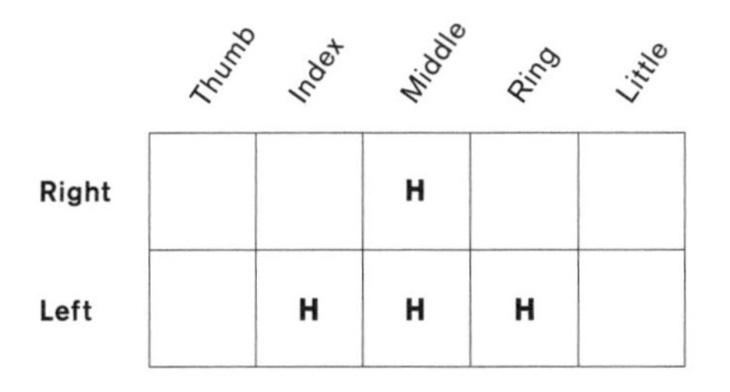

	Thumb	Index	Middle	Ring	Little
Right			**H**		
Left		**H**	**H**	**H**	

Fingerprint Profile: Left index finger + left middle finger or both middle fingers + left ring finger as the highest ranking fingerprints (Passion + Business Integrity + Innovation = The Pioneer in Business)

The Pioneering Artist

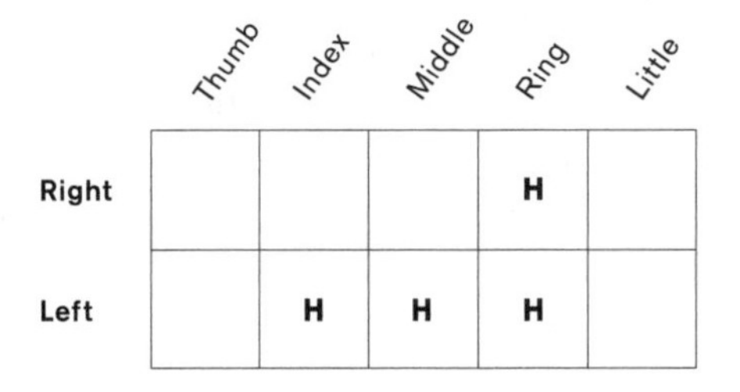

	Thumb	Index	Middle	Ring	Little
Right				**H**	
Left		**H**	**H**	**H**	

Fingerprint Profile: Left index finger + left middle finger + left ring finger or both ring fingers as the highest ranking fingerprints (Passion + Integrity + Creative Innovation = The Pioneering Artist)

The Pioneer is the only archetypal combination that is left ring finger–based. Combining three separate yet related themes—live your passions, personal integrity, and convert the skeptics—The Pioneer, among all life-purpose combinations, has the greatest need to go against the grain, ever striving for freedom of expression. This is both the good news and the bad.

The Frontier Beckons Let's start with the good news. If you are a Pioneer, opportunities abound. First to arrive in a new territory, you get to pick the best spot for your own homestead and you get to name the mountains and streams. I remember when my wife, Alana, and I arrived at the most popular hiking trail in all of Alaska. We were wondering if we needed to reserve a campsite or motel; to our utter surprise, it was almost deserted. There was this one guy with a mountain bike rental shack.

"Isn't this the most popular hike in the entire state?" we asked. "Where are all the KFCs and T-Shirt stores? How did you get this concession?"

"I had been hiking and biking here for five years when a couple of years ago I just went ahead and built the shack myself," he said. "No paperwork. Nobody's bothered me about it. I'm adding sandwiches and cold drinks this spring. Just to give you an idea about this place: my friend moved up here six years ago, decided to get into politics, got twenty-three votes, became mayor, and now he is in the state legislature. No connections, no money; didn't matter."

Sounds good. Is there any bad news to contend with? Actually, there is. Go your own way and find out quickly why everyone else is not. You may have to invent your own industry, creating everything from scratch. It might not be easy to get financing either. Banks like to invest in proven commodities with track records. Living without a motel or McDonald's nearby is pure and resplendent, but what are you going to do if there's a blizzard? And that is not the hard part.

"What is the hard part then?" you may ask. The hard part is going it alone with the knowledge that you will have to prove yourself ten times over to get anyone to take you even slightly seriously, that even your closest friends and family are unlikely to appreciate what you are up to until many moons have passed, that you are almost guaranteed to doubt your own convictions along the way. That is the hard part, pilgrim. Yet, if these are your fingerprints, this is your path.

Summary Like all life purposes, the good news and the bad news are two sides of the same coin. With these fingerprints, the thrill is going against the crowd and, in the long run, having the crowd agree that you were right all along. To succeed as a Pioneer, you will have to know and trust your own instincts when everyone thinks you are wrong.

Dealing with Disapproval

The Left Ring Finger as the Life Lesson

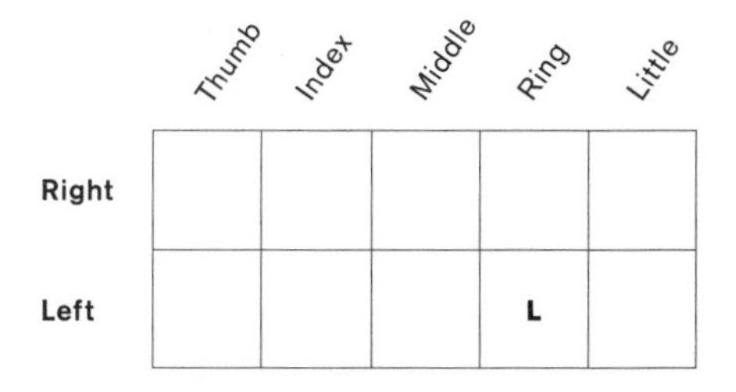

Fingerprint Profile: Left ring finger as the lowest ranking print

Life Lesson: Dealing with Disapproval

Life-Fulfillment Formula: Don't let possible rejections keep you from the life you want.

The left ring finger as the life purpose asks its owner to brave the road less traveled for the life purpose to shine. When the left ring finger is the life lesson, dealing with disapproval is the hardest thing in the world to do, and any road, less traveled or not, is hard to stay on when rejection is a real (or perceived) threat. There are many ways to avoid rejection possibilities, including the strange ways of Caroline.

Caroline "If you can't stand the heat, get out of the kitchen." Harry Truman said that, or was he the one who said, "The buck stops here"? I think he said both. In any event, presidents are not the only ones wrestling with hot kitchens. No matter your life purpose, with this life lesson, extra hot kitchen exercises (dealing with rejection possibilities) are to be expected as you prepare for the rigors of your appointed life task. Caroline's journey to human resources director is a case in point.

As a child, Caroline had always considered herself the odd one out, picking "Rudolph the Red-Nosed Reindeer" as her favorite bedtime story. In high school, her sisters had all the boyfriends; she was the smart one without a date on Friday night. Things got better for Caroline in college as she finally found her niche in politics. Caroline's kitchen temperature was rising with each political argument, and she found she could handle disagreements and even personal attacks with grace. But, after graduation, politics took a back seat, and Caroline found herself adrift.

She spent eleven years writing her thesis while bouncing around several dead-end relationships. After receiving a PhD, Caroline continued speaking out against injustice, still kinda sorta having relationships, not really choosing a career. Eventually, she took a course at the IIHA, and that is how we met. I always liked Caroline. She was smart and funny in a quirky sort of way. But, as I was to learn, she was also treacherous.

Arrange to meet Caroline for lunch on Monday and it was less than fifty-fifty it would actually happen. Caroline always left a vague window of escape available; there was always something that if it came up she might have to cancel, although she didn't think it would. Trying to clarify things led nowhere. It was incredible how obfuscatory she could be. It's just lunch, Caroline. If you want to have lunch on Monday, let's have lunch. If you don't, let's not. It should have been simple, but with Caroline nothing ever was.

I remember the time she signed up for an eight-week, eight-person life-purpose support group. Caroline absolutely guaranteed her attendance despite the fact that her deposit check had somehow failed to materialize. I know now that Caroline was keeping all her options open straight through the first day of class, when she presumably made up her mind to attend or not based upon the weather and her mood of the moment. Caroline did not know and would not have cared that others had been turned away based upon her assurances. That was the last time I would make that mistake with Caroline.

For me, Caroline's behavior was just a nuisance, but for Caroline this was business as usual. I wouldn't be surprised if she had accepted invitations from two different men for dates on the same evening, deciding that day which, if either, to keep. I didn't know whether she had escalated this behavior to two grooms waiting at different churches in tuxedos one Sunday, but from what I eventually learned about Caroline during the life-purpose support group, it would not have shocked me.

The fact is that Caroline could not stand disapproval. It is not as if the rest of the human race relishes the opportunity to be dumped on or rejected, it is just that Caroline is a bit more unconscious than you or I (assuming that you do not have the left ring finger as part of your life lesson). Like Rudolph the Red-Nosed Reindeer, left ring finger life-lesson persons need to learn to deal with rejection possibilities without either selling out or running away.

In Caroline's crazy world, as long as she never pinned herself down, she would remain un-disapproved-of. Of course, Caroline's tactic created extra disapprovals from tuxedoed gentlemen and others. But, the thing is, the disapproval never registered in Caroline's consciousness.

Caroline probably would have remained in the big gaping hole forever had it not been for Cosmo. I don't know what shifted things for Caroline. Maybe with her biological clock ticking away, the time was right. Maybe she just got tired of her life the way it was. All I know is that Cosmo was the best thing that ever happened to Caroline, and he would have none of her shenanigans. Such was his love and so directly did he express it, Caroline found herself bit by bit dropping her silly-little-girl-who-knew-big-words mask and guess what? The Caroline that was hiding one level deeper was a wise-woman high achiever who hated injustice and was willing to work hard to make the world a better place.

Caroline is in her fifties now, the director of human resources for a local township. She sets policy, and last week she had to fire the assistant chief of police. You can say her kitchen is hotter than ever. Although it may seem that it took her a long time to get to her life purpose, Caroline actually had done a good job, considering the path she was on. Left ring finger life-lesson persons are inclined to hide out, as are tented archers (Caroline was in the School of Wisdom). The combination of the two makes for hide-out experts. Her Big Shot life purpose is highly paradoxical here. But then again, who better to take the lead on a dark and stormy night than a Rudolph who had been sitting on the bench for so long without an important role to play?

Summary Caroline and Harry Truman weren't the most popular kids on the block, but they each became effective leaders in their own right, able to keep to their principles in the face of criticism. That is the bottom line for all those with a left ring finger life lesson: don't sell out. Don't let the potential for paralyzing tomato fear keep you from bringing out your talents and capabilities.

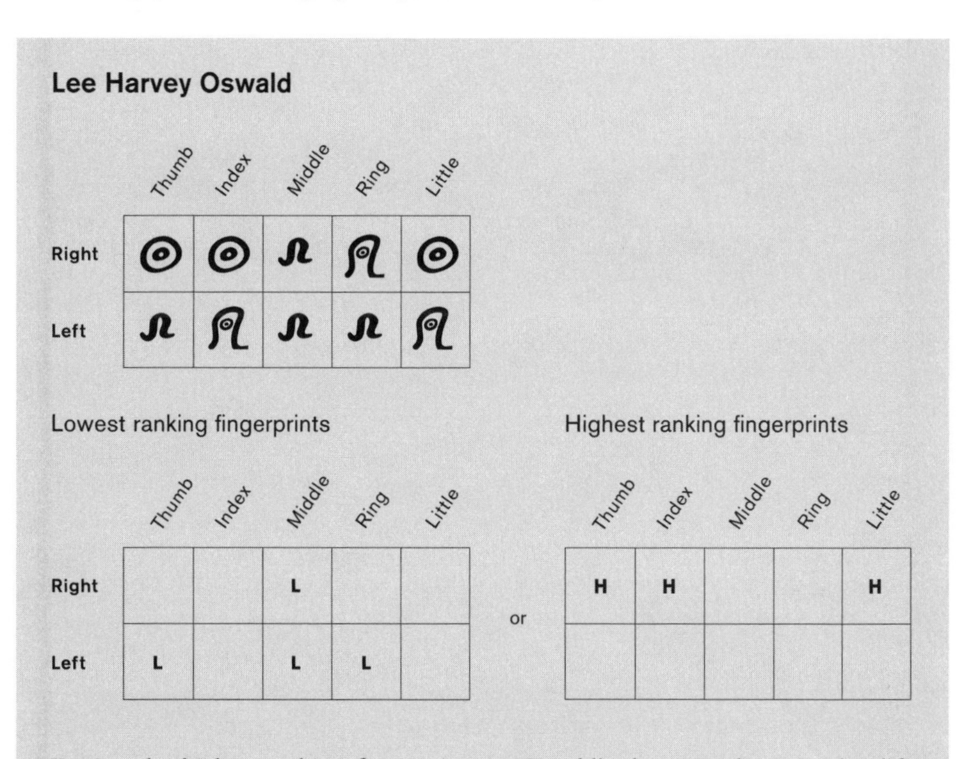

Erasing the highest ranking fingerprints in Oswald's chart reveals a complex life lesson with both middle fingers plus left thumb and left ring finger as the lowest ranking prints. Many of the fingerprint charts listed so far have been chosen for their simplicity: the highest ranking prints or lowest ranking prints appearing in only one or two places. In life, as you will have noted by now if you have taken the fingerprints of your inner circle, things can get much more complicated. Lee Harvey Oswald's chart is not all that unusual in its multiple-finger life lesson.

When multiples occur, the standard procedure is to look first for archetypal combinations. If there are none, then emphasize whichever finger is doubled up (both left and right hands with the same highest or lowest ranking prints). In this case, the middle finger is doubled up, therefore extra weight is placed on Not Being Okay, Issues of Guilt, Appropriate Behaviors, and so on. And that would be correct, up to a point. However, with the left ring finger as part of Oswald's complex life lesson, it will work best to emphasize its role in his life movie. If you do that, placing one-third of the emphasis on Not Okay in the Family or Community (double middle fingers plus left thumb) and the other two-thirds of the weight on feelings of I-Don't-Belong (left ring finger), I believe you get a good approximation of what must have been the dominant theme of the inner dialogue of John F. Kennedy's assassin.

Attempting to live in Russia during the height of the Cold War, handing out Marxist pamphlets on the street corners of New Orleans, stalking episodes, and failed associations with the CIA (regardless of the truth or untruth of conspiracy theories) all point to a man who could never find his place on this planet, anywhere. Conversely, check out Oswald's life purpose: The Big Shot with a Message. Was this how he saw his role in history? Or would his life-purpose inverse, mute small shot, be closer to the truth of his life? Jack Ruby rendered these questions largely unanswerable, but Lee Harvey Oswald's fingerprints offer tantalizing testimony to the inner workings of this mostly shadowy figure who had such an effect on world history.

Susan B. Anthony

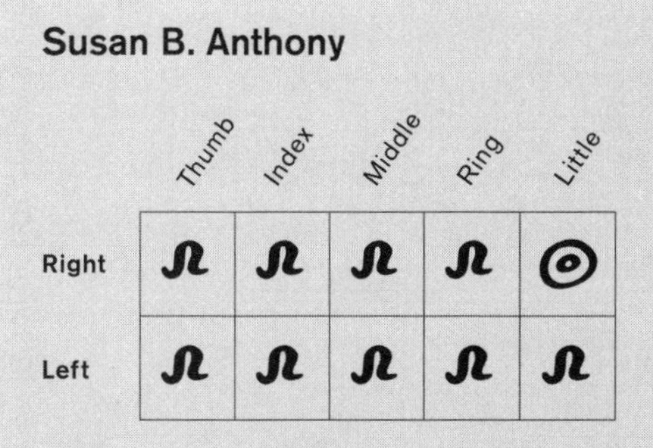

Fingerprint Profile: Right little finger as the highest ranking fingerprint

Life Purpose: A Message from the Heart

Life Lesson: Vulnerability Skills

School: Love

Life-Fulfillment Formula: Speak from the heart and good things are bound to happen.

You are looking at Susan B. Anthony's fingerprint chart. Many with these fingerprints face a tug-of-war between heart (home life) and public communications, but that was never the case for Susan B. Anthony: the two life themes were always joined.

Raised a Quaker, she spent the first fifteen years of her professional life as a teacher. When she was denied permission to speak at temperance rallies because she was a woman, she became outraged and took off on her own lecture tour. Susan B. Anthony had always been in touch with her Message from the Heart, but now she had the fire and charisma to reach her larger audience.

Her topics were women's rights and the abolition of slavery. Like Martin Luther King (see page 202), Susan B. Anthony faced hatred and abuse as she brought a message of inclusion to the masses. Also like King, Anthony needed to reach the hearts as well as the minds of her audience. Her fingerprints remind us that the experiences that we find most unpleasant are often pivotal in our development and can lead us directly toward our life purpose.

Summary The right little finger life purpose often emerges in stages. In the early phase, commonly extending well into a person's thirties, no message is contemplated until some event shifts a person's entire life. Only then does the right little finger life purpose become obvious. If you are under thirty-five and have a highest ranking right little finger, you are encouraged to look at your life for signals that you might have already found your message for the world without realizing it. If you are thirty-five or older, the question often becomes: how far will you go to take your message to the world? Are you willing to put worldwide communications on your front burner?

Persuasion

The Right Little Finger as the Life Purpose in an Archetypal Combination

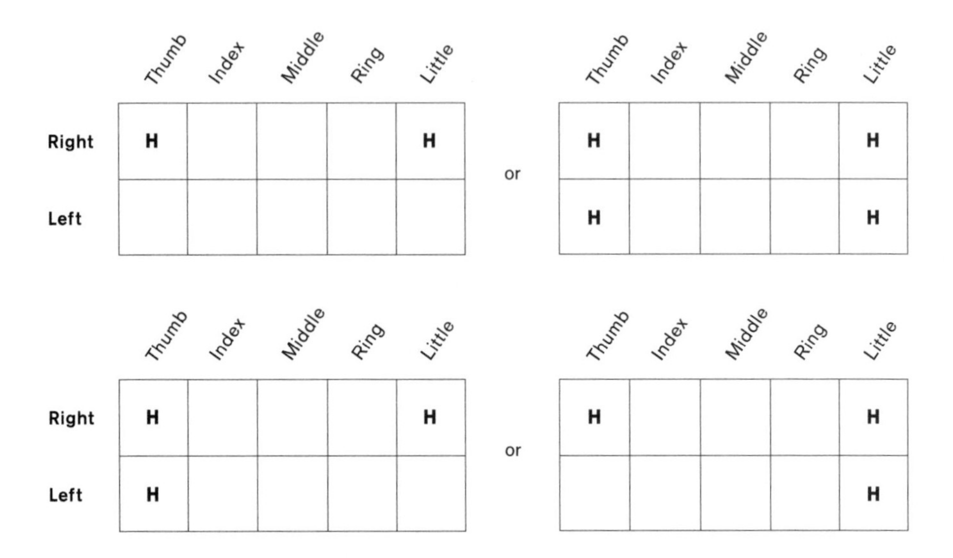

	Thumb	Index	Middle	Ring	Little
Right	H				H
Left					

or

	Thumb	Index	Middle	Ring	Little
Right	H				H
Left	H				H

	Thumb	Index	Middle	Ring	Little
Right	H				H
Left	H				

or

	Thumb	Index	Middle	Ring	Little
Right	H				H
Left					H

Fingerprint Profile: Right thumb or both thumbs + right little finger or both little fingers as the highest ranking prints

Life Purpose: The Persuader

Life-Fulfillment Formula: Use your persuasions skills to make life better for you and others.

Persuasion can operate as a life purpose archetypal combination or, with lowest ranking fingerprints in the same locations, it can also operate as the life lesson (see also The Wing Walker on page 265). In either case, owners of highest or lowest ranking prints in these locations face a world filled with people who very much do not want to be persuaded of anything. They can be sitting on a railroad track with the diesel headed straight for them and still refuse to budge if they sense you are trying to make them do it. Further, you yourself might be one of these people. Yet, if your life purpose is to persuade, you must find it in you to become a Persuader or you will wind up in the big gaping hole. Maybe this story will help you get over any remaining persuasion reluctance you might still possess.

A Little Old Lady It was the late 1970s. I was in the final stages of my financial planning career, reviewing the finances of an eighty-four-year-old woman whose house smelled of dust, death, and stale cat food. The cat food was on the kitchen table, dust was everywhere, and death seemed imminent. She could not afford people food, much less her medicine, she told me as I looked at the hundred thousand dollars she had in the bank at 4 percent interest. Quick math indicated she could live comfortably if her money were in a money market fund (as safe as a bank and paying about 20 percent back then), but her banker had warned her never to listen to anyone who suggested any other financial vehicle except his own.

Before I could decide which rung of hell was appropriate for bankers who were willing to abuse elderly women, I needed to convince her to move her money. She was not all there upstairs, but she was there enough to know someone was trying to persuade her about something, and she was not buying any of it. Four hours later, I had made the toughest sale of my sales career and it carried zero commissions. But I did earn a good story about persuasion's positive possibilities.

Summary The Persuasion life purpose carries a high reluctance factor. Understandably. From the slimy used-car salesman to the slimy politician, we have been burned once too often not to go on alert whenever we feel persuasion is near. Yet, persuasion itself is not good or bad; it depends on what it is being used for. If persuasion is your life purpose, it is your life's goal to be a Persuader and put your persuasion powers to proper use.

True Communications

The Right Little Finger as the Life Lesson

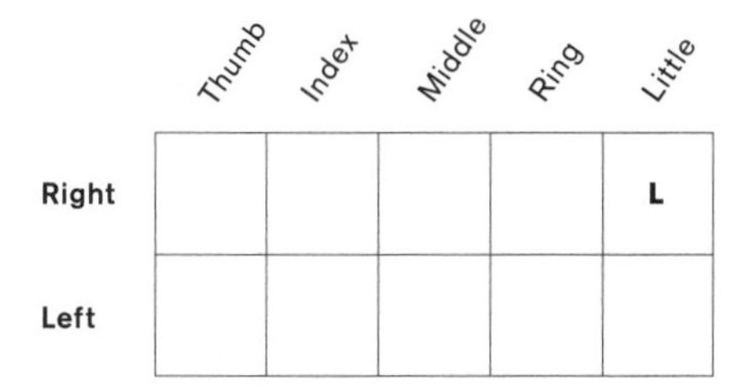

Fingerprint Profile: Right little finger as the lowest ranking fingerprint

Life Lesson: True Communications

Life-Fulfillment Formula: You better ask for what you want, or you might not like what you get.

In the following story, two men with a right little finger life lesson enter into a business relationship. Difficulties come quickly to the surface.

Grant Thinks He's a Thief Ira was a young salesman on the way up. Grant was a sales trainer and popular public speaker. If only Ira had been told that Grant thought himself a thief, Ira might have had an easier time of it. Too bad that wasn't the case. Grant had a right little finger life lesson, so his successful public communications career seemed to suggest he had gotten a good handle on his soul psychology. This was true to some degree, but to Ira's dismay, Grant's true communications consciousness did not extend to all levels of his life.

When Grant had asked Ira to be a presenter at his weeklong sales retreat in Aspen, Ira was thrilled. He would have gladly paid his own expenses and worked for free, but before he could offer to, Grant suggested a fee that easily exceeded anything Ira would have dared imagine. Ira gladly accepted, not realizing that paying his own expenses and working for free were closer to what Grant had in mind.

"What? I can't believe it," Grant said. "Your plane ticket and hotel voucher didn't arrive? I mailed them myself last week." "No," Ira shyly replied, not wanting to add to the great man's upset. He must have so many details to attend to, and Ira was grateful that Grant even took his call personally. "Tell you what, Ira, just put it on your credit card, and we'll work this all out when you get here. I can't wait to introduce you to so-and-so. See you soon."

The seminar turned out to be a great success, but not for Ira. Although listed on the program, blah blah this and blah blah that, Ira never did get to give the presentation he had worked so hard to prepare. It seems Grant had oversold the seminar to the hotel. Short of bodies to pay for rooms he had already agreed to pay for, Grant made up the slack with eager yearlings like Ira. Then, to cover his own profit, he finessed Ira's speaking fees and the fees for half a dozen other presenters. Ira would gladly have offered to work pro bono, and the seminar itself was wonderful. Grant was brilliant and inspiring. He was generous with his time and introductions. Does this seem hard to believe, given the other facts about Grant's behavior? Perhaps, but the longer I've read hands, the more Grant's contradictory behavior makes sense to me.

It wasn't until the last day of the seminar that Ira got filled in on the details. "Grant hasn't paid you yet, has he Ira?" asked Wendy.

"How did you know?"

"Think it through. Did you check with the airlines to see if they had a reservation in your name? You aren't going to be covered for the hotel or whatever presenter fees he promised you either. That's just Grant being Grant. I have known him for years. He can be a fine fellow, and his sales advice is deeply spiritual and eminently practical. That's why I still present at his seminars. But Grant thinks he's a thief. He doesn't realize that he gives so much value to people he doesn't have to steal to get what he wants. I still love him though. Don't take it personally, Ira."

"*Now* you tell me."

Summary Ira *had* taken it personally, but in the end what he learned about true communications, his own and others', was worth the trouble. Next time, Ira vowed, he would speak up sooner, not waiting until circumstances had limited his options and backed him into a corner.

When the right little finger is the life lesson, issues of manipulation often come to the fore. Equally common, however, are issues of proper listening. People in general, and those with this fingerprint configuration in particular, are perfectly capable of hearing what they want to hear regardless of evidence to the contrary. If this is your life lesson, it is worthwhile to double-check with the person on the other end of your conversation to see if what you heard is what was actually spoken.

What I Say Matters

The Right Little Finger as the Life Lesson in an Archetypal Combination

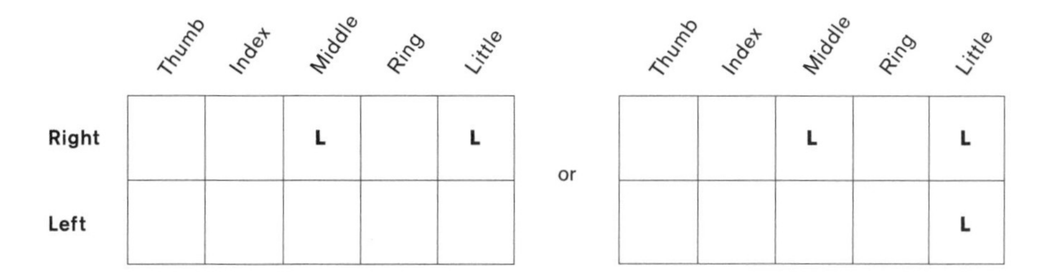

Fingerprint Profile: Right middle finger + right little finger or both little fingers as lowest ranking print(s)

Life Lesson: Nobody Listens to Me (What I Say Matters)

Life-Fulfillment Formula: Believe in the value of what you have to say and speak it out loud.

In its most extreme form, owners of this life lesson are routinely ignored, first by their original families, then by their friends and teachers, and eventually by their spouses and children. The pattern is reinforced to such a degree that it becomes next to impossible to believe in anything that emanates from inside themselves.

In less difficult cases, these folks are challenged to believe in the tangible value of their communications. They have learned to speak up for themselves but are working on integrating the proper work for proper pay piece of their life lesson (the right middle finger element). Ira, in the story just before this one, could be a candidate for this contingent of the WISM family.

Albert Einstein

Albert Einstein had this life lesson and managed to get to its exalted form: important communications to the world. Not that Einstein became the fuzzy-haired, endearing world spokesperson without a couple of battles with this life lesson. As you may or may not know, he didn't learn to speak until the age of three, was not particularly well regarded by his teachers in high school, and although the special and general theories of relativity are the biggest leaps forward in science since Newton, he never did receive the Nobel Prize for either. By the end of his career, most of his colleagues no longer took him seriously. Yet he continued to speak out for the causes he held most dear, and his enduring legacy owes a lot to his public communications. Einstein managed to turn What I Say Matters from nemesis to ally. Good work, Al.

Summary The right middle finger as all or part of the life lesson tends to skewer a person's self-evaluation. When the right middle finger is coupled in lowest ranking with the right little finger or both little fingers, the owner tends to incorrectly evaluate the value of his or her communications. Some people overevaluate their communications, like a boss keeping the troops in a Monday morning sales meeting hours past the point of usefulness. Ignoring the feedback from the sales staff, this What I Say Matters person is locked in a bubble of self-importance with concomitant problems to match.

More common, however, is the person who has something truly valuable to say but does not say it for one reason or another. Included in this category are those who have a product or service to offer but cannot bring themselves to speak up loud enough for the potential customers to hear. I have personally witnessed the devastation this can bring to those who have spent a lifetime developing their craft, only to be ignored by the marketplace.

"Just do it" is the advice to be heeded, but "just do it" doesn't do it. For some, a more extensive inner journey is required to identify, express, and release the shock or trauma keeping those important words locked inside.

The On-Again, Off-Again Healer

The Left Little Finger or Both Little Fingers as the Life Purpose in an Archetypal Combination

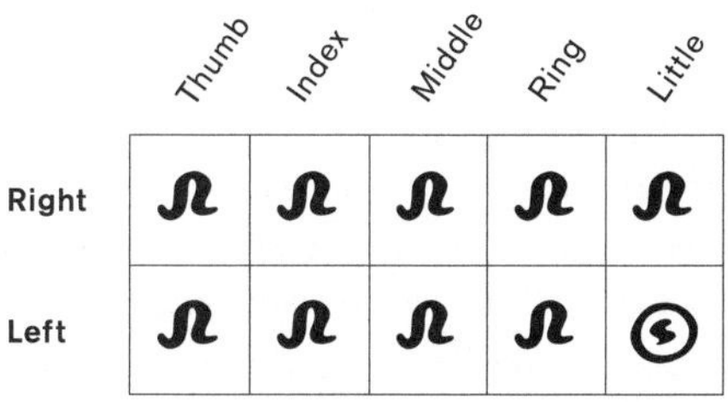

	Thumb	Index	Middle	Ring	Little
Right					
Left					

Fingerprint Profile: The highest-ranking fingerprint is the left little finger, which designates The Healer as the life purpose. However, because in this case the highest-ranking fingerprint is a composite whorl, there is an additional layer of meaning to the life story. Composite whorls are the irregular verbs of fingerprint analysis and they possess several unusual qualities. For one, they are lower ranking than regular whorls, a potentially crucial factor, as with John F. Kennedy (see page 228). Also, they can be thought of as part of the life purpose *and* part of the life lesson. In effect they turn on and off, on and off again. (Harold's story below, and the stories of Gale, Gary, and O Shanti on page 259, will explain the strange workings of the composite whorl in more detail.)

Life Purpose: The Healer (the composite whorl in the "on" position)

Life Lesson: Emotional Explosion or Stuffed Feelings (nine loops with lowest ranking prints). The left little finger operates as part of the life lesson when the composite whorl's "off" switch is triggered. If this happens, The Healer's role is reduced and Intimacy Issues flare up.

School: Love

Life-Fulfillment Formula: Overthrow your emotional baggage and gain access to your Healer with Heart.

The left little finger life purpose focuses on personal growth issues. Those doing well blossom into inner-awareness guides, from therapists to Sunday school teachers to motivational speakers with their own corporate jet. Others, further back on this life path, still struggle to make any sense out of their own lives. If this is your life purpose and you find yourself overwhelmed by life's difficulties, you will do well to keep in mind that you are in training for a life purpose with rewards equal to the difficulties faced in achieving them.

The Herald If The Herald brings a picture to your mind at all it is probably that of a town crier, a medieval eight-o'clock-and-all-is-well-type fellow. However, in earlier times, The Herald had a very different job description. "Herald" comes from the Greek word for "expert sound maker," and referred to the man who spoke the magic words at rituals and ceremonies. As such, the herald was a spiritual leader more akin to a priest or rabbi in today's world. The Herald is one of The Healer subtypes when the left little finger operates as the life purpose. In this example, the left little finger has a composite whorl, and the story becomes more complicated.

As the composite whorl blinks "on," its owner accesses the highest self-awareness qualities of The Herald. Then the composite blinks "off," and the left little finger insight turns into doubt and misinterpretation. It comes back on, it goes back off. On-again, off-again. (Gail, Gary, and O Shanti's stories on page 259 will explain what triggers the on/off switch and how to use it as an ally.)

In its most common form, we find the half-confident part-time Herald, an up-and-coming personal growth practitioner who has a real-world job to pay the rent. In its more exalted form, The Herald becomes completely available on command and the "off" button represents a nonproblematic pastime. A therapist who plays blues piano in a honky-tonk dive on weekends might be a good example. In its negative form, however, the left little finger composite brings forth The Snake Oil Salesman, a spiritual-sounding con artist out for financial or sexual manipulation. Harold, our Herald of the day, somehow managed to fall into all three categories at the same time. Here is his story.

Harold Harold always had an interest in psychology and religion but never quite enough to do more than read books or have long discussions with family and friends. When he was laid off from a software company, he cashed in his stock options and spent six months traveling in India, "monastery hopping," he later told me. His money gone, he thought he would just come back to work in Silicon Valley, but like many others, Harold had not counted on the tech crash of 2000. Six months after his return, he found himself unemployed and living on his credit cards.

A friend suggested becoming a life coach. "It would be easy to fake your way through it," he said. "What do you have to lose? We'll do it together." Harold agreed to give it a try. So Harold and friend pooled their resources and focused on selling themselves to unemployed former techies. They spoke the language, were able to feign empathy in realistic terms, and since there were no regulations or measuring sticks to contend with, how you presented yourself was more important than what you could do for people. Or so Harold and friend believed.

Well, sort of. Friend of Harold lasted three months as a life coach and disappeared to a less expensive state of the union, leaving Harold with a logo and stationery and little else. Harold actually did care about those he was able to sign up for his services, but he felt in over his head and devoted himself to a Become a Life Coach training program at the community college.

I knew none of this when Harold first showed me his hands, his nine loops and left little finger composite trumpeting out his Herald life theme. Harold's hands revealed an analytic personality that had not, as yet, gone very far inward. This trip to uncharted territory would require emotional exploration, and with Harold's mental orientation it was no sure thing that he would be willing to undertake such a journey.

A moment after Harold showed me his hands, a story appeared in my mind's eye, a Hollywood motion picture starring Spencer Tracy. Maybe I was remembering a movie I had seen or was inventing a new one. In any case, in the scene I now visualized, Spencer Tracy is a petty thief trying to run from the coppers. By accident, he finds himself in a monastery and decides it is the perfect hideout. He puts on a hooded robe and walks around, acting like everyone else. A week passes without anyone saying anything to him. Off the sauce and calming down, bit by bit the monastic lifestyle starts to pervade Spencer's consciousness, though he is only a thief in disguise and he plans to leave as soon as the heat lets up.

Bored with the goings-on, Spencer returns to his old digs just to check in on things. He is still wearing his disguise, and a woman stops him on the street and begs for an audience. She must talk to this man of God immediately. Spencer tries to break away but the woman starts to make a fuss and, in his attempt to keep a low profile, Spencer agrees to talk to her. They go inside the nearby church and Spencer hears her out, offering advice as best he can. She tearfully thanks him. Before Spencer can gracefully exit, another parishioner is waiting and then another and another. What can he do? Not wanting to break his cover, he stays until late that night.

Finally alone, or so he thinks, Spencer, exhausted from his labors, makes ready his escape. He notices the golden candlesticks, hesitates for a moment, but decides to leave them. He looks up as he approaches the exit to find it blocked by an older man. The Spencer from a week ago might have pushed him aside, but that Spencer also wouldn't have passed up the golden candlesticks.

The older man thanks Spencer for his good works. Spencer, thinking his disguise is still operational, feigns humility and tries to move on. The older man won't let him. "I know who you are. You robbed and beat up several of my parishioners just in the last year alone. I don't know what has happened to you, but somehow you have been touched by God. I was ready to call the cops when I saw you talking with Mrs. Smith, but I was moved by your faith and sensitivity and I decided not to. You have a place here in our church if you want it."

"But Father, I cannot stay. I am not at all what you think."

"You are exactly what I think you are," the older man said, his eyes as sharp and clear as a desert morning. "Select your life. I do not think you will have another chance."

The story ended there, and as I finished telling it and looked up, I saw that Harold was in tears. Regaining his composure, he told me his story. I was moved. Here was a man who no doubt had spent most of his life in his head, and now he was wrestling with feelings that he had a hard time putting into words. Good for Harold. Emotional expression (his nine loops, finally alive) would, if continued over time, become the gateway into a life-fulfilling, Herald-styled career.

Summary Sooner or later, all those with a left little finger life purpose must visit that part of themselves most resistant to examination. For Harold and his nine loops, this meant exploring his emotional nature. Since the composite whorl on the same finger will sometimes operate as the life lesson, Intimacy Issues are also part of Harold's self-exploration requirement. That was something Harold had not done as yet, but if his genuine emotional display in my office was any indication, this part of Harold's journey was right around the corner.

Public Impact in the Healing Arts

The Left Little Finger as the Life Purpose in an Archetypal Combination

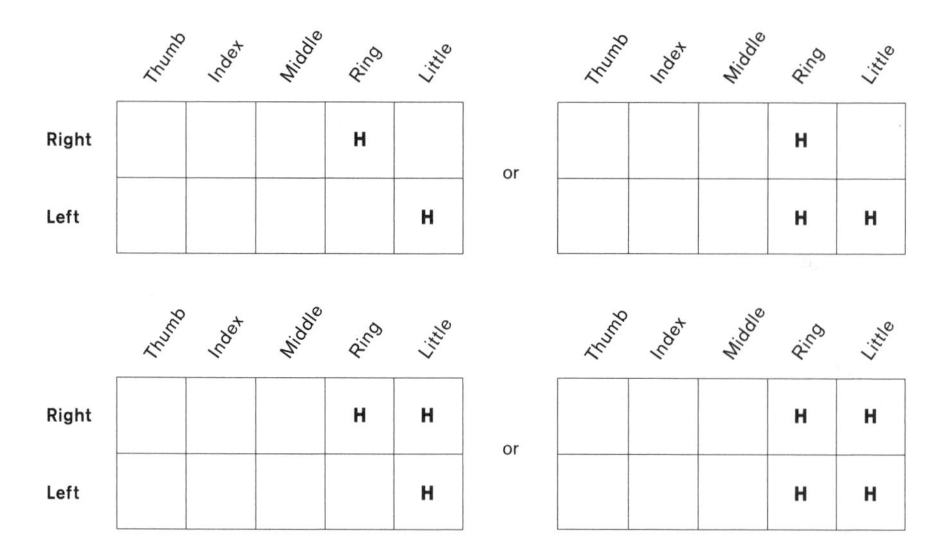

Fingerprint Profile: Right ring finger or both ring fingers + left little finger or both little fingers as highest ranking prints

Life Purpose: Public Impact in the Healing Arts, Inspire the Masses

Life-Fulfillment Formula: Be egoless enough to gain insight, be ego-ish enough to find your appropriate stage.

Public Impact in the Healing Arts (PIHA) is a dualistic life purpose that requires an exquisite balance between the outer world call of the spotlight and inner world hunger for personal growth. Often times, this tug-of-war plays out in the School of Service, with difficult choices to be made between family time, career time, and time for oneself. At their best, PIHAers juggle all three effectively. At their worst, one (or more than one) of the threesome suffers. Let's see what light Justin's story can shed on the PIHA path.

Justin Justin's hands revealed all the equipment you could possibly require to become an accomplished Healer at the Earth University, but his badly bitten nails and other markings indicated he was feeling worn to a nub. Rounding up the usual suspect, my first inclination was to conclude that Justin had gotten himself into the wrong line of work, a common misstep for PIHAers. But theory number one dissolved as Justin described his career. He had a successful therapy practice, he said, one that had supported him nicely for over a decade.

I wondered whether Justin was hiding out from the community at large by overbooking himself with one-on-one sessions, a lurking temptation for owners of these fingerprints. But no, Justin often led workshops and had recently spoken to over three hundred people at a national conference. That appearance had sparked significant interest in his work and invitations to speak at several other venues. I was impressed. Justin's life fit his fingerprints to a T. He should have been harvesting meaning and fulfillment points all over the place, and he was—except in his marriage.

The second Mrs. Justin had a series of requirements that kept him busy all the time. No matter how much he did for his wife, it always seemed less than what she needed. Justin's life lesson was Mr. Not Enough, with an emphasis on the left index finger (Protecting his Boundaries, Standing his Ground). According to the life-fulfillment formula in his fingerprints, learning to say no to his wife (without shutting her out in order to do so) would be the perfect practice ground for the new set of boundary issues Justin was likely to encounter as he moved into the more public phase of his unfolding life purpose.

Summary Mr. Not Enough is the common life lesson for PIHAers and Justin was handling his better than most. Mr. Not Enough had not kept him from his rightful career, nor had it interfered with his branching out and reaching a larger audience. However, Justin's relationship problems indicated there was still some work to do if Mr. Not Enough was to be turned into an ally.

The inclination to ignore the inner growth requirements of this life purpose becomes greatest as the spotlight gets bigger. Mr. Not Enough can be Justin's ally when he provides the Just-Right amount of humility required to keep Justin from getting seduced off course by his own success. In this way, becoming conscious of his life lesson could be just the medicine Justin needs to propel his career forward and possibly improve his marriage at the same time.

This is my own life purpose, one that I embrace happily at this point. Whether I am introducing the elegance and beauty of the fingerprint language to a large audience, or I am brought into the most private affairs of an individual's life to provide comfort and guidance, I am repeatedly thankful for all the rewards this life path has brought me.

If one of the Mr. Not Enoughs has you in his grip, take a moment and consider the role your difficulties have played in your personal development and the large payoff that is possible with these fingerprints.

The Shaman

The Left Little Finger as the Life Purpose in an Archetypal Combination

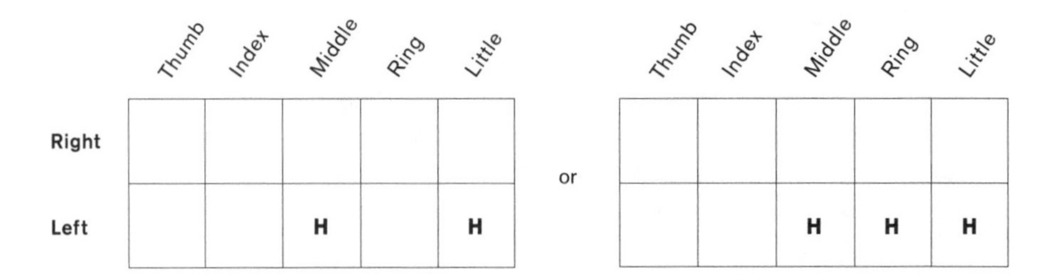

Fingerprint Profile: Left middle finger + left little finger as highest ranking (left ring finger is optional)

Life Purpose: The Shaman (The Mentor + The Healer or The Mentor + The Innovator + The Healer)

Life-Fulfillment Formula: You are a masterful magician, capable of anything. Believe it.

This is the least common of the life purpose archetypal combinations. I have read for only a few dozen of these special people, and in each case, the inner developmental requirements have been extreme. From dealing with the death of a child, to business setbacks, up to and including bankruptcy, the owners of these prints are a brave breed of soul warriors. Of course, it does not always feel that way from the inside.

At their best, advanced Shamans combine the self-awareness skills of The Healer with the integrity of The Mentor, ultimately becoming teachers and role models for self-awareness practitioners. Other Shamans live up to their title in a more literal fashion. Masters of the twilight zone between the real and the unreal, these sorcerers and new age (or old) ceremonial practitioners chant their way to stock market success or lead journeys to the Peruvian jungle in search of ancient wisdoms. Or both in the same week.

The Paradox Principle reveals why this is such a demanding fingerprint chart: before learning the secrets of heightened shamanic awareness, owners of these fingerprints must first explore the zone of false self-awareness (the life-purpose inverse for Shamans). Whether they join an abusive cult, go to work for a company that is preying on human fears for snake oil sales, or avoid these more melodramatic approaches and merely deal with personal deceits never revealed, Shaman trainees pay an expensive tuition to attend the Earth University.

Violeta Breast cancer, that's what the doctor said. Considering that she had never smoked and had eaten health foods since her late teens, it seemed unfair to Violeta that she should have a life-threatening illness while other family members, including the bacon-and-butter-draped-pancake-eaters and the two-pack-a-day persons, did not. "What was God thinking? If it were up to me," Violeta opined, "I might tweak a thing or two around here."

Violeta was alternating between high-spirited optimism ("I am going to beat this thing . . .") and downright defeatism ("What's the use of doing anything?"). Most recently, she had been holed up in her apartment for two weeks, barely talking to anyone. One of her daughters was flying in to go with her to the doctor even though she had stated that she preferred to handle things on her own.

Some Shamans of old blamed the victim if their prayers were ineffective. Today, in front of me, Violeta was blaming herself for all that had transpired in her life. Her divorce, her difficulties with her children, her illness: they all seemed to point to a life that had amounted to nothing.

I knew that given her fingerprints Violeta had performed magic feats at various times during her life. All Shamans do. Whether the magic had been accomplishing a seemingly insurmountable goal or imbuing a friend with positive vibes in the face of tragedy, Shamans alter the fabric of reality with their consciousness. But how much is under my conscious control and how much is not? Where is the line of possibility? Violeta was twirling these questions around and, for the moment at least, seemed bedraggled by the process.

I started in. "It makes sense to doubt your ability to recover from cancer, Violeta. Equally, it makes sense to believe you are going to recover. As of this minute today, you are in a life where both possibilities are completely real, and I guess you will find out which universe you are living in as events unfold. But one thing I do know for sure. You have the power to alter people's experience of their reality, including your own. Whether you use this power to inspire your friends and family, this is a fact of your existence that you are challenged to accept as much as you are challenged to accept your status as a spiritually inclined yet mortal being here at the Earth University."

Violeta's reading was six months ago. She has since had a mastectomy and reunited with her children in a way that would have seemed impossible to her before the current chapter of her life had begun. Regardless of what happens next, Violeta is happier with Violeta than she has ever been, or so she wrote me. Perhaps the experience of getting back something she thought she had lost forever will be an inspiration to Violeta to take the next step on her Shaman's life path.

Violeta really is quite The Magician, you know.

Summary Shamans who have successfully come to terms with their own limiting belief systems eventually learn how to recognize what they actually have power to change and what they do not. Struggling Shamans, on the other hand, repeat their training episodes ad infinitum until they can tell the difference between the still voice of God and the mere illusion of enlightenment. Sometimes grand humiliations are required to accomplish this goal, especially for those whose charts include the left ring finger as part of the mix. In the end, only those who have stared into the most stark of truth mirrors under the most difficult of circumstances earn advanced shaman degrees.

Intimacy Issues, Trust, and Surrender

The Left Little Finger or Both Little Fingers as the Life Lesson in an Archetypal Combination

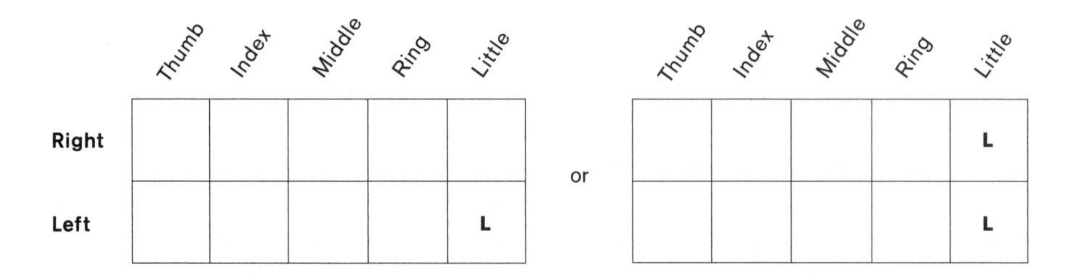

Fingerprint Profile: Left little finger or both little fingers as the lowest ranking print(s)

Life Lesson: Intimacy Issues, Trust, and Surrender

Life-Fulfillment Formula: When is letting go of control the optimal life strategy? Find the answer and change your life.

With the left little finger as the life lesson, your challenge is to surrender to and clearly speak your inner truth and in so doing break a pattern of relationship difficulties (love relationships primarily, but other relationships as well). But how much to say and when? And what is really my inner truth? With this life lesson, errors of inner and outer communications are likely and often take one or more of these three forms: manipulation, abandonment, and codependency.

Manipulation When manipulation appears in my clients' hands they almost invariably tell me how manipulative their partner has been and how much they detest this behavior. Yet manipulation has shown itself in their hands, not their partner's. How can this be?

Barbara reported that she was with her last boyfriend for three months before she found out he was married. Harrumph. Who could blame Barbara for being upset? Bob's deliberate deception was hurtful and disrespectful. If Bob were cornered, he might admit that this was the best way he could think of to get what he wanted from Barbara. So he lied. It worked, even if only temporarily, and now he is off to his next conquest.

Barbara was right; she had been manipulated, not for the first time either. But was it possible that Barbara herself was also a manipulator? Even if she had not attempted to deceive her lover as blatantly as Bob had, was Barbara actually practicing an equivalent form of selective communications, sharing only that part of herself that she felt would get her to the goal that *she* had in mind?

In general, manipulation implies conscious deceit at the expense of another. But in soul psychology, be on the lookout for *unconscious lies by omission*. During our session, Barbara admitted that when she meets a new man her tendency is to focus her full attention on him to the exclusion of all else, her strong independent side hidden from view. Later, when things settle down, her self-contained self emerges. This usually creates a crisis with her no-longer-center-of-all-attention partner and, one thing leading to another, Barbara inevitably finds herself back on her own again, relieved to re-enter her normal life. Relieved, but alone.

Abandonment Issues (Alone and Unloved Forever Fear) Barbara had not been as outright sneaky as her relationship partners, so her own manipulations were not nearly as obvious. Abandonment issues often come with a similar blind spot. As with manipulation, it may look as if your partner is doing the dirty work, but the challenge here is to shift the onus from the other to oneself. Doing so reveals this soul psychology truism: if you are to move beyond abandonment to true communications, you must not abandon yourself.

Many of those involved in this phase of the true communications training program have family histories of abandonment, thus creating a weak base for subsequent relationships. For women, this often means the Absent Daddy Syndrome: emotionally or physically absent fathers who died early, or left the marriage, or were never really emotionally present. These same women may find themselves in adult relationships that mirror their past, unconsciously picking spouses who work all the time or cannot commit. In men, the same pattern often shows up as Too Much Mommy: mothers whose emotional needs dominated the child's existence. If the young boy is too busy trying to be what he thinks will make mommy feel okay, he may grow up into a man who doesn't know what he wants for himself. In both cases, the idea is to recognize and speak up for your own needs, to not abandon yourself unconsciously in relationships.

The gender roles just described are not hard and fast, as Bridget's case suggests. In her reading, Bridget resonated with abandonment fears as an adult (she was twice divorced) but could not relate to the Absent Daddy Syndrome. She had been extremely close to her father and still was. As a matter of fact, he was probably the one person on the planet she felt closest to, she said. Maybe Absent Daddy didn't apply here, I thought to myself, but as Bridget went on to describe how she and her dad watched baseball together, enjoyed talking politics, and often went fishing and hunting, I got the impression that Bridget had learned early on that the best road to love and closeness had been to act like the son daddy had always wanted.

Bridget didn't need to disappoint her dad by not going fishing the next time they got together. But if daddy only saw the part of his daughter that he wanted to see, he would be missing out on a fuller relationship and Bridget would be falling into the self-abandonment trap that had made emotional disconnect and isolation a repeated life theme. Practicing emotional visibility with her dad might open the door toward improved emotional connection with men.

Codependency The third common challenge associated with the left little finger as the life lesson involves codependency. In its most publicized form, the hapless wife of the alcoholic husband cleans up his messes and suffers in silence. The moniker "*co*dependency" acknowledges that each person has a role to play in the substance abuse drama. For our purposes, however, codependency can be expanded to include any form of relationship in which one partner is stuck in the other's life movie, or both are stuck in each other's. The soul psychology perspective is that codependency is a major form of life-purpose avoidance, a place to hang out and pass the time while not consciously grappling with the challenges your own life purpose may present. The good news is that the extreme discomfort of codependency might be just the motivation required to return a person to his or her own life movie. It couldn't be any worse.

Summary The left little finger life lesson usually brings attention to trust and surrender issues in a relationship. Too little surrender and too much surrender are the errors to be expected on the way to Just Right. But at its heart, this life lesson has a deeper philosophical question: how much to exert your influence over events, how much to let go of attachment. Ultimately, the goal is to gain the ability to appropriately surrender to your true inner voice, to allow inner guidance to become your compass until your life matches your life purpose.

When there is no longer any difference between your ego's voice and that still voice within, at this point you have crossed a certain threshold that few have attained. Remember, however, that it is not so much the arrival at such a destination that is the goal, but the journey toward its end and what can be learned along the way; that is the true victory.

The Moon as the Life Purpose

Whorls or peacocks in the Moon elevate this location to life-purpose status. (See the Moon's Life-Purpose Blossoming and Life-Purpose Inverse charts on page 259.) Here we look at three people with composite whorls on the Moon, giving us a chance to further explore the Moon in its good news and bad and allowing a deeper look into the strange world of the composite.

Composite whorls have the unusual quality of blinking on and off, depending on life-lesson progress. For the Moon composite, owners might shift gears seamlessly in and out of the Spiritual Teacher (the Moon Life Purpose Blossoming), like a rabbi who owns a working ranch. In the morning he counsels a family; in the afternoon he takes care of his horses; that evening he leads the prayer service. In this example, the rabbi's life-lesson progress means that the composite whorl switches on and off without a problem. But when life-lesson progress halts, the composite whorl's on/off switch becomes an unconscious roller-coaster ride, as in the case of a manipulative preacher raising money from the faithful for his own illicit purposes. (See the Herald story on page 250 for an example of a composite whorl on the left little finger.)

Gale, Gary, and O Shanti Gale, Gary, and O Shanti each had composite whorls on their Moons, and their varied life experiences cover some of the possibilities inherent in this marking. Gale was forty-two years old and had a five-year-old son from her first marriage. She and Bill had been living together for two years and things were going well until Gale quit her job as a secretary to pursue her spiritual studies. Bill didn't mind Gale's new interests, but he couldn't understand Gale's need to leave all the financial responsibilities on his shoulders. As things got tense, Gale's loop-based life lesson raised its head and she withdrew emotionally from Bill.

On, off, on, off—as Gale continued to ignore her life lesson (emotional authenticity), her composite whorl started to turn her life into an uncomfortable roller-coaster ride. She was in her Moon gaining intuitive insights; then she was out of her Moon, misinterpreting the signs. When composite whorls act up, the only way to stop the mayhem is to return to your life lesson and deal with whatever issue has been swept under the rug. In Gale's case, increased recognition and expression of emotions were called for, but Gale was digging in her heels and becoming more and more remote. She was using her experiences with her first husband as her basis for dealing with Bill, and she was not going to get taken advantage of again. So there.

Unfortunately for Gale, her inappropriate loop response to *this* spousal partner was causing an out-of-control Moon reaction. Over time, her loops stuck on hold, Gale's behaviors became grossly inappropriate. She was alienating the students in her psychic development class and becoming ever more paranoid with family members. Eventually, Gale kicked Bill out, the same week that she was asked to leave the class that had been the center of her life for the last year. Alone, depressed, and lost, Gale would need more than a little remedial looping to get her life back together.

Gary was faring better with his Moon composite. Not fully unlocking his spiritual capabilities but not in Gale's tailspin, Gary was more a C+ student at the Earth University. He was a full decade younger than Gale, and although it was to Gary's advantage to do more work exploring his inner domain, time was on his side. He worked as a stockbroker and played bass guitar on weekends. His wife was the more spiritually inclined of the couple and had introduced him to her meditation teacher. He was considering a class at some point down the road.

O Shanti was the star pupil of this threesome. She had spent several years stuck at the crossroads in her life but had recovered nicely and was now counseling at a hospice. Recently, she had been asked to teach a class to doctors at the hospital, and she was looking forward to the opportunity to bring her healing approach into the mainstream.

Summary Gale, Gary, and O Shanti represent a good sampling of the Moon composite in action. A similar dynamic is at work when the composite whorl appears in any of the ten fingers. The location in question can be part of the life purpose blossoming and also part of the life lesson as well. The key is how the rest of the life lesson is doing. When it is being ignored over time, the composite whorl roller-coaster ride ramps up the discomfort, operating like a truant officer returning wayward students to their appropriate training program.

If you have a composite whorl in any location, see if you can spot the on-again, off-again quality in terms of your life history. Track its easy on, easy off phase; note its not-so-easy on-off phase. Then check your life-lesson progress and compare that to the composite's manifestation in your life. If you can do all this, you have an extra piece of your life-purpose map that you can use for guidance whenever things start to veer out of control.

The composite whorl becomes your ally when, noticing that your life has become an uncomfortable roller-coaster ride, you use this as an opportunity to revisit your life lesson.

Lone Tree on the Plain

Service as the Life Purpose

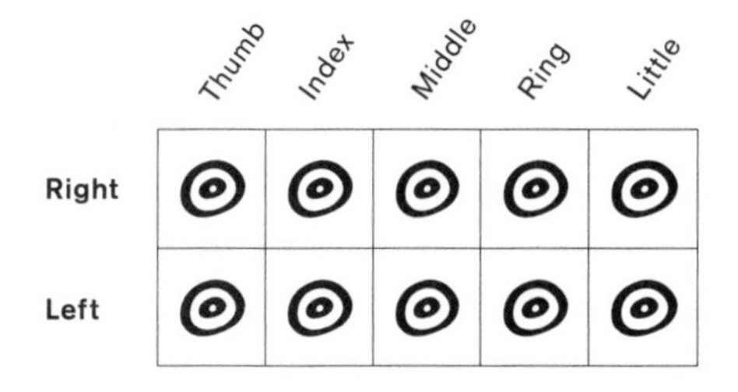

Fingerprint Profile: Whorls on all ten fingers

Life Purpose: Service (Seven or more whorls makes service the life purpose.)

Life Lesson: Self-Indulgence/Servitude (All ten fingerprints must be whorls.)

School: Service

Life-Fulfillment Formula: Go into and out of self-indulgence to find your service-based life.

Having ten whorls represents the most extreme form of duality. The delicious dilemma here is that to reach their fulfillment point (joyous selfless service), owners of ten whorls must first immerse themselves in total selfishness. The title for this life-purpose map comes from Chinese palmistry, signifying a person who is a law unto himself.

Siddhartha, by Hermann Hesse, provides a good literary example of this life path. Young Siddhartha joins a monastery, but his attempt at a spiritual existence, based too much on a mental construct, is bound to collapse. Decades after his monastic period, having lived a mercantile life, he becomes, of all things, a ferryboat man. Who would have sought such employment as the essence of spirituality? Yet Siddhartha finally has a life he truly desires. The point is that with these fingerprints, ultimate fulfillment can come only from service that springs from your inner being as opposed to the doing of good deeds—no matter how wonderful. Let's check out one person's Lone Tree journey and see if we can recognize Siddhartha in a more modern setting.

Peter Pan from Petaluma Al came in for his reading, perspiring heavily. It was not a hot day, but, he explained, he had bicycled in from Petaluma (thirty miles to the north) and needed a moment to freshen up. So freshened, he sat down, and I dived into his hands.

Al's superquick, connect-the-dots intelligence jumped quickly into view. Spotting this, plus several wisdom markers in his line formations, I guessed Al to be a computer consultant or therapist (or some clever combination of both). However, Al's finger spread gave me pause. All the fingers splayed wide apart indicates that the normal restraint of societal mores has little or no influence. Young children often have spread-out fingers. So do Bohemian types, hippies, and back-to-the-land utopians. Clearly, Al was not beholden to normalcy. Add in a missing Career Line to his fingerprint chart with ten whorls, and I knew I was looking at someone who had spent his entire life trying to figure out how to not work for a living—a Peter Pan from Petaluma.

I started to describe the Peter Pan element: clever, charming, fascinated with life, but with no desire to grow up—and Al filled in the details. He was thirty-eight, had sold his software business three years ago, and retired a multimillionaire. He thought he had fulfilled his life dream, but retirement was getting tedious. "It is becoming my job, and I don't *want* a job."

I took Al through the Siddhartha story: his flight from the monastery to become the wine-women-and-song businessman, his triumphant return to spirituality in a new and unpredictable form. "Let's suppose, since you are a ten-whorler, that your life wants to follow a similar path. Can we track that possibility? What if we consider you at work to be equivalent to Siddhartha in the monastery as a youth? You are excited by your possibilities, but eventually you leave for a seemingly opposite existence in which all you do is live out whatever inclination pops to the surface. Siddhartha took decades to weary of this; you took only three years. Eventually, Siddhartha goes back to his roots, but this time because he wants to, not to fulfill some picture in his mind. The parallel is clear. It seems you want back into your prior zone of operation, but this time in a more open-ended form.

"For example, I can imagine you taking business types on magical mystery tours where they learn Peter Pan's secrets: his ability to step outside of what is expected, his eternal playfulness. Then you return them to their regular lives invigorated, in touch with their creativity and their deepest motivations. Of course, you would have to work to build a business like that, but it is Peter Pan–style work, work that could give your life structure and meaning without imprisoning you."

Al beamed. He had had a dream this week, he told me, that essentially contained the same message. The reading over, Al started on his journey home. At least he doesn't have to *row* back to Petaluma, I thought, as I watched him pedal off into the distance.

Summary Peter Pan from Petaluma outlines the life path for those with ten whorls: Phase I, find and express your individualistic nature; Phase II, select service only when that is the truest expression of your heart's desire. Sometimes the owner of these prints is in servitude. Other times service backlash, with all its indulgent excess, seems the only visible motivation. When there is no conflict between what you truly want to do and doing service for others, you have reached the culmination point on this life path. At this point, enlightenment is yours, and any career, including becoming the ferryman like Siddhartha, can be considered the fulfillment of your life purpose.

The Butterfly

Love as the Life Purpose

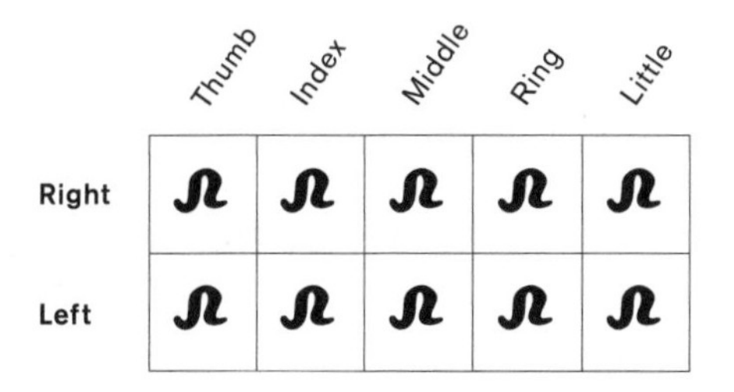

Fingerprint Profile: Loops on all ten fingers

Life Purpose: Love (Seven or more highest ranking loops makes Love the life purpose.)

Life Lesson: Explosion/Stuffed Feelings (Seven or more lowest ranking loops)

School: Love

Life-Fulfillment Formula: Can you bring your capacity to connect with others directly into your own love life?

The all-loops fingerprint chart is one of the most interesting available at the Earth University. From a soul level, owners of this configuration have a total dedication to emotional growth, so you might expect life stories that focus exclusively on relationships. The reality is quite different. On a personality level, you find a dazzling variety of forms. To simplify things, I have selected three representatives of The Butterfly Clan to give an idea of what is possible when someone shows up at the Earth University with ten loops.

Tom Tom was a tall fellow with a calm presence, at peace with himself in a witty and warm way. He was the inventor of Aqua Therapeutics, a trauma-reducing therapy practiced in a warm pool. Camille was another trauma expert who has pioneered a different approach in the same field. Although they had very different personality types, both had The Butterfly life purpose. We'll look at Tom first.

Tom had the elongated, knobby, shoe-box-shaped hands of the philosopher personality type. Advanced philosophers fulfill Freud's ground rules for a good life, finding love and appropriate employment. However, this is a hand type with a high "good life" casualty rate. The overwhelming majority wind up working in a pencil factory or in some other equally inappropriate career. Tom, unlike so many of his Platonic brethren, was not stuck at all. He loved his work and was wonderful at it. But let's not forget the fingerprints. Tom's life purpose was Love and Closeness. Not just Love and Closeness, Love and Closeness as a philosopher type. Ah—here's the rub. His life up to now had been an uplifting journey, but could he open his heart enough to find someone to share his life with?

Camille Unlike Tom, who had put a relationship on the back burner, Camille had married young and was still with her husband of twenty-three years. Everything in her hands identified Camille as a big-hearted sweetie pie, an excellent personality type given her work and life purpose. Advanced sweetie pies have learned how to nourish themselves while taking care of others. It is always a challenge, however, when a person like Camille has a special talent. The heart seeks connection, the special talent begs for action.

"I need more time to write and speak. There are so many people who need help. But I love my family. It is so hard to leave them when I travel."

"Welcome to your life, Camille. It is not just a function of your current circumstances that you feel pulled in these two directions at once."

We sat quietly for a while. "Oh," said Camille, "I see what you mean. No arrangement will make this feeling disappear completely. Hmmm. That is actually quite freeing, you know. I guess I can just go ahead and continue juggling as best I can."

Jasper Jasper is a good representative of the second theme common to these fingerprints. This group of ten-loopers tends to hop from job to job, hence the title: The Butterfly. I met Jasper at his sister JB's fortieth birthday party, a large catered affair held on Paradise Drive. JB was a high-powered businesswoman and a friend. Her brother, Jasper, was the question mark of the family: a nice guy, but at age thirty-eight he had not as yet any idea what he wanted to do with his life. JB had arranged for me to read his hands downstairs that night, while a professional storyteller and percussionist were upstairs entertaining the well heeled.

When we got downstairs, Jasper told me his story. "I love my wife and kids," Jasper said. "I've got a good bunch of pals. The only problem, if you want to call it that, is work. My mom, dad, and sisters are all super-successful types, and I'm basically just hanging out. They keep trying to help me even if I don't feel I need fixing, but if you can tell me anything about a career, I'd sure be glad to hear it." Jasper smiled a friendly smile, and I proceeded to look over his hands.

Hand shape and lines showed no hidden self yearning to breathe free. His fingerprints were all loops: The Butterfly. I have never seen anybody so genuinely happy to receive the news about his life purpose. "That is all I need to hear," Jasper announced. "I wonder what my sister's life purpose is? With all her success, she never seems happy. Is she actually a Butterfly like me?"

Summary Butterflies tend to come in two types: those with a special talent and those without. For the talent-based Butterfly, the challenge is to gain Love and Closeness without giving up the talent. Tom and Camille, though different in personality type, were both in this category and doing well. Those who put their talent on the back burner are usually in worse shape, commonly winding up with relationship difficulties that can be hard to straighten out.

For the Butterfly without the complication of a special talent, the common theme is the personality's inclination to be drawn to and to pull away from Love and Closeness, both at the same time. Like the push-pull toward service in the ten-whorler, the ten-looper's push-pull creates experiences that, if paid attention to, will bring them directly into their right life.

The Wing Walker

Wisdom as the Life Purpose

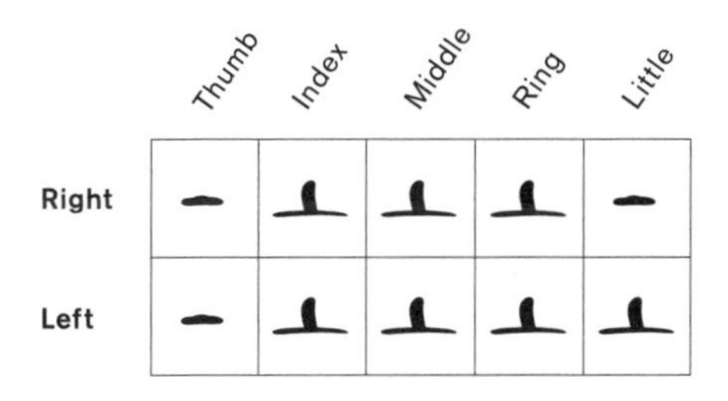

Fingerprint Profile: Seven tented arches, the most I have ever seen

Life Purpose: The Pioneer + The Shaman

Life Lesson: Persuasion

School: Wisdom + Peace

Life-Fulfillment Formula: Overcome your reluctance to persuade and your talents shift people's lives.

The Wing Walker is the title used at the IIHA for anyone with five or more tented arches. These hands are few and far between, but nonetheless memorable. Tented arch owners fear life's diving boards, tending toward an observer lifestyle. Advanced tented archers recognize this fear and cautiously learn to commit. Wing Walkers tend to take an opposite approach to these fingerprints, jumping off every diving board and taking every oversized risk they can find.

Four Wing Walkers Four Wing Walkers will serve as examples for this fingerprint map. The first was a mad scientist type, a fringe player with revolutionary ideas. He had risked his life savings on his controversial research, but now that he had, would he bring his discoveries to whatever establishment stood to benefit or would he keep his ideas to himself? He told me he was more inclined to retreat to a cabin in northern Montana somewhere than to suck up to a bunch of ignoramuses.

The second Wing Walker was a diminutive, white-haired bookstore owner from Zurich who specialized in rare books. We had a long discussion on the history and significance of hand reading. His fingerprints also revealed a Pioneer/Shaman life purpose with a Persuasion life lesson. We wondered together whether his bookstore was his life purpose in action or was it his hideout? Eventually we agreed it was some of each.

Then there was the muckraking journalist who had recently written his third book. It seemed to me he was dealing well with this fingerprint chart. And finally, there was the NLP (neuro-linguistic programming) practitioner whose hands I read at a life-purpose seminar. He used hypnotic regression techniques to help people lose weight, quit smoking, and so on. I thought that an excellent use of persuasion.

Summary The challenge here is to bring your commitment fear into conscious awareness so countermeasures can be employed. If there is "no problem whatsoever" (the standard Wing Walker reply, even though the life purpose is being ignored), there can be no progress on this life path.

Get a Tan

Peace as the Life Purpose

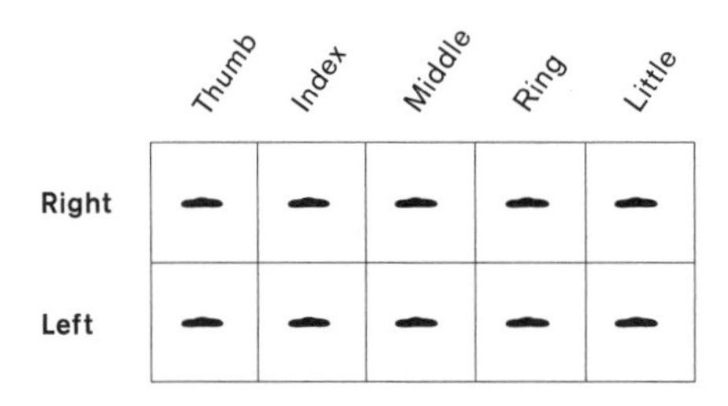

Fingerprint Profile: Arches on all ten fingers

Life Purpose: Peace (Only when all ten prints are arches is the life purpose Peace.)

Life Lesson: Peace (Overextension/Slacking Off)

School: Peace

Life-Fulfillment Formula: Go into total panic; come out to find the rest and relaxation for which your soul aches.

The Get a Tan life purpose is a rare bird that might be the most difficult of all life purposes. For owners of ten arches, the fulfillment point is relaxation, arriving on the Life Is Easy square on life's game board. If you are up on your soul psychology, you can see just what the delicious dilemma would be. The Paradox Principle is going to insist that the owner of these fingerprints uncover whatever is inside that resists fun, pleasure, inner peace. What is this unrest you are experiencing? What's really eating at you? At base, what are you actually worried about?

It takes a brave soul to dive into such waters, and most ten-archers try to avoid the process by hanging out with Ms. Lah-Dee-Dah for a decade or more, before eventually spiraling into a Mr. Sticks and Plates abyss. But do not be deceived by appearances to the contrary. The ten-archer is on a highly spiritual path, digging down to the very depths of hopeless despair in a quest for something on the other side of the existential void.

Connie Connie chain-smoked and chewed gum incessantly, at the same time. She couldn't hold a job (even though she was actually quite competent when not arching out), which is why she eventually found herself living out of her truck. That truck was four months overdue on its registration, and had three bald tires, no windshield wipers, and a generator on its last legs. Connie had to park overnight on a hill to allow the truck to roll down and jump-start itself in the morning. Things would be better if she didn't have five unpaid parking tickets and marijuana in plain sight.

Twenty years later and Connie is a ten-arch success story. She is a drug counselor for inner city kids. Pretty ironic, huh? She is still surrounded by arch behavior, but with her background, who better to help those in need? How did she do it? Every ten-archer I have met not currently in imminent collapse (or still lolling about in Mr. Mellow) has earned every inch of her success. The stories vary, but the paths have been remarkably similar: from Mr. Mellow to feeling completely overwhelmed, overwhelmed to breakdown, breakdown to therapeutic intervention, intervention to recovery, recovery to relapse. Repeat several times. Connie's version was one of the least melodramatic: no hospitalization or incarceration was required, and her therapists used a variety of techniques that, in sum, were just the right tonic. Credit Connie for repeatedly getting back on the wagon.

Summary Connie and her ten-arch brethren are living out that part of each of us forever discomforted by the very struggle of human existence. By bringing to the surface the fear that happiness is an impossibility, the ten-archer serves humanity by showing us that all such wounds, in each of us, have the opportunity to heal.

APPENDIX II

FINGERPRINT HISTORY AND RESEARCH FROM MEDICAL AND HAND ANALYSIS PERSPECTIVES

What then should we be looking for in a fingerprint? The answer might lie in those features that we know are present but that have not yet been analyzed.

—JAMSHED MAVALWALA, *THE STATE OF DERMATOGLYPHICS*

Dr. Harold Cummins, known as the father of *dermatoglyphics*, coined the term for the study of fingerprints and related line and hand shape designations in 1926. His extensive research into the embryonic development of fingerprints is largely responsible for bringing the field to the attention of the medical profession. Noel Jaquin, a contemporary of Cummins, played a similar central role for hand analysts. Since *LifePrints* is a marriage of these two diverse disciplines, it can be instructive to look, albeit briefly, at the history of each. We start our tour of fingerprint history and research thousands of years ago, working our way forward to the present.

EARLY HISTORY

Cave drawings and petroglyph diagrams provide a record of early man's interest in hands; however, the significance of these prehistoric samples is subject to broad interpretation. What can be stated with certainty is that as early as 500 BCE, Babylonian business transactions were recorded on clay tablets that included fingerprints. At approximately the same time, Chinese documents were found to have clay seals imprinted with the fingerprint of the author. Some early pottery is similarly marked. Whether this means it was known that a fingerprint is a certain signature of personal identity cannot be proven one way or the other.

On the hand analysis side, things go back even farther but with less evidence. I have been told by several hand readers versed in Eastern traditions that the study of fingerprints began in India more than five thousand years ago. It is written that Aristotle traveled to India, learned palmistry, and taught it to his pupil Alexander the Great. Any fingerprint system that was in use at that time, however, is beyond our reach today.

Fred Gettings, noted author of *The Book of the Hand*, writes:

> *There is no remembered beginning to an art already old before Aristotle was born . . . [T]he poor fragments . . . which have survived stand as tantalizing evidence of some long-past Golden Age of chiromantic knowledge.* [1]

Perhaps the most bizarre use of fingerprints dates to sixteenth-century China, where the sale of children was concluded by placing their hand- and footprints on bills of sale.[2]

The first official mention of fingerprints in medical literature was in 1684. Dr. Nehemiah Grew lectured the Royal College of Physicians of London about the interesting markings found on human fingertips. As scientists explored the globe in the two centuries following—cataloging animal and plant species and learning about the basic form and function of the human body—the study of fingerprints inched forward.

NOTABLE FINGERPRINT LANDMARKS

1685	Gouard Bidloo	First book with detailed drawings of fingerprints.
1686	Marcello Malpighi	Professor of Anatomy at the University of Barcelona: First observations of fingerprints under a microscope.
1788	J. C. A. Mayer	First to write out basic tenets of fingerprint analysis: "Although the arrangement of skin ridges is never duplicated in two persons, nevertheless, the similarities are closer among some individuals. In others, the differences are marked, yet in spite of their peculiarities of arrangement, all have a certain likeness."[3]
1823	John E. Purkinje	Professor of anatomy at the University of Breslau: First fingerprint classification system.

1833	Sir Charles Bell	Anatomist and author: *The Hand: Its Mechanism and Vital Endowments as Evincing Design.*
1858	Sir William Herschel	British chief administration officer, Bengal, India: First to use fingerprint identification on a mass scale.
1880	Dr. Henry Faulds	Tsukji Hospital, Tokyo; Article in *Nature*: Suggests picking up fingerprints at crime scene.[4]
1883	Mark Twain	*Pudd'nhead Wilson*: Dramatic fingerprint identification secures murder conviction.
1892	Sir Francis Galton	Anthropologist, cousin of Charles Darwin: First practical method of fingerprint identification. Responsible for basic nomenclature; scientific demonstration of permanence of fingerprints; first twins' research.
1897	Harris Hawthorne Wilder	First American to study dermatoglyphics: Named the *a, b, c, d* triradii points; invented the Main Line Index; studied thenar and hypothenar eminences, zones II, III, IV.
1904	Inez Whipple	First serious study of nonhuman prints.
1923	Kristine Bonnevie	First extensive genetic studies.

HAROLD CUMMINS, MD

Sixty years after it was first published, Cummins and Midlo's seminal work, *Finger Prints, Palms and Soles*, remains the standard reference work in dermatoglyphics. Cummins applied himself to all aspects of fingerprint analysis, from anthropology to genetics, and from embryology to the study of malformed hands. He pulled together the diverse work of his predecessors and added original research. His famous Down Syndrome studies predicted a genetic link to the disease based upon the presence of the Simian Crease. Staking his reputation on research that only became established science two decades later cemented his place in history and brought national attention to dermatoglyphics.

Although Cummins stands alone as the giant in his field, other researchers have made significant contributions, including L. S. Penrose, Sarah B. Holt, and Alfred R. Hale.[5] Particularly pertinent to *LifePrints* is the work of John J. Mulvihill, MD, and David W. Smith, MD, whose comprehensive paper concludes that fingerprint formation conforms to volar pad topography.[6] In other words, fingerprints are a map.

COMMON DERMATOGLYPHIC VARIABLES

When a dermatoglyphic study is done, the common practice is to compare one group of individuals to another using a series of common variables. Variables are selected for mathematical purposes only. After the numbers are collected, either the test group shows a high enough degree of variance from controls to be statistically significant or it does not. The following is a list of the most common variables currently in use.

The *a-b* Ridge Count

A triradius is a point where the pattern deviates into three directions. The *a-b* Ridge Count is the number of fingerprint lines between the *a* triradius point under the index finger and the *b* triradius point under the middle finger. Other ridge counts, for instance the *b-c, c-d, a-d* Ridge Counts, are also used, though not nearly as often.

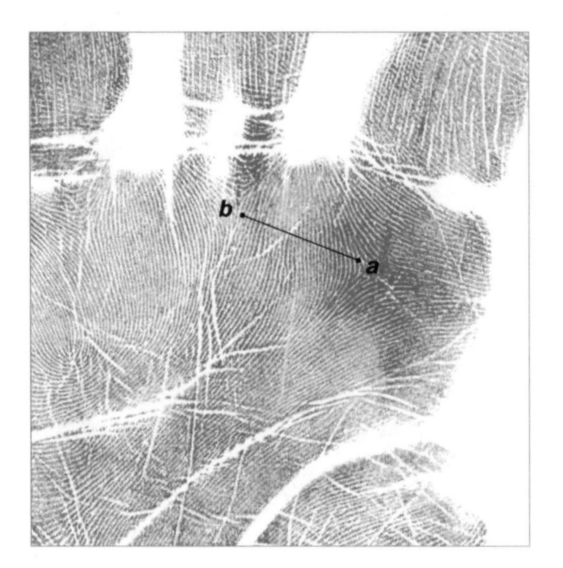

Pattern Intensity

Pattern Intensity is the total number of triradii on all ten fingers. Arches have no triradii; loops have one; whorls have two.

The Arch, Loop, Whorl Sequence, a continuum of fingerprints from the most concentric-circle-at-its-core whorl to the most basic arch, is pictured below.[7]

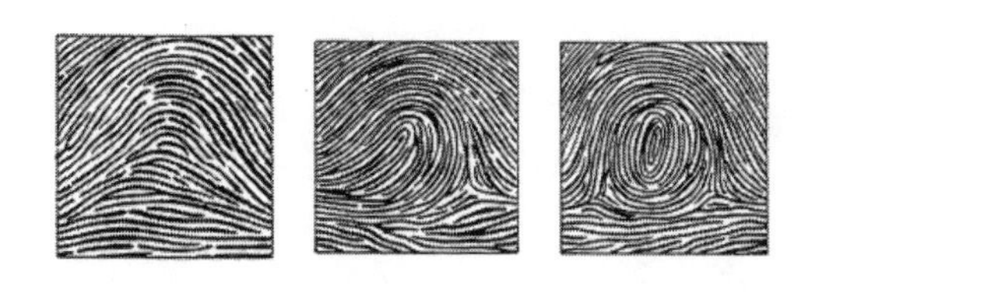

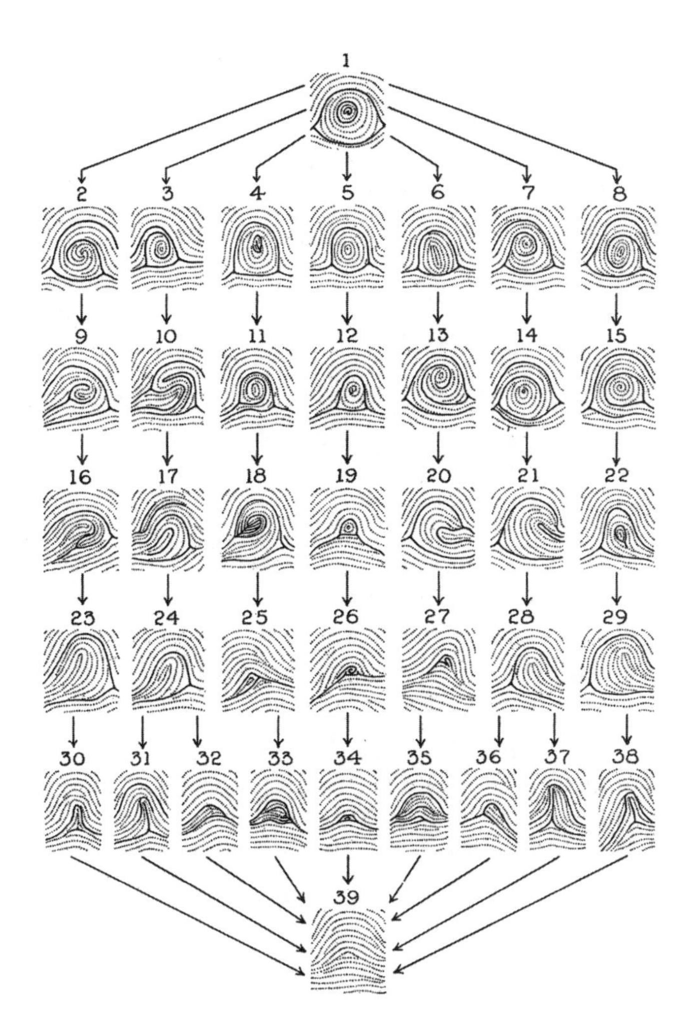

The *atd* Angle

The *atd* Angle is made by connecting the *a, t,* and *d* triradii points. The mean *atd* Angle is approximately 45 to 50 degrees. The *atd* Angle changes as a person ages.

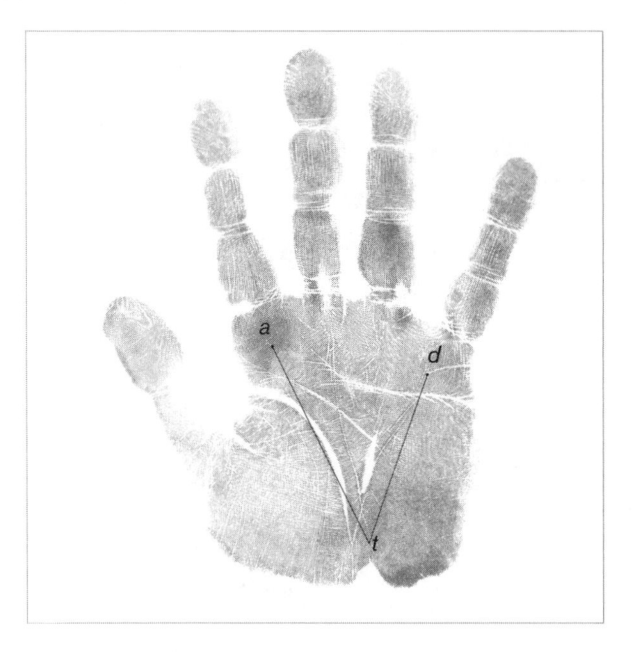

Palmar Crease Line Comparisons

The presence or absence of the Simian Crease is an example of a Palmar Crease Line.

Main Line Index

The Main Line Index is a mathematical formula showing degree of transversality, in other words, how long and tall or short and wide the hand is and how that affects the fingerprints.

Statistical Comparison of Pattern Types

For instance, whorls appear on approximately 25 percent of right thumbs in the general population. What is the percentage of right thumb whorls in Type I diabetics versus Type II diabetics?

The arch-loop-whorl sequence and the statistical comparison of pattern types are the dermatoglyphic variables employed in the LifePrints system.

Comparisons of the Thenar, Hypothenar, and Areas II, III, IV

Whorls appear in the hypothenar area (the Moon) in only six cases per thousand; thenar (Venus) whorls are even less common.

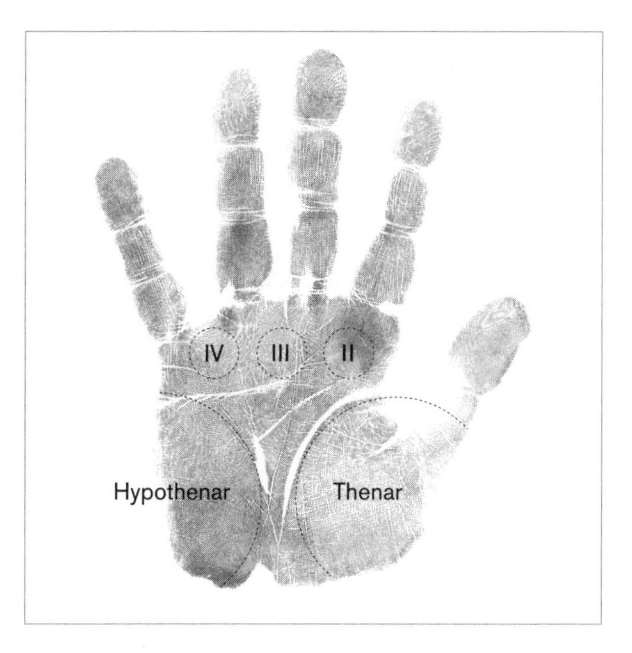

THE STUDY OF PALMAR LINES

When people think of examining the lines on their palm, their first image is that of a fortune teller. Few realize that palmar lines are a historically significant aspect of dermatoglyphics and have been under scientific scrutiny for over a century. Whereas fingerprints are unalterable and easy to classify, line formations change and have proven more difficult to categorize. Nonetheless, numerous studies have linked line patterns to different diseases and psychological conditions.

C. Fere is normally cited as the beginning of the scientific study of line formations.[8] His system merely noted the presence or absence of six different line formations. H. Poch went a step further, adding line intersections in an attempt to correlate embryonic disturbance to line formation.[9] A. Wurth was the first to observe that lines form before the fetal hand can move.[10] Hand lines, it turns out, are not flexion creases as previously thought. G.G. Wendt added a seventh line to the previous system.[11]

Consensus on line classification remained an ephemeral goal, however. The systems in use seemed both too simple to yield valuable results and too difficult to apply. Several new approaches appeared in an attempt to correct these deficiencies. Lieber proposed a much more detailed line classification system, but it proved cumbersome and hardly anyone paid much attention to it.[12]

The most widely quoted expert on palmar line formations is Milton Alter, PhD. Finding all other line classification systems inadequate, he invented his own from scratch. It seemed simple yet more comprehensive and scientific. Starting with four categories of line, he broke each into a few subcategories and statistically compared males and females as well as left and right hands.[13]

Although Alter's system was easily the most thorough and practical of its time and is still referred to as one of the standard works in the field, line formations can be complex, and different observers using Alter's system didn't agree on the presence or absence of lines. Further, Alter himself repeatedly made mistakes of identification.

The most successful system of scientific line classification is Ramesh Chaube's.[14] Whereas earlier systems suffered from lack of detail, too much detail, or substantial errors of identification, Chaube avoids these problems by focusing entirely on the radial point of the three major lines.

This system has produced statistically relevant data in studies of schizophrenia, cancer, tuberculosis, diabetes, and leprosy, and stands as the most useful scientifically accepted line system. Using only a few line variations insures its accuracy. However, for the same reason, Chaube's system is likely to have only limited application.

Johnson and Opitz are responsible for the most thorough comparison of medical and palmistic points of view from the scientific perspective.[15] In their follow-up study of hyperactive and hypoactive children, they conclude, "The inspection of the palm creases should be a routine part of a pediatric examination."[16] Bravo!

Hand readers have been trying to connect with the medical community for years, to marry up if you will, but the scientific community has been playing hard to get. This historical inequality made me even more interested in Johnson and Opitz, but unfortunately they made no use whatsoever of the hand readers' database.

The most logical approach to date was suggested by Dar, Schmidt, and Notowski. In their 1976 study, they write: "As the variability and possible clinical significance of palm crease abnormalities receive greater attention, an accurate and objective method for evaluating palm crease variants is required."[17] It is now 2007 and no one seems to have taken them up on this challenge. Their Latitude/Longitude Coordinates system (reminiscent of Noel Jaquin) lies dormant.[18]

As it now stands, the medical profession is still in search of a workable system of line classification detailed enough to yield significant data yet simple enough to be used by a doctor without specialized training. Perhaps, someday, doctors will discover the system of line identification that has been patiently awaiting their attention for thousands of years.[19]

HAND READERS LOOK AT FINGERPRINTS

We can assume that William Benham, one of the most famous authors on hand reading, would have studied fingerprints had there been more interest during his time. His major work, *The Laws of Scientific Hand Reading*, a six-hundred-page how-to book so detailed as to devote a chapter to reading the hair on the back of the hands, makes no mention of fingerprints whatsoever. Considering that it was originally published in 1899, three years before Scotland Yard accepted fingerprints as conclusive proof of individual identity, this is not surprising. What is surprising is that in his second and last book published thirty years later, *How to Choose Vocation from the Hand*, there is still no reference to fingerprints. Apparently, Benham had fixed his system early on and added little or nothing to it through the years.

It was left to Noel Jaquin, part scientist-part clairvoyant, to introduce fingerprints to Western hand readers. Jaquin's biography makes interesting reading. In 1927 he wrote an article for *Pearson's* magazine that included an offer to analyze any handprints mailed in. Jaquin was hoping to stir up some interest but was completely unprepared for the more than ten thousand responses he received. It took six months, including weekends, but he answered every one. Before he was through, Jaquin would devise a series of medical diagnostic indicators based on skin ridge dissociation and would single-handedly invent the only system of fingerprint analysis widely used by hand readers today.

Nearly every palmistry book that mentions fingerprints reiterates Jaquin's original assertions. Whether it is Terence Dukes in *Chinese Hand Analysis* or Gertrude Hurlimann in her astrologically based *Handlesen ist erlernbar* (two very original and detailed books with premises far different from each other), the fingerprint meanings match Jaquin almost exactly.[20] A whorl appearing on any finger is said to add an individualistic quality, the arch is a sign of crudeness or an elementary nature, the loop provides emotional elasticity, the tented arch signifies a highly strung person, and the composite is repressive and resentful (so I suppose it would be a good idea not to have any of these if you can work that out).[21]

Jaquin's writing is a mixture of personal philosophy, hand reading interpretations, and rambling who-knows-what. His palmistry points include some of the most insightful ever published in any book on the subject. His latitude/longitude approach to the Head and Heart Lines forms the basis for my own system on these two major lines. That being said, not everything written by Jaquin bears up under objective scrutiny.

I came to my conclusion regarding Jaquin's fingerprint system only reluctantly. It is true that on some hands the arches seemed to be part of an elemental psychology and some of my readees with whorls were secretive and individualistic as Jaquin suggests they should be, but other cases stood in full contradiction. Hands with multiple arches sometimes belong to highly refined professors, and some heavily whorled persons constantly bend over backwards to please.

Many hand readers do not use fingerprints at all, and those who employ a Jaquin-based system can usually work their way around these difficulties. They point to this line here and that hand-shape factor there, suggesting that these markings counteract the particular fingerprint in question. In contrast, *LifePrints* suggests that the fingerprints are not one more influence on personality but a separate psychology all its own which interacts with the personality.

Only metaphysician Maurice Cooke suggests anything similar. Cooke sees fingerprints as indicators of past-life lessons learned or unlearned.[22] Whorls on a particular finger indicate the former, arches the latter. This implies that the more arches you have the lower you are on the karmic totem pole, a conclusion that seems narrow and unwarranted, but his philosophy was different enough from Jaquin that I was eager to put Cooke to the test. Unfortunately, his system did not pan out.

Dennis Fairchild's *Humanistic Palmistry* also takes a karmic perspective, but on closer inspection his conclusions are approximately the same as Jaquin's. The same is true for Hutchinson, Fitzherbert, and Jaegers.[23] Each writes extensively about fingerprints, but mostly they organize and extend Jaquin's four typologies, adding hardly anything new to the mix.

As you have read, *LifePrints* operates quite differently: any attempt to interpret a single fingerprint without knowing the other nine prints leads to an incomplete and often erroneous conclusion. Cooke and Jaquin had each seen a piece of the puzzle, but it is clear that neither had read the medical literature on the topographic nature of volar pad formation. Taking this into account would, I believe, have led both men to a more holistically inclusive system.

DOCTORS LOOK AT HAND ANALYSIS

In a similar vein, if any of the medical researchers had given a serious look at hand analysis they would surely have noticed overlapping conclusions and made appropriate use of the ancient art. But few modern doctors have attempted to cross the great divide.

Charlotte Wolfe is one doctor who did. In the 1940s, Wolfe created a detailed and internally consistent hand-shape and line-interpretation system based on the prior works of Dr. Carl Gustav Carus and Dr. N. Vaschide.[24] Though familiar with Cummins's research, she did not go into the psychology of fingerprints at all. Pity.

HAND READERS LOOK AT DERMATOGLYPHICS

The medical literature on palmistry is thin, but what about hand readers studying dermatoglyphics? A good place to start is Ed Campbell.[25] Apparently, Campbell has read almost everything written in English by hand readers on the subject and discusses his findings in his book *The Encyclopedia of Palmistry*. For even greater detail, go to his website: www.Edcampbell.com/PalmD-History.html. Unfortunately, almost everything written in English is pretty much Noel Jaquin's work rephrased by different authors.

Christopher Jones's work is even more comprehensive than Campbell's. His staggering historical compendium on hand reading (www.breathemail.net) dwarfs all other works of its kind.[26] You can find out more about the lives of many of those mentioned so far, though you won't find much more about what fingerprints mean.

Dr. Eugene Schiemann is a contemporary physician who has studied hand reading in depth.[27] His book with Nathaniel Altman is a down-to-earth and comprehensive guide to using the hand as a medical diagnostic tool. He lists various conditions associated with fingerprint combinations, but although he is both a doctor and a hand reader, in regard to fingerprints and psychology, his views are purely Jaquinian.

Martijn van Mensvoort, Arnold Holtzman, and Vernon Mahabel are three other hand readers up on their dermatoglyphics. Van Mensvoort is probably more familiar with medical dermatoglyphics than any hand reader on the planet. His research on autism is of particular note. Holtzman takes a clinical approach and has an extensive website devoted to hand analysis (www.pdc.co.il).[28] Like Wolfe, his system is detailed, internally consistent, and yields useful insights. He does use some dermatoglyphics, but fingerprints are not the focal point of his system. Mahabel, on the other hand, uses fingerprints extensively. Mahabel and I have compared our systems at length and find we agree on many foundation principles while disagreeing on others. Mahabel's introductory book, *The Secret Code in Your Hands* (Mandala Publishing Group), only touches on fingerprints, and the world will have to await future publications to see the depth of his research.

CURRENT TRENDS

So where does that leave dermatoglyphics today? In *The State of Dermatoglyphics*, Ralph M. Garruto, professor of anthropology and neurosciences, sums up the feelings of medical researchers as follows: "The field of dermatoglyphics . . . continues to endure, yet it has not 'flourished' nor has it become irrelevant."[29] In other words: funding has almost disappeared.

Despite the fact that DNA testing has replaced the dermatoglyphic test as the standard in twin studies and other medical research, several scientists struck a positive tone for the future, noting that dermatoglyphics may be in position to become the primary means of assessing complex genetic traits not accessible to DNA analysis. Further, because fingerprints and line formations form during vital stages of fetal development, dermatoglyphic studies are in a unique position to evaluate the effect of toxins on the intrauterine environment.

Dermatoglyphics are still useful for the evaluation of children with suspected genetic disorders and diseases with long latency, slow progression, and late onset. And the new findings that rats have dermatoglyphic patterns opens up a whole new realm of experimental possibilities. Bonnevie, with all her detailed research, had missed this (rat dermatoglyphics are quite small) and until recently, no one had looked.

That being said, the field of dermatoglyphics faces some obvious problems beyond funding. It is interesting to note that most of the difficulties discussed could be ameliorated by merging scanner technology with an updated computer database. Imagine putting your hands on a scanner at your doctor's office and in less than thirty seconds a printout appears with a diagnostic profile (and perhaps even a Life-Prints profile) for you and your physician to discuss. There is absolutely nothing, except perhaps $600,000, keeping this from happening next Thursday.

The history of science is replete with examples of new technologies creating the possibility of new advances: Galileo gets his hands on a telescope, or Loewenhook invents a microscope, and the world is changed. It is exciting to contemplate what will happen when (not if) the study of dermatoglyphics makes use of the routine technological advances already employed by other branches of science.

NOTES

1. Fred Gettings, *The Book of the Hand: An Illustrated History of Palmistry* (London: Paul Hamlyn Ltd., 1965), 159.

2. Harold Cummins and Charles Midlo, *Finger Prints, Palms and Soles* (New York: Dover Publications, Inc., 1961), 7.

3. Ibid., 13.

4. Ibid., 15.

5. According to L. S. Penrose, in "Dermatoglyphic Topography," *Nature* 205 (February 1965): 544, "The permanent configuration is the result of laying a carpet of parallel lines, in some way as economically as possible, over the contours presented by the foetal hand." See also Sarah B. Holt, *The Genetics of Dermal Ridges* (Springfield, IL: Thomas, 1968); and Alfred R. Hale, "Morphogenesis of Volar Skin in the Human Fetus," *American Journal of Anatomy* 91 (1952): 147–73.

6. John J. Mulvihill, MD, and David W. Smith, MD, "The Genesis of Dermatoglyphics," *Journal of Pediatrics* 75, 4 (October 1969).

7. Cummins and Midlo, 62.

8. C. Fere, "Le Lignes Papillaires de la Paume de la Main," *Journal of Anatomy and Physiology* 36, 376–392 (1900).

9. H. Poch, "Uber Handlinien," *Mitteilungen der Anthropologischen Gesellschaft* 55, 133 (1925).

10. A. Wurth, "Die Entsehungder beugerfurchen der menschliche Hohlhand," *Zeitschrift für Morphologie und Anthropologie* 38, 187 (1937).

11. G. G. Wendt, "Zwillingsuntersuchung Uber die Erblichkeit der Handfurchung," *Zeitschrift für Menschliche. Vererbungs und Konstitutionslehre*. 35, 205 (1960).

12. B. Lieber, "Zur Systematik und Klinischen Bedeutung des Menschlichen Handfurchenbildes," *Zeitschrift für Menschliche. Vererbungs und Konstitutionslehre*. 35, 205 (1960).

13. M. Alter, MD, PhD, "Variations in Palmar Creases," *American Journal of Diseases of Children* 120, 426 (1970).

14. R. Chaube and S. Bali, "Palmar Creases and Schizophrenia," *International Symposium on Human Genetics* (Waltair, India: 1971).

15. C. F. Johnson, MD, and E. Opitz, "Single Palmar Crease and Its Clinical Significance in a Child Development Clinic," *Clinical Pediatrics* 10, 7 (1971).

16. C. F. Johnson, MD, and E. Opitz, "Unusual Palm Creases and Unusual Children," *Clinical Pediatrics* 12, 2 (February 1973): 101.

17. H. Dar, R. Schmidt, and H. M. Nitowski, "Topographic Approach for Analysis of Palm Crease Variants," *Journal of Medical Genetics* 13 (1976): 310–13 and "Palmar Crease Variants and Their Clinical Significance: A Study of Newborns at Risk," *Pediatric Research* 11, 103 (1977): 105.

18. Noel Jaquin, *Secrets of Hand Reading* (Bombay: D. B. Taraporevala Sons and Co., Ltd., 1936).

19. Benham does make use of one dermatoglyphic variable, the apex points under the four fingers. Their precise location plays an important role in his system of personality diagnostics. Comte C. de Saint Germain, *The Study of Palmistry for Professional Purposes*, makes largely the same apex observations as did Benham, and two years earlier, but his work is flawed and hard to read, making it less influential in the hand reading community.

20. Hurlimann has some interesting observations on the dermatoglyphic lines that emanate from the triradius points; she is the only hand reader I have found who has written about them.

21. It is particularly interesting that so many modern writers repeat Jaquin's phrase "emotional elasticity" to describe loop psychology. Since approximately 70 percent of fingerprints are loops, is humanity primarily emotionally elastic? Are hands with six loops or fewer underelastic? *LifePrints* also sees loops as emotionally based but not in the same way.

22. Maurice Cook, *Body Signs* (Toronto: Marcus Books, 1982).

23. Beryl B. Hutchinson, *Your Life in Your Hands* (New York: Paperback Library, Inc., 1967); Andrew Fitzherbert, *Hand Psychology* (Garden City, NY: Avery Publishing, 1989); Beverly Jaegers, *Hand Analysis and Dermatoglyphics* (St. Louis, MO: Aries Productions, 1974).

24. Charlotte Wolfe, *Studies in Hand-Reading* (London: Chatto and Windus, 1936).

25. Ed Campbell, *Encyclopedia of Palmistry* (New York: Berkeley Publishing Group, 1996), 98–124.

26. Including Gettings, *The Book of the Hand*, and Andrew Fitzherbert, *The Palmist's Companion* (London: Scarecrow Press, 1992).

27. Eugene Schiemann, MD, with Nathaniel Altman, *Medical Palmistry: A Doctor's Guide to Better Health through Hand Analysis* (Wellingborough, England: Aquarian Press, 1989).

28. The IIHA website, www.handanalysis.net, has an extensive website review of Holtzman's work.

29. Norris M. Durham, Kathleen H. Fox, and Chris C. Plato, eds., *The State of Dermatoglyphics* (Ontario: Edwin Mellen Press, 2000), 360.

INDEX

M

N